DNS Security Extensions RFCs

DNSSEC Specifications

Title: DNSSEC Specifications
Subtitle: DNS Security Extensions RFCs
Publisher: Reed Media Services
Date: September 2009
Website: http://www.reedmedia.net/

ISBN 978-0-9790342-7-5

Contents

Contents

RFC 3007: Secure Domain Name System (DNS) Dynamic Update   29

RFC 3110: RSA/SHA-1 SIGs and RSA KEYs in the Domain Name System (DNS)   37

RFC 3225: Indicating Resolver Support of DNSSEC   43

RFC 3226: DNSSEC and IPv6 A6 Aware Server/Resolver Message Size Requirements   49

RFC 4310: Domain Name System (DNS) Security Extensions Mapping for the Extensible Provisioning Protocol (EPP)　173

RFC 4431: The DNSSEC Lookaside Validation (DLV) DNS Resource Record　193

RFC 4470: Minimally Covering NSEC Records and DNSSEC On-line Signing　197

RFC 4059: Use of SHA-256 in DNSSEC Delegation Signer (DS) Resource Records (RRs)　205

Preface

The *DNSSEC Specifications* book includes the recent (as of September 2009) Internet specifications related to signing DNS resource records.

This book contains copies of RFCs. RFC stands for "Request for Comments" — but these documents actually have already received much review before they are officially published by the Internet Engineering Task Force (IETF). These represent the Internet standards.

This compilation is not official and is provided as a convenience for studying these standards and peer-reviewed suggestions. The definitive versions of these specifications are the plain-text ASCII versions. We have taken great care to make sure that no content changes have been made in this formatted book. Some footnotes and indexing were added to help find information within the book. Spellings, grammar, and punctuation were not changed in this printed book. The original content should be the same. The section numbering also remains the same. Any bibliographic references are listed at the end of the corresponding RFC.

Note that when a RFC refers to an appendix or section number without referring to another document, it implies that it is in the same RFC. (No additional appendices are at the end of this compilation.)

As a quick start to DNSSEC, review the following RFCs contained in this printed book:

- RFC 3833 — Threat Analysis of the Domain Name System (DNS)
- RFC 4033 — DNS Security Introduction and Requirements
- RFC 4034 — Resource Records for the DNS Security Extensions
- RFC 4641 — DNSSEC Operational Practices

Obsolete RFCs

The following RFCs related to DNSSEC are obsolete:

- RFC 2065 "Domain Name System Security Extensions" (January 1997) was obsoleted by RFC 2535 (which is also obsolete).
- RFC 2137 "Secure Domain Name System Dynamic Update" (April 1997) is obsoleted by RFC 3007.
- RFC 2535 "Domain Name System Security Extensions" (March 1999) is obsoleted by RFCs 4033, 4034, and 4035.

- RFC 2537 "RSA/MD5 KEYs and SIGs in the Domain Name System (DNS)" (March 1999) is obsoleted by RFC 3110.

- RFC 2538 "Storing Certificates in the Domain Name System (DNS)" (March 1999) is obsoleted by RFC 4398.

- RFC 2541 "DNS Security Operational Considerations" (March 1999) is obsoleted by RFC 4641.

- RFC 3008 "Domain Name System Security (DNSSEC) Signing Authority" (November 2000) is obsoleted by RFCs 4033, 4034, and 4035.

- RFC 3090 "DNS Security Extension Clarification on Zone Status" (March 2001) is obsoleted by RFCs 4033, 4034, and 4035.

- RFC 3445 "Limiting the Scope of the KEY Resource Record (RR)" (December 2002) is obsoleted by RFCs 4033, 4034, and 4035.

- RFC 3655 "Redefinition of DNS Authenticated Data (AD) bit" (November 2003) is obsoleted by RFCs 4033, 4034, and 4035.

- RFC 3658 "Delegation Signer (DS) Resource Record (RR)" (December 2003) is obsoleted by RFCs 4033, 4034, and 4035.

- RFC 3755 "Legacy Resolver Compatibility for Delegation Signer (DS)" (May 2004) is obsoleted by RFCs 4033, 4034, and 4035.

- RFC 3757 "Domain Name System KEY (DNSKEY) Resource Record (RR) Secure Entry Point (SEP) Flag" (April 2004) is obsoleted by RFCs 4033, 4034, and 4035.

- RFC 3845 "DNS Security (DNSSEC) NextSECure (NSEC) RDATA Format" (August 2004) is obsoleted by RFCs 4033, 4034, and 4035.

DNSSEC Drafts

At the time of this book printing, several Internet-Drafts (I-D) for DNSSEC are in review. These are not official standards, but are works in progress. Drafts are generally only valid proposals for six months. They may be updated, replaced, or obsoleted by other documents at any time.

Current drafts related to DNSSEC are posted at http://tools.ietf.org/wg/dnsext (DNS Extensions Working Group Status) and http://tools.ietf.org/wg/dnsop (Domain Name System Operations Working Group Status).

The following are the abstracts from the recent proposals:

Signaling Cryptographic Algorithm Understanding in DNSSEC

DNS Extensions Working Group
Internet-Draft
Updates: 4035 (if approved)
Intended status: Standards Track
Expires: January 7, 2010

S. Crocker
Shinkuro Inc.
S. Rose
NIST
July 6, 2009

`draft-crocker-dnssec-algo-signal-03.txt`

The DNS Security Extensions (DNSSEC) was developed to provide origin authentication and integrity protection for DNS data by using digital signatures. These digital signatures can be generated using different algorithms. Each digital signature added to a response increases the size of the response, which could result in the response message being truncated. This draft sets out to specify a way for validating end-system resolvers to signal to a server which cryptographic algorithms they prefer in a DNSSEC response by defining an EDNS option to list a client's preferred algorithms.

DNSSEC Operational Practices, Version 2

DNSOP
Internet-Draft
Obsoletes: 2541 (if approved)
Intended status: BCP
Expires: September 8, 2009

O. Kolkman
NLnet Labs
R. Gieben

March 7, 2009

`draft-ietf-dnsop-rfc4641bis-01`

This document describes a set of practices for operating the DNS with security extensions (DNSSEC). The target audience is zone administrators deploying DNSSEC.

The document discusses operational aspects of using keys and signatures in the DNS. It discusses issues of key generation, key storage, signature generation, key rollover, and related policies.

This document obsoletes RFC 2541, as it covers more operational ground and gives more up-to-date requirements with respect to key sizes and the new DNSSEC specification.

Validation of the root trust anchor for the DNS

Network Working Group
Internet-Draft
Intended status: Informational
Expires: October 10, 2009

P. Faltstrom
Cisco
J. Schlyter
Kirei AB
April 8, 2009

`draft-faltstrom-root-trust-anchor-validation-00`

This document describes practical requirements and needs for automatic validation of the root trust anchor for the DNS. It also proposes a mechanism using PGP and/or S/MIME that can be used to fulfil the requirements.

DNSSEC Trust Anchor History Service

DNS Extensions Working Group
Internet-Draft
Intended status: Standards Track
Expires: January 1, 2010

W. Wijngaards
NLnet Labs
June 30, 2009

`draft-wijngaards-dnsext-trust-history-03`

When DNS validators have trusted keys, but have been offline for a longer period, key rollover will fail and they are stuck with stale trust anchors. History service allows validators to query for older DNSKEY RRsets and pick up the rollover trail where they left off.

Validation of the root trust anchor for the DNS

Network Working Group
Internet-Draft
Intended status: Informational
Expires: October 10, 2009

P. Faltstrom
Cisco
J. Schlyter
Kirei AB
April 8, 2009

`draft-faltstrom-root-trust-anchor-validation-00`

This document describes practical requirements and needs for automatic validation of the root trust anchor for the DNS. It also proposes a mechanism using PGP and/or S/MIME that can be used to fulfil the requirements.

Use of GOST signature algorithms in DNSKEY and RRSIG Resource Records for DNSSEC

DNS Extensions working group
Internet-Draft
Intended status: Standards Track
Expires: February 5, 2010

V.Dolmatov, Ed.
Cryptocom Ltd.
August 5, 2009

`draft-dolmatov-dnsext-dnssec-gost-01`

This document describes how to produce GOST signature and hash algorithms DNSKEY and RRSIG resource records for use in the Domain Name System Security Extensions (DNSSEC, RFC 4033, RFC 4034, and RFC 4035).

Clarifications and Implementation Notes for DNSSECbis

Network Working Group
Internet-Draft
Updates: 4033, 4034, 4035, 5155
(if approved)
Intended status: Standards Track
Expires: July 18, 2009

S. Weiler
SPARTA, Inc.
D. Blacka
VeriSign, Inc.
January 14, 2009

`draft-ietf-dnsext-dnssec-bis-updates-08`

This document is a collection of technical clarifications to the DNSSECbis document set. It is meant to serve as a resource to implementors as well as a repository of DNSSECbis errata.

Use of SHA-2 algorithms with RSA in DNSKEY and RRSIG Resource Records for DNSSEC

DNS Extensions working group
Internet-Draft
Intended status: Standards Track
Expires: December 6, 2009

J. Jansen
NLnet Labs
June 4, 2009

`draft-ietf-dnsext-dnssec-rsasha256-14`

This document describes how to produce RSA/SHA-256 and RSA/SHA-512 DNSKEY and RRSIG resource records for use in the Domain Name System Security Extensions (DNSSEC, RFC 4033, RFC 4034, and RFC 4035).

DNSSEC Validator API

DNS Extensions
Internet-Draft
Expires: August 3, 2009

S. Krishnaswamy
A. Hayatnagarkar
SPARTA, Inc.
January 30, 2009

`draft-hayatnagarkar-dnsext-validator-api-07`

The DNS Security Extensions (DNSSEC) provide origin authentication and integrity of DNS data. However, the current resolver Application Programming Interface (API) does not specify how a validating stub resolver should communicate results of DNSSEC processing back to the application. This document describes an API between applications and a validating stub resolver that allows applications to control the DNSSEC validation process and obtain results of DNSSEC processing.

DNSSEC Trust Anchor Configuration and Maintenance

Intended Status: Informational
DNS Operations
Internet-Draft
Expires: September 10, 2009

M. Larson
VeriSign
O. Gudmundsson
OGUD Consulting LLC
March 9, 2009

`draft-ietf-dnsop-dnssec-trust-anchor-03`

This document recommends a preferred format for specifying trust anchors in DNSSEC validating security-aware resolvers and describes how such a resolver should initialize trust anchors for use. This document also describes different mechanisms for keeping trust anchors up to date over time.

Elliptic Curve DSA for DNSSEC

Network Working Group   P. Hoffman
Internet-Draft   VPN Consortium
Intended status: Standards Track   July 6, 2009
Expires: January 7, 2010

```
draft-hoffman-dnssec-ecdsa-00
```

This document describes how to specify Elliptic Curve DSA keys and signatures in DNSSEC. It lists curves of different sizes, and uses the SHA-2 family of hashes for signatures.

DSA with SHA-2 for DNSSEC

Network Working Group   P. Hoffman
Internet-Draft   VPN Consortium
Intended status: Standards Track   July 6, 2009
Expires: January 7, 2010

```
draft-hoffman-dnssec-dsa-sha2-00
```

This document describes how to specify DSA keys and signatures based on SHA-256 with a specific set of parameters in DNSSEC. The keys used are 2048 bits, and have an equivalent security level of 112 bits.

DNSSEC Policy & Practice Statement Framework

Network Working Group   F. Ljunggren
Internet-Draft   Kirei AB
Intended status: Informational   A-M. Eklund-Lowinder
Expires: January 6, 2010   .SE
                                                             July 5, 2009

```
draft-ljunggren-dps-framework-00
```

This document presents a framework to assist writers of DNSSEC policy and practice statements such as registry managers on both TLD and secondary level, who have deployed DNSSEC. DNSSEC is a set of security extensions to the DNS that allows validating DNS answers by to establishing a 'chains of trust' from known public keys to the data being validated.

The aim of this framework is to describe an overall policy for serving secured DNS data and key management. In particular, the framework provides a comprehensive list of topics that potentially (at the writer's discretion) needs to be covered in a DNSSEC policy definition and practice statement.

DNSSEC OK buffer minimum size requirement and error handling

Intended Status: Standard Track
Network Working Group
Internet-Draft
Updates: 4035 (if approved)
Intended status: Standards Track
Expires: December 3, 2009

O. Gudmundsson
Shinkuro, Inc.
June 2009

```
draft-gudmundsson-dnsext-setting-ends0-do-bit-01
```

RFC3226 mandated support for EDNS0 in DNS entities claiming to support either DNS Security Extensions or IPv6 address records. This requirement was motivated because these new features increase the size of DNS messages. If EDNS0 is not supported fall back to TCP will happen, having a detrimental impact on query latency and DNS server load.

Note: The drafts listed above may be expired. They are not official specifications.

DNSSEC Books

For more information about DNSSEC, read the following books from Reed Media Services. The publisher's website is at http://www.reedmedia.net/.

BIND 9 DNS Administration Reference

The definitive documentation for the BIND 9 DNS server covering all the configuration options for *named*, and the syntax and operations for the BIND utilities, including for DNSSEC. (Edited by Jeremy C. Reed. ISBN 978-0-9790342-1-3.)

Beginning DNSSEC by Jeremy C. Reed

A quick introduction to DNSSEC basics, including the BIND tools and configurations to deploy, automate, test, and troubleshoot DNSSEC signed zones.

DNSSEC Howto by Olaf Kolkman

Step-by-step tutorial for configuring a recursive name server to validate answers, securing DNS zones, delegation of signing authority, rolling keys, and server-to-server security and transaction security. Covers BIND, NSD, and Unbound.

RFC 2181
Clarifications to the DNS Specification

Network Working Group
Request for Comments: 2181
Updates: 1034, 1035, 1123
Category: Standards Track

R. Elz
University of Melbourne
R. Bush
RGnet, Inc.

Status of this Memo

1. Abstract

This document considers some areas that have been identified as problems with the specification of the Domain Name System, and proposes remedies for the defects identified. Eight separate issues are considered:

- IP packet header address usage from multi-homed servers,

- TTLs in sets of records with the same name, class, and type,

- correct handling of zone cuts,

- three minor issues concerning SOA records and their use,

- the precise definition of the Time to Live (TTL)

- Use of the TC (truncated) header bit

- the issue of what is an authoritative, or canonical, name,

- and the issue of what makes a valid DNS label.

1

The first six of these are areas where the correct behaviour has been somewhat unclear, we seek to rectify that. The other two are already adequately specified, however the specifications seem to be sometimes ignored. We seek to reinforce the existing specifications.

RFC 2181 Contents

2. Introduction

Several problem areas in the Domain Name System specification [RFC1034, RFC1035] have been noted through the years [RFC1123]. This document addresses several additional problem areas. The issues here are independent. Those issues are the question of which source address a multi-homed DNS server should use when replying to a query, the issue of differing TTLs for DNS records with the same label, class and type, and the issue of canonical names, what they are, how CNAME records relate, what names are legal in what parts of the DNS, and what is the valid syntax of a DNS name.

Clarifications to the DNS specification to avoid these problems are made in this memo. A minor ambiguity in RFC1034 concerned with SOA records is also corrected, as is one in the definition of the TTL (Time To Live) and some possible confusion in use of the TC bit.

3. Terminology

This memo does not use the oft used expressions MUST, SHOULD, MAY, or their negative forms. In some sections it may seem that a specification is worded mildly, and hence some may infer that the specification is optional. That is not correct. Anywhere that this memo suggests that some action should be carried out, or must be carried out, or that some behaviour is acceptable, or not, that is to be considered as a fundamental aspect of this specification, regardless of the specific words used. If some behaviour or action is truly optional, that will be clearly specified by the text.

4. Server Reply Source Address Selection

Most, if not all, DNS clients, expect the address from which a reply is received to be the same address as that to which the query eliciting the reply was sent. This is true for servers acting as clients for the purposes of recursive query resolution, as well as simple resolver clients. The address, along with the identifier (ID) in the reply is used for disambiguating replies, and filtering spurious responses. This may, or may not, have been intended when the DNS was designed, but is now a fact of life.

Some multi-homed hosts running DNS servers generate a reply using a source address that is not the same as the destination address from the client's request packet. Such replies will be discarded by the client because the source address of the reply does not match that of a host to which the client sent the original request. That is, it appears to be an unsolicited response.

4.1. UDP Source Address Selection

To avoid these problems, servers when responding to queries using UDP must cause the reply to be sent with the source address field in the IP header set to the address that was in the destination address field of the IP header of the packet containing the query causing the response. If this would cause the response to be sent from an IP address that is not permitted for this purpose, then the response may be sent from any legal IP address allocated to the server. That address should be chosen to maximise the possibility that the client will be able to use it for further queries. Servers configured in such a way that not all their addresses are equally reachable from all potential clients need take particular care when responding to queries sent to anycast, multicast, or similar, addresses.

4.2. Port Number Selection

Replies to all queries must be directed to the port from which they were sent. When queries are received via TCP this is an inherent part of the transport protocol. For queries received by UDP the server must take note of the source port and use that as the destination port in the response. Replies should always be sent from the port to which they were directed. Except in extraordinary circumstances, this will be the well known port assigned for DNS queries [RFC1700].

5. Resource Record Sets

Each DNS Resource Record (RR) has a label, class, type, and data. It is meaningless for two records to ever have label, class, type and data all equal - servers should suppress such duplicates if encountered. It is however possible for most record types to exist with the same label, class and type, but with different data. Such a group of records is hereby defined to be a Resource Record Set (RRSet).

5.1. Sending RRs from an RRSet

A query for a specific (or non-specific) label, class, and type, will always return all records in the associated RRSet - whether that be one or more RRs. The response must be marked as "truncated" if the entire RRSet will not fit in the response.

5.2. TTLs of RRs in an RRSet

Resource Records also have a time to live (TTL). It is possible for the RRs in an RRSet to have different TTLs. No uses for this have been found that cannot be better accomplished in other ways. This can, however, cause partial replies (not marked "truncated") from a caching server, where the TTLs for some but not all the RRs in the RRSet have expired.

Consequently the use of differing TTLs in an RRSet is hereby deprecated, the TTLs of all RRs in an RRSet must be the same.

Should a client receive a response containing RRs from an RRSet with differing TTLs, it should treat this as an error. If the RRSet concerned is from a non-authoritative source for this data, the client should simply ignore the RRSet, and if the values were required, seek to acquire them from an authoritative source. Clients that are configured to send all queries to one, or more, particular servers should treat those servers as authoritative for this purpose. Should an authoritative source send such a malformed RRSet, the client should treat the RRs for all purposes as if all TTLs in the RRSet had been set to the value of the lowest TTL in the RRSet. In no case may a server send an RRSet with TTLs not all equal.

5.3. DNSSEC Special Cases

Two of the record types added by DNS Security (DNSSEC) [RFC2065] require special attention when considering the formation of Resource Record Sets. Those are the SIG and NXT records. It should be noted that DNS Security is still very new, and there is, as yet, little experience with it. Readers should be prepared for the information related to DNSSEC contained in this document to become outdated as the DNS Security specification matures.[1]

5.3.1. SIG records and RRSets

A SIG record provides signature (validation) data for another RRSet in the DNS.[2] Where a zone has been signed, every RRSet in the zone will have had a SIG record associated with it. The data type of the RRSet is included in the data of the SIG RR, to indicate with which particular RRSet this SIG record is associated. Were the rules above applied, whenever a SIG record was included with a response to validate that response, the SIG records for all other RRSets associated with the appropriate node would also need to be included. In some cases, this could be a very large number of records, not helped by their being rather large RRs.

---

[1]RFCs 4034 and 4035 have an update for this. See pages 109, 120, and 132.

[2]The SIG resource record is no longer used for DNSSEC per now-obsolete RFC 3755 and RFC 4034. The replacement is RRSIG. For details see pages 121 and 109.

Thus, it is specifically permitted for the authority section to contain only those SIG RRs with the "type covered" field equal to the type field of an answer being returned. However, where SIG records are being returned in the answer section, in response to a query for SIG records, or a query for all records associated with a name (type=ANY) the entire SIG RRSet must be included, as for any other RR type.

Servers that receive responses containing SIG records in the authority section, or (probably incorrectly) as additional data, must understand that the entire RRSet has almost certainly not been included. Thus, they must not cache that SIG record in a way that would permit it to be returned should a query for SIG records be received at that server. RFC2065 actually requires that SIG queries be directed only to authoritative servers to avoid the problems that could be caused here, and while servers exist that do not understand the special properties of SIG records, this will remain necessary. However, careful design of SIG record processing in new implementations should permit this restriction to be relaxed in the future, so resolvers do not need to treat SIG record queries specially.

It has been occasionally stated that a received request for a SIG record should be forwarded to an authoritative server, rather than being answered from data in the cache. This is not necessary - a server that has the knowledge of SIG as a special case for processing this way would be better to correctly cache SIG records, taking into account their characteristics. Then the server can determine when it is safe to reply from the cache, and when the answer is not available and the query must be forwarded.

5.3.2. NXT RRs

Next Resource Records (NXT) are even more peculiar.[3] There will only ever be one NXT record in a zone for a particular label, so superficially, the RRSet problem is trivial. However, at a zone cut, both the parent zone, and the child zone (superzone and subzone in RFC2065 terminology) will have NXT records for the same name. Those two NXT records do not form an RRSet, even where both zones are housed at the same server. NXT RRSets always contain just a single RR. Where both NXT records are visible, two RRSets exist. However, servers are not required to treat this as a special case when receiving NXT records in a response. They may elect to notice the existence of two different NXT RRSets, and treat that as they would two different RRSets of any other type. That is, cache one, and ignore the other. Security aware servers will need to correctly process the NXT record in the received response though.

5.4. Receiving RRSets

Servers must never merge RRs from a response with RRs in their cache to form an RRSet. If a response contains data that would form an RRSet with data in a server's cache the server must either ignore the RRs in the response, or discard the entire RRSet currently in the cache, as appropriate. Consequently the issue of TTLs varying between the cache and a response does not cause concern, one will be ignored. That is, one of the data sets is always incorrect if the data from an answer differs from the data in the cache. The challenge for the server is

---

[3]The NXT resource record is obsolete per now-obsolete RFC 3755 and RFC 4034. The replacement is NSEC. For more information, see pages 121 and 114.

to determine which of the data sets is correct, if one is, and retain that, while ignoring the other. Note that if a server receives an answer containing an RRSet that is identical to that in its cache, with the possible exception of the TTL value, it may, optionally, update the TTL in its cache with the TTL of the received answer. It should do this if the received answer would be considered more authoritative (as discussed in the next section) than the previously cached answer.

5.4.1. Ranking data

When considering whether to accept an RRSet in a reply, or retain an RRSet already in its cache instead, a server should consider the relative likely trustworthiness of the various data. An authoritative answer from a reply should replace cached data that had been obtained from additional information in an earlier reply. However additional information from a reply will be ignored if the cache contains data from an authoritative answer or a zone file.

The accuracy of data available is assumed from its source. Trustworthiness shall be, in order from most to least:

- Data from a primary zone file, other than glue data,

- Data from a zone transfer, other than glue,

- The authoritative data included in the answer section of an authoritative reply.

- Data from the authority section of an authoritative answer,

- Glue from a primary zone, or glue from a zone transfer,

- Data from the answer section of a non-authoritative answer, and non-authoritative data from the answer section of authoritative answers,

- Additional information from an authoritative answer, Data from the authority section of a non-authoritative answer, Additional information from non-authoritative answers.

Note that the answer section of an authoritative answer normally contains only authoritative data. However when the name sought is an alias (see section 10.1.1) only the record describing that alias is necessarily authoritative. Clients should assume that other records may have come from the server's cache. Where authoritative answers are required, the client should query again, using the canonical name associated with the alias.

Unauthenticated RRs received and cached from the least trustworthy of those groupings, that is data from the additional data section, and data from the authority section of a non-authoritative answer, should not be cached in such a way that they would ever be returned as answers to a received query. They may be returned as additional information where appropriate. Ignoring this would allow the trustworthiness of relatively untrustworthy data to be increased without cause or excuse.

When DNS security [RFC2065] is in use, and an authenticated reply has been received and verified, the data thus authenticated shall be considered more trustworthy than unauthenticated data of the same type. Note that throughout this document, "authoritative" means a reply with the AA bit set. DNSSEC uses trusted chains of SIG and KEY records[4] to determine the authenticity of data, the AA bit is almost irrelevant. However DNSSEC aware servers must still correctly set the AA bit in responses to enable correct operation with servers that are not security aware (almost all currently).

Note that, glue excluded, it is impossible for data from two correctly configured primary zone files, two correctly configured secondary zones (data from zone transfers) or data from correctly configured primary and secondary zones to ever conflict. Where glue for the same name exists in multiple zones, and differs in value, the nameserver should select data from a primary zone file in preference to secondary, but otherwise may choose any single set of such data. Choosing that which appears to come from a source nearer the authoritative data source may make sense where that can be determined. Choosing primary data over secondary allows the source of incorrect glue data to be discovered more readily, when a problem with such data exists. Where a server can detect from two zone files that one or more are incorrectly configured, so as to create conflicts, it should refuse to load the zones determined to be erroneous, and issue suitable diagnostics.

"Glue" above includes any record in a zone file that is not properly part of that zone, including nameserver records of delegated subzones (NS records), address records that accompany those NS records (A, AAAA, etc), and any other stray data that might appear.

5.5. Sending RRSets (reprise)

A Resource Record Set should only be included once in any DNS reply. It may occur in any of the Answer, Authority, or Additional Information sections, as required. However it should not be repeated in the same, or any other, section, except where explicitly required by a specification. For example, an AXFR response requires the SOA record (always an RRSet containing a single RR) be both the first and last record of the reply. Where duplicates are required this way, the TTL transmitted in each case must be the same.

6. Zone Cuts

The DNS tree is divided into "zones", which are collections of domains that are treated as a unit for certain management purposes. Zones are delimited by "zone cuts". Each zone cut separates a "child" zone (below the cut) from a "parent" zone (above the cut). The domain name that appears at the top of a zone (just below the cut that separates the zone from its parent) is called the zone's "origin". The name of the zone is the same as the name of the domain at the zone's origin. Each zone comprises that subset of the DNS tree that is at or below the zone's origin, and that is above the cuts that separate the zone from its children (if any). The existence of a zone cut is indicated in the parent zone by the existence of NS records specifying the origin of the child zone. A child zone does not contain any explicit reference to its parent.

---

[4]The SIG and KEY resource records are no longer used for DNSSEC per now-obsolete RFC 3755 and RFC 4034. The replacements are RRSIG and DNSKEY – see pages 121, 107, and 109 for details.

6.1. Zone authority

The authoritative servers for a zone are enumerated in the NS records for the origin of the zone, which, along with a Start of Authority (SOA) record are the mandatory records in every zone. Such a server is authoritative for all resource records in a zone that are not in another zone. The NS records that indicate a zone cut are the property of the child zone created, as are any other records for the origin of that child zone, or any sub-domains of it. A server for a zone should not return authoritative answers for queries related to names in another zone, which includes the NS, and perhaps A, records at a zone cut, unless it also happens to be a server for the other zone.

Other than the DNSSEC cases mentioned immediately below, servers should ignore data other than NS records, and necessary A records to locate the servers listed in the NS records, that may happen to be configured in a zone at a zone cut.

6.2. DNSSEC issues

The DNS security mechanisms [RFC2065] complicate this somewhat, as some of the new resource record types added are very unusual when compared with other DNS RRs. In particular the NXT ("next") RR type contains information about which names exist in a zone, and hence which do not, and thus must necessarily relate to the zone in which it exists. The same domain name may have different NXT records in the parent zone and the child zone, and both are valid, and are not an RRSet. See also section 5.3.2.

Since NXT records are intended to be automatically generated, rather than configured by DNS operators, servers may, but are not required to, retain all differing NXT records they receive regardless of the rules in section 5.4.

For a secure parent zone to securely indicate that a subzone is insecure, DNSSEC requires that a KEY RR indicating that the subzone is insecure, and the parent zone's authenticating SIG RR(s) be present in the parent zone, as they by definition cannot be in the subzone. Where a subzone is secure, the KEY and SIG records will be present, and authoritative, in that zone, but should also always be present in the parent zone (if secure).

Note that in none of these cases should a server for the parent zone, not also being a server for the subzone, set the AA bit in any response for a label at a zone cut.

7. SOA RRs

Three minor issues concerning the Start of Zone of Authority (SOA) Resource Record need some clarification.

7.1. Placement of SOA RRs in authoritative answers

RFC1034, in section 3.7, indicates that the authority section of an authoritative answer may contain the SOA record for the zone from which the answer was obtained. When discussing negative caching, RFC1034 section 4.3.4 refers to this technique but mentions the additional section of the response. The former is correct, as is implied by the example shown in section 6.2.5 of RFC1034. SOA records, if added, are to be placed in the authority section.

7.2. TTLs on SOA RRs

It may be observed that in section 3.2.1 of RFC1035, which defines the format of a Resource Record, that the definition of the TTL field contains a throw away line which states that the TTL of an SOA record should always be sent as zero to prevent caching. This is mentioned nowhere else, and has not generally been implemented. Implementations should not assume that SOA records will have a TTL of zero, nor are they required to send SOA records with a TTL of zero.

7.3. The SOA.MNAME field

It is quite clear in the specifications, yet seems to have been widely ignored, that the MNAME field of the SOA record should contain the name of the primary (master) server for the zone identified by the SOA. It should not contain the name of the zone itself. That information would be useless, as to discover it, one needs to start with the domain name of the SOA record - that is the name of the zone.

8. Time to Live (TTL)

The definition of values appropriate to the TTL field in STD 13 is not as clear as it could be, with respect to how many significant bits exist, and whether the value is signed or unsigned. It is hereby specified that a TTL value is an unsigned number, with a minimum value of 0, and a maximum value of 2147483647. That is, a maximum of $2^{31} - 1$. When transmitted, this value shall be encoded in the less significant 31 bits of the 32 bit TTL field, with the most significant, or sign, bit set to zero.

Implementations should treat TTL values received with the most significant bit set as if the entire value received was zero.

Implementations are always free to place an upper bound on any TTL received, and treat any larger values as if they were that upper bound. The TTL specifies a maximum time to live, not a mandatory time to live.

9. The TC (truncated) header bit

The TC bit should be set in responses only when an RRSet is required as a part of the response, but could not be included in its entirety. The TC bit should not be set merely because some extra information could have been included, but there was insufficient room. This includes the results of additional section processing. In such cases the entire RRSet that will not fit in the response should be omitted, and the reply sent as is, with the TC bit clear. If the recipient of the reply needs the omitted data, it can construct a query for that data and send that separately.

Where TC is set, the partial RRSet that would not completely fit may be left in the response. When a DNS client receives a reply with TC set, it should ignore that response, and query again, using a mechanism, such as a TCP connection, that will permit larger replies.

10. Naming issues

It has sometimes been inferred from some sections of the DNS specification [RFC1034, RFC1035] that a host, or perhaps an interface of a host, is permitted exactly one authoritative, or official, name, called the canonical name. There is no such requirement in the DNS.

10.1. CNAME resource records

The DNS CNAME ("canonical name") record exists to provide the canonical name associated with an alias name. There may be only one such canonical name for any one alias. That name should generally be a name that exists elsewhere in the DNS, though there are some rare applications for aliases with the accompanying canonical name undefined in the DNS. An alias name (label of a CNAME record) may, if DNSSEC is in use, have SIG, NXT, and KEY RRs, but may have no other data. That is, for any label in the DNS (any domain name) exactly one of the following is true:

- one CNAME record exists, optionally accompanied by SIG, NXT, and KEY RRs,

- one or more records exist, none being CNAME records,

- the name exists, but has no associated RRs of any type,

- the name does not exist at all.

10.1.1. CNAME terminology

It has been traditional to refer to the label of a CNAME record as "a CNAME". This is unfortunate, as "CNAME" is an abbreviation of "canonical name", and the label of a CNAME record is most certainly not a canonical name. It is, however, an entrenched usage. Care must therefore be taken to be very clear whether the label, or the value (the canonical name) of a CNAME resource record is intended. In this document, the label of a CNAME resource record will always be referred to as an alias.

10.2. PTR records

Confusion about canonical names has lead to a belief that a PTR record should have exactly one RR in its RRSet. This is incorrect, the relevant section of RFC1034 (section 3.6.2) indicates that the value of a PTR record should be a canonical name. That is, it should not be an alias. There is no implication in that section that only one PTR record is permitted for a name. No such restriction should be inferred.

Note that while the value of a PTR record must not be an alias, there is no requirement that the process of resolving a PTR record not encounter any aliases. The label that is being looked up for a PTR value might have a CNAME record. That is, it might be an alias. The value of that CNAME RR, if not another alias, which it should not be, will give the location where the PTR record is found. That record gives the result of the PTR type lookup. This final result, the value of the PTR RR, is the label which must not be an alias.

10.3. MX and NS records

The domain name used as the value of a NS resource record, or part of the value of a MX resource record must not be an alias. Not only is the specification clear on this point, but using an alias in either of these positions neither works as well as might be hoped, nor well fulfills the ambition that may have led to this approach. This domain name must have as its value one or more address records. Currently those will be A records, however in the future other record types giving addressing information may be acceptable. It can also have other RRs, but never a CNAME RR.

Searching for either NS or MX records causes "additional section processing" in which address records associated with the value of the record sought are appended to the answer. This helps avoid needless extra queries that are easily anticipated when the first was made.

Additional section processing does not include CNAME records, let alone the address records that may be associated with the canonical name derived from the alias. Thus, if an alias is used as the value of an NS or MX record, no address will be returned with the NS or MX value. This can cause extra queries, and extra network burden, on every query. It is trivial for the DNS administrator to avoid this by resolving the alias and placing the canonical name directly in the affected record just once when it is updated or installed. In some particular hard cases the lack of the additional section address records in the results of a NS lookup can cause the request to fail.

11. Name syntax

Occasionally it is assumed that the Domain Name System serves only the purpose of mapping Internet host names to data, and mapping Internet addresses to host names. This is not correct, the DNS is a general (if somewhat limited) hierarchical database, and can store almost any kind of data, for almost any purpose.

The DNS itself places only one restriction on the particular labels that can be used to identify resource records. That one restriction relates to the length of the label and the full name. The length of any one label is limited to between 1 and 63 octets. A full domain name is limited to 255 octets (including the separators). The zero length full name is defined as representing the root of the DNS tree, and is typically written and displayed as ".". Those restrictions aside, any binary string whatever can be used as the label of any resource record. Similarly, any binary string can serve as the value of any record that includes a domain name as some or all of its value (SOA, NS, MX, PTR, CNAME, and any others that may be added). Implementations of the DNS protocols must not place any restrictions on the labels that can be used. In particular, DNS servers must not refuse to serve a zone because it contains labels that might not be acceptable to some DNS client programs. A DNS server may be configurable to issue warnings when loading, or even to refuse to load, a primary zone containing labels that might be considered questionable, however this should not happen by default.

Note however, that the various applications that make use of DNS data can have restrictions imposed on what particular values are acceptable in their environment. For example, that any binary label can have an MX record does not imply that any binary name can be used as the host part of an e-mail address. Clients of the DNS can impose whatever restrictions are appropriate to their circumstances on the values they use as keys for DNS lookup requests, and on the values returned by the DNS. If the client has such restrictions, it is solely responsible for validating the data from the DNS to ensure that it conforms before it makes any use of that data.

See also [RFC1123] section 6.1.3.5.

12. Security Considerations

This document does not consider security.

In particular, nothing in section 4 is any way related to, or useful for, any security related purposes.

Section 5.4.1 is also not related to security. Security of DNS data will be obtained by the Secure DNS [RFC2065], which is mostly orthogonal to this memo.

It is not believed that anything in this document adds to any security issues that may exist with the DNS, nor does it do anything to that will necessarily lessen them. Correct implementation of the clarifications in this document might play some small part in limiting the spread of non-malicious bad data in the DNS, but only DNSSEC can help with deliberate attempts to subvert DNS data.

13. References

[RFC1034] Mockapetris, P., "Domain Names - Concepts and Facilities", STD 13, RFC 1034, November 1987.

[RFC1035] Mockapetris, P., "Domain Names - Implementation and Specification", STD 13, RFC 1035, November 1987.

[RFC1123] Braden, R., "Requirements for Internet Hosts - application and support", STD 3, RFC 1123, January 1989.

[RFC1700] Reynolds, J., Postel, J., "Assigned Numbers", STD 2, RFC 1700, October 1994.

[RFC2065] Eastlake, D., Kaufman, C., "Domain Name System Security Extensions", RFC 2065, January 1997.

14. Acknowledgements

This memo arose from discussions in the DNSIND working group of the IETF in 1995 and 1996, the members of that working group are largely responsible for the ideas captured herein. Particular thanks to Donald E. Eastlake, 3rd, and Olafur Gudmundsson, for help with the DNSSEC issues in this document, and to John Gilmore for pointing out where the clarifications were not necessarily clarifying. Bob Halley suggested clarifying the placement of SOA records in authoritative answers, and provided the references. Michael Patton, as usual, and Mark Andrews, Alan Barrett and Stan Barber provided much assistance with many details. Josh Littlefield helped make sure that the clarifications didn't cause problems in some irritating corner cases.

Authors' Addresses

Robert Elz
Computer Science
University of Melbourne
Parkville, Victoria, 3052
Australia.

EMail: kre@munnari.OZ.AU

Randy Bush
RGnet, Inc.
5147 Crystal Springs Drive NE
Bainbridge Island, Washington, 98110
United States.

EMail: randy@psg.com

RFC 2536
DSA KEYs and SIGs in the Domain Name System (DNS)

Network Working Group   D. EastLake
Request for Comments: 2536   IBM
Category: Standards Track   March 1999

Status of this Memo

This document specifies an Internet standards track protocol for the Internet community, and requests discussion and suggestions for improvements. Please refer to the current edition of the "Internet Official Protocol Standards" (STD 1) for the standardization state and status of this protocol. Distribution of this memo is unlimited.

Copyright Notice

Abstract

A standard method for storing US Government Digital Signature Algorithm keys and signatures in the Domain Name System is described which utilizes DNS KEY and SIG resource records.[5]

RFC 2536 Contents

[5]The KEY and SIG resource records are no longer used for DNSSEC per now-obsolete RFC 3755 and RFC 4034. The replacements are DNSKEY and RRSIG – see pages 121 , 107, and 109 for details.

1. Introduction

The Domain Name System (DNS) is the global hierarchical replicated distributed database system for Internet addressing, mail proxy, and other information. The DNS has been extended to include digital signatures and cryptographic keys as described in [RFC 2535]. Thus the DNS can now be secured and can be used for secure key distribution.

This document describes how to store US Government Digital Signature Algorithm (DSA) keys and signatures in the DNS. Familiarity with the US Digital Signature Algorithm is assumed [Schneier]. Implementation of DSA is mandatory for DNS security.

2. DSA KEY Resource Records

DSA public keys are stored in the DNS as KEY RRs using algorithm number 3 [RFC 2535]. The structure of the algorithm specific portion of the RDATA part of this RR is as shown below. These fields, from Q through Y are the "public key" part of the DSA KEY RR.

The period of key validity is not in the KEY RR but is indicated by the SIG RR(s) which signs and authenticates the KEY RR(s) at that domain name.

Field	Size	
T	1	octet
Q	20	octets
P	64 + T*8	octets
G	64 + T*8	octets
Y	64 + T*8	octets

As described in [FIPS 186] and [Schneier]: T is a key size parameter chosen such that $0 <= T <= 8$. (The meaning for algorithm 3 if the T octet is greater than 8 is reserved and the remainder of the RDATA portion may have a different format in that case.) Q is a prime number selected at key generation time such that $2**159 < Q < 2**160$ so Q is always 20 octets long and, as with all other fields, is stored in "big-endian" network order. P, G, and Y are calculated as directed by the FIPS 186 key generation algorithm [Schneier]. P is in the range $2**(511+64T) < P < 2**(512+64T)$ and so is 64 + 8*T octets long. G and Y are quantities modulus P and so can be up to the same length as P and are allocated fixed size fields with the same number of octets as P.

During the key generation process, a random number X must be generated such that $1 <= X <= Q-1$. X is the private key and is used in the final step of public key generation where Y is computed as

$$Y = G{**}X \bmod P$$

3. DSA SIG Resource Records

The signature portion of the SIG RR RDATA area, when using the US Digital Signature Algorithm, is shown below with fields in the order they occur. See [RFC 2535] for fields in the SIG RR RDATA which precede the signature itself.

Field	Size
T	1 octet
R	20 octets
S	20 octets

The data signed is determined as specified in [RFC 2535]. Then the following steps are taken, as specified in [FIPS 186], where Q, P, G, and Y are as specified in the public key [Schneier]:

hash = SHA–1 (data)

Generate a random K such that $0 < K < Q$.

R = (G**K mod P) mod Q

S = (K**(−1) * (hash + X*R)) mod Q

Since Q is 160 bits long, R and S can not be larger than 20 octets, which is the space allocated.

T is copied from the public key. It is not logically necessary in the SIG but is present so that values of $T > 8$ can more conveniently be used as an escape for extended versions of DSA or other algorithms as later specified.

4. Performance Considerations

General signature generation speeds are roughly the same for RSA [RFC 2537] and DSA. With sufficient pre-computation, signature generation with DSA is faster than RSA. Key generation is also faster for DSA. However, signature verification is an order of magnitude slower than RSA when the RSA public exponent is chosen to be small as is recommended for KEY RRs used in domain name system (DNS) data authentication.

Current DNS implementations are optimized for small transfers, typically less than 512 bytes including overhead. While larger transfers will perform correctly and work is underway to make larger transfers more efficient, it is still advisable at this time to make reasonable efforts to minimize the size of KEY RR sets stored within the DNS consistent with adequate security. Keep in mind that in a secure zone, at least one authenticating SIG RR will also be returned.

5. Security Considerations

Many of the general security consideration in [RFC 2535] apply. Keys retrieved from the DNS should not be trusted unless (1) they have been securely obtained from a secure resolver or independently verified by the user and (2) this secure resolver and secure obtainment or independent verification conform to security policies acceptable to the user. As with all cryptographic algorithms, evaluating the necessary strength of the key is essential and dependent on local policy.

The key size limitation of a maximum of 1024 bits (T = 8) in the current DSA standard may limit the security of DSA. For particularly critical applications, implementors are encouraged to consider the range of available algorithms and key sizes.

DSA assumes the ability to frequently generate high quality random numbers. See [RFC 1750] for guidance. DSA is designed so that if manipulated rather than random numbers are used, very high bandwidth covert channels are possible. See [Schneier] and more recent research. The leakage of an entire DSA private key in only two DSA signatures has been demonstrated. DSA provides security only if trusted implementations, including trusted random number generation, are used.

6. IANA Considerations

Allocation of meaning to values of the T parameter that are not defined herein requires an IETF standards actions. It is intended that values unallocated herein be used to cover future extensions of the DSS standard.

References

[FIPS 186] U.S. Federal Information Processing Standard: Digital Signature Standard.

[RFC 1034] Mockapetris, P., "Domain Names - Concepts and Facilities", STD 13, RFC 1034, November 1987.

[RFC 1035] Mockapetris, P., "Domain Names - Implementation and Specification", STD 13, RFC 1035, November 1987.

[RFC 1750] Eastlake, D., Crocker, S. and J. Schiller, "Randomness Recommendations for Security", RFC 1750, December 1994.

[RFC 2535] Eastlake, D., "Domain Name System Security Extensions", RFC 2535, March 1999.

[RFC 2537] Eastlake, D., "RSA/MD5 KEYs and SIGs in the Domain Name System (DNS)", RFC 2537, March 1999.

[Schneier] Schneier, B., "Applied Cryptography Second Edition: protocols, algorithms, and source code in C", 1996.

Author's Address

Donald E. Eastlake 3rd
IBM
65 Shindegan Hill Road, RR #1
Carmel, NY 10512

Phone: +1-914-276-2668(h)
+1-914-784-7913(w)
Fax: +1-914-784-3833(w)
EMail: dee3@us.ibm.com

Full Copyright Statement

RFC 2671
Extension Mechanisms for DNS (EDNS0)

Network Working Group   P. Vixie
Request for Comments: 2671   ISC
Category: Standards Track   August 1999

Status of this Memo

Copyright Notice

Abstract

The Domain Name System's wire protocol includes a number of fixed fields whose range has been or soon will be exhausted and does not allow clients to advertise their capabilities to servers. This document describes backward compatible mechanisms for allowing the protocol to grow.

RFC 2671 Contents

1 - Rationale and Scope

1.1. DNS (see [RFC1035]) specifies a Message Format and within such messages there are standard formats for encoding options, errors, and name compression. The maximum allowable size of a DNS Message is fixed. Many of DNS's protocol limits are too small for uses which are or which are desired to become common. There is no way for implementations to advertise their capabilities.

1.2. Existing clients will not know how to interpret the protocol extensions detailed here. In practice, these clients will be upgraded when they have need of a new feature, and only new features will make use of the extensions. We must however take account of client behaviour in the face of extra fields, and design a fallback scheme for interoperability with these clients.

2 - Affected Protocol Elements

2.1. The DNS Message Header's (see [RFC1035 4.1.1]) second full 16-bit word is divided into a 4-bit OPCODE, a 4-bit RCODE, and a number of 1-bit flags. The original reserved Z bits have been allocated to various purposes, and most of the RCODE values are now in use. More flags and more possible RCODEs are needed.

2.2. The first two bits of a wire format domain label are used to denote the type of the label. [RFC1035 4.1.4] allocates two of the four possible types and reserves the other two. Proposals for use of the remaining types far outnumber those available. More label types are needed.

2.3. DNS Messages are limited to 512 octets in size when sent over UDP. While the minimum maximum reassembly buffer size still allows a limit of 512 octets of UDP payload, most of the hosts now connected to the Internet are able to reassemble larger datagrams. Some mechanism must be created to allow requestors to advertise larger buffer sizes to responders.

3 - Extended Label Types

3.1. The "0 1" label type will now indicate an extended label type, whose value is encoded in the lower six bits of the first octet of a label. All subsequently developed label types should be encoded using an extended label type.

3.2. The "1 1 1 1 1 1" extended label type will be reserved for future expansion of the extended label type code space.

4 - OPT pseudo-RR

4.1. One OPT pseudo-RR can be added to the additional data section of either a request or a response. An OPT is called a pseudo-RR because it pertains to a particular transport level message and not to any actual DNS data. OPT RRs shall never be cached, forwarded, or stored in or loaded from master files. The quantity of OPT pseudo-RRs per message shall be either zero or one, but not greater.

4.2. An OPT RR has a fixed part and a variable set of options expressed as {attribute, value} pairs. The fixed part holds some DNS meta data and also a small collection of new protocol elements which we expect to be so popular that it would be a waste of wire space to encode them as {attribute, value} pairs.

4.3. The fixed part of an OPT RR is structured as follows:

Field Name	Field Type	Description
NAME	domain name	empty (root domain)
TYPE	u_int16_t	OPT
CLASS	u_int16_t	sender's UDP payload size
TTL	u_int32_t	extended RCODE and flags
RDLEN	u_int16_t	describes RDATA
RDATA	octet stream	{attribute, value} pairs

4.4. The variable part of an OPT RR is encoded in its RDATA and is structured as zero or more of the following:

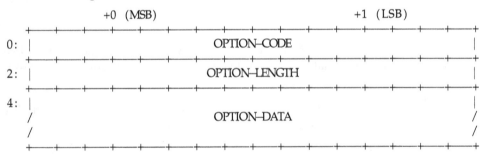

OPTION-CODE (Assigned by IANA.)

OPTION-LENGTH Size (in octets) of OPTION-DATA.

OPTION-DATA Varies per OPTION-CODE.

4.5. The sender's UDP payload size (which OPT stores in the RR CLASS field) is the number of octets of the largest UDP payload that can be reassembled and delivered in the sender's network stack. Note that path MTU, with or without fragmentation, may be smaller than this.

4.5.1. Note that a 512-octet UDP payload requires a 576-octet IP reassembly buffer. Choosing 1280 on an Ethernet connected requestor would be reasonable. The consequence of choosing too large a value may be an ICMP message from an intermediate gateway, or even a silent drop of the response message.

4.5.2. Both requestors and responders are advised to take account of the path's discovered MTU (if already known) when considering message sizes.

4.5.3. The requestor's maximum payload size can change over time, and should therefore not be cached for use beyond the transaction in which it is advertised.

4.5.4. The responder's maximum payload size can change over time, but can be reasonably expected to remain constant between two sequential transactions; for example, a meaningless QUERY to discover a responder's maximum UDP payload size, followed immediately by an UPDATE which takes advantage of this size. (This is considered preferrable to the outright use of TCP for oversized requests, if there is any reason to suspect that the responder implements EDNS, and if a request will not fit in the default 512 payload size limit.)

4.5.5. Due to transaction overhead, it is unwise to advertise an architectural limit as a maximum UDP payload size. Just because your stack can reassemble 64KB datagrams, don't assume that you want to spend more than about 4KB of state memory per ongoing transaction.

4.6. The extended RCODE and flags (which OPT stores in the RR TTL field) are structured as follows:

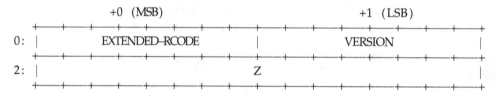

EXTENDED-RCODE Forms upper 8 bits of extended 12-bit RCODE. Note that EXTENDED-RCODE value "0" indicates that an unextended RCODE is in use (values "0" through "15").

VERSION Indicates the implementation level of whoever sets it. Full conformance with this specification is indicated by version "0." Requestors are encouraged to set this to the lowest implemented level capable of expressing a transaction, to minimize the responder and network load of discovering the greatest common implementation level between requestor and responder. A requestor's version numbering strategy should ideally be a run time configuration option.

If a responder does not implement the VERSION level of the request, then it answers with RCODE=BADVERS. All responses will be limited in format to the

VERSION level of the request, but the VERSION of each response will be the highest implementation level of the responder. In this way a requestor will learn the implementation level of a responder as a side effect of every response, including error responses, including RCODE=BADVERS.

Z Set to zero by senders and ignored by receivers, unless modified in a subsequent specification.

5 - Transport Considerations

5.1. The presence of an OPT pseudo-RR in a request should be taken as an indication that the requestor fully implements the given version of EDNS, and can correctly understand any response that conforms to that feature's specification.

5.2. Lack of use of these features in a request must be taken as an indication that the requestor does not implement any part of this specification and that the responder may make no use of any protocol extension described here in its response.

5.3. Responders who do not understand these protocol extensions are expected to send a response with RCODE NOTIMPL, FORMERR, or SERVFAIL. Therefore use of extensions should be "probed" such that a responder who isn't known to support them be allowed a retry with no extensions if it responds with such an RCODE. If a responder's capability level is cached by a requestor, a new probe should be sent periodically to test for changes to responder capability.

6 - Security Considerations

Requestor-side specification of the maximum buffer size may open a new DNS denial of service attack if responders can be made to send messages which are too large for intermediate gateways to forward, thus leading to potential ICMP storms between gateways and responders.

7 - IANA Considerations

The IANA has assigned RR type code 41 for OPT.

It is the recommendation of this document and its working group that IANA create a registry for EDNS Extended Label Types, for EDNS Option Codes, and for EDNS Version Numbers.

This document assigns label type 0b01xxxxxx as "EDNS Extended Label Type." We request that IANA record this assignment.

This document assigns extended label type 0bxx111111 as "Reserved for future extended label types." We request that IANA record this assignment.

This document assigns option code 65535 to "Reserved for future expansion."

This document expands the RCODE space from 4 bits to 12 bits. This will allow IANA to assign more than the 16 distinct RCODE values allowed in [RFC1035].

This document assigns EDNS Extended RCODE "16" to "BADVERS".

IESG approval should be required to create new entries in the EDNS Extended Label Type or EDNS Version Number registries, while any published RFC (including Informational, Experimental, or BCP) should be grounds for allocation of an EDNS Option Code.

8 - Acknowledgements

Paul Mockapetris, Mark Andrews, Robert Elz, Don Lewis, Bob Halley, Donald Eastlake, Rob Austein, Matt Crawford, Randy Bush, and Thomas Narten were each instrumental in creating and refining this specification.

9 - References

[RFC1035] Mockapetris, P., "Domain Names - Implementation and Specification", STD 13, RFC 1035, November 1987.

10 - Author's Address

Paul Vixie
Internet Software Consortium
950 Charter Street
Redwood City, CA 94063

Phone: +1 650 779 7001
EMail: vixie@isc.org

11 - Full Copyright Statement

Acknowledgement

Funding for the RFC Editor function is currently provided by the Internet Society.

RFC 3007
Secure Domain Name System (DNS) Dynamic Update

Network Working Group
Request for Comments: 3007
Updates: 2535, 2136
Obsoletes: 2137
Category: Standards Track

B. Wellington
Nominum
November 2000

Status of this Memo

Copyright Notice

Abstract

This document proposes a method for performing secure Domain Name System (DNS) dynamic updates. The method described here is intended to be flexible and useful while requiring as few changes to the protocol as possible. The authentication of the dynamic update message is separate from later DNSSEC validation of the data. Secure communication based on authenticated requests and transactions is used to provide authorization.

The key words "MUST", "MUST NOT", "REQUIRED", "SHALL", "SHALL NOT", "SHOULD", "SHOULD NOT", "RECOMMENDED", "MAY", and "OPTIONAL" in this document are to be interpreted as described in RFC 2119 [RFC2119].

RFC 3007 Contents

1 - Introduction

This document defines a means to secure dynamic updates of the Domain Name System (DNS), allowing only authorized sources to make changes to a zone's contents. The existing unsecured dynamic update operations form the basis for this work.

Familiarity with the DNS system [RFC1034, RFC1035] and dynamic update [RFC2136] is helpful and is assumed by this document. In addition, knowledge of DNS security extensions [RFC2535], SIG(0) transaction security [RFC2535, RFC2931], and TSIG transaction security [RFC2845] is recommended.

This document updates portions of RFC 2535, in particular section 3.1.2, and RFC 2136. This document obsoletes RFC 2137, an alternate proposal for secure dynamic update, due to implementation experience.

1.1 - Overview of DNS Dynamic Update

DNS dynamic update defines a new DNS opcode and a new interpretation of the DNS message if that opcode is used. An update can specify insertions or deletions of data, along with prerequisites necessary for the updates to occur. All tests and changes for a DNS update request are restricted to a single zone, and are performed at the primary server for the zone. The primary server for a dynamic zone must increment the zone SOA serial number when an update occurs or before the next retrieval of the SOA.

1.2 - Overview of DNS Transaction Security

Exchanges of DNS messages which include TSIG [RFC2845] or SIG(0) [RFC2535, RFC2931] records allow two DNS entities to authenticate DNS requests and responses sent between them. A TSIG MAC (message authentication code) is derived from a shared secret, and a SIG(0) is generated from a private key whose public counterpart is stored in DNS. In both cases, a record containing the message signature/MAC is included as the final resource record in a DNS message. Keyed hashes, used in TSIG, are inexpensive to calculate and verify. Public key encryption, as used in SIG(0), is more scalable as the public keys are stored in DNS.

1.3 - Comparison of data authentication and message authentication

Message based authentication, using TSIG or SIG(0), provides protection for the entire message with a single signing and single verification which, in the case of TSIG, is a relatively inexpensive MAC creation and check. For update requests, this signature can establish, based on policy or key negotiation, the authority to make the request.

DNSSEC SIG records can be used to protect the integrity of individual RRs or RRsets in a DNS message with the authority of the zone owner. However, this cannot sufficiently protect the dynamic update request.

Using SIG records to secure RRsets in an update request is incompatible with the design of update, as described below, and would in any case require multiple expensive public key signatures and verifications.

SIG records do not cover the message header, which includes record counts. Therefore, it is possible to maliciously insert or remove RRsets in an update request without causing a verification failure.

If SIG records were used to protect the prerequisite section, it would be impossible to determine whether the SIGs themselves were a prerequisite or simply used for validation.

In the update section of an update request, signing requests to add an RRset is straightforward, and this signature could be permanently used to protect the data, as specified in [RFC2535]. However, if an RRset is deleted, there is no data for a SIG to cover.

1.4 - Data and message signatures

As specified in [RFC3008], the DNSSEC validation process performed by a resolver MUST NOT process any non-zone keys unless local policy dictates otherwise. When performing secure dynamic update, all zone data modified in a signed zone MUST be signed by a relevant zone key. This completely disassociates authentication of an update request from authentication of the data itself.

The primary usefulness of host and user keys, with respect to DNSSEC, is to authenticate messages, including dynamic updates. Thus, host and user keys MAY be used to generate SIG(0) records to authenticate updates and MAY be used in the TKEY [RFC2930] process to generate TSIG shared secrets. In both cases, no SIG records generated by non-zone keys will be used in a DNSSEC validation process unless local policy dictates.

Authentication of data, once it is present in DNS, only involves DNSSEC zone keys and signatures generated by them.

1.5 - Signatory strength

[RFC2535, section 3.1.2] defines the signatory field of a key as the final 4 bits of the flags field, but does not define its value. This proposal leaves this field undefined. Updating [RFC2535], this field SHOULD be set to 0 in KEY records, and MUST be ignored.

2 - Authentication

TSIG or SIG(0) records MUST be included in all secure dynamic update messages. This allows the server to verifiably determine the originator of a message. If the message contains authentication in the form of a SIG(0), the identity of the sender (that is, the principal) is the owner of the KEY RR that generated the SIG(0). If the message contains a TSIG generated by a statically configured shared secret, the principal is the same as or derived from the shared secret name. If the message contains a TSIG generated by a dynamically configured shared secret, the principal is the same as the one that authenticated the TKEY process; if the TKEY process was unauthenticated, no information is known about the principal, and the associated TSIG shared secret MUST NOT be used for secure dynamic update.

SIG(0) signatures SHOULD NOT be generated by zone keys, since transactions are initiated by a host or user, not a zone.

DNSSEC SIG records (other than SIG(0)) MAY be included in an update message, but MUST NOT be used to authenticate the update request.

If an update fails because it is signed with an unauthorized key, the server MUST indicate failure by returning a message with RCODE REFUSED. Other TSIG, SIG(0), or dynamic update errors are returned as specified in the appropriate protocol description.

3 - Policy

All policy is configured by the zone administrator and enforced by the zone's primary name server. Policy dictates the authorized actions that an authenticated principal can take. Policy checks are based on the principal and the desired action, where the principal is derived from the message signing key and applied to dynamic update messages signed with that key.

The server's policy defines criteria which determine if the key used to sign the update is permitted to perform the requested updates. By default, a principal MUST NOT be permitted to make any changes to zone data; any permissions MUST be enabled though configuration.

The policy is fully implemented in the primary zone server's configuration for several reasons. This removes limitations imposed by encoding policy into a fixed number of bits (such as the KEY RR's signatory field). Policy is only relevant in the server applying it, so there is no reason to expose it. Finally, a change in policy or a new type of policy should not affect the DNS protocol or data format, and should not cause interoperability failures.

3.1 - Standard policies

Implementations SHOULD allow access control policies to use the principal as an authorization token, and MAY also allow policies to grant permission to a signed message regardless of principal.

A common practice would be to restrict the permissions of a principal by domain name. That is, a principal could be permitted to add, delete, or modify entries corresponding to one or more domain names. Implementations SHOULD allow per-name access control, and SHOULD provide a concise representation of the principal's own name, its subdomains, and all names in the zone.

Additionally, a server SHOULD allow restricting updates by RR type, so that a principal could add, delete, or modify specific record types at certain names. Implementations SHOULD allow per-type access control, and SHOULD provide concise representations of all types and all "user" types, where a user type is defined as one that does not affect the operation of DNS itself.

3.1.1 - User types

User types include all data types except SOA, NS, SIG, and NXT. SOA and NS records SHOULD NOT be modified by normal users, since these types create or modify delegation points. The addition of SIG records can lead to attacks resulting in additional workload for resolvers, and the deletion of SIG records could lead to extra work for the server if the zone SIG was deleted. Note that these records are not forbidden, but not recommended for normal users.

NXT records MUST NOT be created, modified, or deleted by dynamic update, as their update may cause instability in the protocol. This is an update to RFC 2136.

Issues concerning updates of KEY records are discussed in the Security Considerations section.

3.2 - Additional policies

Users are free to implement any policies. Policies may be as specific or general as desired, and as complex as desired. They may depend on the principal or any other characteristics of the signed message.

4 - Interaction with DNSSEC

Although this protocol does not change the way updates to secure zones are processed, there are a number of issues that should be clarified.

4.1 - Adding SIGs

An authorized update request MAY include SIG records with each RRset. Since SIG records (except SIG(0) records) MUST NOT be used for authentication of the update message, they are not required.

If a principal is authorized to update SIG records and there are SIG records in the update, the SIG records are added without verification. The server MAY examine SIG records and drop SIGs with a temporal validity period in the past.

4.2 - Deleting SIGs

If a principal is authorized to update SIG records and the update specifies the deletion of SIG records, the server MAY choose to override the authority and refuse the update. For example, the server may allow all SIG records not generated by a zone key to be deleted.

4.3 - Non-explicit updates to SIGs

If the updated zone is secured, the RRset affected by an update operation MUST, at the completion of the update, be signed in accordance with the zone's signing policy. This will usually require one or more SIG records to be generated by one or more zone keys whose private components MUST be online [RFC3008].

When the contents of an RRset are updated, the server MAY delete all associated SIG records, since they will no longer be valid.

4.4 - Effects on the zone

If any changes are made, the server MUST, if necessary, generate a new SOA record and new NXT records, and sign these with the appropriate zone keys. Changes to NXT records by secure dynamic update are explicitly forbidden. SOA updates are allowed, since the maintenance of SOA parameters is outside of the scope of the DNS protocol.

5 - Security Considerations

This document requires that a zone key and possibly other cryptographic secret material be held in an on-line, network-connected host, most likely a name server. This material is at the mercy of host security to remain a secret. Exposing this secret puts DNS data at risk of masquerade attacks. The data at risk is that in both zones served by the machine and delegated from this machine.

Allowing updates of KEY records may lead to undesirable results, since a principal may be allowed to insert a public key without holding the private key, and possibly masquerade as the key owner.

6 - Acknowledgements

The author would like to thank the following people for review and informative comments (in alphabetical order):

Harald Alvestrand
Donald Eastlake
Olafur Gudmundsson

Andreas Gustafsson
Bob Halley
Stuart Kwan
Ed Lewis

7 - References

[RFC1034] Mockapetris, P., "Domain Names - Concepts and Facilities", STD 13, RFC 1034, November 1987.

[RFC1035] Mockapetris, P., "Domain Names - Implementation and Specification", STD 13, RFC 1035, November 1987.

[RFC2136] Vixie (Ed.), P., Thomson, S., Rekhter, Y. and J. Bound, "Dynamic Updates in the Domain Name System", RFC 2136, April 1997.

[RFC2137] Eastlake, D., "Secure Domain Name System Dynamic Update", RFC 2137, April 1997.

[RFC2535] Eastlake, G., "Domain Name System Security Extensions", RFC 2535, March 1999.

[RFC2845] Vixie, P., Gudmundsson, O., Eastlake, D. and B. Wellington, "Secret Key Transaction Signatures for DNS (TSIG)", RFC 2845, May 2000.

[RFC2930] Eastlake, D., "Secret Key Establishment for DNS (TKEY RR)", RFC 2930, September 2000.

[RFC2931] Eastlake, D., "DNS Request and Transaction Signatures (SIG(0)s)", RFC 2931, September 2000.

[RFC3008] Wellington, B., "Domain Name System Security (DNSSEC) Signing Authority", RFC 3008, November 2000.

8 - Author's Address

Brian Wellington
Nominum, Inc.
950 Charter Street
Redwood City, CA 94063

Phone: +1 650 381 6022
EMail: Brian.Wellington@nominum.com

9. Full Copyright Statement

Acknowledgement

Funding for the RFC Editor function is currently provided by the Internet Society.

RFC 3110
RSA/SHA-1 SIGs and RSA KEYs in the Domain Name System (DNS)

Network Working Group   D. Eastlake 3rd
Request for Comments: 3110   Motorola
Obsoletes: 2537   May 2001
Category: Standards Track

Status of this Memo

Copyright Notice

Abstract

This document describes how to produce RSA/SHA1 SIG resource records (RRs) in Section 3 and, so as to completely replace RFC 2537, describes how to produce RSA KEY RRs in Section 2.

Since the adoption of a Proposed Standard for RSA signatures in the DNS (Domain Name Space), advances in hashing have been made. A new DNS signature algorithm is defined to make these advances available in SIG RRs. The use of the previously specified weaker mechanism is deprecated. The algorithm number of the RSA KEY RR is changed to correspond to this new SIG algorithm. No other changes are made to DNS security.

Acknowledgements

Material and comments from the following have been incorporated and are gratefully acknowledged:

Olafur Gudmundsson

The IESG

Charlie Kaufman

Steve Wang

RFC 3110 Contents

1. Introduction

The Domain Name System (DNS) is the global hierarchical replicated distributed database system for Internet addressing, mail proxy, and other information [RFC1034, 1035, etc.]. The DNS has been extended to include digital signatures and cryptographic keys as described in [RFC2535]. Thus the DNS can now be secured and used for secure key distribution.

Familiarity with the RSA and SHA-1 algorithms is assumed [Schneier, FIP180] in this document.

RFC 2537 described how to store RSA keys and RSA/MD5 based signatures in the DNS. However, since the adoption of RFC 2537, continued cryptographic research has revealed hints of weakness in the MD5 [RFC1321] algorithm used in RFC 2537. The SHA1 Secure Hash Algorithm [FIP180], which produces a larger hash, has been developed. By now there has been sufficient experience with SHA1 that it is generally acknowledged to be stronger than MD5. While this stronger hash is probably not needed today in most secure DNS zones, critical zones such a root, most top level domains, and some second and third level domains, are sufficiently valuable targets that it would be negligent not to provide what are generally agreed to be stronger mechanisms. Furthermore, future advances in cryptanalysis and/or computer speeds may require a stronger hash everywhere. In addition, the additional computation required by SHA1 above that required by MD5 is insignificant compared with the computational effort required by the RSA modular exponentiation.

This document describes how to produce RSA/SHA1 SIG RRs in Section 3 and, so as to completely replace RFC 2537, describes how to produce RSA KEY RRs in Section 2.

Implementation of the RSA algorithm in DNS with SHA1 is MANDATORY for DNSSEC. The generation of RSA/MD5 SIG RRs as described in RFC 2537 is NOT RECOMMENDED.

The key words "MUST", "REQUIRED", "SHOULD", "RECOMMENDED", "NOT RECOM-MENDED", and "MAY" in this document are to be interpreted as described in RFC 2119.

2. RSA Public KEY Resource Records

RSA public keys are stored in the DNS as KEY RRs using algorithm number 5 [RFC2535]. The structure of the algorithm specific portion of the RDATA part of such RRs is as shown below.

Field	Size
exponent length	1 or 3 octets (see text)
exponent	as specified by length field
modulus	remaining space

For interoperability, the exponent and modulus are each limited to 4096 bits in length. The public key exponent is a variable length unsigned integer. Its length in octets is represented as one octet if it is in the range of 1 to 255 and by a zero octet followed by a two octet unsigned length if it is longer than 255 bytes. The public key modulus field is a multiprecision unsigned integer. The length of the modulus can be determined from the RDLENGTH and the preceding RDATA fields including the exponent. Leading zero octets are prohibited in the exponent and modulus.

Note: KEY RRs for use with RSA/SHA1 DNS signatures MUST use this algorithm number (rather than the algorithm number specified in the obsoleted RFC 2537).

Note: This changes the algorithm number for RSA KEY RRs to be the same as the new algorithm number for RSA/SHA1 SIGs.

3. RSA/SHA1 SIG Resource Records

RSA/SHA1 signatures are stored in the DNS using SIG resource records (RRs) with algorithm number 5.

The signature portion of the SIG RR RDATA area, when using the RSA/SHA1 algorithm, is calculated as shown below. The data signed is determined as specified in RFC 2535. See RFC 2535 for fields in the SIG RR RDATA which precede the signature itself.

```
hash = SHA1 ( data )

signature = ( 01 | FF* | 00 | prefix | hash ) ** e (mod n)
```

where SHA1 is the message digest algorithm documented in [FIP180], "—" is concatenation, "e" is the private key exponent of the signer, and "n" is the modulus of the signer's public key. 01, FF, and 00 are fixed octets of the corresponding hexadecimal value. "prefix" is the ASN.1 BER SHA1 algorithm designator prefix required in PKCS1 [RFC2437], that is,

    hex 30 21 30 09 06 05 2B 0E 03 02 1A 05 00 04 14

This prefix is included to make it easier to use standard cryptographic libraries. The FF octet MUST be repeated the maximum number of times such that the value of the quantity being exponentiated is one octet shorter than the value of n.

(The above specifications are identical to the corresponding parts of Public Key Cryptographic Standard #1 [RFC2437].)

The size of "n", including most and least significant bits (which will be 1) MUST be not less than 512 bits and not more than 4096 bits. "n" and "e" SHOULD be chosen such that the public exponent is small. These are protocol limits. For a discussion of key size see RFC 2541.

Leading zero bytes are permitted in the RSA/SHA1 algorithm signature.

4. Performance Considerations

General signature generation speeds are roughly the same for RSA and DSA [RFC2536]. With sufficient pre-computation, signature generation with DSA is faster than RSA. Key generation is also faster for DSA. However, signature verification is an order of magnitude slower with DSA when the RSA public exponent is chosen to be small as is recommended for KEY RRs used in domain name system (DNS) data authentication.

A public exponent of 3 minimizes the effort needed to verify a signature. Use of 3 as the public exponent is weak for confidentiality uses since, if the same data can be collected encrypted under three different keys with an exponent of 3 then, using the Chinese Remainder Theorem [NETSEC], the original plain text can be easily recovered. If a key is known to be used only for authentication, as is the case with DNSSEC, then an exponent of 3 is acceptable. However other applications in the future may wish to leverage DNS distributed keys for applications that do require confidentiality. For keys which might have such other uses, a more conservative choice would be 65537 (F4, the fourth fermat number).

Current DNS implementations are optimized for small transfers, typically less than 512 bytes including DNS overhead. Larger transfers will perform correctly and extensions have been standardized [RFC2671] to make larger transfers more efficient, it is still advisable at this time to make reasonable efforts to minimize the size of KEY RR sets stored within the DNS consistent with adequate security. Keep in mind that in a secure zone, at least one authenticating SIG RR will also be returned.

5. IANA Considerations

The DNSSEC algorithm number 5 is allocated for RSA/SHA1 SIG RRs and RSA KEY RRs.

6. Security Considerations

Many of the general security considerations in RFC 2535 apply. Keys retrieved from the DNS should not be trusted unless (1) they have been securely obtained from a secure resolver or independently verified by the user and (2) this secure resolver and secure obtainment or independent verification conform to security policies acceptable to the user. As with all cryptographic algorithms, evaluating the necessary strength of the key is essential and dependent on local policy. For particularly critical applications, implementers are encouraged to consider the range of available algorithms and key sizes. See also RFC 2541, "DNS Security Operational Considerations".

References

[FIP180]   U.S. Department of Commerce, "Secure Hash Standard", FIPS PUB 180-1, 17 Apr 1995.

[NETSEC]   Network Security: PRIVATE Communications in a PUBLIC World, Charlie Kaufman, Radia Perlman, & Mike Speciner, Prentice Hall Series in Computer Networking and Distributed Communications, 1995.

[RFC1034] Mockapetris, P., "Domain Names - Concepts and Facilities", STD 13, RFC 1034, November 1987.

[RFC1035] Mockapetris, P., "Domain Names - Implementation and Specification", STD 13, RFC 1035, November 1987.

[RFC1321] Rivest, R., "The MD5 Message-Digest Algorithm", RFC 1321, April 1992.

[RFC2119] Bradner, S., "Key words for use in RFCs to Indicate Requirement Levels", BCP 14, RFC 2119, March 1997.

[RFC2437] Kaliski, B. and J. Staddon, "PKCS #1: RSA Cryptography Specifications Version 2.0", RFC 2437, October 1998.

[RFC2535] Eastlake, D., "Domain Name System Security Extensions", RFC 2535, March 1999.

[RFC2536] Eastlake, D., "DSA KEYs and SIGs in the Domain Name System (DNS)", RFC 2536, March 1999.

[RFC2537] Eastlake, D., "RSA/MD5 KEYs and SIGs in the Domain Name System (DNS)", RFC 2537, March 1999.

[RFC2541] Eastlake, D., "DNS Security Operational Considerations", RFC 2541, March 1999.

[RFC2671] Vixie, P., "Extension Mechanisms for DNS (EDNS0)", RFC 2671, August 1999.

[Schneier] Bruce Schneier, "Applied Cryptography Second Edition: protocols, algorithms, and source code in C", 1996, John Wiley and Sons, ISBN 0-471-11709-9.

Author's Address

Donald E. Eastlake 3rd
Motorola
155 Beaver Street
Milford, MA 01757 USA

Phone: +1-508-261-5434 (w)
         +1-508-634-2066 (h)
Fax   +1-508-261-4777 (w)
EMail: Donald.Eastlake@motorola.com

Full Copyright Statement

Acknowledgement

Funding for the RFC Editor function is currently provided by the Internet Society.

RFC 3225
Indicating Resolver Support of DNSSEC

Network Working Group
Request for Comments: 3225
Category: Standards Track

D. Conrad
Nominum, Inc.
December 2001

Status of this Memo

This document specifies an Internet standards track protocol for the Internet community, and requests discussion and suggestions for improvements. Please refer to the current edition of the "Internet Official Protocol Standards" (STD 1) for the standardization state and status of this protocol. Distribution of this memo is unlimited.

Copyright Notice

Abstract

In order to deploy DNSSEC (Domain Name System Security Extensions) operationally, DNSSEC aware servers should only perform automatic inclusion of DNSSEC RRs when there is an explicit indication that the resolver can understand those RRs. This document proposes the use of a bit in the EDNS0 header to provide that explicit indication and describes the necessary protocol changes to implement that notification.

RFC 3225 Contents

1. Introduction

DNSSEC [RFC2535] has been specified to provide data integrity and authentication to security aware resolvers and applications through the use of cryptographic digital signatures. However, as DNSSEC is deployed, non-DNSSEC-aware clients will likely query DNSSEC-aware servers. In such situations, the DNSSEC-aware server (responding to a request for data in a signed zone) will respond with SIG, KEY, and/or NXT records. For reasons described in the subsequent section, such responses can have significant negative operational impacts for the DNS infrastructure.

This document discusses a method to avoid these negative impacts, namely DNSSEC-aware servers should only respond with SIG, KEY, and/or NXT RRs when there is an explicit indication from the resolver that it can understand those RRs.

For the purposes of this document, "DNSSEC security RRs" are considered RRs of type SIG, KEY, or NXT.

The key words "MUST", "MUST NOT", "REQUIRED", "SHALL", "SHALL NOT", "SHOULD", "SHOULD NOT", "RECOMMENDED", "MAY", and "OPTIONAL" in this document are to be interpreted as described in [RFC2119].

2. Rationale

Initially, as DNSSEC is deployed, the vast majority of queries will be from resolvers that are not DNSSEC aware and thus do not understand or support the DNSSEC security RRs. When a query from such a resolver is received for a DNSSEC signed zone, the DNSSEC specification indicates the nameserver must respond with the appropriate DNSSEC security RRs. As DNS UDP datagrams are limited to 512 bytes [RFC1035], responses including DNSSEC security RRs have a high probability of resulting in a truncated response being returned and the resolver retrying the query using TCP.

TCP DNS queries result in significant overhead due to connection setup and teardown. Operationally, the impact of these TCP queries will likely be quite detrimental in terms of increased network traffic (typically five packets for a single query/response instead of two), increased latency resulting from the additional round trip times, increased incidences of queries failing due to timeouts, and significantly increased load on nameservers.

In addition, in preliminary and experimental deployment of DNSSEC, there have been reports of non-DNSSEC aware resolvers being unable to handle responses which contain DNSSEC security RRs, resulting in the resolver failing (in the worst case) or entire responses being ignored (in the better case).

Given these operational implications, explicitly notifying the nameserver that the client is prepared to receive (if not understand) DNSSEC security RRs would be prudent.

44

Client-side support of DNSSEC is assumed to be binary – either the client is willing to receive all DNSSEC security RRs or it is not willing to accept any. As such, a single bit is sufficient to indicate client-side DNSSEC support. As effective use of DNSSEC implies the need of EDNS0 [RFC2671], bits in the "classic" (non-EDNS enhanced DNS header) are scarce, and there may be situations in which non-compliant caching or forwarding servers inappropriately copy data from classic headers as queries are passed on to authoritative servers, the use of a bit from the EDNS0 header is proposed.

An alternative approach would be to use the existence of an EDNS0 header as an implicit indication of client-side support of DNSSEC. This approach was not chosen as there may be applications in which EDNS0 is supported but in which the use of DNSSEC is inappropriate.

3. Protocol Changes

The mechanism chosen for the explicit notification of the ability of the client to accept (if not understand) DNSSEC security RRs is using the most significant bit of the Z field on the EDNS0 OPT header in the query. This bit is referred to as the "DNSSEC OK" (DO) bit. In the context of the EDNS0 OPT meta-RR, the DO bit is the first bit of the third and fourth bytes of the "extended RCODE and flags" portion of the EDNS0 OPT meta-RR, structured as follows:

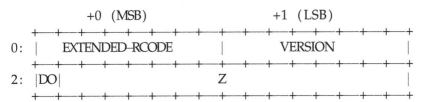

Setting the DO bit to one in a query indicates to the server that the resolver is able to accept DNSSEC security RRs. The DO bit cleared (set to zero) indicates the resolver is unprepared to handle DNSSEC security RRs and those RRs MUST NOT be returned in the response (unless DNSSEC security RRs are explicitly queried for). The DO bit of the query MUST be copied in the response.

More explicitly, DNSSEC-aware nameservers MUST NOT insert SIG, KEY, or NXT RRs to authenticate a response as specified in [RFC2535] unless the DO bit was set on the request. Security records that match an explicit SIG, KEY, NXT, or ANY query, or are part of the zone data for an AXFR or IXFR query, are included whether or not the DO bit was set.

A recursive DNSSEC-aware server MUST set the DO bit on recursive requests, regardless of the status of the DO bit on the initiating resolver request. If the initiating resolver request does not have the DO bit set, the recursive DNSSEC-aware server MUST remove DNSSEC security RRs before returning the data to the client, however cached data MUST NOT be modified.

In the event a server returns a NOTIMP, FORMERR or SERVFAIL response to a query that has the DO bit set, the resolver SHOULD NOT expect DNSSEC security RRs and SHOULD retry the query without EDNS0 in accordance with section 5.3 of [RFC2671].

Security Considerations

The absence of DNSSEC data in response to a query with the DO bit set MUST NOT be taken to mean no security information is available for that zone as the response may be forged or a non-forged response of an altered (DO bit cleared) query.

IANA Considerations

EDNS0 [RFC2671] defines 16 bits as extended flags in the OPT record, these bits are encoded into the TTL field of the OPT record (RFC2671 section 4.6).

This document reserves one of these bits as the OK bit. It is requested that the left most bit be allocated. Thus the USE of the OPT record TTL field would look like

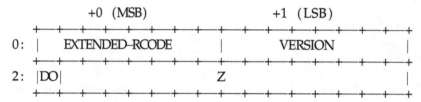

Acknowledgements

This document is based on a rough draft by Bob Halley with input from Olafur Gudmundsson, Andreas Gustafsson, Brian Wellington, Randy Bush, Rob Austein, Steve Bellovin, and Erik Nordmark.

References

[RFC1034] Mockapetris, P., "Domain Names - Concepts and Facilities", STD 13, RFC 1034, November 1987.

[RFC1035] Mockapetris, P., "Domain Names - Implementation and Specifications", STD 13, RFC 1035, November 1987.

[RFC2119] Bradner, S., "Key words for use in RFCs to Indicate Requirement Levels", BCP 14, RFC 2119, March 1997.

[RFC2535] Eastlake, D., "Domain Name System Security Extensions", RFC 2535, March 1999.

[RFC2671] Vixie, P., "Extension Mechanisms for DNS (EDNS0)", RFC 2671, August 1999.

Author's Address

David Conrad
Nominum Inc.
950 Charter Street
Redwood City, CA 94063
USA

Phone: +1 650 381 6003
EMail: david.conrad@nominum.com

Full Copyright Statement

Acknowledgement

Funding for the RFC Editor function is currently provided by the Internet Society.

RFC 3226
DNSSEC and IPv6 A6 Aware Server/Resolver Message Size Requirements

Network Working Group
Request for Comments: 3226
Updates: 2874, 2535
Category: Standards Track

O. Gudmundsson
December 2001

Status of this Memo

This document specifies an Internet standards track protocol for the Internet community, and requests discussion and suggestions for improvements. Please refer to the current edition of the "Internet Official Protocol Standards" (STD 1) for the standardization state and status of this protocol. Distribution of this memo is unlimited.

Copyright Notice

Abstract

This document mandates support for EDNS0 (Extension Mechanisms for DNS) in DNS entities claiming to support either DNS Security Extensions or A6 records. This requirement is necessary because these new features increase the size of DNS messages. If EDNS0 is not supported fall back to TCP will happen, having a detrimental impact on query latency and DNS server load. This document updates RFC 2535 and RFC 2874, by adding new requirements.

RFC 3226 Contents

1. Introduction

Familiarity with the DNS [RFC1034, RFC1035], DNS Security Extensions [RFC2535], EDNS0 [RFC2671] and A6 [RFC2874] is helpful.

STD 13, RFC 1035 Section 2.3.4 requires that DNS messages over UDP have a data payload of 512 octets or less. Most DNS software today will not accept larger UDP datagrams. Any answer that requires more than 512 octets, results in a partial and sometimes useless reply with the Truncation Bit set; in most cases the requester will then retry using TCP. Furthermore, server delivery of truncated responses varies widely and resolver handling of these responses also varies, leading to additional inefficiencies in handling truncation.

Compared to UDP, TCP is an expensive protocol to use for a simple transaction like DNS: a TCP connection requires 5 packets for setup and tear down, excluding data packets, thus requiring at least 3 round trips on top of the one for the original UDP query. The DNS server also needs to keep a state of the connection during this transaction. Many DNS servers answer thousands of queries per second, requiring them to use TCP will cause significant overhead and delays.

1.1. Requirements

The key words "MUST", "REQUIRED", "SHOULD", "RECOMMENDED", and "MAY" in this document are to be interpreted as described in RFC 2119.

2. Motivating factors

2.1. DNSSEC motivations

DNSSEC [RFC2535] secures DNS by adding a Public Key signature on each RR set. These signatures range in size from about 80 octets to 800 octets, most are going to be in the range of 80 to 200 octets. The addition of signatures on each or most RR sets in an answer significantly increases the size of DNS answers from secure zones.

For performance reasons and to reduce load on DNS servers, it is important that security aware servers and resolvers get all the data in Answer and Authority section in one query without truncation. Sending Additional Data in the same query is helpful when the server is authoritative for the data, and this reduces round trips.

DNSSEC OK[OK] specifies how a client can, using EDNS0, indicate that it is interested in receiving DNSSEC records. The OK bit does not eliminate the need for large answers for DNSSEC capable clients.

2.1.1. Message authentication or TSIG motivation

TSIG [RFC2845] allows for the light weight authentication of DNS messages, but increases the size of the messages by at least 70 octets. DNSSEC specifies for computationally expensive message authentication SIG(0) using a standard public key signature. As only one TSIG or SIG(0) can be attached to each DNS answer the size increase of message authentication is not significant, but may still lead to a truncation.

2.2. IPv6 Motivations

IPv6 addresses [RFC2874] are 128 bits and can be represented in the DNS by multiple A6 records, each consisting of a domain name and a bit field. The domain name refers to an address prefix that may require additional A6 RRs to be included in the answer. Answers where the queried name has multiple A6 addresses may overflow a 512-octet UDP packet size.

2.3. Root server and TLD server motivations

The current number of root servers is limited to 13 as that is the maximum number of name servers and their address records that fit in one 512-octet answer for a SOA record. If root servers start advertising A6 or KEY records then the answer for the root NS records will not fit in a single 512-octet DNS message, resulting in a large number of TCP query connections to the root servers. Even if all client resolver query their local name server for information, there are millions of these servers. Each name server must periodically update its information about the high level servers.

For redundancy, latency and load balancing reasons, large numbers of DNS servers are required for some zones. Since the root zone is used by the entire net, it is important to have as many servers as possible. Large TLDs (and many high-visibility SLDs) often have enough servers that either A6 or KEY records would cause the NS response to overflow the 512 byte limit. Note that these zones with large numbers of servers are often exactly those zones that are critical to network operation and that already sustain fairly high loads.

2.4. UDP vs TCP for DNS messages

Given all these factors, it is essential that any implementation that supports DNSSEC and or A6 be able to use larger DNS messages than 512 octets.

The original 512 restriction was put in place to reduce the probability of fragmentation of DNS responses. A fragmented UDP message that suffers a loss of one of the fragments renders the answer useless and the query must be retried. A TCP connection requires a larger number of round trips for establishment, data transfer and tear down, but only the lost data segments are retransmitted.

In the early days a number of IP implementations did not handle fragmentation well, but all modern operating systems have overcome that issue thus sending fragmented messages is fine from that standpoint. The open issue is the effect of losses on fragmented messages. If connection has high loss ratio only TCP will allow reliable transfer of DNS data, most links have low loss ratios thus sending fragmented UDP packet in one round trip is better than establishing a TCP connection to transfer a few thousand octets.

2.5. EDNS0 and large UDP messages

EDNS0 [RFC2671] allows clients to declare the maximum size of UDP message they are willing to handle. Thus, if the expected answer is between 512 octets and the maximum size that the client can accept, the additional overhead of a TCP connection can be avoided.

3. Protocol changes:

This document updates RFC 2535 and RFC 2874, by adding new requirements.

All RFC 2535 compliant servers and resolvers MUST support EDNS0 and advertise message size of at least 1220 octets, but SHOULD advertise message size of 4000. This value might be too low to get full answers for high level servers and successor of this document may require a larger value.

All RFC 2874 compliant servers and resolver MUST support EDNS0 and advertise message size of at least 1024 octets, but SHOULD advertise message size of 2048. The IPv6 datagrams should be 1024 octets, unless the MTU of the path is known. (Note that this is smaller than the minimum IPv6 MTU to allow for some extension headers and/or encapsulation without exceeding the minimum MTU.)

All RFC 2535 and RFC 2874 compliant entities MUST be able to handle fragmented IPv4 and IPv6 UDP packets.

All hosts supporting both RFC 2535 and RFC 2874 MUST use the larger required value in EDNS0 advertisements.

4. Acknowledgments

Harald Alvestrand, Rob Austein, Randy Bush, David Conrad, Andreas Gustafsson, Jun-ichiro itojun Hagino, Bob Halley, Edward Lewis Michael Patton and Kazu Yamamoto were instrumental in motivating and shaping this document.

5. Security Considerations:

There are no additional security considerations other than those in RFC 2671.

6. IANA Considerations:

None

7. References

[RFC1034] Mockapetris, P., "Domain Names - Concepts and Facilities", STD 13, RFC 1034, November 1987.

[RFC1035] Mockapetris, P., "Domain Names - Implementation and Specification", STD 13, RFC 1035, November 1987.

[RFC2535] Eastlake, D. "Domain Name System Security Extensions", RFC 2535, March 1999.

[RFC2671] Vixie, P., "Extension Mechanisms for DNS (EDNS0)", RFC 2671, August 1999.

[RFC2845] Vixie, P., Gudmundsson, O., Eastlake, D. and B. Wellington, "Secret Key Transaction Authentication for DNS (TSIG)", RFC 2845, May 2000.

[RFC2874] Crawford, M. and C. Huitema, "DNS Extensions to Support IPv6 Address Aggregation and Renumbering", RFC 2874, July 2000.

[RFC3225] Conrad, D., "Indicating Resolver Support of DNSSEC", RFC 3225, December 2001.

8. Author Address

Olafur Gudmundsson
3826 Legation Street, NW
Washington, DC 20015
USA

EMail: ogud@ogud.com

9. Full Copyright Statement

copied, published and distributed, in whole or in part, without restriction of any kind, provided that the above copyright notice and this paragraph are included on all such copies and derivative works. However, this document itself may not be modified in any way, such as by removing the copyright notice or references to the Internet Society or other Internet organizations, except as needed for the purpose of developing Internet standards in which case the procedures for copyrights defined in the Internet Standards process must be followed, or as required to translate it into languages other than English.

The limited permissions granted above are perpetual and will not be revoked by the Internet Society or its successors or assigns.

This document and the information contained herein is provided on an "AS IS" basis and THE INTERNET SOCIETY AND THE INTERNET ENGINEERING TASK FORCE DISCLAIMS ALL WARRANTIES, EXPRESS OR IMPLIED, INCLUDING BUT NOT LIMITED TO ANY WARRANTY THAT THE USE OF THE INFORMATION HEREIN WILL NOT INFRINGE ANY RIGHTS OR ANY IMPLIED WARRANTIES OF MERCHANTABILITY OR FITNESS FOR A PARTICULAR PURPOSE.

Acknowledgement

Funding for the RFC Editor function is currently provided by the Internet Society.

RFC 3364
Tradeoffs in Domain Name System (DNS) Support for Internet Protocol version 6 (IPv6)

Network Working Group
Request for Comments: 3364
Updates: 2673, 2874
Category: Informational

R. Austein
Bourgeois Dilettant
August 2002

Status of this Memo

Copyright Notice

Abstract

The IETF has two different proposals on the table for how to do DNS support for IPv6, and has thus far failed to reach a clear consensus on which approach is better. This note attempts to examine the pros and cons of each approach, in the hope of clarifying the debate so that we can reach closure and move on.

RFC 3364 Contents

Introduction

RFC 1886 [RFC1886] specified straightforward mechanisms to support IPv6 addresses in the DNS. These mechanisms closely resemble the mechanisms used to support IPv4, with a minor improvement to the reverse mapping mechanism based on experience with CIDR. RFC 1886 is currently listed as a Proposed Standard.

RFC 2874 [RFC2874] specified enhanced mechanisms to support IPv6 addresses in the DNS. These mechanisms provide new features that make it possible for an IPv6 address stored in the DNS to be broken up into multiple DNS resource records in ways that can reflect the network topology underlying the address, thus making it possible for the data stored in the DNS to reflect certain kinds of network topology changes or routing architectures that are either impossible or more difficult to represent without these mechanisms. RFC 2874 is also currently listed as a Proposed Standard.

Both of these Proposed Standards were the output of the IPNG Working Group. Both have been implemented, although implementation of [RFC1886] is more widespread, both because it was specified earlier and because it's simpler to implement.

There's little question that the mechanisms proposed in [RFC2874] are more general than the mechanisms proposed in [RFC1886], and that these enhanced mechanisms might be valuable if IPv6's evolution goes in certain directions. The questions are whether we really need the more general mechanism, what new usage problems might come along with the enhanced mechanisms, and what effect all this will have on IPv6 deployment.

The one thing on which there does seem to be widespread agreement is that we should make up our minds about all this Real Soon Now.

Main Advantages of Going with A6

While the A6 RR proposed in [RFC2874] is very general and provides a superset of the functionality provided by the AAAA RR in [RFC1886], many of the features of A6 can also be implemented with AAAA RRs via preprocessing during zone file generation.

There is one specific area where A6 RRs provide something that cannot be provided using AAAA RRs: A6 RRs can represent addresses in which a prefix portion of the address can change without any action (or perhaps even knowledge) by the parties controlling the DNS zone containing the terminal portion (least significant bits) of the address. This includes both so-called "rapid renumbering" scenarios (where an entire network's prefix may change very quickly) and routing architectures such as the former "GSE" proposal [GSE] (where the "routing goop" portion of an address may be subject to change without warning). A6 RRs do not completely remove the need to update leaf zones during all renumbering events (for example, changing ISPs would usually require a change to the upward delegation pointer), but careful use of A6 RRs could keep the number of RRs that need to change during such an event to a minimum.

Note that constructing AAAA RRs via preprocessing during zone file generation requires exactly the sort of information that A6 RRs store in the DNS. This begs the question of where the hypothetical preprocessor obtains that information if it's not getting it from the DNS.

Note also that the A6 RR, when restricted to its zero-length-prefix form ("A6 0"), is semantically equivalent to an AAAA RR (with one "wasted" octet in the wire representation), so anything that can be done with an AAAA RR can also be done with an A6 RR.

Main Advantages of Going with AAAA

The AAAA RR proposed in [RFC1886], while providing only a subset of the functionality provided by the A6 RR proposed in [RFC2874], has two main points to recommend it:

- AAAA RRs are essentially identical (other than their length) to IPv4's A RRs, so we have more than 15 years of experience to help us predict the usage patterns, failure scenarios and so forth associated with AAAA RRs.

- The AAAA RR is "optimized for read", in the sense that, by storing a complete address rather than making the resolver fetch the address in pieces, it minimizes the effort involved in fetching addresses from the DNS (at the expense of increasing the effort involved in injecting new data into the DNS).

Less Compelling Arguments in Favor of A6

Since the A6 RR allows a zone administrator to write zone files whose description of addresses maps to the underlying network topology, A6 RRs can be construed as a "better" way of representing addresses than AAAA. This may well be a useful capability, but in and of itself it's more of an argument for better tools for zone administrators to use when constructing zone files than a justification for changing the resolution protocol used on the wire.

Less Compelling Arguments in Favor of AAAA

Some of the pressure to go with AAAA instead of A6 appears to be based on the wider deployment of AAAA. Since it is possible to construct transition tools (see discussion of AAAA synthesis, later in this note), this does not appear to be a compelling argument if A6 provides features that we really need.

Another argument in favor of AAAA RRs over A6 RRs appears to be that the A6 RR's advanced capabilities increase the number of ways in which a zone administrator could build a non-working configuration. While operational issues are certainly important, this is more of argument that we need better tools for zone administrators than it is a justification for turning away from A6 if A6 provides features that we really need.

Potential Problems with A6

The enhanced capabilities of the A6 RR, while interesting, are not in themselves justification for choosing A6 if we don't really need those capabilities. The A6 RR is "optimized for write", in the sense that, by making it possible to store fragmented IPv6 addresses in the DNS, it makes it possible to reduce the effort that it takes to inject new data into the DNS (at the expense of increasing the effort involved in fetching data from the DNS). This may be justified if we expect the effort involved in maintaining AAAA-style DNS entries to be prohibitive, but in general, we expect the DNS data to be read more frequently than it is written, so we need to evaluate this particular tradeoff very carefully.

There are also several potential issues with A6 RRs that stem directly from the feature that makes them different from AAAA RRs: the ability to build up address via chaining.

Resolving a chain of A6 RRs involves resolving a series of what are almost independent queries, but not quite. Each of these sub-queries takes some non-zero amount of time, unless the answer happens to be in the resolver's local cache already. Assuming that resolving an AAAA RR takes time T as a baseline, we can guess that, on the average, it will take something approaching time N*T to resolve an N-link chain of A6 RRs, although we would expect to see a fairly good caching factor for the A6 fragments representing the more significant bits of an address. This leaves us with two choices, neither of which is very good: we can decrease the amount of time that the resolver is willing to wait for each fragment, or we can increase the amount of time that a resolver is willing to wait before returning failure to a client. What little data we have on this subject suggests that users are already impatient with the length of time it takes to resolve A RRs in the IPv4 Internet, which suggests that they are not likely to be patient with significantly longer delays in the IPv6 Internet. At the same time, terminating queries prematurely is both a waste of resources and another source of user frustration. Thus, we are forced to conclude that indiscriminate use of long A6 chains is likely to lead to problems.

To make matters worse, the places where A6 RRs are likely to be most critical for rapid renumbering or GSE-like routing are situations where the prefix name field in the A6 RR points to a target that is not only outside the DNS zone containing the A6 RR, but is administered by a different organization (for example, in the case of an end user's site, the prefix name will most likely point to a name belonging to an ISP that provides connectivity for the site).

While pointers out of zone are not a problem per se, pointers to other organizations are somewhat more difficult to maintain and less susceptible to automation than pointers within a single organization would be. Experience both with glue RRs and with PTR RRs in the IN-ADDR.ARPA tree suggests that many zone administrators do not really understand how to set up and maintain these pointers properly, and we have no particular reason to believe that these zone administrators will do a better job with A6 chains than they do today. To be fair, however, the alternative case of building AAAA RRs via preprocessing before loading zones has many of the same problems; at best, one can claim that using AAAA RRs for this purpose would allow DNS clients to get the wrong answer somewhat more efficiently than with A6 RRs.

Finally, assuming near total ignorance of how likely a query is to fail, the probability of failure with an N-link A6 chain would appear to be roughly proportional to N, since each of the queries involved in resolving an A6 chain would have the same probability of failure as a single AAAA query. Note again that this comment applies to failures in the the process of resolving a query, not to the data obtained via that process. Arguably, in an ideal world, A6 RRs would increase the probability of the answer a client (finally) gets being right, assuming that nothing goes wrong in the query process, but we have no real idea how to quantify that assumption at this point even to the hand-wavey extent used elsewhere in this note.

One potential problem that has been raised in the past regarding A6 RRs turns out not to be a serious issue. The A6 design includes the possibility of there being more than one A6 RR matching the prefix name portion of a leaf A6 RR. That is, an A6 chain may not be a simple linked list, it may in fact be a tree, where each branch represents a possible prefix. Some critics of A6 have been concerned that this will lead to a wild expansion of queries, but this turns out not to be a problem if a resolver simply follows the "bounded work per query" rule described in RFC 1034 (page 35). That rule applies to all work resulting from attempts to process a query, regardless of whether it's a simple query, a CNAME chain, an A6 tree, or an infinite loop. The client may not get back a useful answer in cases where the zone has been configured badly, but a proper implementation should not produce a query explosion as a result of processing even the most perverse A6 tree, chain, or loop.

Interactions with DNSSEC

One of the areas where AAAA and A6 RRs differ is in the precise details of how they interact with DNSSEC. The following comments apply only to non-zero-prefix A6 RRs (A6 0 RRs, once again, are semantically equivalent to AAAA RRs).

Other things being equal, the time it takes to re-sign all of the addresses in a zone after a renumbering event is longer with AAAA RRs than with A6 RRs (because each address record has to be re-signed rather than just signing a common prefix A6 RR and a few A6 0 RRs associated with the zone's name servers). Note, however, that in general this does not present a serious scaling problem, because the re-signing is performed in the leaf zones.

Other things being equal, there's more work involved in verifying the signatures received back for A6 RRs, because each address fragment has a separate associated signature. Similarly, a DNS message containing a set of A6 address fragments and their associated signatures will be larger than the equivalent packet with a single AAAA (or A6 0) and a single associated signature.

Since AAAA RRs cannot really represent rapid renumbering or GSE-style routing scenarios very well, it should not be surprising that DNSSEC signatures of AAAA RRs are also somewhat problematic. In cases where the AAAA RRs would have to be changing very quickly to keep up with prefix changes, the time required to re-sign the AAAA RRs may be prohibitive.

Empirical testing by Bill Sommerfeld [Sommerfeld] suggests that 333MHz Celeron laptop with 128KB L2 cache and 64MB RAM running the BIND-9 dnssec-signzone program under NetBSD can generate roughly 40 1024-bit RSA signatures per second. Extrapolating from this, assuming one A RR, one AAAA RR, and one NXT RR per host, this suggests that it would take this laptop a few hours to sign a zone listing $10^{**}5$ hosts, or about a day to sign a zone listing $10^{**}6$ hosts using AAAA RRs.

This suggests that the additional effort of re-signing a large zone full of AAAA RRs during a re-numbering event, while noticeable, is only likely to be prohibitive in the rapid renumbering case where AAAA RRs don't work well anyway.

Interactions with Dynamic Update

DNS dynamic update appears to work equally well for AAAA or A6 RRs, with one minor exception: with A6 RRs, the dynamic update client needs to know the prefix length and prefix name. At present, no mechanism exists to inform a dynamic update client of these values, but presumably such a mechanism could be provided via an extension to DHCP, or some other equivalent could be devised.

Transition from AAAA to A6 Via AAAA Synthesis

While AAAA is at present more widely deployed than A6, it is possible to transition from AAAA-aware DNS software to A6-aware DNS software. A rough plan for this was presented at IETF-50 in Minneapolis and has been discussed on the ipng mailing list. So if the IETF concludes that A6's enhanced capabilities are necessary, it should be possible to transition from AAAA to A6.

The details of this transition have been left to a separate document, but the general idea is that the resolver that is performing iterative resolution on behalf of a DNS client program could synthesize AAAA RRs representing the result of performing the equivalent A6 queries. Note that in this case it is not possible to generate an equivalent DNSSEC signature for the AAAA RR, so clients that care about performing DNSSEC validation for themselves would have to issue A6 queries directly rather than relying on AAAA synthesis.

Bitlabels

While the differences between AAAA and A6 RRs have generated most of the discussion to date, there are also two proposed mechanisms for building the reverse mapping tree (the IPv6 equivalent of IPv4's IN-ADDR.ARPA tree).

[RFC1886] proposes a mechanism very similar to the IN-ADDR.ARPA mechanism used for IPv4 addresses: the RR name is the hexadecimal representation of the IPv6 address, reversed and concatenated with a well-known suffix, broken up with a dot between each hexadecimal digit. The resulting DNS names are somewhat tedious for humans to type, but are very easy for programs to generate. Making each hexadecimal digit a separate label means that delegation on arbitrary bit boundaries will result in a maximum of 16 NS RRsets per label level; again, the mechanism is somewhat tedious for humans, but is very easy to program. As with IPv4's IN-ADDR.ARPA tree, the one place where this scheme is weak is in handling delegations in the least significant label; however, since there appears to be no real need to delegate the least significant four bits of an IPv6 address, this does not appear to be a serious restriction.

[RFC2874] proposed a radically different way of naming entries in the reverse mapping tree: rather than using textual representations of addresses, it proposes to use a new kind of DNS label (a "bit label") to represent binary addresses directly in the DNS. This has the advantage of being significantly more compact than the textual representation, and arguably might have been a better solution for DNS to use for this purpose if it had been designed into the protocol from the outset. Unfortunately, experience to date suggests that deploying a new DNS label type is very hard: all of the DNS name servers that are authoritative for any portion of the name in question must be upgraded before the new label type can be used, as must any resolvers involved in the resolution process. Any name server that has not been upgraded to understand the new label type will reject the query as being malformed.

Since the main benefit of the bit label approach appears to be an ability that we don't really need (delegation in the least significant four bits of an IPv6 address), and since the upgrade problem is likely to render bit labels unusable until a significant portion of the DNS code base has been upgraded, it is difficult to escape the conclusion that the textual solution is good enough.

DNAME RRs

[RFC2874] also proposes using DNAME RRs as a way of providing the equivalent of A6's fragmented addresses in the reverse mapping tree. That is, by using DNAME RRs, one can write zone files for the reverse mapping tree that have the same ability to cope with rapid renumbering or GSE-style routing that the A6 RR offers in the main portion of the DNS tree. Consequently, the need to use DNAME in the reverse mapping tree appears to be closely tied to the need to use fragmented A6 in the main tree: if one is necessary, so is the other, and if one isn't necessary, the other isn't either.

Other uses have also been proposed for the DNAME RR, but since they are outside the scope of the IPv6 address discussion, they will not be addressed here.

Recommendation

Distilling the above feature comparisons down to their key elements, the important questions appear to be:

(a) Is IPv6 going to do rapid renumbering or GSE-like routing?

(b) Is the reverse mapping tree for IPv6 going to require delegation in the least significant four bits of the address?

Question (a) appears to be the key to the debate. This is really a decision for the IPv6 community to make, not the DNS community.

Question (b) is also for the IPv6 community to make, but it seems fairly obvious that the answer is "no".

Recommendations based on these questions:

(1) If the IPv6 working groups seriously intend to specify and deploy rapid renumbering or GSE-like routing, we should transition to using the A6 RR in the main tree and to using DNAME RRs as necessary in the reverse tree.

(2) Otherwise, we should keep the simpler AAAA solution in the main tree and should not use DNAME RRs in the reverse tree.

(3) In either case, the reverse tree should use the textual representation described in [RFC1886] rather than the bit label representation described in [RFC2874].

(4) If we do go to using A6 RRs in the main tree and to using DNAME RRs in the reverse tree, we should write applicability statements and implementation guidelines designed to discourage excessively complex uses of these features; in general, any network that can be described adequately using A6 0 RRs and without using DNAME RRs should be described that way, and the enhanced features should be used only when absolutely necessary, at least until we have much more experience with them and have a better understanding of their failure modes.

Security Considerations

This note compares two mechanisms with similar security characteristics, but there are a few security implications to the choice between these two mechanisms:

(1) The two mechanisms have similar but not identical interactions with DNSSEC. Please see the section entitled "Interactions with DNSSEC" (above) for a discussion of these issues.

(2) To the extent that operational complexity is the enemy of security, the tradeoffs in operational complexity discussed throughout this note have an impact on security.

(3) To the extent that protocol complexity is the enemy of security, the additional protocol complexity of [RFC2874] as compared to [RFC1886] has some impact on security.

IANA Considerations

None, since all of these RR types have already been allocated.

Acknowledgments

This note is based on a number of discussions both public and private over a period of (at least) eight years, but particular thanks go to Alain Durand, Bill Sommerfeld, Christian Huitema, Jun-ichiro itojun Hagino, Mark Andrews, Matt Crawford, Olafur Gudmundsson, Randy Bush, and Sue Thomson, none of whom are responsible for what the author did with their ideas.

References

[RFC1886] Thomson, S. and C. Huitema, "DNS Extensions to support IP version 6", RFC 1886, December 1995.

[RFC2874] Crawford, M. and C. Huitema, "DNS Extensions to Support IPv6 Address Aggregation and Renumbering", RFC 2874, July 2000.

[Sommerfeld] Private message to the author from Bill Sommerfeld dated 21 March 2001, summarizing the result of experiments he performed on a copy of the MIT.EDU zone.

[GSE] "GSE" was an evolution of the so-called "8+8" proposal discussed by the IPng working group in 1996 and 1997. The GSE proposal itself was written up as an Internet-Draft, which has long since expired. Readers interested in the details and history of GSE should review the IPng working group's mailing list archives and minutes from that period.

Author's Address

Rob Austein

EMail: sra@hactrn.net

Full Copyright Statement

that the above copyright notice and this paragraph are included on all such copies and derivative works. However, this document itself may not be modified in any way, such as by removing the copyright notice or references to the Internet Society or other Internet organizations, except as needed for the purpose of developing Internet standards in which case the procedures for copyrights defined in the Internet Standards process must be followed, or as required to translate it into languages other than English.

The limited permissions granted above are perpetual and will not be revoked by the Internet Society or its successors or assigns.

This document and the information contained herein is provided on an "AS IS" basis and THE INTERNET SOCIETY AND THE INTERNET ENGINEERING TASK FORCE DISCLAIMS ALL WARRANTIES, EXPRESS OR IMPLIED, INCLUDING BUT NOT LIMITED TO ANY WARRANTY THAT THE USE OF THE INFORMATION HEREIN WILL NOT INFRINGE ANY RIGHTS OR ANY IMPLIED WARRANTIES OF MERCHANTABILITY OR FITNESS FOR A PARTICULAR PURPOSE.

Acknowledgement

Funding for the RFC Editor function is currently provided by the Internet Society.

RFC 3597
Handling of Unknown DNS Resource Record (RR) Types

Network Working Group
Request for Comments: 3597
Category: Standards Track

A. Gustafsson
Nominum Inc.
September 2003

Status of this Memo

Copyright Notice

Abstract

Extending the Domain Name System (DNS) with new Resource Record (RR) types currently requires changes to name server software. This document specifies the changes necessary to allow future DNS implementations to handle new RR types transparently.

RFC 3597 Contents

1. Introduction

The DNS is designed to be extensible to support new services through the introduction of new resource record (RR) types. In practice, deploying a new RR type currently requires changes to the name server software not only at the authoritative DNS server that is providing the new information and the client making use of it, but also at all slave servers for the zone containing it, and in some cases also at caching name servers and forwarders used by the client.

Because the deployment of new server software is slow and expensive, the potential of the DNS in supporting new services has never been fully realized. This memo proposes changes to name servers and to procedures for defining new RR types aimed at simplifying the future deployment of new RR types.

The key words "MUST", "MUST NOT", "REQUIRED", "SHALL", "SHALL NOT", "SHOULD", "SHOULD NOT", "RECOMMENDED", "MAY", and "OPTIONAL" in this document are to be interpreted as described in [RFC 2119].

2. Definition

An "RR of unknown type" is an RR whose RDATA format is not known to the DNS implementation at hand, and whose type is not an assigned QTYPE or Meta-TYPE as specified in [RFC 2929] (section 3.1) nor within the range reserved in that section for assignment only to QTYPEs and Meta-TYPEs. Such an RR cannot be converted to a type-specific text format, compressed, or otherwise handled in a type-specific way.

In the case of a type whose RDATA format is class specific, an RR is considered to be of unknown type when the RDATA format for that combination of type and class is not known.

3. Transparency

To enable new RR types to be deployed without server changes, name servers and resolvers MUST handle RRs of unknown type transparently. That is, they must treat the RDATA section of such RRs as unstructured binary data, storing and transmitting it without change [RFC1123].

To ensure the correct operation of equality comparison (section 6) and of the DNSSEC canonical form (section 7) when an RR type is known to some but not all of the servers involved, servers MUST also exactly preserve the RDATA of RRs of known type, except for changes due to compression or decompression where allowed by section 4 of this memo. In particular, the character case of domain names that are not subject to compression MUST be preserved.

4. Domain Name Compression

RRs containing compression pointers in the RDATA part cannot be treated transparently, as the compression pointers are only meaningful within the context of a DNS message. Transparently copying the RDATA into a new DNS message would cause the compression pointers to point at the corresponding location in the new message, which now contains unrelated data. This would cause the compressed name to be corrupted.

To avoid such corruption, servers MUST NOT compress domain names embedded in the RDATA of types that are class-specific or not well-known. This requirement was stated in [RFC1123] without defining the term "well-known"; it is hereby specified that only the RR types defined in [RFC1035] are to be considered "well-known".

The specifications of a few existing RR types have explicitly allowed compression contrary to this specification: [RFC2163] specified that compression applies to the PX RR, and [RFC2535] allowed compression in SIG RRs and NXT RRs records. Since this specification disallows compression in these cases, it is an update to [RFC2163] (section 4) and [RFC2535] (sections 4.1.7 and 5.2).

Receiving servers MUST decompress domain names in RRs of well-known type, and SHOULD also decompress RRs of type RP, AFSDB, RT, SIG, PX, NXT, NAPTR, and SRV (although the current specification of the SRV RR in [RFC2782] prohibits compression, [RFC2052] mandated it, and some servers following that earlier specification are still in use).

Future specifications for new RR types that contain domain names within their RDATA MUST NOT allow the use of name compression for those names, and SHOULD explicitly state that the embedded domain names MUST NOT be compressed.

As noted in [RFC1123], the owner name of an RR is always eligible for compression.

5. Text Representation

In the "type" field of a master file line, an unknown RR type is represented by the word "TYPE" immediately followed by the decimal RR type number, with no intervening whitespace. In the "class" field, an unknown class is similarly represented as the word "CLASS" immediately followed by the decimal class number.

This convention allows types and classes to be distinguished from each other and from TTL values, allowing the "[<TTL>] [<class>] <type> <RDATA>" and "[<class>] [<TTL>] <type> <RDATA>" forms of [RFC1035] to both be unambiguously parsed.

The RDATA section of an RR of unknown type is represented as a sequence of white space separated words as follows:

The special token \# (a backslash immediately followed by a hash sign), which identifies the RDATA as having the generic encoding defined herein rather than a traditional type-specific encoding.

An unsigned decimal integer specifying the RDATA length in octets.

Zero or more words of hexadecimal data encoding the actual RDATA field, each containing an even number of hexadecimal digits.

If the RDATA is of zero length, the text representation contains only the \# token and the single zero representing the length.

An implementation MAY also choose to represent some RRs of known type using the above generic representations for the type, class and/or RDATA, which carries the benefit of making the resulting master file portable to servers where these types are unknown. Using the generic representation for the RDATA of an RR of known type can also be useful in the case of an RR type where the text format varies depending on a version, protocol, or similar field (or several) embedded in the RDATA when such a field has a value for which no text format is known, e.g., a LOC RR [RFC1876] with a VERSION other than 0.

Even though an RR of known type represented in the \# format is effectively treated as an unknown type for the purpose of parsing the RDATA text representation, all further processing by the server MUST treat it as a known type and take into account any applicable type-specific rules regarding compression, canonicalization, etc.

The following are examples of RRs represented in this manner, illustrating various combinations of generic and type-specific encodings for the different fields of the master file format:

```
a.example.    CLASS32    TYPE731      \# 6  abcd (
                                      ef 01 23 45  )
b.example.    HS         TYPE62347    \# 0
e.example.    IN         A            \# 4  0A000001
e.example.    CLASS1     TYPE1        10.0.0.2
```

6. Equality Comparison

Certain DNS protocols, notably Dynamic Update [RFC2136], require RRs to be compared for equality. Two RRs of the same unknown type are considered equal when their RDATA is bitwise equal. To ensure that the outcome of the comparison is identical whether the RR is known to the server or not, specifications for new RR types MUST NOT specify type-specific comparison rules.

This implies that embedded domain names, being included in the overall bitwise comparison, are compared in a case-sensitive manner.

As a result, when a new RR type contains one or more embedded domain names, it is possible to have multiple RRs owned by the same name that differ only in the character case of the embedded domain name(s). This is similar to the existing possibility of multiple TXT records differing only in character case, and not expected to cause any problems in practice.

7. DNSSEC Canonical Form and Ordering

DNSSEC defines a canonical form and ordering for RRs [RFC2535] (section 8.1). In that canonical form, domain names embedded in the RDATA are converted to lower case.

The downcasing is necessary to ensure the correctness of DNSSEC signatures when case distinctions in domain names are lost due to compression, but since it requires knowledge of the presence and position of embedded domain names, it cannot be applied to unknown types.

To ensure continued consistency of the canonical form of RR types where compression is allowed, and for continued interoperability with existing implementations that already implement the [RFC2535] canonical form and apply it to their known RR types, the canonical form remains unchanged for all RR types whose whose initial publication as an RFC was prior to the initial publication of this specification as an RFC (RFC 3597).

As a courtesy to implementors, it is hereby noted that the complete set of such previously published RR types that contain embedded domain names, and whose DNSSEC canonical form therefore involves downcasing according to the DNS rules for character comparisons, consists of the RR types NS, MD, MF, CNAME, SOA, MB, MG, MR, PTR, HINFO, MINFO, MX, HINFO, RP, AFSDB, RT, SIG, PX, NXT, NAPTR, KX, SRV, DNAME, and A6.

This document specifies that for all other RR types (whether treated as unknown types or treated as known types according to an RR type definition RFC more recent than RFC 3597), the canonical form is such that no downcasing of embedded domain names takes place, and otherwise identical to the canonical form specified in [RFC2535] section 8.1.

Note that the owner name is always set to lower case according to the DNS rules for character comparisons, regardless of the RR type.

The DNSSEC canonical RR ordering is as specified in [RFC2535] section 8.3, where the octet sequence is the canonical form as revised by this specification.

8. Additional Section Processing

Unknown RR types cause no additional section processing. Future RR type specifications MAY specify type-specific additional section processing rules, but any such processing MUST be optional as it can only be performed by servers for which the RR type in case is known.

9. IANA Considerations

This document does not require any IANA actions.

10. Security Considerations

This specification is not believed to cause any new security problems, nor to solve any existing ones.

11. Normative References

[RFC1034] Mockapetris, P., "Domain Names - Concepts and Facilities", STD 13, RFC 1034, November 1987.

[RFC1035] Mockapetris, P., "Domain Names - Implementation and Specifications", STD 13, RFC 1035, November 1987.

[RFC1123] Braden, R., Ed., "Requirements for Internet Hosts – Application and Support", STD 3, RFC 1123, October 1989.

[RFC2119] Bradner, S., "Key words for use in RFCs to Indicate Requirement Levels", BCP 14, RFC 2119, March 1997.

[RFC2535] Eastlake, D., "Domain Name System Security Extensions", RFC 2535, March 1999.

[RFC2163] Allocchio, C., "Using the Internet DNS to Distribute MIXER Conformant Global Address Mapping (MCGAM)", RFC 2163, January 1998.

[RFC2929] Eastlake, D., Brunner-Williams, E. and B. Manning, "Domain Name System (DNS) IANA Considerations", BCP 42, RFC 2929, September 2000.

12. Informative References

[RFC1876] Davis, C., Vixie, P., Goodwin, T. and I. Dickinson, "A Means for Expressing Location Information in the Domain Name System", RFC 1876, January 1996.

[RFC2052] Gulbrandsen, A. and P. Vixie, "A DNS RR for specifying the location of services (DNS SRV)", RFC 2052, October 1996.

[RFC2136] Vixie, P., Ed., Thomson, S., Rekhter, Y. and J. Bound, "Dynamic Updates in the Domain Name System (DNS UPDATE)", RFC 2136, April 1997.

[RFC2782] Gulbrandsen, A., Vixie, P. and L. Esibov, "A DNS RR for specifying the location of services (DNS SRV)", RFC 2782, February 2000.

13. Intellectual Property Statement

The IETF takes no position regarding the validity or scope of any intellectual property or other rights that might be claimed to pertain to the implementation or use of the technology described in this document or the extent to which any license under such rights might or might not be available; neither does it represent that it has made any effort to identify any such rights. Information on the IETF's procedures with respect to rights in standards-track and standards-related documentation can be found in BCP-11. Copies of claims of rights made available for publication and any assurances of licenses to be made available, or the result of an attempt made to obtain a general license or permission for the use of such proprietary rights by implementors or users of this specification can be obtained from the IETF Secretariat.

The IETF invites any interested party to bring to its attention any copyrights, patents or patent applications, or other proprietary rights which may cover technology that may be required to practice this standard. Please address the information to the IETF Executive Director.

14. Author's Address

Andreas Gustafsson
Nominum, Inc.
2385 Bay Rd
Redwood City, CA 94063
USA

Phone: +1 650 381 6004
EMail: gson@nominum.com

15. Full Copyright Statement

Acknowledgement

Funding for the RFC Editor function is currently provided by the Internet Society.

RFC 3833
Threat Analysis of the Domain Name System (DNS)

Network Working Group
Request for Comments: 3833
Category: Informational

D. Atkins
IHTFP Consulting
R. Austein
ISC
August 2004

Status of this Memo

Copyright Notice

Abstract

Although the DNS Security Extensions (DNSSEC) have been under development for most of the last decade, the IETF has never written down the specific set of threats against which DNSSEC is designed to protect. Among other drawbacks, this cart-before-the-horse situation has made it difficult to determine whether DNSSEC meets its design goals, since its design goals are not well specified. This note attempts to document some of the known threats to the DNS, and, in doing so, attempts to measure to what extent (if any) DNSSEC is a useful tool in defending against these threats.

RFC 3833 Contents

1. Introduction

The earliest organized work on DNSSEC within the IETF was an open design team meeting organized by members of the DNS working group in November 1993 at the 28th IETF meeting in Houston. The broad outlines of DNSSEC as we know it today are already clear in Jim Galvin's summary of the results of that meeting [Galvin93]:

- While some participants in the meeting were interested in protecting against disclosure of DNS data to unauthorized parties, the design team made an explicit decision that "DNS data is 'public'", and ruled all threats of data disclosure explicitly out of scope for DNSSEC.

- While some participants in the meeting were interested in authentication of DNS clients and servers as a basis for access control, this work was also ruled out of scope for DNSSEC per se.

- Backwards compatibility and co-existence with "insecure DNS" was listed as an explicit requirement.

- The resulting list of desired security services was

  1) data integrity, and

  2) data origin authentication.

- The design team noted that a digital signature mechanism would support the desired services.

While a number of detail decisions were yet to be made (and in some cases remade after implementation experience) over the subsequent decade, the basic model and design goals have remained fixed.

Nowhere, however, does any of the DNSSEC work attempt to specify in any detail the sorts of attacks against which DNSSEC is intended to protect, or the reasons behind the list of desired security services that came out of the Houston meeting. For that, we have to go back to a paper originally written by Steve Bellovin in 1990 but not published until 1995, for reasons that Bellovin explained in the paper's epilogue [Bellovin95].

While it may seem a bit strange to publish the threat analysis a decade after starting work on the protocol designed to defend against it, that is, nevertheless, what this note attempts to do. Better late than never.

This note assumes that the reader is familiar with both the DNS and with DNSSEC, and does not attempt to provide a tutorial on either. The DNS documents most relevant to the subject of this note are: [RFC1034], [RFC1035], section 6.1 of [RFC1123], [RFC2181], [RFC2308], [RFC2671], [RFC2845], [RFC2930], [RFC3007], and [RFC2535].

For purposes of discussion, this note uses the term "DNSSEC" to refer to the core hierarchical public key and signature mechanism specified in the DNSSEC documents, and refers to TKEY and TSIG as separate mechanisms, even though channel security mechanisms such as TKEY and TSIG are also part of the larger problem of "securing DNS" and thus are often considered part of the overall set of "DNS security extensions". This is an arbitrary distinction that in part reflects the way in which the protocol has evolved (introduction of a putatively simpler channel security model for certain operations such as zone transfers and dynamic update requests), and perhaps should be changed in a future revision of this note.

2. Known Threats

There are several distinct classes of threats to the DNS, most of which are DNS-related instances of more general problems, but a few of which are specific to peculiarities of the DNS protocol.

2.1. Packet Interception

Some of the simplest threats against DNS are various forms of packet interception: monkey-in-the-middle attacks, eavesdropping on requests combined with spoofed responses that beat the real response back to the resolver, and so forth. In any of these scenarios, the attacker can simply tell either party (usually the resolver) whatever it wants that party to believe. While packet interception attacks are far from unique to DNS, DNS's usual behavior of sending an entire query or response in a single unsigned, unencrypted UDP packet makes these attacks particularly easy for any bad guy with the ability to intercept packets on a shared or transit network.

To further complicate things, the DNS query the attacker intercepts may just be a means to an end for the attacker: the attacker might even choose to return the correct result in the answer section of a reply message while using other parts of the message to set the stage for something more complicated, for example, a name chaining attack (see section 2.3).

While it certainly would be possible to sign DNS messages using a channel security mechanism such as TSIG or IPsec, or even to encrypt them using IPsec, this would not be a very good solution for interception attacks. First, this approach would impose a fairly high processing cost per DNS message, as well as a very high cost associated with establishing and maintaining bilateral trust relationships between all the parties that might be involved in resolving any particular query. For heavily used name servers (such as the servers for the root zone), this cost would almost certainly be prohibitively high. Even more important, however, is that the underlying trust model in such a design would be wrong, since at best it would only provide a hop-by-hop integrity check on DNS messages and would not provide any sort of end-to-end integrity check between the producer of DNS data (the zone administrator) and the consumer of DNS data (the application that triggered the query).

By contrast, DNSSEC (when used properly) does provide an end-to-end data integrity check, and is thus a much better solution for this class of problems during basic DNS lookup operations.

TSIG does have its place in corners of the DNS protocol where there's a specific trust relationship between a particular client and a particular server, such as zone transfer, dynamic update, or a resolver (stub or otherwise) that is not going to check all the DNSSEC signatures itself.

Note that DNSSEC does not provide any protection against modification of the DNS message header, so any properly paranoid resolver must:

- Perform all of the DNSSEC signature checking on its own,

- Use TSIG (or some equivalent mechanism) to ensure the integrity of its communication with whatever name servers it chooses to trust, or

- Resign itself to the possibility of being attacked via packet interception (and via other techniques discussed below).

2.2. ID Guessing and Query Prediction

Since DNS is for the most part used over UDP/IP, it is relatively easy for an attacker to generate packets which will match the transport protocol parameters. The ID field in the DNS header is only a 16-bit field and the server UDP port associated with DNS is a well-known value, so there are only $2^{**}32$ possible combinations of ID and client UDP port for a given client and server. This is not a particularly large range, and is not sufficient to protect against a brute force search; furthermore, in practice both the client UDP port and the ID can often be predicted from previous traffic, and it is not uncommon for the client port to be a known fixed value as well (due to firewalls or other restrictions), thus frequently reducing the search space to a range smaller than $2^{**}16$.

By itself, ID guessing is not enough to allow an attacker to inject bogus data, but combined with knowledge (or guesses) about QNAMEs and QTYPEs for which a resolver might be querying, this leaves the resolver only weakly defended against injection of bogus responses.

Since this attack relies on predicting a resolver's behavior, it's most likely to be successful when the victim is in a known state, whether because the victim rebooted recently, or because the victim's behavior has been influenced by some other action by the attacker, or because the victim is responding (in a predictable way) to some third party action known to the attacker.

This attack is both more and less difficult for the attacker than the simple interception attack described above: more difficult, because the attack only works when the attacker guesses correctly; less difficult, because the attacker doesn't need to be on a transit or shared network.

In most other respects, this attack is similar to a packet interception attack. A resolver that checks DNSSEC signatures will be able to detect the forged response; resolvers that do not perform DNSSEC signature checking themselves should use TSIG or some equivalent mechanism to ensure the integrity of their communication with a recursive name server that does perform DNSSEC signature checking.

2.3. Name Chaining

Perhaps the most interesting class of DNS-specific threats are the name chaining attacks. These are a subset of a larger class of name-based attacks, sometimes called "cache poisoning" attacks. Most name-based attacks can be partially mitigated by the long-standing defense of checking RRs in response messages for relevance to the original query, but such defenses do not catch name chaining attacks. There are several variations on the basic attack, but what they all have in common is that they all involve DNS RRs whose RDATA portion (right hand side) includes a DNS name (or, in a few cases, something that is not a DNS name but which directly maps to a DNS name). Any such RR is, at least in principle, a hook that lets an attacker feed bad data into a victim's cache, thus potentially subverting subsequent decisions based on DNS names.

The worst examples in this class of RRs are CNAME, NS, and DNAME RRs because they can redirect a victim's query to a location of the attacker's choosing. RRs like MX and SRV are somewhat less dangerous, but in principle they can also be used to trigger further lookups at a location of the attacker's choosing. Address RR types such as A or AAAA don't have DNS names in their RDATA, but since the IN-ADDR.ARPA and IP6.ARPA trees are indexed using a DNS encoding of IPv4 and IPv6 addresses, these record types can also be used in a name chaining attack.

The general form of a name chaining attack is something like this:

- Victim issues a query, perhaps at the instigation of the attacker or some third party; in some cases the query itself may be unrelated to the name under attack (that is, the attacker is just using this query as a means to inject false information about some other name).

- Attacker injects response, whether via packet interception, query guessing, or by being a legitimate name server that's involved at some point in the process of answering the query that the victim issued.

- Attacker's response includes one or more RRs with DNS names in their RDATA; depending on which particular form this attack takes, the object may be to inject false data associated with those names into the victim's cache via the Additional section of this response, or may be to redirect the next stage of the query to a server of the attacker's choosing (in order to inject more complex lies into the victim's cache than will fit easily into a single response, or in order to place the lies in the Authority or Answer section of a response where they will have a better chance of sneaking past a resolver's defenses).

Any attacker who can insert resource records into a victim's cache can almost certainly do some kind of damage, so there are cache poisoning attacks which are not name chaining attacks in the sense discussed here. However, in the case of name chaining attacks, the cause and effect relationship between the initial attack and the eventual result may be significantly more complex than in the other forms of cache poisoning, so name chaining attacks merit special attention.

The common thread in all of the name chaining attacks is that response messages allow the attacker to introduce arbitrary DNS names of the attacker's choosing and provide further information that the attacker claims is associated with those names; unless the victim has better knowledge of the data associated with those names, the victim is going to have a hard time defending against this class of attacks.

This class of attack is particularly insidious given that it's quite easy for an attacker to provoke a victim into querying for a particular name of the attacker's choosing, for example, by embedding a link to a 1x1-pixel "web bug" graphic in a piece of Text/HTML mail to the victim. If the victim's mail reading program attempts to follow such a link, the result will be a DNS query for a name chosen by the attacker.

DNSSEC should provide a good defense against most (all?) variations on this class of attack. By checking signatures, a resolver can determine whether the data associated with a name really was inserted by the delegated authority for that portion of the DNS name space. More precisely, a resolver can determine whether the entity that injected the data had access to an allegedly secret key whose corresponding public key appears at an expected location in the DNS name space with an expected chain of parental signatures that start with a public key of which the resolver has prior knowledge.

DNSSEC signatures do not cover glue records, so there's still a possibility of a name chaining attack involving glue, but with DNSSEC it is possible to detect the attack by temporarily accepting the glue in order to fetch the signed authoritative version of the same data, then checking the signatures on the authoritative version.

2.4. Betrayal By Trusted Server

Another variation on the packet interception attack is the trusted server that turns out not to be so trustworthy, whether by accident or by intent. Many client machines are only configured with stub resolvers, and use trusted servers to perform all of their DNS queries on their behalf. In many cases the trusted server is furnished by the user's ISP and advertised to the client via DHCP or PPP options. Besides accidental betrayal of this trust relationship (via server bugs, successful server break-ins, etc), the server itself may be configured to give back answers that are not what the user would expect, whether in an honest attempt to help the user or to promote some other goal such as furthering a business partnership between the ISP and some third party.

This problem is particularly acute for frequent travelers who carry their own equipment and expect it to work in much the same way wherever they go. Such travelers need trustworthy DNS service without regard to who operates the network into which their equipment is currently plugged or what brand of middle boxes the local infrastructure might use.

While the obvious solution to this problem would be for the client to choose a more trustworthy server, in practice this may not be an option for the client. In many network environments a client machine has only a limited set of recursive name servers from which to choose, and none of them may be particularly trustworthy. In extreme cases, port filtering or other forms of packet interception may prevent the client host from being able to run an iterative resolver even if the owner of the client machine is willing and able to do so. Thus, while the initial source of this problem is not a DNS protocol attack per se, this sort of betrayal is a threat to DNS clients, and simply switching to a different recursive name server is not an adequate defense.

Viewed strictly from the DNS protocol standpoint, the only difference between this sort of betrayal and a packet interception attack is that in this case the client has voluntarily sent its request to the attacker. The defense against this is the same as with a packet interception attack: the resolver must either check DNSSEC signatures itself or use TSIG (or equivalent) to authenticate the server that it has chosen to trust. Note that use of TSIG does not by itself guarantee that a name server is at all trustworthy: all TSIG can do is help a resolver protect its communication with a name server that it has already decided to trust for other reasons. Protecting a resolver's communication with a server that's giving out bogus answers is not particularly useful.

Also note that if the stub resolver does not trust the name server that is doing work on its behalf and wants to check the DNSSEC signatures itself, the resolver really does need to have independent knowledge of the DNSSEC public key(s) it needs in order to perform the check. Usually the public key for the root zone is enough, but in some cases knowledge of additional keys may also be appropriate.

It is difficult to escape the conclusion that a properly paranoid resolver must always perform its own signature checking, and that this rule even applies to stub resolvers.

2.5. Denial of Service

As with any network service (or, indeed, almost any service of any kind in any domain of discourse), DNS is vulnerable to denial of service attacks. DNSSEC does not help this, and may in fact make the problem worse for resolvers that check signatures, since checking signatures both increases the processing cost per DNS message and in some cases can also increase the number of messages needed to answer a query. TSIG (and similar mechanisms) have equivalent problems.

DNS servers are also at risk of being used as denial of service amplifiers, since DNS response packets tend to be significantly longer than DNS query packets. Unsurprisingly, DNSSEC doesn't help here either.

2.6. Authenticated Denial of Domain Names

Much discussion has taken place over the question of authenticated denial of domain names. The particular question is whether there is a requirement for authenticating the non-existence of a name. The issue is whether the resolver should be able to detect when an attacker removes RRs from a response.

General paranoia aside, the existence of RR types whose absence causes an action other than immediate failure (such as missing MX and SRV RRs, which fail over to A RRs) constitutes a real threat. Arguably, in some cases, even the absence of an RR might be considered a problem. The question remains: how serious is this threat? Clearly the threat does exist; general paranoia says that some day it'll be on the front page of some major newspaper, even if we cannot conceive of a plausible scenario involving this attack today. This implies that some mitigation of this risk is required.

Note that it's necessary to prove the non-existence of applicable wildcard RRs as part of the authenticated denial mechanism, and that, in a zone that is more than one label deep, such a proof may require proving the non-existence of multiple discrete sets of wildcard RRs.

DNSSEC does include mechanisms which make it possible to determine which authoritative names exist in a zone, and which authoritative resource record types exist at those names. The DNSSEC protections do not cover non-authoritative data such as glue records.

2.7. Wildcards

Much discussion has taken place over whether and how to provide data integrity and data origin authentication for "wildcard" DNS names. Conceptually, RRs with wildcard names are patterns for synthesizing RRs on the fly according to the matching rules described in section 4.3.2 of RFC 1034. While the rules that control the behavior of wildcard names have a few quirks that can make them a trap for the unwary zone administrator, it's clear that a number of sites make heavy use of wildcard RRs, particularly wildcard MX RRs.

In order to provide the desired services for wildcard RRs, we need to do two things:

- We need a way to attest to the existence of the wildcard RR itself (that is, we need to show that the synthesis rule exists), and

- We need a way to attest to the non-existence of any RRs which, if they existed, would make the wildcard RR irrelevant according to the synthesis rules that govern the way in which wildcard RRs are used (that is, we need to show that the synthesis rule is applicable).

Note that this makes the wildcard mechanisms dependent upon the authenticated denial mechanism described in the previous section.

DNSSEC includes mechanisms along the lines described above, which make it possible for a resolver to verify that a name server applied the wildcard expansion rules correctly when generating an answer.

3. Weaknesses of DNSSEC

DNSSEC has some problems of its own:

- DNSSEC is complex to implement and includes some nasty edge cases at the zone cuts that require very careful coding. Testbed experience to date suggests that trivial zone configuration errors or expired keys can cause serious problems for a DNSSEC-aware resolver, and that the current protocol's error reporting capabilities may leave something to be desired.

- DNSSEC significantly increases the size of DNS response packets; among other issues, this makes DNSSEC-aware DNS servers even more effective as denial of service amplifiers.

- DNSSEC answer validation increases the resolver's work load, since a DNSSEC-aware resolver will need to perform signature validation and in some cases will also need to issue further queries. This increased workload will also increase the time it takes to get an answer back to the original DNS client, which is likely to trigger both timeouts and re-queries in some cases. Arguably, many current DNS clients are already too impatient even before taking the further delays that DNSSEC will impose into account, but that topic is beyond the scope of this note.

- Like DNS itself, DNSSEC's trust model is almost totally hierarchical. While DNSSEC does allow resolvers to have special additional knowledge of public keys beyond those for the root, in the general case the root key is the one that matters. Thus any compromise in any of the zones between the root and a particular target name can damage DNSSEC's ability to protect the integrity of data owned by that target name. This is not a change, since insecure DNS has the same model.

- Key rollover at the root is really hard. Work to date has not even come close to adequately specifying how the root key rolls over, or even how it's configured in the first place.

- DNSSEC creates a requirement of loose time synchronization between the validating resolver and the entity creating the DNSSEC signatures. Prior to DNSSEC, all time-related actions in DNS could be performed by a machine that only knew about "elapsed" or "relative" time. Because the validity period of a DNSSEC signature is based on "absolute" time, a validating resolver must have the same concept of absolute time as the zone signer in order to determine whether the signature is within its validity period or has expired. An attacker that can change a resolver's opinion of the current absolute time can fool the resolver using expired signatures. An attacker that can change the zone signer's opinion of the current absolute time can fool the zone signer into generating signatures whose validity period does not match what the signer intended.

- The possible existence of wildcard RRs in a zone complicates the authenticated denial mechanism considerably. For most of the decade that DNSSEC has been under development these issues were poorly understood. At various times there have been questions as to whether the authenticated denial mechanism is completely airtight and whether it would be worthwhile to optimize the authenticated denial mechanism for the common case in which wildcards are not present in a zone. However, the main problem is just the inherent complexity of the wildcard mechanism itself. This complexity probably makes the code for generating and checking authenticated denial attestations somewhat fragile, but since the alternative of giving up wildcards entirely is not practical due to widespread use, we are going to have to live with wildcards. The question just becomes one of whether or not the proposed optimizations would make DNSSEC's mechanisms more or less fragile.

- Even with DNSSEC, the class of attacks discussed in section 2.4 is not easy to defeat. In order for DNSSEC to be effective in this case, it must be possible to configure the resolver to expect certain categories of DNS records to be signed. This may require manual configuration of the resolver, especially during the initial DNSSEC rollout period when the resolver cannot reasonably expect the root and TLD zones to be signed.

4. Topics for Future Work

This section lists a few subjects not covered above which probably need additional study, additional mechanisms, or both.

4.1. Interactions With Other Protocols

The above discussion has concentrated exclusively on attacks within the boundaries of the DNS protocol itself, since those are (some of) the problems against which DNSSEC was intended to protect. There are, however, other potential problems at the boundaries where DNS interacts with other protocols.

4.2. Securing DNS Dynamic Update

DNS dynamic update opens a number of potential problems when combined with DNSSEC. Dynamic update of a non-secure zone can use TSIG to authenticate the updating client to the server. While TSIG does not scale very well (it requires manual configuration of shared keys between the DNS name server and each TSIG client), it works well in a limited or closed environment such as a DHCP server updating a local DNS name server.

Major issues arise when trying to use dynamic update on a secure zone. TSIG can similarly be used in a limited fashion to authenticate the client to the server, but TSIG only protects DNS transactions, not the actual data, and the TSIG is not inserted into the DNS zone, so resolvers cannot use the TSIG as a way of verifying the changes to the zone. This means that either:

a) The updating client must have access to a zone-signing key in order to sign the update before sending it to the server, or

b) The DNS name server must have access to an online zone-signing key in order to sign the update.

In either case, a zone-signing key must be available to create signed RRsets to place in the updated zone. The fact that this key must be online (or at least available) is a potential security risk.

Dynamic update also requires an update to the SERIAL field of the zone's SOA RR. In theory, this could also be handled via either of the above options, but in practice (a) would almost certainly be extremely fragile, so (b) is the only workable mechanism.

There are other threats in terms of describing the policy of who can make what changes to which RRsets in the zone. The current access control scheme in Secure Dynamic Update is fairly limited. There is no way to give fine-grained access to updating DNS zone information to multiple entities, each of whom may require different kinds of access. For example, Alice may need to be able to add new nodes to the zone or change existing nodes, but not remove them; Bob may need to be able to remove zones but not add them; Carol may need to be able to add, remove, or modify nodes, but only A records.

Scaling properties of the key management problem here are a particular concern that needs more study.

4.3. Securing DNS Zone Replication

As discussed in previous sections, DNSSEC per se attempts to provide data integrity and data origin authentication services on top of the normal DNS query protocol. Using the terminology discussed in [RFC3552], DNSSEC provides "object security" for the normal DNS query protocol. For purposes of replicating entire DNS zones, however, DNSSEC does not provide object security, because zones include unsigned NS RRs and glue at delegation points. Use of TSIG to protect zone transfer (AXFR or IXFR) operations provides "channel security", but still does not provide object security for complete zones. The trust relationships involved in zone transfer are still very much a hop-by-hop matter of name server operators trusting other name server operators rather than an end-to-end matter of name server operators trusting zone administrators.

Zone object security was not an explicit design goal of DNSSEC, so failure to provide this service should not be a surprise. Nevertheless, there are some zone replication scenarios for which this would be a very useful additional service, so this seems like a useful area for future work. In theory it should not be difficult to add zone object security as a backwards compatible enhancement to the existing DNSSEC model, but the DNSEXT WG has not yet discussed either the desirability of or the requirements for such an enhancement.

5. Conclusion

Based on the above analysis, the DNSSEC extensions do appear to solve a set of problems that do need to be solved, and are worth deploying.

Security Considerations

This entire document is about security considerations of the DNS. The authors believe that deploying DNSSEC will help to address some, but not all, of the known threats to the DNS.

Acknowledgments

This note is based both on previous published works by others and on a number of discussions both public and private over a period of many years, but particular thanks go to

Jaap Akkerhuis,
Steve Bellovin,
Dan Bernstein,
Randy Bush,
Steve Crocker,
Olafur Gudmundsson,
Russ Housley,
Rip Loomis,

Allison Mankin,
Paul Mockapetris,
Thomas Narten
Mans Nilsson,
Pekka Savola,
Paul Vixie,
Xunhua Wang,
and any other members of the DNS, DNSSEC, DNSIND, and DNSEXT working groups whose names and contributions the authors have forgotten, none of whom are responsible for what the authors did with their ideas.

As with any work of this nature, the authors of this note acknowledge that we are standing on the toes of those who have gone before us. Readers interested in this subject may also wish to read [Bellovin95], [Schuba93], and [Vixie95].

Normative References

[RFC1034] Mockapetris, P., "Domain names - concepts and facilities", STD 13, RFC 1034, November 1987.

[RFC1035] Mockapetris, P., "Domain names - implementation and specification", STD 13, RFC 1035, November 1987.

[RFC1123] Braden, R., "Requirements for Internet Hosts - Application and Support", STD 3, RFC 1123, October 1989.

[RFC2181] Elz, R. and R. Bush, "Clarifications to the DNS Specification", RFC 2181, July 1997.

[RFC2308] Andrews, M., "Negative Caching of DNS Queries (DNS NCACHE)", RFC 2308, March 1998.

[RFC2671] Vixie, P., "Extension Mechanisms for DNS (EDNS0)", RFC 2671, August 1999.

[RFC2845] Vixie, P., Gudmundsson, O., Eastlake 3rd, D., and B. Wellington, "Secret Key Transaction Authentication for DNS (TSIG)", RFC 2845, May 2000.

[RFC2930] Eastlake 3rd, D., "Secret Key Establishment for DNS (TKEY RR)", RFC 2930, September 2000.

[RFC3007] Wellington, B., "Secure Domain Name System (DNS) Dynamic Update", RFC 3007, November 2000.

[RFC2535] Eastlake 3rd, D., "Domain Name System Security Extensions", RFC 2535, March 1999.

Informative References

[RFC3552] Rescorla, E. and B. Korver, "Guidelines for Writing RFC Text on Security Considerations", BCP 72, RFC 3552, July 2003.

[Bellovin95] Bellovin, S., "Using the Domain Name System for System Break-Ins", Proceedings of the Fifth Usenix Unix Security Symposium, June 1995.

[Galvin93] Design team meeting summary message posted to dns-security@tis.com mailing list by Jim Galvin on 19 November 1993.

[Schuba93] Schuba, C., "Addressing Weaknesses in the Domain Name System Protocol", Master's thesis, Purdue University Department of Computer Sciences, August 1993.

[Vixie95] Vixie, P, "DNS and BIND Security Issues", Proceedings of the Fifth Usenix Unix Security Symposium, June 1995.

Authors' Addresses

Derek Atkins
IHTFP Consulting, Inc.
6 Farragut Ave
Somerville, MA 02144
USA

EMail: derek@ihtfp.com

Rob Austein
Internet Systems Consortium
950 Charter Street
Redwood City, CA 94063
USA

EMail: sra@isc.org

Full Copyright Statement

Intellectual Property

The IETF takes no position regarding the validity or scope of any Intellectual Property Rights or other rights that might be claimed to pertain to the implementation or use of the technology described in this document or the extent to which any license under such rights might or might not be available; nor does it represent that it has made any independent effort to identify any such rights. Information on the procedures with respect to rights in RFC documents can be found in BCP 78 and BCP 79.

Copies of IPR disclosures made to the IETF Secretariat and any assurances of licenses to be made available, or the result of an attempt made to obtain a general license or permission for the use of such proprietary rights by implementers or users of this specification can be obtained from the IETF on-line IPR repository at http://www.ietf.org/ipr.

The IETF invites any interested party to bring to its attention any copyrights, patents or patent applications, or other proprietary rights that may cover technology that may be required to implement this standard. Please address the information to the IETF at ietf-ipr@ietf.org.

Acknowledgement

Funding for the RFC Editor function is currently provided by the Internet Society.

RFC 4033
DNS Security Introduction and Requirements

Network Working Group

Request for Comments: 4033
Obsoletes: 2535, 3008, 3090, 3445, 3655, 3658,
3755, 3757, 3845
Updates: 1034, 1035, 2136, 2181, 2308, 3225,
3007, 3597, 3226
Category: Standards Track

R. Arends
Telematica Instituut
R. Austein
ISC
M. Larson
VeriSign
D. Massey
Colorado State University
S. Rose
NIST
March 2005

Status of This Memo

This document specifies an Internet standards track protocol for the Internet community, and requests discussion and suggestions for improvements. Please refer to the current edition of the "Internet Official Protocol Standards" (STD 1) for the standardization state and status of this protocol. Distribution of this memo is unlimited.

Copyright Notice

Copyright (C) The Internet Society (2005).

Abstract

The Domain Name System Security Extensions (DNSSEC) add data origin authentication and data integrity to the Domain Name System. This document introduces these extensions and describes their capabilities and limitations. This document also discusses the services that the DNS security extensions do and do not provide. Last, this document describes the interrelationships between the documents that collectively describe DNSSEC.

RFC 4033 Contents

1. Introduction

This document introduces the Domain Name System Security Extensions (DNSSEC). This document and its two companion documents ([RFC4034] and [RFC4035]) update, clarify, and refine the security extensions defined in [RFC2535] and its predecessors. These security extensions consist of a set of new resource record types and modifications to the existing DNS protocol ([RFC1035]). The new records and protocol modifications are not fully described in this document, but are described in a family of documents outlined in Section 10. Sections 3 and 4 describe the capabilities and limitations of the security extensions in greater detail. Section 5 discusses the scope of the document set. Sections 6, 7, 8, and 9 discuss the effect that these security extensions will have on resolvers, stub resolvers, zones, and name servers.

This document and its two companions obsolete [RFC2535], [RFC3008], [RFC3090], [RFC3445], [RFC3655], [RFC3658], [RFC3755], [RFC3757], and [RFC3845]. This document set also updates but does not obsolete [RFC1034], [RFC1035], [RFC2136], [RFC2181], [RFC2308], [RFC3225], [RFC3007], [RFC3597], and the portions of [RFC3226] that deal with DNSSEC.

The DNS security extensions provide origin authentication and integrity protection for DNS data, as well as a means of public key distribution. These extensions do not provide confidentiality.

2. Definitions of Important DNSSEC Terms

This section defines a number of terms used in this document set. Because this is intended to be useful as a reference while reading the rest of the document set, first-time readers may wish to skim this section quickly, read the rest of this document, and then come back to this section.

Authentication Chain: An alternating sequence of DNS public key (DNSKEY) RRsets and Delegation Signer (DS) RRsets forms a chain of signed data, with each link in the chain vouching for the next. A DNSKEY RR is used to verify the signature covering a DS RR and allows the DS RR to be authenticated. The DS RR contains a hash of another DNSKEY RR and this new DNSKEY RR is authenticated by matching the hash in the DS RR. This new DNSKEY RR in turn authenticates another DNSKEY RRset and, in turn, some DNSKEY RR in this set may be used to authenticate another DS RR, and so forth until the chain finally ends with a DNSKEY RR whose corresponding private key signs the desired DNS data. For example, the root DNSKEY RRset can be used to authenticate the DS RRset for "example." The "example." DS RRset contains a hash that matches some "example." DNSKEY, and this DNSKEY's corresponding private key signs the "example." DNSKEY RRset. Private key counterparts of the "example." DNSKEY RRset sign data records such as "www.example." and DS RRs for delegations such as "subzone.example."

Authentication Key: A public key that a security-aware resolver has verified and can therefore use to authenticate data. A security-aware resolver can obtain authentication keys in three ways. First, the resolver is generally configured to know about at least one public key; this configured data is usually either the public key itself or a hash of the public key as found in the DS RR (see "trust anchor"). Second, the resolver may use an authenticated public key to verify a DS RR and the DNSKEY RR to which the DS RR refers. Third, the resolver may be able to determine that a new public key has been signed by the private key corresponding to another public key that the resolver has verified. Note that the resolver must always be guided by local policy when deciding whether to authenticate a new public key, even if the local policy is simply to authenticate any new public key for which the resolver is able verify the signature.

Authoritative RRset: Within the context of a particular zone, an RRset is "authoritative" if and only if the owner name of the RRset lies within the subset of the name space that is at or below the zone apex and at or above the cuts that separate the zone from its children, if any. All RRsets at the zone apex are authoritative, except for certain RRsets at this domain name that, if present, belong to this zone's parent. These RRset could include a DS RRset, the NSEC RRset referencing this DS RRset (the "parental NSEC"), and RRSIG RRs associated with these RRsets, all of which are authoritative in the parent zone. Similarly, if this zone contains any delegation points, only the parental NSEC RRset, DS RRsets, and any RRSIG RRs associated with these RRsets are authoritative for this zone.

Delegation Point: Term used to describe the name at the parental side of a zone cut. That is, the delegation point for "foo.example" would be the foo.example node in the "example" zone (as opposed to the zone apex of the "foo.example" zone). See also zone apex.

Island of Security: Term used to describe a signed, delegated zone that does not have an authentication chain from its delegating parent. That is, there is no DS RR containing a hash of a DNSKEY RR for the island in its delegating parent zone (see [RFC4034]). An island of security is served by security-aware name servers and may provide authentication chains to any delegated child zones. Responses from an island of security or its descendents can only be authenticated if its authentication keys can be authenticated by some trusted means out of band from the DNS protocol.

Key Signing Key (KSK): An authentication key that corresponds to a private key used to sign one or more other authentication keys for a given zone. Typically, the private key corresponding to a key signing key will sign a zone signing key, which in turn has a corresponding private key that will sign other zone data. Local policy may require that the zone signing key be changed frequently, while the key signing key may have a longer validity period in order to provide a more stable secure entry point into the zone. Designating an authentication key as a key signing key is purely an operational issue: DNSSEC validation does not distinguish between key signing keys and other DNSSEC authentication keys, and it is possible to use a single key as both a key signing key and a zone signing key. Key signing keys are discussed in more detail in [RFC3757]. Also see zone signing key.

Non-Validating Security-Aware Stub Resolver: A security-aware stub resolver that trusts one or more security-aware recursive name servers to perform most of the tasks discussed in this document set on its behalf. In particular, a non-validating security-aware stub resolver is an entity that sends DNS queries, receives DNS responses, and is capable of establishing an appropriately secured channel to a security-aware recursive name server that will provide these services on behalf of the security-aware stub resolver. See also security-aware stub resolver, validating security-aware stub resolver.

Non-Validating Stub Resolver: A less tedious term for a non-validating security-aware stub resolver.

Security-Aware Name Server: An entity acting in the role of a name server (defined in section 2.4 of [RFC1034]) that understands the DNS security extensions defined in this document set. In particular, a security-aware name server is an entity that receives DNS queries, sends DNS responses, supports the EDNS0 ([RFC2671]) message size extension and the DO bit ([RFC3225]), and supports the RR types and message header bits defined in this document set.

Security-Aware Recursive Name Server: An entity that acts in both the security-aware name server and security-aware resolver roles. A more cumbersome but equivalent phrase would be "a security-aware name server that offers recursive service".

Security-Aware Resolver: An entity acting in the role of a resolver (defined in section 2.4 of [RFC1034]) that understands the DNS security extensions defined in this document set. In particular, a security-aware resolver is an entity that sends DNS queries, receives DNS responses, supports the EDNS0 ([RFC2671]) message size extension and the DO bit ([RFC3225]), and is capable of using the RR types and message header bits defined in this document set to provide DNSSEC services.

Security-Aware Stub Resolver: An entity acting in the role of a stub resolver (defined in section 5.3.1 of [RFC1034]) that has enough of an understanding the DNS security extensions defined in this document set to provide additional services not available from a security-oblivious stub resolver. Security-aware stub resolvers may be either "validating" or "non-validating", depending on whether the stub resolver attempts to verify DNSSEC signatures on its own or trusts a friendly security-aware name server to do so. See also validating stub resolver, non-validating stub resolver.

Security-Oblivious <anything>: An <anything> that is not "security-aware".

Signed Zone: A zone whose RRsets are signed and that contains properly constructed DNSKEY, Resource Record Signature (RRSIG), Next Secure (NSEC), and (optionally) DS records.

Trust Anchor: A configured DNSKEY RR or DS RR hash of a DNSKEY RR. A validating security-aware resolver uses this public key or hash as a starting point for building the authentication chain to a signed DNS response. In general, a validating resolver will have to obtain the initial values of its trust anchors via some secure or trusted means outside the DNS protocol. Presence of a trust anchor also implies that the resolver should expect the zone to which the trust anchor points to be signed.

Unsigned Zone: A zone that is not signed.

Validating Security-Aware Stub Resolver: A security-aware resolver that sends queries in recursive mode but that performs signature validation on its own rather than just blindly trusting an upstream security-aware recursive name server. See also security-aware stub resolver, non-validating security-aware stub resolver.

Validating Stub Resolver: A less tedious term for a validating security-aware stub resolver.

Zone Apex: Term used to describe the name at the child's side of a zone cut. See also delegation point.

Zone Signing Key (ZSK): An authentication key that corresponds to a private key used to sign a zone. Typically, a zone signing key will be part of the same DNSKEY RRset as the key signing key whose corresponding private key signs this DNSKEY RRset, but the zone signing key is used for a slightly different purpose and may differ from the key signing key in other ways, such as validity lifetime. Designating an authentication key as a zone signing key is purely an operational issue; DNSSEC validation does not distinguish between zone signing keys and other DNSSEC authentication keys, and it is possible to use a single key as both a key signing key and a zone signing key. See also key signing key.

3. Services Provided by DNS Security

The Domain Name System (DNS) security extensions provide origin authentication and integrity assurance services for DNS data, including mechanisms for authenticated denial of existence of DNS data. These mechanisms are described below.

These mechanisms require changes to the DNS protocol. DNSSEC adds four new resource record types: Resource Record Signature (RRSIG), DNS Public Key (DNSKEY), Delegation Signer (DS), and Next Secure (NSEC). It also adds two new message header bits: Checking Disabled (CD) and Authenticated Data (AD). In order to support the larger DNS message sizes that result from adding the DNSSEC RRs, DNSSEC also requires EDNS0 support ([RFC2671]). Finally, DNSSEC requires support for the DNSSEC OK (DO) EDNS header bit ([RFC3225]) so that a security-aware resolver can indicate in its queries that it wishes to receive DNSSEC RRs in response messages.

These services protect against most of the threats to the Domain Name System described in [RFC3833]. Please see Section 12 for a discussion of the limitations of these extensions.

3.1. Data Origin Authentication and Data Integrity

DNSSEC provides authentication by associating cryptographically generated digital signatures with DNS RRsets. These digital signatures are stored in a new resource record, the RRSIG record. Typically, there will be a single private key that signs a zone's data, but multiple keys are possible. For example, there may be keys for each of several different digital signature algorithms. If a security-aware resolver reliably learns a zone's public key, it can authenticate that zone's signed data. An important DNSSEC concept is that the key that signs a zone's data is associated with the zone itself and not with the zone's authoritative name servers. (Public keys for DNS transaction authentication mechanisms may also appear in zones, as described in [RFC2931], but DNSSEC itself is concerned with object security of DNS data, not channel security of DNS transactions. The keys associated with transaction security may be stored in different RR types. See [RFC3755] for details.)

A security-aware resolver can learn a zone's public key either by having a trust anchor configured into the resolver or by normal DNS resolution. To allow the latter, public keys are stored in a new type of resource record, the DNSKEY RR. Note that the private keys used to sign zone data must be kept secure and should be stored offline when practical. To discover a public key reliably via DNS resolution, the target key itself has to be signed by either a configured authentication key or another key that has been authenticated previously. Security-aware resolvers authenticate zone information by forming an authentication chain from a newly learned public key back to a previously known authentication public key, which in turn either has been configured into the resolver or must have been learned and verified previously. Therefore, the resolver must be configured with at least one trust anchor.

If the configured trust anchor is a zone signing key, then it will authenticate the associated zone; if the configured key is a key signing key, it will authenticate a zone signing key. If the configured trust anchor is the hash of a key rather than the key itself, the resolver may have to obtain the key via a DNS query. To help security-aware resolvers establish this authentication chain, security-aware name servers attempt to send the signature(s) needed to authenticate a zone's public key(s) in the DNS reply message along with the public key itself, provided that there is space available in the message.

The Delegation Signer (DS) RR type simplifies some of the administrative tasks involved in signing delegations across organizational boundaries. The DS RRset resides at a delegation point in a parent zone and indicates the public key(s) corresponding to the private key(s) used to self-sign the DNSKEY RRset at the delegated child zone's apex. The administrator of the child zone, in turn, uses the private key(s) corresponding to one or more of the public keys in this DNSKEY RRset to sign the child zone's data. The typical authentication chain is therefore DNSKEY->[DS->DNSKEY]*->RRset, where "*" denotes zero or more DS->DNSKEY subchains. DNSSEC permits more complex authentication chains, such as additional layers of DNSKEY RRs signing other DNSKEY RRs within a zone.

A security-aware resolver normally constructs this authentication chain from the root of the DNS hierarchy down to the leaf zones based on configured knowledge of the public key for the root. Local policy, however, may also allow a security-aware resolver to use one or more configured public keys (or hashes of public keys) other than the root public key, may not provide configured knowledge of the root public key, or may prevent the resolver from using particular public keys for arbitrary reasons, even if those public keys are properly signed with verifiable signatures. DNSSEC provides mechanisms by which a security-aware resolver can determine whether an RRset's signature is "valid" within the meaning of DNSSEC. In the final analysis, however, authenticating both DNS keys and data is a matter of local policy, which may extend or even override the protocol extensions defined in this document set. See Section 5 for further discussion.

3.2. Authenticating Name and Type Non-Existence

The security mechanism described in Section 3.1 only provides a way to sign existing RRsets in a zone. The problem of providing negative responses with the same level of authentication and integrity requires the use of another new resource record type, the NSEC record. The NSEC record allows a security-aware resolver to authenticate a negative reply for either name or type non-existence with the same mechanisms used to authenticate other DNS replies. Use of NSEC records requires a canonical representation and ordering for domain names in zones. Chains of NSEC records explicitly describe the gaps, or "empty space", between domain names in a zone and list the types of RRsets present at existing names. Each NSEC record is signed and authenticated using the mechanisms described in Section 3.1.

4. Services Not Provided by DNS Security

DNS was originally designed with the assumptions that the DNS will return the same answer to any given query regardless of who may have issued the query, and that all data in the DNS is thus visible. Accordingly, DNSSEC is not designed to provide confidentiality, access control lists, or other means of differentiating between inquirers.

DNSSEC provides no protection against denial of service attacks. Security-aware resolvers and security-aware name servers are vulnerable to an additional class of denial of service attacks based on cryptographic operations. Please see Section 12 for details.

The DNS security extensions provide data and origin authentication for DNS data. The mechanisms outlined above are not designed to protect operations such as zone transfers and dynamic update ([RFC2136], [RFC3007]). Message authentication schemes described in [RFC2845] and [RFC2931] address security operations that pertain to these transactions.

5. Scope of the DNSSEC Document Set and Last Hop Issues

The specification in this document set defines the behavior for zone signers and security-aware name servers and resolvers in such a way that the validating entities can unambiguously determine the state of the data.

A validating resolver can determine the following 4 states:

Secure: The validating resolver has a trust anchor, has a chain of trust, and is able to verify all the signatures in the response.

Insecure: The validating resolver has a trust anchor, a chain of trust, and, at some delegation point, signed proof of the non-existence of a DS record. This indicates that subsequent branches in the tree are provably insecure. A validating resolver may have a local policy to mark parts of the domain space as insecure.

Bogus: The validating resolver has a trust anchor and a secure delegation indicating that subsidiary data is signed, but the response fails to validate for some reason: missing signatures, expired signatures, signatures with unsupported algorithms, data missing that the relevant NSEC RR says should be present, and so forth.

Indeterminate: There is no trust anchor that would indicate that a specific portion of the tree is secure. This is the default operation mode.

This specification only defines how security-aware name servers can signal non-validating stub resolvers that data was found to be bogus (using RCODE=2, "Server Failure"; see [RFC4035]).

There is a mechanism for security-aware name servers to signal security-aware stub resolvers that data was found to be secure (using the AD bit; see [RFC4035]).

This specification does not define a format for communicating why responses were found to be bogus or marked as insecure. The current signaling mechanism does not distinguish between indeterminate and insecure states.

A method for signaling advanced error codes and policy between a security-aware stub resolver and security-aware recursive nameservers is a topic for future work, as is the interface between a security-aware resolver and the applications that use it. Note, however, that the lack of the specification of such communication does not prohibit deployment of signed zones or the deployment of security aware recursive name servers that prohibit propagation of bogus data to the applications.

6. Resolver Considerations

A security-aware resolver has to be able to perform cryptographic functions necessary to verify digital signatures using at least the mandatory-to-implement algorithm(s). Security-aware resolvers must also be capable of forming an authentication chain from a newly learned zone back to an authentication key, as described above. This process might require additional queries to intermediate DNS zones to obtain necessary DNSKEY, DS, and RRSIG records. A security-aware resolver should be configured with at least one trust anchor as the starting point from which it will attempt to establish authentication chains.

If a security-aware resolver is separated from the relevant authoritative name servers by a recursive name server or by any sort of intermediary device that acts as a proxy for DNS, and if the recursive name server or intermediary device is not security-aware, the security-aware resolver may not be capable of operating in a secure mode. For example, if a security-aware resolver's packets are routed through a network address translation (NAT) device that includes a DNS proxy that is not security-aware, the security-aware resolver may find it difficult or impossible to obtain or validate signed DNS data. The security-aware resolver may have a particularly difficult time obtaining DS RRs in such a case, as DS RRs do not follow the usual DNS rules for ownership of RRs at zone cuts. Note that this problem is not specific to NATs: any security-oblivious DNS software of any kind between the security-aware resolver and the authoritative name servers will interfere with DNSSEC.

If a security-aware resolver must rely on an unsigned zone or a name server that is not security aware, the resolver may not be able to validate DNS responses and will need a local policy on whether to accept unverified responses.

A security-aware resolver should take a signature's validation period into consideration when determining the TTL of data in its cache, to avoid caching signed data beyond the validity period of the signature. However, it should also allow for the possibility that the security-aware resolver's own clock is wrong. Thus, a security-aware resolver that is part of a security-aware recursive name server will have to pay careful attention to the DNSSEC "checking disabled" (CD) bit ([RFC4034]). This is in order to avoid blocking valid signatures from getting through to other security-aware resolvers that are clients of this recursive name server. See [RFC4035] for how a secure recursive server handles queries with the CD bit set.

7. Stub Resolver Considerations

Although not strictly required to do so by the protocol, most DNS queries originate from stub resolvers. Stub resolvers, by definition, are minimal DNS resolvers that use recursive query mode to offload most of the work of DNS resolution to a recursive name server. Given the widespread use of stub resolvers, the DNSSEC architecture has to take stub resolvers into account, but the security features needed in a stub resolver differ in some respects from those needed in a security-aware iterative resolver.

Even a security-oblivious stub resolver may benefit from DNSSEC if the recursive name servers it uses are security-aware, but for the stub resolver to place any real reliance on DNSSEC services, the stub resolver must trust both the recursive name servers in question and the communication channels between itself and those name servers. The first of these issues is a local policy issue: in essence, a security-oblivious stub resolver has no choice but to place itself at the mercy of the recursive name servers that it uses, as it does not perform DNSSEC validity checks on its own. The second issue requires some kind of channel security mechanism; proper use of DNS transaction authentication mechanisms such as SIG(0) ([RFC2931]) or TSIG ([RFC2845]) would suffice, as would appropriate use of IPsec. Particular implementations may have other choices available, such as operating system specific interprocess communication mechanisms. Confidentiality is not needed for this channel, but data integrity and message authentication are.

A security-aware stub resolver that does trust both its recursive name servers and its communication channel to them may choose to examine the setting of the Authenticated Data (AD) bit in the message header of the response messages it receives. The stub resolver can use this flag bit as a hint to find out whether the recursive name server was able to validate signatures for all of the data in the Answer and Authority sections of the response.

There is one more step that a security-aware stub resolver can take if, for whatever reason, it is not able to establish a useful trust relationship with the recursive name servers that it uses: it can perform its own signature validation by setting the Checking Disabled (CD) bit in its query messages. A validating stub resolver is thus able to treat the DNSSEC signatures as trust relationships between the zone administrators and the stub resolver itself.

8. Zone Considerations

There are several differences between signed and unsigned zones. A signed zone will contain additional security-related records (RRSIG, DNSKEY, DS, and NSEC records). RRSIG and NSEC records may be generated by a signing process prior to serving the zone. The RRSIG records that accompany zone data have defined inception and expiration times that establish a validity period for the signatures and the zone data the signatures cover.

8.1. TTL Values vs. RRSIG Validity Period

It is important to note the distinction between a RRset's TTL value and the signature validity period specified by the RRSIG RR covering that RRset. DNSSEC does not change the definition or function of the TTL value, which is intended to maintain database coherency in caches. A caching resolver purges RRsets from its cache no later than the end of the time period specified by the TTL fields of those RRsets, regardless of whether the resolver is security-aware.

The inception and expiration fields in the RRSIG RR ([RFC4034]), on the other hand, specify the time period during which the signature can be used to validate the covered RRset. The signatures associated with signed zone data are only valid for the time period specified by these fields in the RRSIG RRs in question. TTL values cannot extend the validity period of signed RRsets in a resolver's cache, but the resolver may use the time remaining before expiration of the signature validity period of a signed RRset as an upper bound for the TTL of the signed RRset and its associated RRSIG RR in the resolver's cache.

8.2. New Temporal Dependency Issues for Zones

Information in a signed zone has a temporal dependency that did not exist in the original DNS protocol. A signed zone requires regular maintenance to ensure that each RRset in the zone has a current valid RRSIG RR. The signature validity period of an RRSIG RR is an interval during which the signature for one particular signed RRset can be considered valid, and the signatures of different RRsets in a zone may expire at different times. Re-signing one or more RRsets in a zone will change one or more RRSIG RRs, which will in turn require incrementing the zone's SOA serial number to indicate that a zone change has occurred and re-signing the SOA RRset itself. Thus, re-signing any RRset in a zone may also trigger DNS NOTIFY messages and zone transfer operations.

9. Name Server Considerations

A security-aware name server should include the appropriate DNSSEC records (RRSIG, DNSKEY, DS, and NSEC) in all responses to queries from resolvers that have signaled their willingness to receive such records via use of the DO bit in the EDNS header, subject to message size limitations. Because inclusion of these DNSSEC RRs could easily cause UDP message truncation and fallback to TCP, a security-aware name server must also support the EDNS "sender's UDP payload" mechanism.

If possible, the private half of each DNSSEC key pair should be kept offline, but this will not be possible for a zone for which DNS dynamic update has been enabled. In the dynamic update case, the primary master server for the zone will have to re-sign the zone when it is updated, so the private key corresponding to the zone signing key will have to be kept online. This is an example of a situation in which the ability to separate the zone's DNSKEY RRset into zone signing key(s) and key signing key(s) may be useful, as the key signing key(s) in such a case can still be kept offline and may have a longer useful lifetime than the zone signing key(s).

By itself, DNSSEC is not enough to protect the integrity of an entire zone during zone transfer operations, as even a signed zone contains some unsigned, nonauthoritative data if the zone has any children. Therefore, zone maintenance operations will require some additional mechanisms (most likely some form of channel security, such as TSIG, SIG(0), or IPsec).

10. DNS Security Document Family

The DNSSEC document set can be partitioned into several main groups, under the larger umbrella of the DNS base protocol documents.

The "DNSSEC protocol document set" refers to the three documents that form the core of the DNS security extensions:

1. DNS Security Introduction and Requirements (this document)

2. Resource Records for DNS Security Extensions [RFC4034]

3. Protocol Modifications for the DNS Security Extensions [RFC4035]

Additionally, any document that would add to or change the core DNS Security extensions would fall into this category. This includes any future work on the communication between security-aware stub resolvers and upstream security-aware recursive name servers.

The "Digital Signature Algorithm Specification" document set refers to the group of documents that describe how specific digital signature algorithms should be implemented to fit the

DNSSEC resource record format. Each document in this set deals with a specific digital signature algorithm. Please see the appendix on "DNSSEC Algorithm and Digest Types" in [RFC4034] for a list of the algorithms that were defined when this core specification was written.

The "Transaction Authentication Protocol" document set refers to the group of documents that deal with DNS message authentication, including secret key establishment and verification. Although not strictly part of the DNSSEC specification as defined in this set of documents, this group is noted because of its relationship to DNSSEC.

The final document set, "New Security Uses", refers to documents that seek to use proposed DNS Security extensions for other security related purposes. DNSSEC does not provide any direct security for these new uses but may be used to support them. Documents that fall in this category include those describing the use of DNS in the storage and distribution of certificates ([RFC2538]).

11. IANA Considerations

This overview document introduces no new IANA considerations. Please see [RFC4034] for a complete review of the IANA considerations introduced by DNSSEC.

12. Security Considerations

This document introduces DNS security extensions and describes the document set that contains the new security records and DNS protocol modifications. The extensions provide data origin authentication and data integrity using digital signatures over resource record sets. This section discusses the limitations of these extensions.

In order for a security-aware resolver to validate a DNS response, all zones along the path from the trusted starting point to the zone containing the response zones must be signed, and all name servers and resolvers involved in the resolution process must be security-aware, as defined in this document set. A security-aware resolver cannot verify responses originating from an unsigned zone, from a zone not served by a security-aware name server, or for any DNS data that the resolver is only able to obtain through a recursive name server that is not security-aware. If there is a break in the authentication chain such that a security-aware resolver cannot obtain and validate the authentication keys it needs, then the security-aware resolver cannot validate the affected DNS data.

This document briefly discusses other methods of adding security to a DNS query, such as using a channel secured by IPsec or using a DNS transaction authentication mechanism such as TSIG ([RFC2845]) or SIG(0) ([RFC2931]), but transaction security is not part of DNSSEC per se.

A non-validating security-aware stub resolver, by definition, does not perform DNSSEC signature validation on its own and thus is vulnerable both to attacks on (and by) the security-aware recursive name servers that perform these checks on its behalf and to attacks on its communication with those security-aware recursive name servers. Non-validating security-aware stub resolvers should use some form of channel security to defend against the latter threat. The only known defense against the former threat would be for the security-aware stub resolver to perform its own signature validation, at which point, again by definition, it would no longer be a non-validating security-aware stub resolver.

DNSSEC does not protect against denial of service attacks. DNSSEC makes DNS vulnerable to a new class of denial of service attacks based on cryptographic operations against security-aware resolvers and security-aware name servers, as an attacker can attempt to use DNSSEC mechanisms to consume a victim's resources. This class of attacks takes at least two forms. An attacker may be able to consume resources in a security-aware resolver's signature validation code by tampering with RRSIG RRs in response messages or by constructing needlessly complex signature chains. An attacker may also be able to consume resources in a security-aware name server that supports DNS dynamic update, by sending a stream of update messages that force the security-aware name server to re-sign some RRsets in the zone more frequently than would otherwise be necessary.

Due to a deliberate design choice, DNSSEC does not provide confidentiality.

DNSSEC introduces the ability for a hostile party to enumerate all the names in a zone by following the NSEC chain. NSEC RRs assert which names do not exist in a zone by linking from existing name to existing name along a canonical ordering of all the names within a zone. Thus, an attacker can query these NSEC RRs in sequence to obtain all the names in a zone. Although this is not an attack on the DNS itself, it could allow an attacker to map network hosts or other resources by enumerating the contents of a zone.

DNSSEC introduces significant additional complexity to the DNS and thus introduces many new opportunities for implementation bugs and misconfigured zones. In particular, enabling DNSSEC signature validation in a resolver may cause entire legitimate zones to become effectively unreachable due to DNSSEC configuration errors or bugs.

DNSSEC does not protect against tampering with unsigned zone data. Non-authoritative data at zone cuts (glue and NS RRs in the parent zone) are not signed. This does not pose a problem when validating the authentication chain, but it does mean that the non-authoritative data itself is vulnerable to tampering during zone transfer operations. Thus, while DNSSEC can provide data origin authentication and data integrity for RRsets, it cannot do so for zones, and other mechanisms (such as TSIG, SIG(0), or IPsec) must be used to protect zone transfer operations.

Please see [RFC4034] and [RFC4035] for additional security considerations.

13. Acknowledgements

This document was created from the input and ideas of the members of the DNS Extensions Working Group. Although explicitly listing everyone who has contributed during the decade in which DNSSEC has been under development would be impossible, the editors would particularly like to thank the following people for their contributions to and comments on this document set: Jaap Akkerhuis, Mark Andrews, Derek Atkins, Roy Badami, Alan Barrett, Dan Bernstein, David Blacka, Len Budney, Randy Bush, Francis Dupont, Donald Eastlake, Robert

Elz, Miek Gieben, Michael Graff, Olafur Gudmundsson, Gilles Guette, Andreas Gustafsson, Jun-ichiro Itojun Hagino, Phillip Hallam-Baker, Bob Halley, Ted Hardie, Walter Howard, Greg Hudson, Christian Huitema, Johan Ihren, Stephen Jacob, Jelte Jansen, Simon Josefsson, Andris Kalnozols, Peter Koch, Olaf Kolkman, Mark Kosters, Suresh Krishnaswamy, Ben Laurie, David Lawrence, Ted Lemon, Ed Lewis, Ted Lindgreen, Josh Littlefield, Rip Loomis, Bill Manning, Russ Mundy, Thomas Narten, Mans Nilsson, Masataka Ohta, Mike Patton, Rob Payne, Jim Reid, Michael Richardson, Erik Rozendaal, Marcos Sanz, Pekka Savola, Jakob Schlyter, Mike StJohns, Paul Vixie, Sam Weiler, Brian Wellington, and Suzanne Woolf.

No doubt the above list is incomplete. We apologize to anyone we left out.

14. References

14.1. Normative References

[RFC1034] Mockapetris, P., "Domain names - concepts and facilities", STD 13, RFC 1034, November 1987.

[RFC1035] Mockapetris, P., "Domain names - implementation and specification", STD 13, RFC 1035, November 1987.

[RFC2535] Eastlake 3rd, D., "Domain Name System Security Extensions", RFC 2535, March 1999.

[RFC2671] Vixie, P., "Extension Mechanisms for DNS (EDNS0)", RFC 2671, August 1999.

[RFC3225] Conrad, D., "Indicating Resolver Support of DNSSEC", RFC 3225, December 2001.

[RFC3226] Gudmundsson, O., "DNSSEC and IPv6 A6 aware server/resolver message size requirements", RFC 3226, December 2001.

[RFC3445] Massey, D. and S. Rose, "Limiting the Scope of the KEY Resource Record (RR)", RFC 3445, December 2002.

[RFC4034] Arends, R., Austein, R., Larson, M., Massey, D., and S. Rose, "Resource Records for DNS Security Extensions", RFC 4034, March 2005.

[RFC4035] Arends, R., Austein, R., Larson, M., Massey, D., and S. Rose, "Protocol Modifications for the DNS Security Extensions", RFC 4035, March 2005.

14.2. Informative References

[RFC2136] Vixie, P., Thomson, S., Rekhter, Y., and J. Bound, "Dynamic Updates in the Domain Name System (DNS UPDATE)", RFC 2136, April 1997.

[RFC2181] Elz, R. and R. Bush, "Clarifications to the DNS Specification", RFC 2181, July 1997.

[RFC2308] Andrews, M., "Negative Caching of DNS Queries (DNS NCACHE)", RFC 2308, March 1998.

[RFC2538] Eastlake 3rd, D. and O. Gudmundsson, "Storing Certificates in the Domain Name System (DNS)", RFC 2538, March 1999.

[RFC2845] Vixie, P., Gudmundsson, O., Eastlake 3rd, D., and B. Wellington, "Secret Key Transaction Authentication for DNS (TSIG)", RFC 2845, May 2000.

[RFC2931] Eastlake 3rd, D., "DNS Request and Transaction Signatures (SIG(0)s)", RFC 2931, September 2000.

[RFC3007] Wellington, B., "Secure Domain Name System (DNS) Dynamic Update", RFC 3007, November 2000.

[RFC3008] Wellington, B., "Domain Name System Security (DNSSEC) Signing Authority", RFC 3008, November 2000.

[RFC3090] Lewis, E., "DNS Security Extension Clarification on Zone Status", RFC 3090, March 2001.

[RFC3597] Gustafsson, A., "Handling of Unknown DNS Resource Record (RR) Types", RFC 3597, September 2003.

[RFC3655] Wellington, B. and O. Gudmundsson, "Redefinition of DNS Authenticated Data (AD) bit", RFC 3655, November 2003.

[RFC3658] Gudmundsson, O., "Delegation Signer (DS) Resource Record (RR)", RFC 3658, December 2003.

[RFC3755] Weiler, S., "Legacy Resolver Compatibility for Delegation Signer (DS)", RFC 3755, May 2004.

[RFC3757] Kolkman, O., Schlyter, J., and E. Lewis, "Domain Name System KEY (DNSKEY) Resource Record (RR) Secure Entry Point (SEP) Flag", RFC 3757, April 2004.

[RFC3833] Atkins, D. and R. Austein, "Threat Analysis of the Domain Name System (DNS)", RFC 3833, August 2004.

[RFC3845] Schlyter, J., "DNS Security (DNSSEC) NextSECure (NSEC) RDATA Format", RFC 3845, August 2004.

Authors' Addresses

Roy Arends
Telematica Instituut
Brouwerijstraat 1
7523 XC Enschede
NL

EMail: roy.arends@telin.nl

Rob Austein
Internet Systems Consortium

950 Charter Street
Redwood City, CA 94063
USA

EMail: sra@isc.org

Matt Larson
VeriSign, Inc.
21345 Ridgetop Circle
Dulles, VA 20166-6503
USA

EMail: mlarson@verisign.com

Dan Massey
Colorado State University
Department of Computer Science
Fort Collins, CO 80523-1873

EMail: massey@cs.colostate.edu

Scott Rose
National Institute for Standards and Technology
100 Bureau Drive
Gaithersburg, MD 20899-8920
USA

EMail: scott.rose@nist.gov

Full Copyright Statement

Intellectual Property

not be available; nor does it represent that it has made any independent effort to identify any such rights. Information on the procedures with respect to rights in RFC documents can be found in BCP 78 and BCP 79.

Copies of IPR disclosures made to the IETF Secretariat and any assurances of licenses to be made available, or the result of an attempt made to obtain a general license or permission for the use of such proprietary rights by implementers or users of this specification can be obtained from the IETF on-line IPR repository at http://www.ietf.org/ipr.

The IETF invites any interested party to bring to its attention any copyrights, patents or patent applications, or other proprietary rights that may cover technology that may be required to implement this standard. Please address the information to the IETF at ietf-ipr@ietf.org.

Acknowledgement

Funding for the RFC Editor function is currently provided by the Internet Society.

RFC 4034
Resource Records for the DNS Security Extensions

Network Working Group
Request for Comments: 4034
Obsoletes: 2535, 3008, 3090, 3445, 3655, 3658,
3755, 3757, 3845
Updates: 1034, 1035, 2136, 2181, 2308, 3225,
3007, 3597, 3226
Category: Standards Track

R. Arends
Telematica Instituut
R. Austein
ISC
M. Larson
VeriSign
D. Massey
Colorado State University
S. Rose
NIST
March 2005

Status of This Memo

This document specifies an Internet standards track protocol for the Internet community, and requests discussion and suggestions for improvements. Please refer to the current edition of the "Internet Official Protocol Standards" (STD 1) for the standardization state and status of this protocol. Distribution of this memo is unlimited.

Copyright Notice

Abstract

This document is part of a family of documents that describe the DNS Security Extensions (DNSSEC). The DNS Security Extensions are a collection of resource records and protocol modifications that provide source authentication for the DNS. This document defines the public key (DNSKEY), delegation signer (DS), resource record digital signature (RRSIG), and authenticated denial of existence (NSEC) resource records. The purpose and format of each resource record is described in detail, and an example of each resource record is given.

This document obsoletes RFC 2535 and incorporates changes from all updates to RFC 2535.

RFC 4034 Contents

1. Introduction

The DNS Security Extensions (DNSSEC) introduce four new DNS resource record types: DNS Public Key (DNSKEY), Resource Record Signature (RRSIG), Next Secure (NSEC), and Delegation Signer (DS). This document defines the purpose of each resource record (RR), the RR's RDATA format, and its presentation format (ASCII representation).

1.1. Background and Related Documents

This document is part of a family of documents defining DNSSEC, which should be read together as a set.

[RFC4033] contains an introduction to DNSSEC and definition of common terms; the reader is assumed to be familiar with this document. [RFC4033] also contains a list of other documents updated by and obsoleted by this document set.

[RFC4035] defines the DNSSEC protocol operations.

The reader is also assumed to be familiar with the basic DNS concepts described in [RFC1034], [RFC1035], and the subsequent documents that update them, particularly [RFC2181] and [RFC2308].

This document defines the DNSSEC resource records. All numeric DNS type codes given in this document are decimal integers.

1.2. Reserved Words

The key words "MUST", "MUST NOT", "REQUIRED", "SHALL", "SHALL NOT", "SHOULD", "SHOULD NOT", "RECOMMENDED", "MAY", and "OPTIONAL" in this document are to be interpreted as described in [RFC2119].

2. The DNSKEY Resource Record

DNSSEC uses public key cryptography to sign and authenticate DNS resource record sets (RRsets). The public keys are stored in DNSKEY resource records and are used in the DNSSEC authentication process described in [RFC4035]: A zone signs its authoritative RRsets by using a private key and stores the corresponding public key in a DNSKEY RR. A resolver can then use the public key to validate signatures covering the RRsets in the zone, and thus to authenticate them.

The DNSKEY RR is not intended as a record for storing arbitrary public keys and MUST NOT be used to store certificates or public keys that do not directly relate to the DNS infrastructure.

The Type value for the DNSKEY RR type is 48.

The DNSKEY RR is class independent.

The DNSKEY RR has no special TTL requirements.

2.1. DNSKEY RDATA Wire Format

The RDATA for a DNSKEY RR consists of a 2 octet Flags Field, a 1 octet Protocol Field, a 1 octet Algorithm Field, and the Public Key Field.

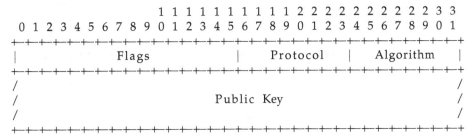

2.1.1. The Flags Field

Bit 7 of the Flags field is the Zone Key flag. If bit 7 has value 1, then the DNSKEY record holds a DNS zone key, and the DNSKEY RR's owner name MUST be the name of a zone. If bit 7 has value 0, then the DNSKEY record holds some other type of DNS public key and MUST NOT be used to verify RRSIGs that cover RRsets.

Bit 15 of the Flags field is the Secure Entry Point flag, described in [RFC3757]. If bit 15 has value 1, then the DNSKEY record holds a key intended for use as a secure entry point. This flag is only intended to be a hint to zone signing or debugging software as to the intended use of this DNSKEY record; validators MUST NOT alter their behavior during the signature validation process in any way based on the setting of this bit. This also means that a DNSKEY RR with the SEP bit set would also need the Zone Key flag set in order to be able to generate signatures legally. A DNSKEY RR with the SEP set and the Zone Key flag not set MUST NOT be used to verify RRSIGs that cover RRsets.

Bits 0-6 and 8-14 are reserved: these bits MUST have value 0 upon creation of the DNSKEY RR and MUST be ignored upon receipt.

2.1.2. The Protocol Field

The Protocol Field MUST have value 3, and the DNSKEY RR MUST be treated as invalid during signature verification if it is found to be some value other than 3.

2.1.3. The Algorithm Field

The Algorithm field identifies the public key's cryptographic algorithm and determines the format of the Public Key field. A list of DNSSEC algorithm types can be found in Appendix A.1

2.1.4. The Public Key Field

The Public Key Field holds the public key material. The format depends on the algorithm of the key being stored and is described in separate documents.

2.1.5. Notes on DNSKEY RDATA Design

Although the Protocol Field always has value 3, it is retained for backward compatibility with early versions of the KEY record.

2.2. The DNSKEY RR Presentation Format

The presentation format of the RDATA portion is as follows:

The Flag field MUST be represented as an unsigned decimal integer. Given the currently defined flags, the possible values are: 0, 256, and 257.

The Protocol Field MUST be represented as an unsigned decimal integer with a value of 3.

The Algorithm field MUST be represented either as an unsigned decimal integer or as an algorithm mnemonic as specified in Appendix A.1.

The Public Key field MUST be represented as a Base64 encoding of the Public Key. Whitespace is allowed within the Base64 text. For a definition of Base64 encoding, see [RFC3548].

2.3. DNSKEY RR Example

The following DNSKEY RR stores a DNS zone key for example.com.

```
example.com. 86400 IN DNSKEY 256 3 5 ( AQPSKmynfzW4kyBv015MUG2DeIQ3
                                        Cbl+BBZH4b/0PY1kxkmvHjcZc8no
                                        kfzj31GajIQKY+5CptLr3buXA10h
                                        WqTkF7H6RfoRqXQeogmMHfpftf6z
                                        Mv1LyBUgia7za6ZEzOJBOztyvhjL
                                        742iU/TpPSEDhm2SNKLijfUppn1U
                                        aNvv4w==   )
```

The first four text fields specify the owner name, TTL, Class, and RR type (DNSKEY). Value 256 indicates that the Zone Key bit (bit 7) in the Flags field has value 1. Value 3 is the fixed Protocol value. Value 5 indicates the public key algorithm. Appendix A.1 identifies algorithm type 5 as RSA/SHA1 and indicates that the format of the RSA/SHA1 public key field is defined in [RFC3110]. The remaining text is a Base64 encoding of the public key.

3. The RRSIG Resource Record

DNSSEC uses public key cryptography to sign and authenticate DNS resource record sets (RRsets). Digital signatures are stored in RRSIG resource records and are used in the DNSSEC authentication process described in [RFC4035]. A validator can use these RRSIG RRs to authenticate RRsets from the zone. The RRSIG RR MUST only be used to carry verification material (digital signatures) used to secure DNS operations.

An RRSIG record contains the signature for an RRset with a particular name, class, and type. The RRSIG RR specifies a validity interval for the signature and uses the Algorithm, the Signer's Name, and the Key Tag to identify the DNSKEY RR containing the public key that a validator can use to verify the signature.

Because every authoritative RRset in a zone must be protected by a digital signature, RRSIG RRs must be present for names containing a CNAME RR. This is a change to the traditional DNS specification [RFC1034], which stated that if a CNAME is present for a name, it is the only type allowed at that name. A RRSIG and NSEC (see Section 4) MUST exist for the same name as a CNAME resource record in a signed zone.

The Type value for the RRSIG RR type is 46.

The RRSIG RR is class independent.

An RRSIG RR MUST have the same class as the RRset it covers.

The TTL value of an RRSIG RR MUST match the TTL value of the RRset it covers. This is an exception to the [RFC2181] rules for TTL values of individual RRs within a RRset: individual RRSIG RRs with the same owner name will have different TTL values if the RRsets they cover have different TTL values.

3.1. RRSIG RDATA Wire Format

The RDATA for an RRSIG RR consists of a 2 octet Type Covered field, a 1 octet Algorithm field, a 1 octet Labels field, a 4 octet Original TTL field, a 4 octet Signature Expiration field, a 4 octet Signature Inception field, a 2 octet Key tag, the Signer's Name field, and the Signature field.

```
                          1 1 1 1 1 1 1 1 1 1 2 2 2 2 2 2 2 2 2 2 3 3
      0 1 2 3 4 5 6 7 8 9 0 1 2 3 4 5 6 7 8 9 0 1 2 3 4 5 6 7 8 9 0 1
     +-+-+-+-+-+-+-+-+-+-+-+-+-+-+-+-+-+-+-+-+-+-+-+-+-+-+-+-+-+-+-+-+
     |        Type Covered           |  Algorithm    |     Labels    |
     +-+-+-+-+-+-+-+-+-+-+-+-+-+-+-+-+-+-+-+-+-+-+-+-+-+-+-+-+-+-+-+-+
     |                         Original  TTL                         |
     +-+-+-+-+-+-+-+-+-+-+-+-+-+-+-+-+-+-+-+-+-+-+-+-+-+-+-+-+-+-+-+-+
     |                      Signature  Expiration                    |
     +-+-+-+-+-+-+-+-+-+-+-+-+-+-+-+-+-+-+-+-+-+-+-+-+-+-+-+-+-+-+-+-+
     |                      Signature  Inception                     |
     +-+-+-+-+-+-+-+-+-+-+-+-+-+-+-+-+-+-+-+-+-+-+-+-+-+-+-+-+-+-+-+-+
     |            Key Tag            |                               /
     +-+-+-+-+-+-+-+-+-+-+-+-+-+-+-+-+         Signer's Name          /
     /                                                               /
     +-+-+-+-+-+-+-+-+-+-+-+-+-+-+-+-+-+-+-+-+-+-+-+-+-+-+-+-+-+-+-+-+
     /                                                               /
     /                          Signature                            /
     /                                                               /
     +-+-+-+-+-+-+-+-+-+-+-+-+-+-+-+-+-+-+-+-+-+-+-+-+-+-+-+-+-+-+-+-+
```

3.1.1. The Type Covered Field

The Type Covered field identifies the type of the RRset that is covered by this RRSIG record.

3.1.2. The Algorithm Number Field

The Algorithm Number field identifies the cryptographic algorithm used to create the signature. A list of DNSSEC algorithm types can be found in Appendix A.1

3.1.3. The Labels Field

The Labels field specifies the number of labels in the original RRSIG RR owner name. The significance of this field is that a validator uses it to determine whether the answer was synthesized from a wildcard. If so, it can be used to determine what owner name was used in generating the signature.

To validate a signature, the validator needs the original owner name that was used to create the signature. If the original owner name contains a wildcard label ("*"), the owner name may have been expanded by the server during the response process, in which case the validator will have to reconstruct the original owner name in order to validate the signature. [RFC4035] describes how to use the Labels field to reconstruct the original owner name.

The value of the Labels field MUST NOT count either the null (root) label that terminates the owner name or the wildcard label (if present). The value of the Labels field MUST be less than or equal to the number of labels in the RRSIG owner name. For example, "www.example.com." has a Labels field value of 3, and "*.example.com." has a Labels field value of 2. Root (".") has a Labels field value of 0.

Although the wildcard label is not included in the count stored in the Labels field of the RRSIG RR, the wildcard label is part of the RRset's owner name when the signature is generated or verified.

3.1.4. Original TTL Field

The Original TTL field specifies the TTL of the covered RRset as it appears in the authoritative zone.

The Original TTL field is necessary because a caching resolver decrements the TTL value of a cached RRset. In order to validate a signature, a validator requires the original TTL. [RFC4035] describes how to use the Original TTL field value to reconstruct the original TTL.

3.1.5. Signature Expiration and Inception Fields

The Signature Expiration and Inception fields specify a validity period for the signature. The RRSIG record MUST NOT be used for authentication prior to the inception date and MUST NOT be used for authentication after the expiration date.

The Signature Expiration and Inception field values specify a date and time in the form of a 32-bit unsigned number of seconds elapsed since 1 January 1970 00:00:00 UTC, ignoring leap seconds, in network byte order. The longest interval that can be expressed by this format without wrapping is approximately 136 years. An RRSIG RR can have an Expiration field value that is numerically smaller than the Inception field value if the expiration field value is near the 32-bit wrap-around point or if the signature is long lived. Because of this, all comparisons involving these fields MUST use "Serial number arithmetic", as defined in [RFC1982]. As a direct consequence, the values contained in these fields cannot refer to dates more than 68 years in either the past or the future.

3.1.6. The Key Tag Field

The Key Tag field contains the key tag value of the DNSKEY RR that validates this signature, in network byte order. Appendix B explains how to calculate Key Tag values.

3.1.7. The Signer's Name Field

The Signer's Name field value identifies the owner name of the DNSKEY RR that a validator is supposed to use to validate this signature. The Signer's Name field MUST contain the name of the zone of the covered RRset. A sender MUST NOT use DNS name compression on the Signer's Name field when transmitting a RRSIG RR.

3.1.8. The Signature Field

The Signature field contains the cryptographic signature that covers the RRSIG RDATA (excluding the Signature field) and the RRset specified by the RRSIG owner name, RRSIG class, and RRSIG Type Covered field. The format of this field depends on the algorithm in use, and these formats are described in separate companion documents.

3.1.8.1. Signature Calculation

A signature covers the RRSIG RDATA (excluding the Signature Field) and covers the data RRset specified by the RRSIG owner name, RRSIG class, and RRSIG Type Covered fields. The RRset is in canonical form (see Section 6), and the set RR(1),...RR(n) is signed as follows:

signature = sign(RRSIG_RDATA — RR(1) — RR(2)...) where

> "—" denotes concatenation;
>
> RRSIG_RDATA is the wire format of the RRSIG RDATA fields with the Signer's Name field in canonical form and the Signature field excluded;
>
> RR(i) = owner — type — class — TTL — RDATA length — RDATA
>
> > "owner" is the fully qualified owner name of the RRset in canonical form (for RRs with wildcard owner names, the wildcard label is included in the owner name);
> >
> > Each RR MUST have the same owner name as the RRSIG RR;
> >
> > Each RR MUST have the same class as the RRSIG RR;
> >
> > Each RR in the RRset MUST have the RR type listed in the RRSIG RR's Type Covered field;
> >
> > Each RR in the RRset MUST have the TTL listed in the RRSIG Original TTL Field;
> >
> > Any DNS names in the RDATA field of each RR MUST be in canonical form; and
> >
> > The RRset MUST be sorted in canonical order.

See Sections 6.2 and 6.3 for details on canonical form and ordering of RRsets.

3.2. The RRSIG RR Presentation Format

The presentation format of the RDATA portion is as follows:

The Type Covered field is represented as an RR type mnemonic. When the mnemonic is not known, the TYPE representation as described in [RFC3597], Section 5, MUST be used.

The Algorithm field value MUST be represented either as an unsigned decimal integer or as an algorithm mnemonic, as specified in Appendix A.1.

The Labels field value MUST be represented as an unsigned decimal integer.

The Original TTL field value MUST be represented as an unsigned decimal integer.

The Signature Expiration Time and Inception Time field values MUST be represented either as an unsigned decimal integer indicating seconds since 1 January 1970 00:00:00 UTC, or in the form YYYYMMDDHHmmSS in UTC, where:

> YYYY is the year (0001-9999, but see Section 3.1.5);
>
> MM is the month number (01-12);
>
> DD is the day of the month (01-31);
>
> HH is the hour, in 24 hour notation (00-23);
>
> mm is the minute (00-59); and
>
> SS is the second (00-59).

Note that it is always possible to distinguish between these two formats because the YYYYM-MDDHHmmSS format will always be exactly 14 digits, while the decimal representation of a 32-bit unsigned integer can never be longer than 10 digits.

The Key Tag field MUST be represented as an unsigned decimal integer.

The Signer's Name field value MUST be represented as a domain name.

The Signature field is represented as a Base64 encoding of the signature. Whitespace is allowed within the Base64 text. See Section 2.2.

3.3. RRSIG RR Example

The following RRSIG RR stores the signature for the A RRset of host.example.com:

```
host.example.com. 86400 IN RRSIG A 5 3 86400 20030322173103 (
                    20030220173103 2642 example.com.
                    oJB1W6WNGv+ldvQ3WDG0MQkg5IEhjRip8WTr
                    PYGv07h108dUKGMeDPKijVCHX3DDKdfb+v6o
                    B9wfuh3DTJXUAfI/M0zmO/zz8bW0Rznl8O3t
                    GNazPwQKkRN20XPXV6nwwfoXmJQbsLNrLfkG
                    J5D6fwFm8nN+6pBzeDQfsS3Ap3o= )
```

The first four fields specify the owner name, TTL, Class, and RR type (RRSIG). The "A" represents the Type Covered field. The value 5 identifies the algorithm used (RSA/SHA1) to create the signature. The value 3 is the number of Labels in the original owner name. The value 86400 in the RRSIG RDATA is the Original TTL for the covered A RRset. 20030322173103 and 20030220173103 are the expiration and inception dates, respectively. 2642 is the Key Tag, and example.com. is the Signer's Name. The remaining text is a Base64 encoding of the signature.

Note that combination of RRSIG RR owner name, class, and Type Covered indicates that this RRSIG covers the "host.example.com" A RRset. The Label value of 3 indicates that no wildcard expansion was used. The Algorithm, Signer's Name, and Key Tag indicate that this signature can be authenticated using an example.com zone DNSKEY RR whose algorithm is 5 and whose key tag is 2642.

4. The NSEC Resource Record

The NSEC resource record lists two separate things: the next owner name (in the canonical ordering of the zone) that contains authoritative data or a delegation point NS RRset, and the set of RR types present at the NSEC RR's owner name [RFC3845]. The complete set of NSEC RRs in a zone indicates which authoritative RRsets exist in a zone and also form a chain of authoritative owner names in the zone. This information is used to provide authenticated denial of existence for DNS data, as described in [RFC4035].

Because every authoritative name in a zone must be part of the NSEC chain, NSEC RRs must be present for names containing a CNAME RR. This is a change to the traditional DNS specification [RFC1034], which stated that if a CNAME is present for a name, it is the only type allowed at that name. An RRSIG (see Section 3) and NSEC MUST exist for the same name as does a CNAME resource record in a signed zone.

See [RFC4035] for discussion of how a zone signer determines precisely which NSEC RRs it has to include in a zone.

The type value for the NSEC RR is 47.

The NSEC RR is class independent.

The NSEC RR SHOULD have the same TTL value as the SOA minimum TTL field. This is in the spirit of negative caching ([RFC2308]).

4.1. NSEC RDATA Wire Format

The RDATA of the NSEC RR is as shown below:

```
                      1 1 1 1 1 1 1 1 1 1 2 2 2 2 2 2 2 2 2 2 3 3
  0 1 2 3 4 5 6 7 8 9 0 1 2 3 4 5 6 7 8 9 0 1 2 3 4 5 6 7 8 9 0 1
 +-+-+-+-+-+-+-+-+-+-+-+-+-+-+-+-+-+-+-+-+-+-+-+-+-+-+-+-+-+-+-+-+
 /                      Next  Domain  Name                       /
 +-+-+-+-+-+-+-+-+-+-+-+-+-+-+-+-+-+-+-+-+-+-+-+-+-+-+-+-+-+-+-+-+
 /                       Type  Bit  Maps                         /
 +-+-+-+-+-+-+-+-+-+-+-+-+-+-+-+-+-+-+-+-+-+-+-+-+-+-+-+-+-+-+-+-+
```

4.1.1. The Next Domain Name Field

The Next Domain field contains the next owner name[6] (in the canonical ordering of the zone) that has authoritative data or contains a delegation point NS RRset; see Section 6.1 for an

---

[6]This is updated by RFC 4470. See page 199.

explanation of canonical ordering. The value of the Next Domain Name field in the last NSEC record in the zone is the name of the zone apex (the owner name of the zone's SOA RR). This indicates that the owner name of the NSEC RR is the last name in the canonical ordering of the zone.

A sender MUST NOT use DNS name compression on the Next Domain Name field when transmitting an NSEC RR.

Owner names of RRsets for which the given zone is not authoritative (such as glue records) MUST NOT be listed in the Next Domain Name unless at least one authoritative RRset exists at the same owner name.

4.1.2. The Type Bit Maps Field

The Type Bit Maps field identifies the RRset types that exist at the NSEC RR's owner name.

The RR type space is split into 256 window blocks, each representing the low-order 8 bits of the 16-bit RR type space. Each block that has at least one active RR type is encoded using a single octet window number (from 0 to 255), a single octet bitmap length (from 1 to 32) indicating the number of octets used for the window block's bitmap, and up to 32 octets (256 bits) of bitmap.

Blocks are present in the NSEC RR RDATA in increasing numerical order.

Type Bit Maps Field = (Window Block # — Bitmap Length — Bitmap)+

where "—" denotes concatenation.

Each bitmap encodes the low-order 8 bits of RR types within the window block, in network bit order. The first bit is bit 0. For window block 0, bit 1 corresponds to RR type 1 (A), bit 2 corresponds to RR type 2 (NS), and so forth. For window block 1, bit 1 corresponds to RR type 257, and bit 2 to RR type 258. If a bit is set, it indicates that an RRset of that type is present for the NSEC RR's owner name. If a bit is clear, it indicates that no RRset of that type is present for the NSEC RR's owner name.

Bits representing pseudo-types MUST be clear, as they do not appear in zone data. If encountered, they MUST be ignored upon being read.

Blocks with no types present MUST NOT be included. Trailing zero octets in the bitmap MUST be omitted. The length of each block's bitmap is determined by the type code with the largest numerical value, within that block, among the set of RR types present at the NSEC RR's owner name. Trailing zero octets not specified MUST be interpreted as zero octets.

The bitmap for the NSEC RR at a delegation point requires special attention. Bits corresponding to the delegation NS RRset and the RR types for which the parent zone has authoritative data MUST be set; bits corresponding to any non-NS RRset for which the parent is not authoritative MUST be clear.

A zone MUST NOT include an NSEC RR for any domain name that only holds glue records.

4.1.3. Inclusion of Wildcard Names in NSEC RDATA

If a wildcard owner name appears in a zone, the wildcard label ("*") is treated as a literal symbol and is treated the same as any other owner name for the purposes of generating NSEC RRs. Wildcard owner names appear in the Next Domain Name field without any wildcard expansion. [RFC4035] describes the impact of wildcards on authenticated denial of existence.

4.2. The NSEC RR Presentation Format

The presentation format of the RDATA portion is as follows:

The Next Domain Name field is represented as a domain name.

The Type Bit Maps field is represented as a sequence of RR type mnemonics. When the mnemonic is not known, the TYPE representation described in [RFC3597], Section 5, MUST be used.

4.3. NSEC RR Example

The following NSEC RR identifies the RRsets associated with alfa.example.com. and identifies the next authoritative name after alfa.example.com.

```
alfa.example.com.  86400  IN  NSEC  host.example.com.  (
                                  A MX RRSIG NSEC TYPE1234 )
```

The first four text fields specify the name, TTL, Class, and RR type (NSEC). The entry host.example.com. is the next authoritative name after alfa.example.com. in canonical order. The A, MX, RRSIG, NSEC, and TYPE1234 mnemonics indicate that there are A, MX, RRSIG, NSEC, and TYPE1234 RRsets associated with the name alfa.example.com.

The RDATA section of the NSEC RR above would be encoded as:

```
0x04 'h'  'o'  's'  't'
0x07 'e'  'x'  'a'  'm'  'p'  'l'  'e'
0x03 'c'  'o'  'm'  0x00
0x00 0x06 0x40 0x01 0x00 0x00 0x00 0x03
0x04 0x1b 0x00 0x00 0x00 0x00 0x00 0x00
0x00 0x00 0x00 0x00 0x00 0x00 0x00 0x00
0x00 0x00 0x00 0x00 0x00 0x00 0x00 0x00
0x00 0x00 0x00 0x00 0x20
```

Assuming that the validator can authenticate this NSEC record, it could be used to prove that beta.example.com does not exist, or to prove that there is no AAAA record associated with alfa.example.com. Authenticated denial of existence is discussed in [RFC4035].

5. The DS Resource Record

The DS Resource Record refers to a DNSKEY RR and is used in the DNS DNSKEY authentication process. A DS RR refers to a DNSKEY RR by storing the key tag, algorithm number, and a digest of the DNSKEY RR. Note that while the digest should be sufficient to identify the public key, storing the key tag and key algorithm helps make the identification process more efficient. By authenticating the DS record, a resolver can authenticate the DNSKEY RR to which the DS record points. The key authentication process is described in [RFC4035].

The DS RR and its corresponding DNSKEY RR have the same owner name, but they are stored in different locations. The DS RR appears only on the upper (parental) side of a delegation, and is authoritative data in the parent zone. For example, the DS RR for "example.com" is stored in the "com" zone (the parent zone) rather than in the "example.com" zone (the child zone). The corresponding DNSKEY RR is stored in the "example.com" zone (the child zone). This simplifies DNS zone management and zone signing but introduces special response processing requirements for the DS RR; these are described in [RFC4035].

The type number for the DS record is 43.

The DS resource record is class independent.

The DS RR has no special TTL requirements.

5.1. DS RDATA Wire Format

The RDATA for a DS RR consists of a 2 octet Key Tag field, a 1 octet Algorithm field, a 1 octet Digest Type field, and a Digest field.

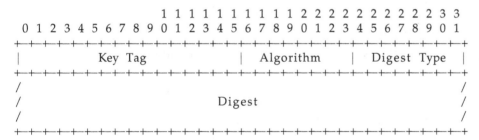

5.1.1. The Key Tag Field

The Key Tag field lists the key tag of the DNSKEY RR referred to by the DS record, in network byte order.

The Key Tag used by the DS RR is identical to the Key Tag used by RRSIG RRs. Appendix B describes how to compute a Key Tag.

5.1.2. The Algorithm Field

The Algorithm field lists the algorithm number of the DNSKEY RR referred to by the DS record.

The algorithm number used by the DS RR is identical to the algorithm number used by RRSIG and DNSKEY RRs. Appendix A.1 lists the algorithm number types.

5.1.3. The Digest Type Field

The DS RR refers to a DNSKEY RR by including a digest of that DNSKEY RR. The Digest Type field identifies the algorithm used to construct the digest. Appendix A.2 lists the possible digest algorithm types.

5.1.4. The Digest Field

The DS record refers to a DNSKEY RR by including a digest of that DNSKEY RR.

The digest is calculated by concatenating the canonical form of the fully qualified owner name of the DNSKEY RR with the DNSKEY RDATA, and then applying the digest algorithm.

digest = digest_algorithm(DNSKEY owner name — DNSKEY RDATA);

"—" denotes concatenation

DNSKEY RDATA = Flags — Protocol — Algorithm — Public Key.

The size of the digest may vary depending on the digest algorithm and DNSKEY RR size. As of the time of this writing, the only defined digest algorithm is SHA-1, which produces a 20 octet digest.

5.2. Processing of DS RRs When Validating Responses

The DS RR links the authentication chain across zone boundaries, so the DS RR requires extra care in processing. The DNSKEY RR referred to in the DS RR MUST be a DNSSEC zone key. The DNSKEY RR Flags MUST have Flags bit 7 set. If the DNSKEY flags do not indicate a DNSSEC zone key, the DS RR (and the DNSKEY RR it references) MUST NOT be used in the validation process.

5.3. The DS RR Presentation Format

The presentation format of the RDATA portion is as follows:

The Key Tag field MUST be represented as an unsigned decimal integer.

The Algorithm field MUST be represented either as an unsigned decimal integer or as an algorithm mnemonic specified in Appendix A.1.

The Digest Type field MUST be represented as an unsigned decimal integer.

The Digest MUST be represented as a sequence of case-insensitive hexadecimal digits. Whitespace is allowed within the hexadecimal text.

5.4. DS RR Example

The following example shows a DNSKEY RR and its corresponding DS RR.

```
dskey.example.com.  86400  IN  DNSKEY  256  3  5  ( AQOeiiR0GOMYkDshWoSKz9Xz
                                          fwJr1AYtsmx3TGkJaNXVbfi/
                                          2pHm822aJ5iI9BMzNXxeYCmZ
                                          DRD99WYwYqUSdjMmmAphXdvx
                                          egXd/M5+X7OrzKBaMbCVdFLU
                                          Uh6DhweJBjEVv5f2wwjM9Xzc
                                          nOf+EPbtG9DMBmADjFDc2w/r
                                          ljwvFw==
                                          ) ;  key id = 60485

dskey.example.com.  86400  IN  DS  60485  5  1  ( 2BB183AF5F22588179A53B0A
                                          98631FAD1A292118 )
```

The first four text fields specify the name, TTL, Class, and RR type (DS). Value 60485 is the key tag for the corresponding "dskey.example.com." DNSKEY RR, and value 5 denotes the algorithm used by this "dskey.example.com." DNSKEY RR. The value 1 is the algorithm used to construct the digest, and the rest of the RDATA text is the digest in hexadecimal.

6. Canonical Form and Order of Resource Records

This section defines a canonical form for resource records, a canonical ordering of DNS names, and a canonical ordering of resource records within an RRset. A canonical name order is required to construct the NSEC name chain. A canonical RR form and ordering within an RRset are required in order to construct and verify RRSIG RRs.

6.1. Canonical DNS Name Order

For the purposes of DNS security, owner names are ordered by treating individual labels as unsigned left-justified octet strings. The absence of a octet sorts before a zero value octet, and uppercase US-ASCII letters are treated as if they were lowercase US-ASCII letters.

To compute the canonical ordering of a set of DNS names, start by sorting the names according to their most significant (rightmost) labels. For names in which the most significant label is identical, continue sorting according to their next most significant label, and so forth.

For example, the following names are sorted in canonical DNS name order. The most significant label is "example". At this level, "example" sorts first, followed by names ending in "a.example", then by names ending "z.example". The names within each level are sorted in the same way.

example

a.example

yljkjljk.a.example

Z.a.example

zABC.a.EXAMPLE

z.example

\001.z.example

*.z.example

\200.z.example

6.2. Canonical RR Form

For the purposes of DNS security, the canonical form of an RR is the wire format of the RR where:

1. every domain name in the RR is fully expanded (no DNS name compression) and fully qualified;

2. all uppercase US-ASCII letters in the owner name of the RR are replaced by the corresponding lowercase US-ASCII letters;

3. if the type of the RR is NS, MD, MF, CNAME, SOA, MB, MG, MR, PTR, HINFO, MINFO, MX, HINFO, RP, AFSDB, RT, SIG, PX, NXT, NAPTR, KX, SRV, DNAME, A6, RRSIG, or NSEC, all uppercase US-ASCII letters in the DNS names contained within the RDATA are replaced by the corresponding lowercase US-ASCII letters;

4. if the owner name of the RR is a wildcard name, the owner name is in its original unexpanded form, including the "*" label (no wildcard substitution); and

5. the RR's TTL is set to its original value as it appears in the originating authoritative zone or the Original TTL field of the covering RRSIG RR.

6.3. Canonical RR Ordering within an RRset

For the purposes of DNS security, RRs with the same owner name, class, and type are sorted by treating the RDATA portion of the canonical form of each RR as a left-justified unsigned octet sequence in which the absence of an octet sorts before a zero octet.

[RFC2181] specifies that an RRset is not allowed to contain duplicate records (multiple RRs with the same owner name, class, type, and RDATA). Therefore, if an implementation detects duplicate RRs when putting the RRset in canonical form, it MUST treat this as a protocol error. If the implementation chooses to handle this protocol error in the spirit of the robustness principle (being liberal in what it accepts), it MUST remove all but one of the duplicate RR(s) for the purposes of calculating the canonical form of the RRset.

7. IANA Considerations

This document introduces no new IANA considerations, as all of the protocol parameters used in this document have already been assigned by previous specifications. However, since the evolution of DNSSEC has been long and somewhat convoluted, this section attempts to describe the current state of the IANA registries and other protocol parameters that are (or once were) related to DNSSEC.

Please refer to [RFC4035] for additional IANA considerations.

DNS Resource Record Types: [RFC2535] assigned types 24, 25, and 30 to the SIG, KEY, and NXT RRs, respectively. [RFC3658] assigned DNS Resource Record Type 43 to DS. [RFC3755] assigned types 46, 47, and 48 to the RRSIG, NSEC, and DNSKEY RRs, respectively. [RFC3755] also marked type 30 (NXT) as Obsolete and restricted use of types 24 (SIG) and 25 (KEY) to the "SIG(0)" transaction security protocol described in [RFC2931] and to the transaction KEY Resource Record described in [RFC2930].

DNS Security Algorithm Numbers: [RFC2535] created an IANA registry for DNSSEC Resource Record Algorithm field numbers and assigned values 1-4 and 252-255. [RFC3110] assigned value 5. [RFC3755] altered this registry to include flags for each entry regarding its use with the DNS security extensions. Each algorithm entry could refer to an algorithm that can be used for zone signing, transaction security (see [RFC2931]), or both. Values 6-251 are available for assignment by IETF standards action ([RFC3755]). See Appendix A for a full listing of the DNS Security Algorithm Numbers entries at the time of this writing and their status for use in DNSSEC.

[RFC3658] created an IANA registry for DNSSEC DS Digest Types and assigned value 0 to reserved and value 1 to SHA-1.

KEY Protocol Values: [RFC2535] created an IANA Registry for KEY Protocol Values, but [RFC3445] reassigned all values other than 3 to reserved and closed this IANA registry. The registry remains closed, and all KEY and DNSKEY records are required to have a Protocol Octet value of 3.

Flag bits in the KEY and DNSKEY RRs: [RFC3755] created an IANA registry for the DNSSEC KEY and DNSKEY RR flag bits. Initially, this registry only contains assignments for bit 7 (the ZONE bit) and bit 15 (the Secure Entry Point flag (SEP) bit; see [RFC3757]). As stated in [RFC3755], bits 0-6 and 8-14 are available for assignment by IETF Standards Action.

8. Security Considerations

This document describes the format of four DNS resource records used by the DNS security extensions and presents an algorithm for calculating a key tag for a public key. Other than the items described below, the resource records themselves introduce no security considerations. Please see [RFC4033] and [RFC4035] for additional security considerations related to the use of these records.

The DS record points to a DNSKEY RR by using a cryptographic digest, the key algorithm type, and a key tag. The DS record is intended to identify an existing DNSKEY RR, but it is theoretically possible for an attacker to generate a DNSKEY that matches all the DS fields. The probability of constructing a matching DNSKEY depends on the type of digest algorithm in use. The only currently defined digest algorithm is SHA-1, and the working group believes that constructing a public key that would match the algorithm, key tag, and SHA-1 digest given in a DS record would be a sufficiently difficult problem that such an attack is not a serious threat at this time.

The key tag is used to help select DNSKEY resource records efficiently, but it does not uniquely identify a single DNSKEY resource record. It is possible for two distinct DNSKEY RRs to have the same owner name, the same algorithm type, and the same key tag. An implementation that uses only the key tag to select a DNSKEY RR might select the wrong public key in some circumstances. Please see Appendix B for further details.

The table of algorithms in Appendix A and the key tag calculation algorithms in Appendix B include the RSA/MD5 algorithm for completeness, but the RSA/MD5 algorithm is NOT RECOMMENDED, as explained in [RFC3110].

9. Acknowledgements

This document was created from the input and ideas of the members of the DNS Extensions Working Group and working group mailing list. The editors would like to express their thanks for the comments and suggestions received during the revision of these security extension specifications. Although explicitly listing everyone who has contributed during the decade in which DNSSEC has been under development would be impossible, [RFC4033] includes a list of some of the participants who were kind enough to comment on these documents.

10. References

10.1. Normative References

[RFC1034] Mockapetris, P., "Domain names - concepts and facilities", STD 13, RFC 1034, November 1987.

[RFC1035] Mockapetris, P., "Domain names - implementation and specification", STD 13, RFC 1035, November 1987.

[RFC1982] Elz, R. and R. Bush, "Serial Number Arithmetic", RFC 1982, August 1996.

[RFC2119] Bradner, S., "Key words for use in RFCs to Indicate Requirement Levels", BCP 14, RFC 2119, March 1997.

[RFC2181] Elz, R. and R. Bush, "Clarifications to the DNS Specification", RFC 2181, July 1997.

[RFC2308] Andrews, M., "Negative Caching of DNS Queries (DNS NCACHE)", RFC 2308, March 1998.

[RFC2536] Eastlake 3rd, D., "DSA KEYs and SIGs in the Domain Name System (DNS)", RFC 2536, March 1999.

[RFC2931] Eastlake 3rd, D., "DNS Request and Transaction Signatures (SIG(0)s)", RFC 2931, September 2000.

[RFC3110] Eastlake 3rd, D., "RSA/SHA-1 SIGs and RSA KEYs in the Domain Name System (DNS)", RFC 3110, May 2001.

[RFC3445] Massey, D. and S. Rose, "Limiting the Scope of the KEY Resource Record (RR)", RFC 3445, December 2002.

[RFC3548] Josefsson, S., "The Base16, Base32, and Base64 Data Encodings", RFC 3548, July 2003.

[RFC3597] Gustafsson, A., "Handling of Unknown DNS Resource Record (RR) Types", RFC 3597, September 2003.

[RFC3658] Gudmundsson, O., "Delegation Signer (DS) Resource Record (RR)", RFC 3658, December 2003.

[RFC3755] Weiler, S., "Legacy Resolver Compatibility for Delegation Signer (DS)", RFC 3755, May 2004.

[RFC3757] Kolkman, O., Schlyter, J., and E. Lewis, "Domain Name System KEY (DNSKEY) Resource Record (RR) Secure Entry Point (SEP) Flag", RFC 3757, April 2004.

[RFC4033] Arends, R., Austein, R., Larson, M., Massey, D., and S. Rose, "DNS Security Introduction and Requirements", RFC 4033, March 2005.

[RFC4035] Arends, R., Austein, R., Larson, M., Massey, D., and S. Rose, "Protocol Modifications for the DNS Security Extensions", RFC 4035, March 2005.

10.2. Informative References

[RFC2535] Eastlake 3rd, D., "Domain Name System Security Extensions", RFC 2535, March 1999.

[RFC2537] Eastlake 3rd, D., "RSA/MD5 KEYs and SIGs in the Domain Name System (DNS)", RFC 2537, March 1999.

[RFC2539] Eastlake 3rd, D., "Storage of Diffie-Hellman Keys in the Domain Name System (DNS)", RFC 2539, March 1999.

[RFC2930] Eastlake 3rd, D., "Secret Key Establishment for DNS (TKEY RR)", RFC 2930, September 2000.

[RFC3845] Schlyter, J., "DNS Security (DNSSEC) NextSECure (NSEC) RDATA Format", RFC 3845, August 2004.

Appendix A. DNSSEC Algorithm and Digest Types

The DNS security extensions are designed to be independent of the underlying cryptographic algorithms. The DNSKEY, RRSIG, and DS resource records all use a DNSSEC Algorithm Number to identify the cryptographic algorithm in use by the resource record. The DS resource record also specifies a Digest Algorithm Number to identify the digest algorithm used to construct the DS record. The currently defined Algorithm and Digest Types are listed below. Additional Algorithm or Digest Types could be added as advances in cryptography warrant them.

A DNSSEC aware resolver or name server MUST implement all MANDATORY algorithms.

A.1. DNSSEC Algorithm Types

The DNSKEY, RRSIG, and DS RRs use an 8-bit number to identify the security algorithm being used. These values are stored in the "Algorithm number" field in the resource record RDATA.

Some algorithms are usable only for zone signing (DNSSEC), some only for transaction security mechanisms (SIG(0) and TSIG), and some for both. Those usable for zone signing may appear in DNSKEY, RRSIG, and DS RRs. Those usable for transaction security would be present in SIG(0) and KEY RRs, as described in [RFC2931].

Value	Algorithm [Mnemonic]	Zone Signing	References	Status
0	reserved			
1	RSA/MD5 [RSAMD5]	n	[RFC2537]	NOT RECOMMENDED
2	Diffie–Hellman [DH]	n	[RFC2539]	–
3	DSA/SHA–1 [DSA]	y	[RFC2536]	OPTIONAL
4	Elliptic Curve [ECC]		TBA	–
5	RSA/SHA–1 [RSASHA1]	y	[RFC3110]	MANDATORY
252	Indirect [INDIRECT]	n		–
253	Private [PRIVATEDNS]	y	see below	OPTIONAL
254	Private [PRIVATEOID]	y	see below	OPTIONAL
255	reserved			

6 - 251 Available for assignment by IETF Standards Action.

A.1.1. Private Algorithm Types

Algorithm number 253 is reserved for private use and will never be assigned to a specific algorithm. The public key area in the DNSKEY RR and the signature area in the RRSIG RR begin with a wire encoded domain name, which MUST NOT be compressed. The domain name indicates the private algorithm to use, and the remainder of the public key area is determined by that algorithm. Entities should only use domain names they control to designate their private algorithms.

Algorithm number 254 is reserved for private use and will never be assigned to a specific algorithm. The public key area in the DNSKEY RR and the signature area in the RRSIG RR begin with an unsigned length byte followed by a BER encoded Object Identifier (ISO OID) of that length. The OID indicates the private algorithm in use, and the remainder of the area is whatever is required by that algorithm. Entities should only use OIDs they control to designate their private algorithms.

A.2. DNSSEC Digest Types

A "Digest Type" field in the DS resource record types identifies the cryptographic digest algorithm used by the resource record. The following table lists the currently defined digest algorithm types.

VALUE	Algorithm	STATUS
0	Reserved	–
1	SHA–1	MANDATORY
2–255	Unassigned	–

Appendix B. Key Tag Calculation

The Key Tag field in the RRSIG and DS resource record types provides a mechanism for selecting a public key efficiently. In most cases, a combination of owner name, algorithm, and key tag can efficiently identify a DNSKEY record. Both the RRSIG and DS resource records have corresponding DNSKEY records. The Key Tag field in the RRSIG and DS records can be used to help select the corresponding DNSKEY RR efficiently when more than one candidate DNSKEY RR is available.

However, it is essential to note that the key tag is not a unique identifier. It is theoretically possible for two distinct DNSKEY RRs to have the same owner name, the same algorithm, and the same key tag. The key tag is used to limit the possible candidate keys, but it does not uniquely identify a DNSKEY record. Implementations MUST NOT assume that the key tag uniquely identifies a DNSKEY RR.

The key tag is the same for all DNSKEY algorithm types except algorithm 1 (please see Appendix B.1 for the definition of the key tag for algorithm 1). The key tag algorithm is the sum of the wire format of the DNSKEY RDATA broken into 2 octet groups. First, the RDATA (in wire format) is treated as a series of 2 octet groups. These groups are then added together, ignoring any carry bits.

A reference implementation of the key tag algorithm is as an ANSI C function is given below, with the RDATA portion of the DNSKEY RR is used as input. It is not necessary to use the following reference code verbatim, but the numerical value of the Key Tag MUST be identical to what the reference implementation would generate for the same input.

Please note that the algorithm for calculating the Key Tag is almost but not completely identical to the familiar ones-complement checksum used in many other Internet protocols. Key Tags MUST be calculated using the algorithm described here rather than the ones complement checksum.

The following ANSI C reference implementation calculates the value of a Key Tag. This reference implementation applies to all algorithm types except algorithm 1 (see Appendix B.1). The input is the wire format of the RDATA portion of the DNSKEY RR. The code is written for clarity, not efficiency.

```
/*
 * Assumes that int is at least 16 bits.
 * First octet of the key tag is the most significant 8 bits of the
 * return value;
 * Second octet of the key tag is the least significant 8 bits of the
 * return value.
 */

unsigned int
keytag (
        unsigned char key[],    /* the RDATA part of the DNSKEY RR */
        unsigned int keysize    /* the RDLENGTH */
      )
{
        unsigned long ac;       /* assumed to be 32 bits or larger */
        int i;                  /* loop index */

        for ( ac = 0, i = 0; i < keysize; ++i )
                ac += (i & 1) ? key[i] : key[i] << 8;
        ac += (ac >> 16) & 0xFFFF;
        return ac & 0xFFFF;
}
```

B.1. Key Tag for Algorithm 1 (RSA/MD5)

The key tag for algorithm 1 (RSA/MD5) is defined differently from the key tag for all other algorithms, for historical reasons. For a DNSKEY RR with algorithm 1, the key tag is defined to be the most significant 16 bits of the least significant 24 bits in the public key modulus (in other words, the 4th to last and 3rd to last octets of the public key modulus).

Please note that Algorithm 1 is NOT RECOMMENDED.

Authors' Addresses

Roy Arends
Telematica Instituut
Brouwerijstraat 1
7523 XC Enschede
NL

EMail: roy.arends@telin.nl

Rob Austein
Internet Systems Consortium

950 Charter Street
Redwood City, CA 94063
USA

EMail: sra@isc.org

Matt Larson
VeriSign, Inc.
21345 Ridgetop Circle
Dulles, VA 20166-6503
USA

EMail: mlarson@verisign.com

Dan Massey
Colorado State University
Department of Computer Science
Fort Collins, CO 80523-1873

EMail: massey@cs.colostate.edu

Scott Rose
National Institute for Standards and Technology
100 Bureau Drive
Gaithersburg, MD 20899-8920
USA

EMail: scott.rose@nist.gov

Full Copyright Statement

Intellectual Property

not be available; nor does it represent that it has made any independent effort to identify any such rights. Information on the procedures with respect to rights in RFC documents can be found in BCP 78 and BCP 79.

Copies of IPR disclosures made to the IETF Secretariat and any assurances of licenses to be made available, or the result of an attempt made to obtain a general license or permission for the use of such proprietary rights by implementers or users of this specification can be obtained from the IETF on-line IPR repository at http://www.ietf.org/ipr.

The IETF invites any interested party to bring to its attention any copyrights, patents or patent applications, or other proprietary rights that may cover technology that may be required to implement this standard. Please address the information to the IETF at ietf-ipr@ietf.org.

Acknowledgement

Funding for the RFC Editor function is currently provided by the Internet Society.

RFC 4035
Protocol Modifications for the DNS Security Extensions

Network Working Group
Request for Comments: 4035
Obsoletes: 2535, 3008, 3090, 3445, 3655, 3658,
3755, 3757, 3845
Updates: 1034, 1035, 2136, 2181, 2308, 3225,
3007, 3597, 3226
Category: Standards Track

R. Arends
Telematica Instituut
R. Austein
ISC
M. Larson
VeriSign
D. Massey
Colorado State University
S. Rose
NIST
March 2005

Status of This Memo

This document specifies an Internet standards track protocol for the Internet community, and requests discussion and suggestions for improvements. Please refer to the current edition of the "Internet Official Protocol Standards" (STD 1) for the standardization state and status of this protocol. Distribution of this memo is unlimited.

Copyright Notice

Abstract

This document is part of a family of documents that describe the DNS Security Extensions (DNSSEC). The DNS Security Extensions are a collection of new resource records and protocol modifications that add data origin authentication and data integrity to the DNS. This document describes the DNSSEC protocol modifications. This document defines the concept of a signed zone, along with the requirements for serving and resolving by using DNSSEC. These techniques allow a security-aware resolver to authenticate both DNS resource records and authoritative DNS error indications.

This document obsoletes RFC 2535 and incorporates changes from all updates to RFC 2535.

RFC 4035 Contents

1. Introduction

The DNS Security Extensions (DNSSEC) are a collection of new resource records and protocol modifications that add data origin authentication and data integrity to the DNS. This document defines the DNSSEC protocol modifications. Section 2 of this document defines the concept of a signed zone and lists the requirements for zone signing. Section 3 describes the modifications to authoritative name server behavior necessary for handling signed zones. Section 4 describes the behavior of entities that include security-aware resolver functions. Finally, Section 5 defines how to use DNSSEC RRs to authenticate a response.

1.1. Background and Related Documents

This document is part of a family of documents defining DNSSEC that should be read together as a set.

[RFC4033] contains an introduction to DNSSEC and definitions of common terms; the reader is assumed to be familiar with this document. [RFC4033] also contains a list of other documents updated by and obsoleted by this document set.

[RFC4034] defines the DNSSEC resource records.

The reader is also assumed to be familiar with the basic DNS concepts described in [RFC1034], [RFC1035], and the subsequent documents that update them; particularly, [RFC2181] and [RFC2308].

This document defines the DNSSEC protocol operations.

1.2. Reserved Words

The key words "MUST", "MUST NOT", "REQUIRED", "SHALL", "SHALL NOT", "SHOULD", "SHOULD NOT", "RECOMMENDED", "MAY", and "OPTIONAL" in this document are to be interpreted as described in [RFC2119].

2. Zone Signing

DNSSEC introduces the concept of signed zones. A signed zone includes DNS Public Key (DNSKEY), Resource Record Signature (RRSIG), Next Secure (NSEC), and (optionally) Delegation Signer (DS) records according to the rules specified in Sections 2.1, 2.2, 2.3, and 2.4, respectively. A zone that does not include these records according to the rules in this section is an unsigned zone.

DNSSEC requires a change to the definition of the CNAME resource record ([RFC1035]). Section 2.5 changes the CNAME RR to allow RRSIG and NSEC RRs to appear at the same owner name as does a CNAME RR.

DNSSEC specifies the placement of two new RR types, NSEC and DS, which can be placed at the parental side of a zone cut (that is, at a delegation point). This is an exception to the general prohibition against putting data in the parent zone at a zone cut. Section 2.6 describes this change.

2.1. Including DNSKEY RRs in a Zone

To sign a zone, the zone's administrator generates one or more public/private key pairs and uses the private key(s) to sign authoritative RRsets in the zone. For each private key used to create RRSIG RRs in a zone, the zone SHOULD include a zone DNSKEY RR containing the corresponding public key. A zone key DNSKEY RR MUST have the Zone Key bit of the flags RDATA field set (see Section 2.1.1 of [RFC4034]). Public keys associated with other DNS operations MAY be stored in DNSKEY RRs that are not marked as zone keys but MUST NOT be used to verify RRSIGs.

If the zone administrator intends a signed zone to be usable other than as an island of security, the zone apex MUST contain at least one DNSKEY RR to act as a secure entry point into the zone. This secure entry point could then be used as the target of a secure delegation via a corresponding DS RR in the parent zone (see [RFC4034]).

2.2. Including RRSIG RRs in a Zone

For each authoritative RRset in a signed zone, there MUST be at least one RRSIG record that meets the following requirements:

- The RRSIG owner name is equal to the RRset owner name.

- The RRSIG class is equal to the RRset class.

- The RRSIG Type Covered field is equal to the RRset type.

- The RRSIG Original TTL field is equal to the TTL of the RRset.

- The RRSIG RR's TTL is equal to the TTL of the RRset.

- The RRSIG Labels field is equal to the number of labels in the RRset owner name, not counting the null root label and not counting the leftmost label if it is a wildcard.

- The RRSIG Signer's Name field is equal to the name of the zone containing the RRset.

- The RRSIG Algorithm, Signer's Name, and Key Tag fields identify a zone key DNSKEY record at the zone apex.

The process for constructing the RRSIG RR for a given RRset is described in [RFC4034]. An RRset MAY have multiple RRSIG RRs associated with it. Note that as RRSIG RRs are closely tied to the RRsets whose signatures they contain, RRSIG RRs, unlike all other DNS RR types, do not form RRsets. In particular, the TTL values among RRSIG RRs with a common owner name do not follow the RRset rules described in [RFC2181].

An RRSIG RR itself MUST NOT be signed, as signing an RRSIG RR would add no value and would create an infinite loop in the signing process.

The NS RRset that appears at the zone apex name MUST be signed, but the NS RRsets that appear at delegation points (that is, the NS RRsets in the parent zone that delegate the name to the child zone's name servers) MUST NOT be signed. Glue address RRsets associated with delegations MUST NOT be signed.

There MUST be an RRSIG for each RRset using at least one DNSKEY of each algorithm in the zone apex DNSKEY RRset. The apex DNSKEY RRset itself MUST be signed by each algorithm appearing in the DS RRset located at the delegating parent (if any).

2.3. Including NSEC RRs in a Zone

Each owner name in the zone that has authoritative data or a delegation point NS RRset MUST have an NSEC resource record. The format of NSEC RRs and the process for constructing the NSEC RR for a given name is described in [RFC4034].

The TTL value for any NSEC RR SHOULD be the same as the minimum TTL value field in the zone SOA RR.

An NSEC record (and its associated RRSIG RRset) MUST NOT be the only RRset at any particular owner name. That is, the signing process MUST NOT create NSEC or RRSIG RRs for owner name nodes that were not the owner name of any RRset before the zone was signed.[7] The main reasons for this are a desire for namespace consistency between signed and unsigned versions of the same zone and a desire to reduce the risk of response inconsistency in security oblivious recursive name servers.

The type bitmap of every NSEC resource record in a signed zone MUST indicate the presence of both the NSEC record itself and its corresponding RRSIG record.

---

[7]This is updated by RFC 4470. See page 199.

The difference between the set of owner names that require RRSIG records and the set of owner names that require NSEC records is subtle and worth highlighting. RRSIG records are present at the owner names of all authoritative RRsets. NSEC records are present at the owner names of all names for which the signed zone is authoritative and also at the owner names of delegations from the signed zone to its children. Neither NSEC nor RRSIG records are present (in the parent zone) at the owner names of glue address RRsets. Note, however, that this distinction is for the most part visible only during the zone signing process, as NSEC RRsets are authoritative data and are therefore signed. Thus, any owner name that has an NSEC RRset will have RRSIG RRs as well in the signed zone.

The bitmap for the NSEC RR at a delegation point requires special attention. Bits corresponding to the delegation NS RRset and any RRsets for which the parent zone has authoritative data MUST be set; bits corresponding to any non-NS RRset for which the parent is not authoritative MUST be clear.

2.4. Including DS RRs in a Zone

The DS resource record establishes authentication chains between DNS zones. A DS RRset SHOULD be present at a delegation point when the child zone is signed. The DS RRset MAY contain multiple records, each referencing a public key in the child zone used to verify the RRSIGs in that zone. All DS RRsets in a zone MUST be signed, and DS RRsets MUST NOT appear at a zone's apex.

A DS RR SHOULD point to a DNSKEY RR that is present in the child's apex DNSKEY RRset, and the child's apex DNSKEY RRset SHOULD be signed by the corresponding private key. DS RRs that fail to meet these conditions are not useful for validation, but because the DS RR and its corresponding DNSKEY RR are in different zones, and because the DNS is only loosely consistent, temporary mismatches can occur.

The TTL of a DS RRset SHOULD match the TTL of the delegating NS RRset (that is, the NS RRset from the same zone containing the DS RRset).

Construction of a DS RR requires knowledge of the corresponding DNSKEY RR in the child zone, which implies communication between the child and parent zones. This communication is an operational matter not covered by this document.

2.5. Changes to the CNAME Resource Record

If a CNAME RRset is present at a name in a signed zone, appropriate RRSIG and NSEC RRsets are REQUIRED at that name. A KEY RRset at that name for secure dynamic update purposes is also allowed ([RFC3007]). Other types MUST NOT be present at that name.

This is a modification to the original CNAME definition given in [RFC1034]. The original definition of the CNAME RR did not allow any other types to coexist with a CNAME record, but a signed zone requires NSEC and RRSIG RRs for every authoritative name. To resolve this conflict, this specification modifies the definition of the CNAME resource record to allow it to coexist with NSEC and RRSIG RRs.

2.6. DNSSEC RR Types Appearing at Zone Cuts

DNSSEC introduced two new RR types that are unusual in that they can appear at the parental side of a zone cut. At the parental side of a zone cut (that is, at a delegation point), NSEC RRs are REQUIRED at the owner name. A DS RR could also be present if the zone being delegated is signed and seeks to have a chain of authentication to the parent zone. This is an exception to the original DNS specification ([RFC1034]), which states that only NS RRsets could appear at the parental side of a zone cut.

This specification updates the original DNS specification to allow NSEC and DS RR types at the parent side of a zone cut. These RRsets are authoritative for the parent when they appear at the parent side of a zone cut.

2.7. Example of a Secure Zone

Appendix A shows a complete example of a small signed zone.

3. Serving

This section describes the behavior of entities that include security-aware name server functions. In many cases such functions will be part of a security-aware recursive name server, but a security-aware authoritative name server has some of the same requirements. Functions specific to security-aware recursive name servers are described in Section 3.2; functions specific to authoritative servers are described in Section 3.1.

In the following discussion, the terms "SNAME", "SCLASS", and "STYPE" are as used in [RFC1034].

A security-aware name server MUST support the EDNS0 ([RFC2671]) message size extension, MUST support a message size of at least 1220 octets, and SHOULD support a message size of 4000 octets. As IPv6 packets can only be fragmented by the source host, a security aware name server SHOULD take steps to ensure that UDP datagrams it transmits over IPv6 are fragmented, if necessary, at the minimum IPv6 MTU, unless the path MTU is known. Please see [RFC1122], [RFC2460], and [RFC3226] for further discussion of packet size and fragmentation issues.

A security-aware name server that receives a DNS query that does not include the EDNS OPT pseudo-RR or that has the DO bit clear MUST treat the RRSIG, DNSKEY, and NSEC RRs as it would any other RRset and MUST NOT perform any of the additional processing described below. Because the DS RR type has the peculiar property of only existing in the parent zone at delegation points, DS RRs always require some special processing, as described in Section 3.1.4.1.

Security aware name servers that receive explicit queries for security RR types that match the content of more than one zone that it serves (for example, NSEC and RRSIG RRs above and below a delegation point where the server is authoritative for both zones) should behave self-consistently. As long as the response is always consistent for each query to the name server, the name server MAY return one of the following:

- The above-delegation RRsets.

- The below-delegation RRsets.

- Both above and below-delegation RRsets.

- Empty answer section (no records).

- Some other response.

- An error.

DNSSEC allocates two new bits in the DNS message header: the CD (Checking Disabled) bit and the AD (Authentic Data) bit. The CD bit is controlled by resolvers; a security-aware name server MUST copy the CD bit from a query into the corresponding response. The AD bit is controlled by name servers; a security-aware name server MUST ignore the setting of the AD bit in queries. See Sections 3.1.6, 3.2.2, 3.2.3, 4, and 4.9 for details on the behavior of these bits.

A security aware name server that synthesizes CNAME RRs from DNAME RRs as described in [RFC2672] SHOULD NOT generate signatures for the synthesized CNAME RRs.

3.1. Authoritative Name Servers

Upon receiving a relevant query that has the EDNS ([RFC2671]) OPT pseudo-RR DO bit ([RFC3225]) set, a security-aware authoritative name server for a signed zone MUST include additional RRSIG, NSEC, and DS RRs, according to the following rules:

- RRSIG RRs that can be used to authenticate a response MUST be included in the response according to the rules in Section 3.1.1.

- NSEC RRs that can be used to provide authenticated denial of existence MUST be included in the response automatically according to the rules in Section 3.1.3.

- Either a DS RRset or an NSEC RR proving that no DS RRs exist MUST be included in referrals automatically according to the rules in Section 3.1.4.

These rules only apply to responses where the semantics convey information about the presence or absence of resource records. That is, these rules are not intended to rule out responses such as RCODE 4 ("Not Implemented") or RCODE 5 ("Refused").

DNSSEC does not change the DNS zone transfer protocol. Section 3.1.5 discusses zone transfer requirements.

3.1.1. Including RRSIG RRs in a Response

When responding to a query that has the DO bit set, a security-aware authoritative name server SHOULD attempt to send RRSIG RRs that a security-aware resolver can use to authenticate the RRsets in the response. A name server SHOULD make every attempt to keep the RRset and its associated RRSIG(s) together in a response. Inclusion of RRSIG RRs in a response is subject to the following rules:

- When placing a signed RRset in the Answer section, the name server MUST also place its RRSIG RRs in the Answer section. The RRSIG RRs have a higher priority for inclusion than any other RRsets that may have to be included. If space does not permit inclusion of these RRSIG RRs, the name server MUST set the TC bit.

- When placing a signed RRset in the Authority section, the name server MUST also place its RRSIG RRs in the Authority section. The RRSIG RRs have a higher priority for inclusion than any other RRsets that may have to be included. If space does not permit inclusion of these RRSIG RRs, the name server MUST set the TC bit.

- When placing a signed RRset in the Additional section, the name server MUST also place its RRSIG RRs in the Additional section. If space does not permit inclusion of both the RRset and its associated RRSIG RRs, the name server MAY retain the RRset while dropping the RRSIG RRs. If this happens, the name server MUST NOT set the TC bit solely because these RRSIG RRs didn't fit.

3.1.2. Including DNSKEY RRs in a Response

When responding to a query that has the DO bit set and that requests the SOA or NS RRs at the apex of a signed zone, a security-aware authoritative name server for that zone MAY return the zone apex DNSKEY RRset in the Additional section. In this situation, the DNSKEY RRset and associated RRSIG RRs have lower priority than does any other information that would be placed in the additional section. The name server SHOULD NOT include the DNSKEY RRset unless there is enough space in the response message for both the DNSKEY RRset and its associated RRSIG RR(s). If there is not enough space to include these DNSKEY and RRSIG RRs, the name server MUST omit them and MUST NOT set the TC bit solely because these RRs didn't fit (see Section 3.1.1).

3.1.3. Including NSEC RRs in a Response

When responding to a query that has the DO bit set, a security-aware authoritative name server for a signed zone MUST include NSEC RRs in each of the following cases:

No Data: The zone contains RRsets that exactly match <SNAME, SCLASS> but does not contain any RRsets that exactly match <SNAME, SCLASS, STYPE>.

Name Error: The zone does not contain any RRsets that match <SNAME, SCLASS> either exactly or via wildcard name expansion.

Wildcard Answer: The zone does not contain any RRsets that exactly match <SNAME, SCLASS> but does contain an RRset that matches <SNAME, SCLASS, STYPE> via wildcard name expansion.

Wildcard No Data: The zone does not contain any RRsets that exactly match <SNAME, SCLASS> and does contain one or more RRsets that match <SNAME, SCLASS> via wildcard name expansion, but does not contain any RRsets that match <SNAME, SCLASS, STYPE> via wildcard name expansion.

In each of these cases, the name server includes NSEC RRs in the response to prove that an exact match for <SNAME, SCLASS, STYPE> was not present in the zone and that the response that the name server is returning is correct given the data in the zone.

3.1.3.1. Including NSEC RRs: No Data Response

If the zone contains RRsets matching <SNAME, SCLASS> but contains no RRset matching <SNAME, SCLASS, STYPE>, then the name server MUST include the NSEC RR for <SNAME, SCLASS> along with its associated RRSIG RR(s) in the Authority section of the response (see Section 3.1.1). If space does not permit inclusion of the NSEC RR or its associated RRSIG RR(s), the name server MUST set the TC bit (see Section 3.1.1).

Since the search name exists, wildcard name expansion does not apply to this query, and a single signed NSEC RR suffices to prove that the requested RR type does not exist.

3.1.3.2. Including NSEC RRs: Name Error Response

If the zone does not contain any RRsets matching <SNAME, SCLASS> either exactly or via wildcard name expansion, then the name server MUST include the following NSEC RRs in the Authority section, along with their associated RRSIG RRs:

- An NSEC RR proving that there is no exact match for <SNAME, SCLASS>.

- An NSEC RR proving that the zone contains no RRsets that would match <SNAME, SCLASS> via wildcard name expansion.

In some cases, a single NSEC RR may prove both of these points. If it does, the name server SHOULD only include the NSEC RR and its RRSIG RR(s) once in the Authority section.

If space does not permit inclusion of these NSEC and RRSIG RRs, the name server MUST set the TC bit (see Section 3.1.1).

The owner names of these NSEC and RRSIG RRs are not subject to wildcard name expansion when these RRs are included in the Authority section of the response.

Note that this form of response includes cases in which SNAME corresponds to an empty non-terminal name within the zone (a name that is not the owner name for any RRset but that is the parent name of one or more RRsets).

3.1.3.3. Including NSEC RRs: Wildcard Answer Response

If the zone does not contain any RRsets that exactly match <SNAME, SCLASS> but does contain an RRset that matches <SNAME, SCLASS, STYPE> via wildcard name expansion, the name server MUST include the wildcard-expanded answer and the corresponding wildcard-expanded RRSIG RRs in the Answer section and MUST include in the Authority section an NSEC RR and associated RRSIG RR(s) proving that the zone does not contain a closer match for <SNAME, SCLASS>. If space does not permit inclusion of the answer, NSEC and RRSIG RRs, the name server MUST set the TC bit (see Section 3.1.1).

3.1.3.4. Including NSEC RRs: Wildcard No Data Response

This case is a combination of the previous cases. The zone does not contain an exact match for <SNAME, SCLASS>, and although the zone does contain RRsets that match <SNAME, SCLASS> via wildcard expansion, none of those RRsets matches STYPE. The name server MUST include the following NSEC RRs in the Authority section, along with their associated RRSIG RRs:

- An NSEC RR proving that there are no RRsets matching STYPE at the wildcard owner name that matched <SNAME, SCLASS> via wildcard expansion.

- An NSEC RR proving that there are no RRsets in the zone that would have been a closer match for <SNAME, SCLASS>.

In some cases, a single NSEC RR may prove both of these points. If it does, the name server SHOULD only include the NSEC RR and its RRSIG RR(s) once in the Authority section.

The owner names of these NSEC and RRSIG RRs are not subject to wildcard name expansion when these RRs are included in the Authority section of the response.

If space does not permit inclusion of these NSEC and RRSIG RRs, the name server MUST set the TC bit (see Section 3.1.1).

3.1.3.5. Finding the Right NSEC RRs

As explained above, there are several situations in which a security-aware authoritative name server has to locate an NSEC RR that proves that no RRsets matching a particular SNAME exist. Locating such an NSEC RR within an authoritative zone is relatively simple, at least in concept. The following discussion assumes that the name server is authoritative for the zone that would have held the non-existent RRsets matching SNAME. The algorithm below is written for clarity, not for efficiency.

To find the NSEC that proves that no RRsets matching name N exist in the zone Z that would have held them, construct a sequence, S, consisting of the owner names of every RRset in Z, sorted into canonical order ([RFC4034]), with no duplicate names. Find the name M that would have immediately preceded N in S if any RRsets with owner name N had existed. M is the owner name of the NSEC RR that proves that no RRsets exist with owner name N.

The algorithm for finding the NSEC RR that proves that a given name is not covered by any applicable wildcard is similar but requires an extra step. More precisely, the algorithm for finding the NSEC proving that no RRsets exist with the applicable wildcard name is precisely the same as the algorithm for finding the NSEC RR that proves that RRsets with any other owner name do not exist. The part that's missing is a method of determining the name of the non-existent applicable wildcard. In practice, this is easy, because the authoritative name server has already checked for the presence of precisely this wildcard name as part of step (1)(c) of the normal lookup algorithm described in Section 4.3.2 of [RFC1034].

3.1.4. Including DS RRs in a Response

When responding to a query that has the DO bit set, a security-aware authoritative name server returning a referral includes DNSSEC data along with the NS RRset.

If a DS RRset is present at the delegation point, the name server MUST return both the DS RRset and its associated RRSIG RR(s) in the Authority section along with the NS RRset.

If no DS RRset is present at the delegation point, the name server MUST return both the NSEC RR that proves that the DS RRset is not present and the NSEC RR's associated RRSIG RR(s) along with the NS RRset. The name server MUST place the NS RRset before the NSEC RRset and its associated RRSIG RR(s).

Including these DS, NSEC, and RRSIG RRs increases the size of referral messages and may cause some or all glue RRs to be omitted. If space does not permit inclusion of the DS or NSEC RRset and associated RRSIG RRs, the name server MUST set the TC bit (see Section 3.1.1).

3.1.4.1. Responding to Queries for DS RRs

The DS resource record type is unusual in that it appears only on the parent zone's side of a zone cut. For example, the DS RRset for the delegation of "foo.example" is stored in the "example" zone rather than in the "foo.example" zone. This requires special processing rules for both name servers and resolvers, as the name server for the child zone is authoritative for the name at the zone cut by the normal DNS rules but the child zone does not contain the DS RRset.

A security-aware resolver sends queries to the parent zone when looking for a needed DS RR at a delegation point (see Section 4.2). However, special rules are necessary to avoid confusing security-oblivious resolvers which might become involved in processing such a query (for example, in a network configuration that forces a security-aware resolver to channel its queries through a security-oblivious recursive name server). The rest of this section describes how a security-aware name server processes DS queries in order to avoid this problem.

The need for special processing by a security-aware name server only arises when all the following conditions are met:

- The name server has received a query for the DS RRset at a zone cut.

- The name server is authoritative for the child zone.

- The name server is not authoritative for the parent zone.

- The name server does not offer recursion.

In all other cases, the name server either has some way of obtaining the DS RRset or could not have been expected to have the DS RRset even by the pre-DNSSEC processing rules, so the name server can return either the DS RRset or an error response according to the normal processing rules.

If all the above conditions are met, however, the name server is authoritative for SNAME but cannot supply the requested RRset. In this case, the name server MUST return an authoritative "no data" response showing that the DS RRset does not exist in the child zone's apex. See Appendix B.8 for an example of such a response.

3.1.5. Responding to Queries for Type AXFR or IXFR

DNSSEC does not change the DNS zone transfer process. A signed zone will contain RRSIG, DNSKEY, NSEC, and DS resource records, but these records have no special meaning with respect to a zone transfer operation.

An authoritative name server is not required to verify that a zone is properly signed before sending or accepting a zone transfer. However, an authoritative name server MAY choose to reject the entire zone transfer if the zone fails to meet any of the signing requirements described in Section 2. The primary objective of a zone transfer is to ensure that all authoritative name servers have identical copies of the zone. An authoritative name server that chooses to perform its own zone validation MUST NOT selectively reject some RRs and accept others.

DS RRsets appear only on the parental side of a zone cut and are authoritative data in the parent zone. As with any other authoritative RRset, the DS RRset MUST be included in zone transfers of the zone in which the RRset is authoritative data. In the case of the DS RRset, this is the parent zone.

NSEC RRs appear in both the parent and child zones at a zone cut and are authoritative data in both the parent and child zones. The parental and child NSEC RRs at a zone cut are never identical to each other, as the NSEC RR in the child zone's apex will always indicate the presence of the child zone's SOA RR whereas the parental NSEC RR at the zone cut will never indicate the presence of an SOA RR. As with any other authoritative RRs, NSEC RRs MUST be included in zone transfers of the zone in which they are authoritative data. The parental NSEC RR at a zone cut MUST be included in zone transfers of the parent zone, and the NSEC at the zone apex of the child zone MUST be included in zone transfers of the child zone.

RRSIG RRs appear in both the parent and child zones at a zone cut and are authoritative in whichever zone contains the authoritative RRset for which the RRSIG RR provides the signature. That is, the RRSIG RR for a DS RRset or a parental NSEC RR at a zone cut will be authoritative in the parent zone, and the RRSIG for any RRset in the child zone's apex will be authoritative in the child zone. Parental and child RRSIG RRs at a zone cut will never be identical to each other, as the Signer's Name field of an RRSIG RR in the child zone's apex will indicate a DNSKEY RR in the child zone's apex whereas the same field of a parental RRSIG RR at the zone cut will indicate a DNSKEY RR in the parent zone's apex. As with any other authoritative RRs, RRSIG RRs MUST be included in zone transfers of the zone in which they are authoritative data.

3.1.6. The AD and CD Bits in an Authoritative Response

The CD and AD bits are designed for use in communication between security-aware resolvers and security-aware recursive name servers. These bits are for the most part not relevant to query processing by security-aware authoritative name servers.

A security-aware name server does not perform signature validation for authoritative data during query processing, even when the CD bit is clear. A security-aware name server SHOULD clear the CD bit when composing an authoritative response.

A security-aware name server MUST NOT set the AD bit in a response unless the name server considers all RRsets in the Answer and Authority sections of the response to be authentic. A security-aware name server's local policy MAY consider data from an authoritative zone to be authentic without further validation. However, the name server MUST NOT do so unless the name server obtained the authoritative zone via secure means (such as a secure zone transfer mechanism) and MUST NOT do so unless this behavior has been configured explicitly.

A security-aware name server that supports recursion MUST follow the rules for the CD and AD bits given in Section 3.2 when generating a response that involves data obtained via recursion.

3.2. Recursive Name Servers

As explained in [RFC4033], a security-aware recursive name server is an entity that acts in both the security-aware name server and security-aware resolver roles. This section uses the terms "name server side" and "resolver side" to refer to the code within a security-aware recursive name server that implements the security-aware name server role and the code that implements the security-aware resolver role, respectively.

The resolver side follows the usual rules for caching and negative caching that would apply to any security-aware resolver.

3.2.1. The DO Bit

The resolver side of a security-aware recursive name server MUST set the DO bit when sending requests, regardless of the state of the DO bit in the initiating request received by the name server side. If the DO bit in an initiating query is not set, the name server side MUST strip any authenticating DNSSEC RRs from the response but MUST NOT strip any DNSSEC RR types that the initiating query explicitly requested.

3.2.2. The CD Bit

The CD bit exists in order to allow a security-aware resolver to disable signature validation in a security-aware name server's processing of a particular query.

The name server side MUST copy the setting of the CD bit from a query to the corresponding response.

The name server side of a security-aware recursive name server MUST pass the state of the CD bit to the resolver side along with the rest of an initiating query, so that the resolver side will know whether it is required to verify the response data it returns to the name server side. If the CD bit is set, it indicates that the originating resolver is willing to perform whatever authentication its local policy requires. Thus, the resolver side of the recursive name server need not perform authentication on the RRsets in the response. When the CD bit is set, the recursive name server SHOULD, if possible, return the requested data to the originating resolver, even if the recursive name server's local authentication policy would reject the records in question. That is, by setting the CD bit, the originating resolver has indicated that it takes responsibility for performing its own authentication, and the recursive name server should not interfere.

If the resolver side implements a BAD cache (see Section 4.7) and the name server side receives a query that matches an entry in the resolver side's BAD cache, the name server side's response depends on the state of the CD bit in the original query. If the CD bit is set, the name server side SHOULD return the data from the BAD cache; if the CD bit is not set, the name server side MUST return RCODE 2 (server failure).

The intent of the above rule is to provide the raw data to clients that are capable of performing their own signature verification checks while protecting clients that depend on the resolver side of a security-aware recursive name server to perform such checks. Several of the possible reasons why signature validation might fail involve conditions that may not apply equally to the recursive name server and the client that invoked it. For example, the recursive name server's clock may be set incorrectly, or the client may have knowledge of a relevant island of security that the recursive name server does not share. In such cases, "protecting" a client that is capable of performing its own signature validation from ever seeing the "bad" data does not help the client.

3.2.3. The AD Bit

The name server side of a security-aware recursive name server MUST NOT set the AD bit in a response unless the name server considers all RRsets in the Answer and Authority sections of the response to be authentic. The name server side SHOULD set the AD bit if and only if the resolver side considers all RRsets in the Answer section and any relevant negative response RRs in the Authority section to be authentic. The resolver side MUST follow the procedure described in Section 5 to determine whether the RRs in question are authentic. However, for backward compatibility, a recursive name server MAY set the AD bit when a response includes unsigned CNAME RRs if those CNAME RRs demonstrably could have been synthesized from an authentic DNAME RR that is also included in the response according to the synthesis rules described in [RFC2672].

3.3. Example DNSSEC Responses

See Appendix B for example response packets.

4. Resolving

This section describes the behavior of entities that include security-aware resolver functions. In many cases such functions will be part of a security-aware recursive name server, but a stand-alone security-aware resolver has many of the same requirements. Functions specific to security-aware recursive name servers are described in Section 3.2.

4.1. EDNS Support

A security-aware resolver MUST include an EDNS ([RFC2671]) OPT pseudo-RR with the DO ([RFC3225]) bit set when sending queries.

A security-aware resolver MUST support a message size of at least 1220 octets, SHOULD support a message size of 4000 octets, and MUST use the "sender's UDP payload size" field in the EDNS OPT pseudo-RR to advertise the message size that it is willing to accept. A security-aware resolver's IP layer MUST handle fragmented UDP packets correctly regardless of whether any such fragmented packets were received via IPv4 or IPv6. Please see [RFC1122], [RFC2460], and [RFC3226] for discussion of these requirements.[8]

4.2. Signature Verification Support

A security-aware resolver MUST support the signature verification mechanisms described in Section 5 and SHOULD apply them to every received response, except when:

- the security-aware resolver is part of a security-aware recursive name server, and the response is the result of recursion on behalf of a query received with the CD bit set;

- the response is the result of a query generated directly via some form of application interface that instructed the security-aware resolver not to perform validation for this query; or

- validation for this query has been disabled by local policy.

A security-aware resolver's support for signature verification MUST include support for verification of wildcard owner names.

Security-aware resolvers MAY query for missing security RRs in an attempt to perform validation; implementations that choose to do so must be aware that the answers received may not be sufficient to validate the original response. For example, a zone update may have changed (or deleted) the desired information between the original and follow-up queries.

When attempting to retrieve missing NSEC RRs that reside on the parental side at a zone cut, a security-aware iterative-mode resolver MUST query the name servers for the parent zone, not the child zone.

When attempting to retrieve a missing DS, a security-aware iterative-mode resolver MUST query the name servers for the parent zone, not the child zone. As explained in Section 3.1.4.1, security-aware name servers need to apply special processing rules to handle the DS RR, and in some situations the resolver may also need to apply special rules to locate the name servers for the parent zone if the resolver does not already have the parent's NS RRset. To locate the parent NS RRset, the resolver can start with the delegation name, strip off the leftmost label, and query for an NS RRset by that name. If no NS RRset is present at that name, the resolver then strips off the leftmost remaining label and retries the query for that name, repeating this process of walking up the tree until it either finds the NS RRset or runs out of labels.

---

[8]The DNSSEC OK min bufsize Internet-Draft proposes to update this.

4.3. Determining Security Status of Data

A security-aware resolver MUST be able to determine whether it should expect a particular RRset to be signed. More precisely, a security-aware resolver must be able to distinguish between four cases:

Secure: An RRset for which the resolver is able to build a chain of signed DNSKEY and DS RRs from a trusted security anchor to the RRset. In this case, the RRset should be signed and is subject to signature validation, as described above.

Insecure: An RRset for which the resolver knows that it has no chain of signed DNSKEY and DS RRs from any trusted starting point to the RRset. This can occur when the target RRset lies in an unsigned zone or in a descendent of an unsigned zone. In this case, the RRset may or may not be signed, but the resolver will not be able to verify the signature.

Bogus: An RRset for which the resolver believes that it ought to be able to establish a chain of trust but for which it is unable to do so, either due to signatures that for some reason fail to validate or due to missing data that the relevant DNSSEC RRs indicate should be present. This case may indicate an attack but may also indicate a configuration error or some form of data corruption.

Indeterminate: An RRset for which the resolver is not able to determine whether the RRset should be signed, as the resolver is not able to obtain the necessary DNSSEC RRs. This can occur when the security-aware resolver is not able to contact security-aware name servers for the relevant zones.

4.4. Configured Trust Anchors

A security-aware resolver MUST be capable of being configured with at least one trusted public key or DS RR and SHOULD be capable of being configured with multiple trusted public keys or DS RRs. Since a security-aware resolver will not be able to validate signatures without such a configured trust anchor, the resolver SHOULD have some reasonably robust mechanism for obtaining such keys when it boots; examples of such a mechanism would be some form of non-volatile storage (such as a disk drive) or some form of trusted local network configuration mechanism.

Note that trust anchors also cover key material that is updated in a secure manner. This secure manner could be through physical media, a key exchange protocol, or some other out-of-band means.

4.5. Response Caching

A security-aware resolver SHOULD cache each response as a single atomic entry containing the entire answer, including the named RRset and any associated DNSSEC RRs. The resolver SHOULD discard the entire atomic entry when any of the RRs contained in it expire. In most cases the appropriate cache index for the atomic entry will be the triple <QNAME, QTYPE, QCLASS>, but in cases such as the response form described in Section 3.1.3.2 the appropriate cache index will be the double <QNAME,QCLASS>.

The reason for these recommendations is that, between the initial query and the expiration of the data from the cache, the authoritative data might have been changed (for example, via dynamic update).

There are two situations for which this is relevant:

1. By using the RRSIG record, it is possible to deduce that an answer was synthesized from a wildcard. A security-aware recursive name server could store this wildcard data and use it to generate positive responses to queries other than the name for which the original answer was first received.

2. NSEC RRs received to prove the non-existence of a name could be reused by a security-aware resolver to prove the non-existence of any name in the name range it spans.

In theory, a resolver could use wildcards or NSEC RRs to generate positive and negative responses (respectively) until the TTL or signatures on the records in question expire. However, it seems prudent for resolvers to avoid blocking new authoritative data or synthesizing new data on their own. Resolvers that follow this recommendation will have a more consistent view of the namespace.

4.6. Handling of the CD and AD Bits

A security-aware resolver MAY set a query's CD bit in order to indicate that the resolver takes responsibility for performing whatever authentication its local policy requires on the RRsets in the response. See Section 3.2 for the effect this bit has on the behavior of security-aware recursive name servers.

A security-aware resolver MUST clear the AD bit when composing query messages to protect against buggy name servers that blindly copy header bits that they do not understand from the query message to the response message.

A resolver MUST disregard the meaning of the CD and AD bits in a response unless the response was obtained by using a secure channel or the resolver was specifically configured to regard the message header bits without using a secure channel.

4.7. Caching BAD Data

While many validation errors will be transient, some are likely to be more persistent, such as those caused by administrative error (failure to re-sign a zone, clock skew, and so forth). Since requerying will not help in these cases, validating resolvers might generate a significant amount of unnecessary DNS traffic as a result of repeated queries for RRsets with persistent validation failures.

To prevent such unnecessary DNS traffic, security-aware resolvers MAY cache data with invalid signatures, with some restrictions.

Conceptually, caching such data is similar to negative caching ([RFC2308]), except that instead of caching a valid negative response, the resolver is caching the fact that a particular answer failed to validate. This document refers to a cache of data with invalid signatures as a "BAD cache".

Resolvers that implement a BAD cache MUST take steps to prevent the cache from being useful as a denial-of-service attack amplifier, particularly the following:

- Since RRsets that fail to validate do not have trustworthy TTLs, the implementation MUST assign a TTL. This TTL SHOULD be small, in order to mitigate the effect of caching the results of an attack.

- In order to prevent caching of a transient validation failure (which might be the result of an attack), resolvers SHOULD track queries that result in validation failures and SHOULD only answer from the BAD cache after the number of times that responses to queries for that particular <QNAME, QTYPE, QCLASS> have failed to validate exceeds a threshold value.

Resolvers MUST NOT return RRsets from the BAD cache unless the resolver is not required to validate the signatures of the RRsets in question under the rules given in Section 4.2 of this document. See Section 3.2.2 for discussion of how the responses returned by a security-aware recursive name server interact with a BAD cache.

4.8. Synthesized CNAMEs

A validating security-aware resolver MUST treat the signature of a valid signed DNAME RR as also covering unsigned CNAME RRs that could have been synthesized from the DNAME RR, as described in [RFC2672], at least to the extent of not rejecting a response message solely because it contains such CNAME RRs. The resolver MAY retain such CNAME RRs in its cache or in the answers it hands back, but is not required to do so.

4.9. Stub Resolvers

A security-aware stub resolver MUST support the DNSSEC RR types, at least to the extent of not mishandling responses just because they contain DNSSEC RRs.

4.9.1. Handling of the DO Bit

A non-validating security-aware stub resolver MAY include the DNSSEC RRs returned by a security-aware recursive name server as part of the data that the stub resolver hands back to the application that invoked it, but is not required to do so. A non-validating stub resolver that seeks to do this will need to set the DO bit in order to receive DNSSEC RRs from the recursive name server.

A validating security-aware stub resolver MUST set the DO bit, because otherwise it will not receive the DNSSEC RRs it needs to perform signature validation.

4.9.2. Handling of the CD Bit

A non-validating security-aware stub resolver SHOULD NOT set the CD bit when sending queries unless it is requested by the application layer, as by definition, a non-validating stub resolver depends on the security-aware recursive name server to perform validation on its behalf.

A validating security-aware stub resolver SHOULD set the CD bit, because otherwise the security-aware recursive name server will answer the query using the name server's local policy, which may prevent the stub resolver from receiving data that would be acceptable to the stub resolver's local policy.

4.9.3. Handling of the AD Bit

A non-validating security-aware stub resolver MAY chose to examine the setting of the AD bit in response messages that it receives in order to determine whether the security-aware recursive name server that sent the response claims to have cryptographically verified the data in the Answer and Authority sections of the response message. Note, however, that the responses received by a security-aware stub resolver are heavily dependent on the local policy of the security-aware recursive name server. Therefore, there may be little practical value in checking the status of the AD bit, except perhaps as a debugging aid. In any case, a security-aware stub resolver MUST NOT place any reliance on signature validation allegedly performed on its behalf, except when the security-aware stub resolver obtained the data in question from a trusted security-aware recursive name server via a secure channel.

A validating security-aware stub resolver SHOULD NOT examine the setting of the AD bit in response messages, as, by definition, the stub resolver performs its own signature validation regardless of the setting of the AD bit.

5. Authenticating DNS Responses

To use DNSSEC RRs for authentication, a security-aware resolver requires configured knowledge of at least one authenticated DNSKEY or DS RR. The process for obtaining and authenticating this initial trust anchor is achieved via some external mechanism. For example, a resolver could use some off-line authenticated exchange to obtain a zone's DNSKEY RR or to obtain a DS RR that identifies and authenticates a zone's DNSKEY RR. The remainder of this section assumes that the resolver has somehow obtained an initial set of trust anchors.

An initial DNSKEY RR can be used to authenticate a zone's apex DNSKEY RRset. To authenticate an apex DNSKEY RRset by using an initial key, the resolver MUST:

1.   verify that the initial DNSKEY RR appears in the apex DNSKEY RRset, and that the DNSKEY RR has the Zone Key Flag (DNSKEY RDATA bit 7) set; and

2.   verify that there is some RRSIG RR that covers the apex DNSKEY RRset, and that the combination of the RRSIG RR and the initial DNSKEY RR authenticates the DNSKEY RRset. The process for using an RRSIG RR to authenticate an RRset is described in Section 5.3.

Once the resolver has authenticated the apex DNSKEY RRset by using an initial DNSKEY RR, delegations from that zone can be authenticated by using DS RRs. This allows a resolver to start from an initial key and use DS RRsets to proceed recursively down the DNS tree, obtaining other apex DNSKEY RRsets. If the resolver were configured with a root DNSKEY RR, and if every delegation had a DS RR associated with it, then the resolver could obtain and validate any apex DNSKEY RRset. The process of using DS RRs to authenticate referrals is described in Section 5.2.

Section 5.3 shows how the resolver can use DNSKEY RRs in the apex DNSKEY RRset and RRSIG RRs from the zone to authenticate any other RRsets in the zone once the resolver has authenticated a zone's apex DNSKEY RRset. Section 5.4 shows how the resolver can use authenticated NSEC RRsets from the zone to prove that an RRset is not present in the zone.

When a resolver indicates support for DNSSEC (by setting the DO bit), a security-aware name server should attempt to provide the necessary DNSKEY, RRSIG, NSEC, and DS RRsets in a response (see Section 3). However, a security-aware resolver may still receive a response that lacks the appropriate DNSSEC RRs, whether due to configuration issues such as an upstream security-oblivious recursive name server that accidentally interferes with DNSSEC RRs or due to a deliberate attack in which an adversary forges a response, strips DNSSEC RRs from a response, or modifies a query so that DNSSEC RRs appear not to be requested. The absence of DNSSEC data in a response MUST NOT by itself be taken as an indication that no authentication information exists.

A resolver SHOULD expect authentication information from signed zones. A resolver SHOULD believe that a zone is signed if the resolver has been configured with public key information for the zone, or if the zone's parent is signed and the delegation from the parent contains a DS RRset.

5.1. Special Considerations for Islands of Security

Islands of security (see [RFC4033]) are signed zones for which it is not possible to construct an authentication chain to the zone from its parent. Validating signatures within an island of security requires that the validator have some other means of obtaining an initial authenticated zone key for the island. If a validator cannot obtain such a key, it SHOULD switch to operating as if the zones in the island of security are unsigned.

All the normal processes for validating responses apply to islands of security. The only difference between normal validation and validation within an island of security is in how the validator obtains a trust anchor for the authentication chain.

5.2. Authenticating Referrals

Once the apex DNSKEY RRset for a signed parent zone has been authenticated, DS RRsets can be used to authenticate the delegation to a signed child zone. A DS RR identifies a DNSKEY RR in the child zone's apex DNSKEY RRset and contains a cryptographic digest of the child zone's DNSKEY RR. Use of a strong cryptographic digest algorithm ensures that it is computationally infeasible for an adversary to generate a DNSKEY RR that matches the digest. Thus, authenticating the digest allows a resolver to authenticate the matching DNSKEY RR.

The resolver can then use this child DNSKEY RR to authenticate the entire child apex DNSKEY RRset.

Given a DS RR for a delegation, the child zone's apex DNSKEY RRset can be authenticated if all of the following hold:

- The DS RR has been authenticated using some DNSKEY RR in the parent's apex DNSKEY RRset (see Section 5.3).

- The Algorithm and Key Tag in the DS RR match the Algorithm field and the key tag of a DNSKEY RR in the child zone's apex DNSKEY RRset, and, when the DNSKEY RR's owner name and RDATA are hashed using the digest algorithm specified in the DS RR's Digest Type field, the resulting digest value matches the Digest field of the DS RR.

- The matching DNSKEY RR in the child zone has the Zone Flag bit set, the corresponding private key has signed the child zone's apex DNSKEY RRset, and the resulting RRSIG RR authenticates the child zone's apex DNSKEY RRset.

If the referral from the parent zone did not contain a DS RRset, the response should have included a signed NSEC RRset proving that no DS RRset exists for the delegated name (see Section 3.1.4). A security-aware resolver MUST query the name servers for the parent zone for the DS RRset if the referral includes neither a DS RRset nor a NSEC RRset proving that the DS RRset does not exist (see Section 4).

If the validator authenticates an NSEC RRset that proves that no DS RRset is present for this zone, then there is no authentication path leading from the parent to the child. If the resolver has an initial DNSKEY or DS RR that belongs to the child zone or to any delegation below the child zone, this initial DNSKEY or DS RR MAY be used to re-establish an authentication path. If no such initial DNSKEY or DS RR exists, the validator cannot authenticate RRsets in or below the child zone.

If the validator does not support any of the algorithms listed in an authenticated DS RRset, then the resolver has no supported authentication path leading from the parent to the child. The resolver should treat this case as it would the case of an authenticated NSEC RRset proving that no DS RRset exists, as described above.

Note that, for a signed delegation, there are two NSEC RRs associated with the delegated name. One NSEC RR resides in the parent zone and can be used to prove whether a DS RRset exists for the delegated name. The second NSEC RR resides in the child zone and identifies which RRsets are present at the apex of the child zone. The parent NSEC RR and child NSEC RR can always be distinguished because the SOA bit will be set in the child NSEC RR and clear in the parent NSEC RR. A security-aware resolver MUST use the parent NSEC RR when attempting to prove that a DS RRset does not exist.

If the resolver does not support any of the algorithms listed in an authenticated DS RRset, then the resolver will not be able to verify the authentication path to the child zone. In this case, the resolver SHOULD treat the child zone as if it were unsigned.

5.3. Authenticating an RRset with an RRSIG RR

A validator can use an RRSIG RR and its corresponding DNSKEY RR to attempt to authenticate RRsets. The validator first checks the RRSIG RR to verify that it covers the RRset, has a valid time interval, and identifies a valid DNSKEY RR. The validator then constructs the canonical form of the signed data by appending the RRSIG RDATA (excluding the Signature Field) with the canonical form of the covered RRset. Finally, the validator uses the public key and signature to authenticate the signed data. Sections 5.3.1, 5.3.2, and 5.3.3 describe each step in detail.

5.3.1. Checking the RRSIG RR Validity

A security-aware resolver can use an RRSIG RR to authenticate an RRset if all of the following conditions hold:

- The RRSIG RR and the RRset MUST have the same owner name and the same class.
- The RRSIG RR's Signer's Name field MUST be the name of the zone that contains the RRset.
- The RRSIG RR's Type Covered field MUST equal the RRset's type.
- The number of labels in the RRset owner name MUST be greater than or equal to the value in the RRSIG RR's Labels field.
- The validator's notion of the current time MUST be less than or equal to the time listed in the RRSIG RR's Expiration field.
- The validator's notion of the current time MUST be greater than or equal to the time listed in the RRSIG RR's Inception field.
- The RRSIG RR's Signer's Name, Algorithm, and Key Tag fields MUST match the owner name, algorithm, and key tag for some DNSKEY RR in the zone's apex DNSKEY RRset.
- The matching DNSKEY RR MUST be present in the zone's apex DNSKEY RRset, and MUST have the Zone Flag bit (DNSKEY RDATA Flag bit 7) set.

It is possible for more than one DNSKEY RR to match the conditions above. In this case, the validator cannot predetermine which DNSKEY RR to use to authenticate the signature, and it MUST try each matching DNSKEY RR until either the signature is validated or the validator has run out of matching public keys to try.

Note that this authentication process is only meaningful if the validator authenticates the DNSKEY RR before using it to validate signatures. The matching DNSKEY RR is considered to be authentic if:

- the apex DNSKEY RRset containing the DNSKEY RR is considered authentic; or
- the RRset covered by the RRSIG RR is the apex DNSKEY RRset itself, and the DNSKEY RR either matches an authenticated DS RR from the parent zone or matches a trust anchor.

5.3.2. Reconstructing the Signed Data

Once the RRSIG RR has met the validity requirements described in Section 5.3.1, the validator has to reconstruct the original signed data. The original signed data includes RRSIG RDATA (excluding the Signature field) and the canonical form of the RRset. Aside from being ordered, the canonical form of the RRset might also differ from the received RRset due to DNS name compression, decremented TTLs, or wildcard expansion. The validator should use the following to reconstruct the original signed data:

> signed_data = RRSIG_RDATA — RR(1) — RR(2)... where

> "—" denotes concatenation

> RRSIG_RDATA is the wire format of the RRSIG RDATA fields with the Signature field excluded and the Signer's Name in canonical form.

> RR(i) = name — type — class — OrigTTL — RDATA length — RDATA

>> name is calculated according to the function below

>> class is the RRset's class

>> type is the RRset type and all RRs in the class

>> OrigTTL is the value from the RRSIG Original TTL field

>> All names in the RDATA field are in canonical form The set of all RR(i) is sorted into canonical order.

> To calculate the name:

>> let rrsig_labels = the value of the RRSIG Labels field

>> let fqdn = RRset's fully qualified domain name in canonical form

>> let fqdn_labels = Label count of the fqdn above.

>> if rrsig_labels = fqdn_labels,
>> name = fqdn

>> if rrsig_labels < fqdn_labels,
>> name = "*." — the rightmost rrsig_label labels of the fqdn

>> if rrsig_labels > fqdn_labels
>> the RRSIG RR did not pass the necessary validation checks and MUST NOT be used to authenticate this RRset.

The canonical forms for names and RRsets are defined in [RFC4034].

NSEC RRsets at a delegation boundary require special processing. There are two distinct NSEC RRsets associated with a signed delegated name. One NSEC RRset resides in the parent zone, and specifies which RRsets are present at the parent zone. The second NSEC RRset resides at the child zone and identifies which RRsets are present at the apex in the child zone. The parent NSEC RRset and child NSEC RRset can always be distinguished as only a child

NSEC RR will indicate that an SOA RRset exists at the name. When reconstructing the original NSEC RRset for the delegation from the parent zone, the NSEC RRs MUST NOT be combined with NSEC RRs from the child zone. When reconstructing the original NSEC RRset for the apex of the child zone, the NSEC RRs MUST NOT be combined with NSEC RRs from the parent zone.

Note that each of the two NSEC RRsets at a delegation point has a corresponding RRSIG RR with an owner name matching the delegated name, and each of these RRSIG RRs is authoritative data associated with the same zone that contains the corresponding NSEC RRset. If necessary, a resolver can tell these RRSIG RRs apart by checking the Signer's Name field.

5.3.3. Checking the Signature

Once the resolver has validated the RRSIG RR as described in Section 5.3.1 and reconstructed the original signed data as described in Section 5.3.2, the validator can attempt to use the cryptographic signature to authenticate the signed data, and thus (finally!) authenticate the RRset.

The Algorithm field in the RRSIG RR identifies the cryptographic algorithm used to generate the signature. The signature itself is contained in the Signature field of the RRSIG RDATA, and the public key used to verify the signature is contained in the Public Key field of the matching DNSKEY RR(s) (found in Section 5.3.1). [RFC4034] provides a list of algorithm types and provides pointers to the documents that define each algorithm's use.

Note that it is possible for more than one DNSKEY RR to match the conditions in Section 5.3.1. In this case, the validator can only determine which DNSKEY RR is correct by trying each matching public key until the validator either succeeds in validating the signature or runs out of keys to try.

If the Labels field of the RRSIG RR is not equal to the number of labels in the RRset's fully qualified owner name, then the RRset is either invalid or the result of wildcard expansion. The resolver MUST verify that wildcard expansion was applied properly before considering the RRset to be authentic. Section 5.3.4 describes how to determine whether a wildcard was applied properly.

If other RRSIG RRs also cover this RRset, the local resolver security policy determines whether the resolver also has to test these RRSIG RRs and how to resolve conflicts if these RRSIG RRs lead to differing results.

If the resolver accepts the RRset as authentic, the validator MUST set the TTL of the RRSIG RR and each RR in the authenticated RRset to a value no greater than the minimum of:

- the RRset's TTL as received in the response;

- the RRSIG RR's TTL as received in the response;

- the value in the RRSIG RR's Original TTL field; and

- the difference of the RRSIG RR's Signature Expiration time and the current time.

5.3.4. Authenticating a Wildcard Expanded RRset Positive Response

If the number of labels in an RRset's owner name is greater than the Labels field of the covering RRSIG RR, then the RRset and its covering RRSIG RR were created as a result of wildcard expansion. Once the validator has verified the signature, as described in Section 5.3, it must take additional steps to verify the non-existence of an exact match or closer wildcard match for the query. Section 5.4 discusses these steps.

Note that the response received by the resolver should include all NSEC RRs needed to authenticate the response (see Section 3.1.3).

5.4. Authenticated Denial of Existence

A resolver can use authenticated NSEC RRs to prove that an RRset is not present in a signed zone. Security-aware name servers should automatically include any necessary NSEC RRs for signed zones in their responses to security-aware resolvers.

Denial of existence is determined by the following rules:

- If the requested RR name matches the owner name of an authenticated NSEC RR, then the NSEC RR's type bit map field lists all RR types present at that owner name, and a resolver can prove that the requested RR type does not exist by checking for the RR type in the bit map. If the number of labels in an authenticated NSEC RR's owner name equals the Labels field of the covering RRSIG RR, then the existence of the NSEC RR proves that wildcard expansion could not have been used to match the request.

- If the requested RR name would appear after an authenticated NSEC RR's owner name and before the name listed in that NSEC RR's Next Domain Name field according to the canonical DNS name order defined in [RFC4034], then no RRsets with the requested name exist in the zone. However, it is possible that a wildcard could be used to match the requested RR owner name and type, so proving that the requested RRset does not exist also requires proving that no possible wildcard RRset exists that could have been used to generate a positive response.

In addition, security-aware resolvers MUST authenticate the NSEC RRsets that comprise the non-existence proof as described in Section 5.3.

To prove the non-existence of an RRset, the resolver must be able to verify both that the queried RRset does not exist and that no relevant wildcard RRset exists. Proving this may require more than one NSEC RRset from the zone. If the complete set of necessary NSEC RRsets is not present in a response (perhaps due to message truncation), then a security-aware resolver MUST resend the query in order to attempt to obtain the full collection of NSEC RRs necessary to verify the non-existence of the requested RRset. As with all DNS operations, however, the resolver MUST bound the work it puts into answering any particular query.

Since a validated NSEC RR proves the existence of both itself and its corresponding RRSIG RR, a validator MUST ignore the settings of the NSEC and RRSIG bits in an NSEC RR.

5.5. Resolver Behavior When Signatures Do Not Validate

If for whatever reason none of the RRSIGs can be validated, the response SHOULD be considered BAD. If the validation was being done to service a recursive query, the name server MUST return RCODE 2 to the originating client. However, it MUST return the full response if and only if the original query had the CD bit set. Also see Section 4.7 on caching responses that do not validate.

5.6. Authentication Example

Appendix C shows an example of the authentication process.

6. IANA Considerations

[RFC4034] contains a review of the IANA considerations introduced by DNSSEC. The following are additional IANA considerations discussed in this document:

[RFC2535] reserved the CD and AD bits in the message header. The meaning of the AD bit was redefined in [RFC3655], and the meaning of both the CD and AD bit are restated in this document. No new bits in the DNS message header are defined in this document.

[RFC2671] introduced EDNS, and [RFC3225] reserved the DNSSEC OK bit and defined its use. The use is restated but not altered in this document.

7. Security Considerations

This document describes how the DNS security extensions use public key cryptography to sign and authenticate DNS resource record sets. Please see [RFC4033] for terminology and general security considerations related to DNSSEC; see [RFC4034] for considerations specific to the DNSSEC resource record types.

An active attacker who can set the CD bit in a DNS query message or the AD bit in a DNS response message can use these bits to defeat the protection that DNSSEC attempts to provide to security-oblivious recursive-mode resolvers. For this reason, use of these control bits by a security-aware recursive-mode resolver requires a secure channel. See Sections 3.2.2 and 4.9 for further discussion.

The protocol described in this document attempts to extend the benefits of DNSSEC to security-oblivious stub resolvers. However, as recovery from validation failures is likely to be specific to particular applications, the facilities that DNSSEC provides for stub resolvers may prove inadequate. Operators of security-aware recursive name servers will have to pay close attention to the behavior of the applications that use their services when choosing a local validation policy; failure to do so could easily result in the recursive name server accidentally denying service to the clients it is intended to support.

8. Acknowledgements

This document was created from the input and ideas of the members of the DNS Extensions Working Group and working group mailing list. The editors would like to express their thanks for the comments and suggestions received during the revision of these security extension specifications. Although explicitly listing everyone who has contributed during the decade in which DNSSEC has been under development would be impossible, [RFC4033] includes a list of some of the participants who were kind enough to comment on these documents.

9. References

9.1. Normative References

[RFC1034] Mockapetris, P., "Domain names - concepts and facilities", STD 13, RFC 1034, November 1987.

[RFC1035] Mockapetris, P., "Domain names - implementation and specification", STD 13, RFC 1035, November 1987.

[RFC1122] Braden, R., "Requirements for Internet Hosts - Communication Layers", STD 3, RFC 1122, October 1989.

[RFC2119] Bradner, S., "Key words for use in RFCs to Indicate Requirement Levels", BCP 14, RFC 2119, March 1997.

[RFC2181] Elz, R. and R. Bush, "Clarifications to the DNS Specification", RFC 2181, July 1997.

[RFC2460] Deering, S. and R. Hinden, "Internet Protocol, Version 6 (IPv6) Specification", RFC 2460, December 1998.

[RFC2671] Vixie, P., "Extension Mechanisms for DNS (EDNS0)", RFC 2671, August 1999.

[RFC2672] Crawford, M., "Non-Terminal DNS Name Redirection", RFC 2672, August 1999.

[RFC3225] Conrad, D., "Indicating Resolver Support of DNSSEC", RFC 3225, December 2001.

[RFC3226] Gudmundsson, O., "DNSSEC and IPv6 A6 aware server/resolver message size requirements", RFC 3226, December 2001.

[RFC4033] Arends, R., Austein, R., Larson, M., Massey, D., and S. Rose, "DNS Security Introduction and Requirements", RFC 4033, March 2005.

[RFC4034] Arends, R., Austein, R., Larson, M., Massey, D., and S. Rose, "Resource Records for DNS Security Extensions", RFC 4034, March 2005.

9.2. Informative References

[RFC2308] Andrews, M., "Negative Caching of DNS Queries (DNS NCACHE)", RFC 2308, March 1998.

[RFC2535] Eastlake 3rd, D., "Domain Name System Security Extensions", RFC 2535, March 1999.

[RFC3007] Wellington, B., "Secure Domain Name System (DNS) Dynamic Update", RFC 3007, November 2000.

[RFC3655] Wellington, B. and O. Gudmundsson, "Redefinition of DNS Authenticated Data (AD) bit", RFC 3655, November 2003.

Appendix A. Signed Zone Example

The following example shows a (small) complete signed zone.

```
example.         3600 IN SOA ns1.example. bugs.x.w.example. (
                      1081539377
                      3600
                      300
                      3600000
                      3600
                      )
                 3600 RRSIG  SOA 5 1 3600 20040509183619 (
                      20040409183619 38519 example.
                      ONx0k36rcjaxYtcNgq6iQnpNV5+drqYAsC9h
                      7TSJaHCqbhE67Sr6aH2xDUGcqQWu/n0UVzrF
                      vkgO9ebarZ0GWDKcuwlM6eNB5SiX2K74l5LW
                      DA7S/Un/IbtDq4Ay8NMNLQI7Dw7n4p8/rjkB
                      jV7j86HyQgM5e7+miRAz8V01b0I= )
                 3600 NS     ns1.example.
                 3600 NS     ns2.example.
                 3600 RRSIG  NS 5 1 3600 20040509183619 (
                      20040409183619 38519 example.
                      gl13F00f2U0R+SWiXXLHwsMY+qStYy5k6zfd
                      EuivWc+wd1fmbNCyql0Tk7lHTX6UOxc8AgNf
                      4ISFve8XqF4q+o9qlnqIzmppU3LiNeKT4FZ8
                      RO5urFOvoMRTbQxW3U0hXWuggE4g3ZpsHv48
                      0HjMeRaZB/FRPGfJPajngcq6Kwg= )
                 3600 MX     1 xx.example.
                 3600 RRSIG  MX 5 1 3600 20040509183619 (
                      20040409183619 38519 example.
                      HyDHYVT5KHSZ7HtO/vypumPmSZQrcOP3tzWB
                      2qaKkHVPfau/DgLgS/IKENkYOGL95G4N+NzE
                      VyNU8dcTOckT+ChPcGeVjguQ7a3Ao9Z/ZkUO
                      6gmmUW4b89rz1PUxW4jzUxj66PTwoVtUU/iM
                      W6OISukd1EQt7a0kygkg+PEDxdI= )
```

```
                  3600 NSEC   a.example. NS SOA MX RRSIG NSEC DNSKEY
                  3600 RRSIG  NSEC 5 1 3600 20040509183619 (
                              20040409183619 38519 example.
                              O0k558jHhyrC97ISHnislm4kLMW48C7U7cBm
                              FTfhke5iVqNRVTB1STLMpgpbDIC9hcryoO0V
                              Z9ME5xPzUEhbvGnHd5sfzgFVeGxr5Nyyq4tW
                              SDBgIBiLQUv1ivy29vhXy7WgR62dPrZ0PWvm
                              jfFJ5arXf4nPxp/kEowGgBRzY/U= )
                  3600 DNSKEY 256 3 5 (
                              AQOy1bZVvpPqhg4j7EJoM9rI3ZmyEx2OzDBV
                              rZy/lvI5CQePxXHZS4i8dANH4DX3tbHol61e
                              k8EFMcsGXxKciJFHyhl94C+NwILQdzsUlSFo
                              vBZsyl/NX6yEbtw/xN9ZNcrbYvgjjZ/UVPZI
                              ySFNsgEYvh0z2542lzMKR4Dh8uZffQ==
                              )
                  3600 DNSKEY 257 3 5 (
                              AQOeX7+baTmvpVHb2CcLnL1dMRWbuscRvHXl
                              LnXwDzvqp4tZVKp1sZMepFb8MvxhhW3y/0QZ
                              syCjczGJ1qk8vJe52iOhInKROVLRwxGpMfzP
                              RLMlGybr51bOV/1se0ODacj3DomyB4QB5gKT
                              Yot/K9alk5/j8vfd4jWCWD+E1Sze0Q==
                              )
                  3600 RRSIG  DNSKEY 5 1 3600 20040509183619 (
                              20040409183619 9465 example.
                              ZxgauAuIj+k1YoVEOSlZfx41fcmKzTFHoweZ
                              xYnz99JVQZJ33wFS0Q0jcP7VXKkaElXk9nYJ
                              XevO/7nAbo88iWsMkSpSR6jWzYYKwfrBI/L9
                              hjYmyVO9m6FjQ7uwM4dCP/bIuV/DKqOAK9NY
                              NC3AHfvCV1Tp4VKDqxqG7R5tTVM= )
                  3600 RRSIG  DNSKEY 5 1 3600 20040509183619 (
                              20040409183619 38519 example.
                              eGL0s90glUqcOmloo/2y+bSzyEfKVOQViD9Z
                              DNhLz/Yn9CQZlDVRJffACQDAUhXpU/oP34ri
                              bKBpysRXosczFrKqS5Oa0bzMOfXCXup9qHAp
                              eFIku28Vqfr8Nt7cigZLxjK+u0Ws/4lIRjKk
                              7z5OXogYVaFzHKillDt3HRxHIZM= )
a.example.        3600 IN NS  ns1.a.example.
                  3600 IN NS  ns2.a.example.
                  3600 DS     57855 5 1 (
                              B6DCD485719ADCA18E5F3D48A2331627FDD3
                              636B )
                  3600 RRSIG  DS 5 2 3600 20040509183619 (
                              20040409183619 38519 example.
                              oXIKit/QtdG64J/CB+Gi8dOvnwRvqrto1AdQ
                              oRkAN15FP3iZ7suB7gvTBmXzCjL7XUgQVcoH
                              kdhyCuzp8W9qJHgRUSwKKkczSyuL64nhgjuD
                              EML8l9wlWVsl7PR2VnZduM9bLyBhaaPmRKX/
                              Fm+v6ccF2EGNLRiY08kdkz+XHHo= )
                  3600 NSEC   ai.example. NS DS RRSIG NSEC
                  3600 RRSIG  NSEC 5 2 3600 20040509183619 (
                              20040409183619 38519 example.
```

```
                            cOlYgqJLqlRqmBQ3iap2SyIsK4O5aqpKSoba
                            U9fQ5SMApZmHfq3AgLflkrkXRXvgxTQSKkG2
                            039/cRUs6Jk/25+fi7Xr5nOVJsb0lq4zsB3I
                            BBdjyGDAHE0F5ROJj87996vJupdm1fbH481g
                            sdkOW6Zyqtz3Zos8N0BBkEx+2G4= )
ns1.a.example.  3600 IN A   192.0.2.5
ns2.a.example.  3600 IN A   192.0.2.6
ai.example.     3600 IN A   192.0.2.9
                3600 RRSIG  A 5 2 3600 20040509183619 (
                            20040409183619 38519 example.
                            pAOtzLP2MU0tDJUwHOKE5FPIIHmdYsCgTb5B
                            ERGgpnJluA9ixOyf6xxVCgrEJW0WNZSsJicd
                            hBHXfDmAGKUajUUlYSAH8tS4Znrhyymlvk3u
                            ArDu2wfT130e9UHnumaHHMpUTosKe22PblOy
                            6zrTpg9FkS0XGVmYRvOTNYx2HvQ= )
                3600 HINFO  "KLH-10" "ITS"
                3600 RRSIG  HINFO 5 2 3600 20040509183619 (
                            20040409183619 38519 example.
                            Iq/RGCbBdKzcYzlGE4ovbr5YcB+ezxbZ9W0l
                            e/7WqyvhOO9J16HxhhL7VY/IKmTUY0GGdcfh
                            ZEOCkf4lEykZF9NPok1/R/fWrtzNp8jobuY7
                            AZEcZadp1WdDF3jc2/ndCa5XZhLKD3JzOsBw
                            FvL8sqlS5QS6FY/ijFEDnI4RkZA= )
                3600 AAAA   2001:db8::f00:baa9
                3600 RRSIG  AAAA 5 2 3600 20040509183619 (
                            20040409183619 38519 example.
                            nLcpFuXdT35AcE+EoafOUkl69KB+/e56XmFK
                            kewXG2IadYLKAOBIoR5+VoQV3XgTcofTJNsh
                            1rnF6Eav2zpZB3byI6yo2bwY8MNkr4A7cL9T
                            dMmDwV/hWFKsbGBsj8xSCN/caEL2CWY/5XP2
                            sZM6QjBBLmukH30+w1z3h8PUP2o= )
                3600 NSEC   b.example. A HINFO AAAA RRSIG NSEC
                3600 RRSIG  NSEC 5 2 3600 20040509183619 (
                            20040409183619 38519 example.
                            QoshyPevLcJ/xcRpEtMft1uoIrcrieVcc9pG
                            CScIn5Glnib40T6ayVOimXwdSTZ/8ISXGj4p
                            P8Sh0PlA6olZQ84L453/BUqB8BpdOGky4hsN
                            3AGcLEv1Gr0QMvirQaFcjzOECfnGyBm+wpFL
                            AhS+JOVfDI/79QtyTI0SaDWcg8U= )
b.example.      3600 IN NS  ns1.b.example.
                3600 IN NS  ns2.b.example.
                3600 NSEC   ns1.example. NS RRSIG NSEC
                3600 RRSIG  NSEC 5 2 3600 20040509183619 (
                            20040409183619 38519 example.
                            GNuxHn844wfmUhPzGWKJCPY5ttEX/RfjDoOx
                            9ueK1PtYkOWKOOdiJ/PJKCYB3hYX+858dDWS
                            xb2qnV/LSTCNVBnkm6owOpysY97MVj5VQEWs
                            0lm9tFoqjcptQkmQKYPrwUnCSNwvvclSF1xZ
                            vhRXgWT7OuFXldoCG6TfVFMs9xE= )
ns1.b.example.  3600 IN A   192.0.2.7
ns2.b.example.  3600 IN A   192.0.2.8
```

```
ns1.example.    3600 IN A    192.0.2.1
                3600 RRSIG   A 5 2 3600 20040509183619 (
                             20040409183619 38519 example.
                             F1C9HVhIcs10cZU09G5yIVfKJy5yRQQ3qVet
                             5pGhp82pzhAOMZ3K22JnmK4c+IjUeFp/to06
                             im5FVpHtbFisdjyPq84bhTv8vrXt5AB1wNB+
                             +iAqvIfdgW4sFNC6oADb1hK8QNauw9VePJhK
                             v/iVXSYC0b7mPSU+EOlknFpVECs= )
                3600 NSEC    ns2.example. A RRSIG NSEC
                3600 RRSIG   NSEC 5 2 3600 20040509183619 (
                             20040409183619 38519 example.
                             I4hj+Kt6+8rCcHcUdolks2S+Wzri9h3fHas8
                             1rGN/eILdJHN7JpV6lLGPIh/8fIBkfvdyWnB
                             jjf1q3O7JgYO1UdI7FvBNWqaaEPJK3UkddBq
                             ZIaLi8Qr2XHkjq38BeQsbp8X0+6h4ETWSGT8
                             IZaIGBLryQWGLw6Y6X8dqhlnxJM= )
ns2.example.    3600 IN A    192.0.2.2
                3600 RRSIG   A 5 2 3600 20040509183619 (
                             20040409183619 38519 example.
                             V7cQRw1TR+knlaL1z/psxlS1PcD37JJDaCMq
                             Qo6/u1qFQu6x+wuDHRH22Ap9ulJPQjFwMKOu
                             yfPGQPC8KzGdE3vt5snFEAoE1Vn3mQqtu7SO
                             6amIjk13Kj/jyJ4nGmdRIc/3cM3ipXFhNTKq
                             rdhx8SZ0yy4ObIRzIzvBFLiSS8o= )
                3600 NSEC    *.w.example. A RRSIG NSEC
                3600 RRSIG   NSEC 5 2 3600 20040509183619 (
                             20040409183619 38519 example.
                             N0QzHvaJf5NRw1rE9uxS1Ltb2LZ73Qb9bKGE
                             VyaISkqzGpP3jYJXZJPVTq4UVEsgT3CgeHvb
                             3QbeJ5Dfb2V9NGCHj/OvF/LBxFFWwhLwzngH
                             l+bQAgAcMsLu/nL3nDi1y/JSQjAcdZNDl4bw
                             Ymx28EtgIpo9A0qmP08rMBqs1Jw= )
*.w.example.    3600 IN MX   1 ai.example.
                3600 RRSIG   MX 5 2 3600 20040509183619 (
                             20040409183619 38519 example.
                             OMK8rAZlepfzLWW75Dxd63jy2wswESzxDKG2
                             f9AMN1CytCd10cYISAxfAdvXSZ7xujKAtPbc
                             tvOQ2ofO7AZJ+d01EeeQTVBPq4/6KCWhqe2X
                             TjnkVLNvvhnc0u28aoSsG0+4InvkkOHknKxw
                             4kX18MMR34i8lC36SR5xBni8vHI= )
                3600 NSEC    x.w.example. MX RRSIG NSEC
                3600 RRSIG   NSEC 5 2 3600 20040509183619 (
                             20040409183619 38519 example.
                             r/mZnRC3I/VIcrelgIcteSxDhtsdlTDt8ng9
                             HSBlABOlzLxQtfgTnn8f+aOwJIAFe1Ee5RvU
                             5cVhQJNP5XpXMJHfyps8tVvfxSAXfahpYqtx
                             91gsmcV/1V9/bZAG55CefP9cM4Z9Y9NT9XQ8
                             s1InQ2UoIv6tJEaaKkP701j8OLA= )
x.w.example.    3600 IN MX   1 xx.example.
                3600 RRSIG   MX 5 3 3600 20040509183619 (
                             20040409183619 38519 example.
```

```
                                  Il2WTZ+Bkv+OytBx4LItNW5mjB4RCwhOO8y1
                                  XzPHZmZUTVYL7LaA63f6T9ysVBzJRI3KRjAP
                                  H3U1qaYnDoN1DrWqmi9RJe4FoObkbcdm7P3I
                                  kx70ePCoFgRz1Yq+bVVXCvGuAU4xALv3W/Y1
                                  jNSlwZ2mSWKHfxFQxPtLj8s32+k= )
            3600 NSEC             x.y.w.example. MX RRSIG NSEC
            3600 RRSIG            NSEC 5 3 3600 20040509183619 (
                                  20040409183619 38519 example.
                                  aRbpHftxggzgMXdDlym9SsADqMZovZZl2QWK
                                  vw8J0tZEUNQByH5Qfnf5N1FqH/pS46UA7A4E
                                  mcWBN9PUA1pdPY6RVeaRlZlCr1IkVctvbtaI
                                  NJuBba/VHm+pebTbKcAPIvL9tBOoh+to1h6e
                                  IjgiM8PXkBQtxPq37wDKALkyn7Q= )
x.y.w.example. 3600 IN MX         1 xx.example.
            3600 RRSIG            MX 5 4 3600 20040509183619 (
                                  20040409183619 38519 example.
                                  k2bJHbwP5LH5qN4is39UiPzjAWYmJA38Hhia
                                  t7i9t7nbX/e0FPnvDSQXzcK7UL+zrVA+3MDj
                                  q1ub4q3SZgcbLMgexxIW3Va//LVrxkP6Xupq
                                  GtOB9prkK54QTl/qZTXfMQpW480YOvVknhvb
                                  +gLcMZBnHJ326nb/TOOmrqNmQQE= )
            3600 NSEC             xx.example. MX RRSIG NSEC
            3600 RRSIG            NSEC 5 4 3600 20040509183619 (
                                  20040409183619 38519 example.
                                  OvE6WUzN2ziieJcvKPWbCAyXyP6ef8cr6Csp
                                  ArVSTzKSquNwbezZmkU7E34o5lmb6CWSSSpg
                                  xw098kNUFnHcQf/LzY2zqRomubrNQhJTiDTX
                                  a0ArunJQCzPjOYq5t0SLjm6qp6McJI1AP5Vr
                                  QoKqJDCLnoAlcPOPKAm/jJkn3jk= )
xx.example. 3600 IN A             192.0.2.10
            3600 RRSIG            A 5 2 3600 20040509183619 (
                                  20040409183619 38519 example.
                                  kBF4YxMGWF0D8r0cztL+2fWWOvNlU/GYSpYP
                                  7SoKoNQ4fZKyk+weWGlKLIUM+uE1zjVTPXoa
                                  0Z6WG0oZp46rkl1EzMcdMgoaeUzzAJ2BMq+Y
                                  VdxG9IK1yZkYGY9AgbTOGPoAgbJyO9EPULsx
                                  kbIDV6GPPSZVusnZU6OMgdgzHV4= )
            3600 HINFO            "KLH-10" "TOPS-20"
            3600 RRSIG            HINFO 5 2 3600 20040509183619 (
                                  20040409183619 38519 example.
                                  GY2PLSXmMHkWHfLdggiox8+chWpeMNJLkML0
                                  t+U/SXSUsoUdR91KNdNUkTDWamwcF8oFRjhq
                                  BcPZ6EqrF+vl5v5oGuvSF7U52epfVTC+wWF8
                                  3yCUeUw8YklhLWlvk8gQ15YKth0ITQy8/wI+
                                  RgNvuwbioFSEuv2pNlkq0goYxNY= )
            3600 AAAA             2001:db8::f00:baaa
            3600 RRSIG            AAAA 5 2 3600 20040509183619 (
                                  20040409183619 38519 example.
                                  Zzj0yodDxcBLnnOIwDsuKo5WqiaK24DlKg9C
                                  aGaxDFiKgKobUj2jilYQHpGFn2poFRetZd4z
                                  ulyQkssz2QHrVrPuTMS22knudCiwP4LWpVTr
```

```
                    U4zfeA+rDz9stmSBP/4PekH/x2IoAYnwctd/
                    xS9cL2QgW7FChw16mzlkH6/vsfs= )
    3600 NSEC       example. A HINFO AAAA RRSIG NSEC
    3600 RRSIG      NSEC 5 2 3600 20040509183619 (
                    20040409183619 38519 example.
                    ZFWUln6Avc8bmGl5GFjD3BwT530DUZKHNuoY
                    9A8lgXYyrxu+pqgFiRVbyZRQvVB5pccEOT3k
                    mvHgEa/HzbDB4PIYY79W+VHrgOxzdQGGCZzi
                    asXrpSGOWwSOElghPnMIi8xdF7qtCntr382W
                    GghLahumFIpg4MO3LS/prgzVVWo= )
```

The apex DNSKEY set includes two DNSKEY RRs, and the DNSKEY RDATA Flags indicate that each of these DNSKEY RRs is a zone key. One of these DNSKEY RRs also has the SEP flag set and has been used to sign the apex DNSKEY RRset; this is the key that should be hashed to generate a DS record to be inserted into the parent zone. The other DNSKEY is used to sign all the other RRsets in the zone.

The zone includes a wildcard entry, "*.w.example". Note that the name "*.w.example" is used in constructing NSEC chains, and that the RRSIG covering the "*.w.example" MX RRset has a label count of 2.

The zone also includes two delegations. The delegation to "b.example" includes an NS RRset, glue address records, and an NSEC RR; note that only the NSEC RRset is signed. The delegation to "a.example" provides a DS RR; note that only the NSEC and DS RRsets are signed.

Appendix B. Example Responses

The examples in this section show response messages using the signed zone example in Appendix A.

B.1. Answer

A successful query to an authoritative server.

```
;; Header: QR AA DO RCODE=0
;;
;; Question
x.w.example.            IN MX

;; Answer
x.w.example.     3600 IN MX  1 xx.example.
x.w.example.     3600 RRSIG  MX 5 3 3600 20040509183619 (
                             20040409183619 38519 example.
                             Il2WTZ+Bkv+OytBx4LItNW5mjB4RCwhOO8y1
                             XzPHZmZUTVYL7LaA63f6T9ysVBzJRI3KRjAP
                             H3U1qaYnDoN1DrWqmi9RJe4FoObkbcdm7P3I
                             kx70ePCoFgRz1Yq+bVVXCvGuAU4xALv3W/Y1
```

```
                                  jNSlwZ2mSWKHfxFQxPtLj8s32+k=  )

;; Authority
example.           3600 NS       ns1.example.
example.           3600 NS       ns2.example.
example.           3600 RRSIG    NS 5 1 3600 20040509183619 (
                                 20040409183619 38519 example.
                                 gl13F00f2U0R+SWiXXLHwsMY+qStYy5k6zfd
                                 EuivWc+wd1fmbNCyql0Tk7lHTX6UOxc8AgNf
                                 4ISFve8XqF4q+o9qlnqIzmppU3LiNeKT4FZ8
                                 RO5urFOvoMRTbQxW3U0hXWuggE4g3ZpsHv48
                                 0HjMeRaZB/FRPGfJPajngcq6Kwg=  )

;; Additional
xx.example.        3600 IN A     192.0.2.10
xx.example.        3600 RRSIG    A 5 2 3600 20040509183619 (
                                 20040409183619 38519 example.
                                 kBF4YxMGWF0D8r0cztL+2fWWOvNlU/GYSpYP
                                 7SoKoNQ4fZKyk+weWGlKLIUM+uE1zjVTPXoa
                                 0Z6WG0oZp46rkl1EzMcdMgoaeUzzAJ2BMq+Y
                                 VdxG9IK1yZkYGY9AgbTOGPoAgbJyO9EPULsx
                                 kbIDV6GPPSZVusnZU6OMgdgzHV4=  )
xx.example.        3600 AAAA     2001:db8::f00:baaa
xx.example.        3600 RRSIG    AAAA 5 2 3600 20040509183619 (
                                 20040409183619 38519 example.
                                 Zzj0yodDxcBLnnOIwDsuKo5WqiaK24DlKg9C
                                 aGaxDFiKgKobUj2jilYQHpGFn2poFRetZd4z
                                 ulyQkssz2QHrVrPuTMS22knudCiwP4LWpVTr
                                 U4zfeA+rDz9stmSBP/4PekH/x2IoAYnwctd/
                                 xS9cL2QgW7FChw16mzlkH6/vsfs=  )
ns1.example.       3600 IN A     192.0.2.1
ns1.example.       3600 RRSIG    A 5 2 3600 20040509183619 (
                                 20040409183619 38519 example.
                                 F1C9HVhIcs10cZU09G5yIVfKJy5yRQQ3qVet
                                 5pGhp82pzhAOMZ3K22JnmK4c+IjUeFp/to06
                                 im5FVpHtbFisdjyPq84bhTv8vrXt5AB1wNB+
                                 +iAqvIfdgW4sFNC6oADb1hK8QNauw9VePJhK
                                 v/iVXSYC0b7mPSU+EOlknFpVECs=  )
ns2.example.       3600 IN A     192.0.2.2
ns2.example.       3600 RRSIG    A 5 2 3600 20040509183619 (
                                 20040409183619 38519 example.
                                 V7cQRw1TR+knlaL1z/psxlS1PcD37JJDaCMq
                                 Qo6/u1qFQu6x+wuDHRH22Ap9ulJPQjFwMKOu
                                 yfPGQPC8KzGdE3vt5snFEAoE1Vn3mQqtu7SO
                                 6amIjk13Kj/jyJ4nGmdRIc/3cM3ipXFhNTKq
                                 rdhx8SZ0yy4ObIRzIzvBFLiSS8o=  )
```

B.2. Name Error

An authoritative name error. The NSEC RRs prove that the name does not exist and that no covering wildcard exists.

```
;;  Header: QR AA DO RCODE=3
;;
;;  Question
ml.example.            IN A

;;  Answer
;;  (empty)

;;  Authority
example.          3600 IN SOA  ns1.example.  bugs.x.w.example.  (
                               1081539377
                               3600
                               300
                               3600000
                               3600
                               )
example.          3600 RRSIG   SOA 5 1 3600 20040509183619 (
                               20040409183619 38519 example.
                               ONx0k36rcjaxYtcNgq6iQnpNV5+drqYAsC9h
                               7TSJaHCqbhE67Sr6aH2xDUGcqQWu/n0UVzrF
                               vkgO9ebarZ0GWDKcuwlM6eNB5SiX2K74l5LW
                               DA7S/Un/IbtDq4Ay8NMNLQI7Dw7n4p8/rjkB
                               jV7j86HyQgM5e7+miRAz8V01b0I=  )
b.example.        3600 NSEC    ns1.example. NS RRSIG NSEC
b.example.        3600 RRSIG   NSEC 5 2 3600 20040509183619 (
                               20040409183619 38519 example.
                               GNuxHn844wfmUhPzGWKJCPY5ttEX/RfjDoOx
                               9ueK1PtYkOWKOOdiJ/PJKCYB3hYX+858dDWS
                               xb2qnV/LSTCNVBnkm6owOpysY97MVj5VQEWs
                               0lm9tFoqjcptQkmQKYPrwUnCSNwvvclSF1xZ
                               vhRXgWT7OuFXldoCG6TfVFMs9xE=  )
example.          3600 NSEC    a.example. NS SOA MX RRSIG NSEC DNSKEY
example.          3600 RRSIG   NSEC 5 1 3600 20040509183619 (
                               20040409183619 38519 example.
                               O0k558jHhyrC97ISHnislm4kLMW48C7U7cBm
                               FTfhke5iVqNRVTB1STLMpgpbDIC9hcryoO0V
                               Z9ME5xPzUEhbvGnHd5sfzgFVeGxr5Nyyq4tW
                               SDBgIBiLQUv1ivy29vhXy7WgR62dPrZ0PWvm
                               jfFJ5arXf4nPxp/kEowGgBRzY/U=  )

;;  Additional
;;  (empty)
```

B.3. No Data Error

A "no data" response. The NSEC RR proves that the name exists and that the requested RR type does not.

```
;; Header: QR AA DO RCODE=0
;;
;; Question
ns1.example.            IN MX

;; Answer
;; (empty)

;; Authority
example.          3600 IN SOA ns1.example. bugs.x.w.example. (
                              1081539377
                              3600
                              300
                              3600000
                              3600
                              )
example.          3600 RRSIG  SOA 5 1 3600 20040509183619 (
                              20040409183619 38519 example.
                              ONx0k36rcjaxYtcNgq6iQnpNV5+drqYAsC9h
                              7TSJaHCqbhE67Sr6aH2xDUGcqQWu/n0UVzrF
                              vkgO9ebarZ0GWDKcuwlM6eNB5SiX2K74l5LW
                              DA7S/Un/IbtDq4Ay8NMNLQI7Dw7n4p8/rjkB
                              jV7j86HyQgM5e7+miRAz8V01b0I= )
ns1.example.      3600 NSEC   ns2.example. A RRSIG NSEC
ns1.example.      3600 RRSIG  NSEC 5 2 3600 20040509183619 (
                              20040409183619 38519 example.
                              I4hj+Kt6+8rCcHcUdolks2S+Wzri9h3fHas8
                              1rGN/eILdJHN7JpV6lLGPIh/8fIBkfvdyWnB
                              jjf1q3O7JgYO1UdI7FvBNWqaaEPJK3UkddBq
                              ZIaLi8Qr2XHkjq38BeQsbp8X0+6h4ETWSGT8
                              IZaIGBLryQWGLw6Y6X8dqhlnxJM= )

;; Additional
;; (empty)
```

B.4. Referral to Signed Zone

Referral to a signed zone. The DS RR contains the data which the resolver will need to validate the corresponding DNSKEY RR in the child zone's apex.

```
;; Header: QR DO RCODE=0
;;
;; Question
mc.a.example.           IN MX
```

```
;;  Answer
;;  (empty)

;;  Authority
a.example.          3600  IN  NS    ns1.a.example.
a.example.          3600  IN  NS    ns2.a.example.
a.example.          3600  DS        57855  5  1  (
                                    B6DCD485719ADCA18E5F3D48A2331627FDD3
                                    636B )
a.example.          3600  RRSIG     DS 5 2 3600 20040509183619 (
                                    20040409183619 38519 example.
                                    oXIKit/QtdG64J/CB+Gi8dOvnwRvqrto1AdQ
                                    oRkAN15FP3iZ7suB7gvTBmXzCjL7XUgQVcoH
                                    kdhyCuzp8W9qJHgRUSwKKkczSyuL64nhgjuD
                                    EML8l9wlWVsl7PR2VnZduM9bLyBhaaPmRKX/
                                    Fm+v6ccF2EGNLRiY08kdkz+XHHo= )

;;  Additional
ns1.a.example.  3600  IN  A    192.0.2.5
ns2.a.example.  3600  IN  A    192.0.2.6
```

B.5. Referral to Unsigned Zone

Referral to an unsigned zone. The NSEC RR proves that no DS RR for this delegation exists in the parent zone.

```
;;  Header: QR DO RCODE=0
;;
;;  Question
mc.b.example.          IN  MX

;;  Answer
;;  (empty)

;;  Authority
b.example.          3600  IN  NS    ns1.b.example.
b.example.          3600  IN  NS    ns2.b.example.
b.example.          3600  NSEC      ns1.example. NS RRSIG NSEC
b.example.          3600  RRSIG     NSEC 5 2 3600 20040509183619 (
                                    20040409183619 38519 example.
                                    GNuxHn844wfmUhPzGWKJCPY5ttEX/RfjDoOx
                                    9ueK1PtYkOWKOOdiJ/PJKCYB3hYX+858dDWS
                                    xb2qnV/LSTCNVBnkm6owOpysY97MVj5VQEWs
                                    01m9tFoqjcptQkmQKYPrwUnCSNwvvclSF1xZ
                                    vhRXgWT7OuFXldoCG6TfVFMs9xE= )
;;  Additional
ns1.b.example.  3600  IN  A    192.0.2.7
ns2.b.example.  3600  IN  A    192.0.2.8
```

B.6. Wildcard Expansion

A successful query that was answered via wildcard expansion. The label count in the answer's RRSIG RR indicates that a wildcard RRset was expanded to produce this response, and the NSEC RR proves that no closer match exists in the zone.

```
;; Header: QR AA DO RCODE=0
;;
;; Question
a.z.w.example.        IN MX

;; Answer
a.z.w.example. 3600 IN MX   1 ai.example.
a.z.w.example. 3600 RRSIG   MX 5 2 3600 20040509183619 (
                            20040409183619 38519 example.
                            OMK8rAZlepfzLWW75Dxd63jy2wswESzxDKG2
                            f9AMN1CytCd10cYISAxfAdvXSZ7xujKAtPbc
                            tvOQ2ofO7AZJ+d01EeeQTVBPq4/6KCWhqe2X
                            TjnkVLNvvhnc0u28aoSsG0+4InvkkOHknKxw
                            4kX18MMR34i8lC36SR5xBni8vHI= )

;; Authority
example.        3600 NS     ns1.example.
example.        3600 NS     ns2.example.
example.        3600 RRSIG  NS 5 1 3600 20040509183619 (
                            20040409183619 38519 example.
                            gl13F00f2U0R+SWiXXLHwsMY+qStYy5k6zfd
                            EuivWc+wd1fmbNCyql0Tk7lHTX6UOxc8AgNf
                            4ISFve8XqF4q+o9qlnqIzmppU3LiNeKT4FZ8
                            RO5urFOvoMRTbQxW3U0hXWuggE4g3ZpsHv48
                            0HjMeRaZB/FRPGfJPajngcq6Kwg= )
x.y.w.example. 3600 NSEC    xx.example. MX RRSIG NSEC
x.y.w.example. 3600 RRSIG   NSEC 5 4 3600 20040509183619 (
                            20040409183619 38519 example.
                            OvE6WUzN2ziieJcvKPWbCAyXyP6ef8cr6Csp
                            ArVSTzKSquNwbezZmkU7E34o5lmb6CWSSSpg
                            xw098kNUFnHcQf/LzY2zqRomubrNQhJTiDTX
                            a0ArunJQCzPjOYq5t0SLjm6qp6McJI1AP5Vr
                            QoKqJDCLnoAlcPOPKAm/jJkn3jk= )

;; Additional
ai.example.    3600 IN A    192.0.2.9
ai.example.    3600 RRSIG   A 5 2 3600 20040509183619 (
                            20040409183619 38519 example.
                            pAOtzLP2MU0tDJUwHOKE5FPIIHmdYsCgTb5B
                            ERGgpnJluA9ixOyf6xxVCgrEJW0WNZSsJicd
                            hBHXfDmAGKUajUUlYSAH8tS4Znrhyymlvk3u
                            ArDu2wfT130e9UHnumaHHMpUTosKe22PblOy
                            6zrTpg9FkS0XGVmYRvOTNYx2HvQ= )
ai.example.    3600 AAAA    2001:db8::f00:baa9
ai.example.    3600 RRSIG   AAAA 5 2 3600 20040509183619 (
                            20040409183619 38519 example.
```

```
nLcpFuXdT35AcE+EoafOUkl69KB+/e56XmFK
kewXG2IadYLKAOBIoR5+VoQV3XgTcofTJNsh
1rnF6Eav2zpZB3byI6yo2bwY8MNkr4A7cL9T
dMmDwV/hWFKsbGBsj8xSCN/caEL2CWY/5XP2
sZM6QjBBLmukH30+w1z3h8PUP2o=  )
```

B.7. Wildcard No Data Error

A "no data" response for a name covered by a wildcard. The NSEC RRs prove that the matching wildcard name does not have any RRs of the requested type and that no closer match exists in the zone.

```
;; Header: QR AA DO RCODE=0
;;
;; Question
a.z.w.example.          IN AAAA

;; Answer
;; (empty)

;; Authority
example.           3600 IN SOA ns1.example. bugs.x.w.example. (
                             1081539377
                             3600
                             300
                             3600000
                             3600
                             )
example.           3600 RRSIG SOA 5 1 3600 20040509183619 (
                             20040409183619 38519 example.
                             ONx0k36rcjaxYtcNgq6iQnpNV5+drqYAsC9h
                             7TSJaHCqbhE67Sr6aH2xDUGcqQWu/n0UVzrF
                             vkgO9ebarZ0GWDKcuwlM6eNB5SiX2K74l5LW
                             DA7S/Un/IbtDq4Ay8NMNLQI7Dw7n4p8/rjkB
                             jV7j86HyQgM5e7+miRAz8V01b0I=  )
x.y.w.example. 3600 NSEC   xx.example. MX RRSIG NSEC
x.y.w.example. 3600 RRSIG  NSEC 5 4 3600 20040509183619 (
                             20040409183619 38519 example.
                             OvE6WUzN2ziieJcvKPWbCAyXyP6ef8cr6Csp
                             ArVSTzKSquNwbezZmkU7E34o5lmb6CWSSSpg
                             xw098kNUFnHcQf/LzY2zqRomubrNQhJTiDTX
                             a0ArunJQCzPjOYq5t0SLjm6qp6McJI1AP5Vr
                             QoKqJDCLnoAlcPOPKAm/jJkn3jk=  )
*.w.example.   3600 NSEC   x.w.example. MX RRSIG NSEC
*.w.example.   3600 RRSIG  NSEC 5 2 3600 20040509183619 (
                             20040409183619 38519 example.
                             r/mZnRC3I/VIcrelgIcteSxDhtsdlTDt8ng9
                             HSBlABOlzLxQtfgTnn8f+aOwJIAFe1Ee5RvU
                             5cVhQJNP5XpXMJHfyps8tVvfxSAXfahpYqtx
                             91gsmcV/1V9/bZAG55CefP9cM4Z9Y9NT9XQ8
```

167

                              s1InQ2UoIv6tJEaaKkP701j8OLA=)

```
;; Additional
;; (empty)
```

B.8. DS Child Zone No Data Error

A "no data" response for a QTYPE=DS query that was mistakenly sent to a name server for the child zone.

```
;; Header: QR AA DO RCODE=0
;;
;; Question
example.                IN DS

;; Answer
;; (empty)

;; Authority
example.         3600 IN SOA ns1.example. bugs.x.w.example. (
                             1081539377
                             3600
                             300
                             3600000
                             3600
                             )
example.         3600 RRSIG  SOA 5 1 3600 20040509183619 (
                             20040409183619 38519 example.
                             ONx0k36rcjaxYtcNgq6iQnpNV5+drqYAsC9h
                             7TSJaHCqbhE67Sr6aH2xDUGcqQWu/n0UVzrF
                             vkgO9ebarZ0GWDKcuwlM6eNB5SiX2K74l5LW
                             DA7S/Un/IbtDq4Ay8NMNLQI7Dw7n4p8/rjkB
                             jV7j86HyQgM5e7+miRAz8V01b0I= )
example.         3600 NSEC   a.example. NS SOA MX RRSIG NSEC DNSKEY
example.         3600 RRSIG  NSEC 5 1 3600 20040509183619 (
                             20040409183619 38519 example.
                             O0k558jHhyrC97ISHnislm4kLMW48C7U7cBm
                             FTfhke5iVqNRVTB1STLMpgpbDIC9hcryoO0V
                             Z9ME5xPzUEhbvGnHd5sfzgFVeGxr5Nyyq4tW
                             SDBgIBiLQUv1ivy29vhXy7WgR62dPrZ0PWvm
                             jfFJ5arXf4nPxp/kEowGgBRzY/U= )

;; Additional
;; (empty)
```

Appendix C. Authentication Examples

The examples in this section show how the response messages in Appendix B are authenticated.

C.1. Authenticating an Answer

The query in Appendix B.1 returned an MX RRset for "x.w.example.com". The corresponding RRSIG indicates that the MX RRset was signed by an "example" DNSKEY with algorithm 5 and key tag 38519. The resolver needs the corresponding DNSKEY RR in order to authenticate this answer. The discussion below describes how a resolver might obtain this DNSKEY RR.

The RRSIG indicates the original TTL of the MX RRset was 3600, and, for the purpose of authentication, the current TTL is replaced by 3600. The RRSIG labels field value of 3 indicates that the answer was not the result of wildcard expansion. The "x.w.example.com" MX RRset is placed in canonical form, and, assuming the current time falls between the signature inception and expiration dates, the signature is authenticated.

C.1.1. Authenticating the Example DNSKEY RR

This example shows the logical authentication process that starts from the a configured root DNSKEY (or DS RR) and moves down the tree to authenticate the desired "example" DNSKEY RR. Note that the logical order is presented for clarity. An implementation may choose to construct the authentication as referrals are received or to construct the authentication chain only after all RRsets have been obtained, or in any other combination it sees fit. The example here demonstrates only the logical process and does not dictate any implementation rules.

We assume the resolver starts with a configured DNSKEY RR for the root zone (or a configured DS RR for the root zone). The resolver checks whether this configured DNSKEY RR is present in the root DNSKEY RRset (or whether the DS RR matches some DNSKEY in the root DNSKEY RRset), whether this DNSKEY RR has signed the root DNSKEY RRset, and whether the signature lifetime is valid. If all these conditions are met, all keys in the DNSKEY RRset are considered authenticated. The resolver then uses one (or more) of the root DNSKEY RRs to authenticate the "example" DS RRset. Note that the resolver may have to query the root zone to obtain the root DNSKEY RRset or "example" DS RRset.

Once the DS RRset has been authenticated using the root DNSKEY, the resolver checks the "example" DNSKEY RRset for some "example" DNSKEY RR that matches one of the authenticated "example" DS RRs. If such a matching "example" DNSKEY is found, the resolver checks whether this DNSKEY RR has signed the "example" DNSKEY RRset and the signature lifetime is valid. If these conditions are met, all keys in the "example" DNSKEY RRset are considered authenticated.

Finally, the resolver checks that some DNSKEY RR in the "example" DNSKEY RRset uses algorithm 5 and has a key tag of 38519. This DNSKEY is used to authenticate the RRSIG included in the response. If multiple "example" DNSKEY RRs match this algorithm and key tag, then each DNSKEY RR is tried, and the answer is authenticated if any of the matching DNSKEY RRs validate the signature as described above.

C.2. Name Error

The query in Appendix B.2 returned NSEC RRs that prove that the requested data does not exist and no wildcard applies. The negative reply is authenticated by verifying both NSEC

RRs. The NSEC RRs are authenticated in a manner identical to that of the MX RRset discussed above.

C.3. No Data Error

The query in Appendix B.3 returned an NSEC RR that proves that the requested name exists, but the requested RR type does not exist. The negative reply is authenticated by verifying the NSEC RR. The NSEC RR is authenticated in a manner identical to that of the MX RRset discussed above.

C.4. Referral to Signed Zone

The query in Appendix B.4 returned a referral to the signed "a.example." zone. The DS RR is authenticated in a manner identical to that of the MX RRset discussed above. This DS RR is used to authenticate the "a.example" DNSKEY RRset.

Once the "a.example" DS RRset has been authenticated using the "example" DNSKEY, the resolver checks the "a.example" DNSKEY RRset for some "a.example" DNSKEY RR that matches the DS RR. If such a matching "a.example" DNSKEY is found, the resolver checks whether this DNSKEY RR has signed the "a.example" DNSKEY RRset and whether the signature lifetime is valid. If all these conditions are met, all keys in the "a.example" DNSKEY RRset are considered authenticated.

C.5. Referral to Unsigned Zone

The query in Appendix B.5 returned a referral to an unsigned "b.example." zone. The NSEC proves that no authentication leads from "example" to "b.example", and the NSEC RR is authenticated in a manner identical to that of the MX RRset discussed above.

C.6. Wildcard Expansion

The query in Appendix B.6 returned an answer that was produced as a result of wildcard expansion. The answer section contains a wildcard RRset expanded as it would be in a traditional DNS response, and the corresponding RRSIG indicates that the expanded wildcard MX RRset was signed by an "example" DNSKEY with algorithm 5 and key tag 38519. The RRSIG indicates that the original TTL of the MX RRset was 3600, and, for the purpose of authentication, the current TTL is replaced by 3600. The RRSIG labels field value of 2 indicates that the answer is the result of wildcard expansion, as the "a.z.w.example" name contains 4 labels. The name "a.z.w.w.example" is replaced by "*.w.example", the MX RRset is placed in canonical form, and, assuming that the current time falls between the signature inception and expiration dates, the signature is authenticated.

The NSEC proves that no closer match (exact or closer wildcard) could have been used to answer this query, and the NSEC RR must also be authenticated before the answer is considered valid.

C.7. Wildcard No Data Error

The query in Appendix B.7 returned NSEC RRs that prove that the requested data does not exist and no wildcard applies. The negative reply is authenticated by verifying both NSEC RRs.

C.8. DS Child Zone No Data Error

The query in Appendix B.8 returned NSEC RRs that shows the requested was answered by a child server ("example" server). The NSEC RR indicates the presence of an SOA RR, showing that the answer is from the child . Queries for the "example" DS RRset should be sent to the parent servers ("root" servers).

Authors' Addresses

Roy Arends
Telematica Instituut
Brouwerijstraat 1
7523 XC Enschede
NL

EMail: roy.arends@telin.nl

Rob Austein
Internet Systems Consortium
950 Charter Street
Redwood City, CA 94063
USA

EMail: sra@isc.org

Matt Larson
VeriSign, Inc.
21345 Ridgetop Circle
Dulles, VA 20166-6503
USA

EMail: mlarson@verisign.com

Dan Massey
Colorado State University
Department of Computer Science
Fort Collins, CO 80523-1873

EMail: massey@cs.colostate.edu

Scott Rose
National Institute for Standards and Technology
100 Bureau Drive

Gaithersburg, MD 20899-8920
USA

EMail: scott.rose@nist.gov

Full Copyright Statement

Intellectual Property

Acknowledgement

Funding for the RFC Editor function is currently provided by the Internet Society.

RFC 4310
Domain Name System (DNS) Security Extensions Mapping for the Extensible Provisioning Protocol (EPP)

Network Working Group
Request for Comments: 4310
Category: Standards Track

S. Hollenbeck
VeriSign, Inc.
November 2005

Status of this Memo

This document specifies an Internet standards track protocol for the Internet community, and requests discussion and suggestions for improvements. Please refer to the current edition of the "Internet Official Protocol Standards" (STD 1) for the standardization state and status of this protocol. Distribution of this memo is unlimited.

Copyright Notice

Copyright (C) The Internet Society (2005).

Abstract

This document describes an Extensible Provisioning Protocol (EPP) extension mapping for the provisioning and management of Domain Name System security extensions (DNSSEC) for domain names stored in a shared central repository. Specified in XML, this mapping extends the EPP domain name mapping to provide additional features required for the provisioning of DNS security extensions.

RFC 4310 Contents

1. Introduction

This document describes an extension mapping for version 1.0 of the Extensible Provisioning Protocol (EPP) described in RFC 3730 [1]. This mapping, an extension of the domain name mapping described in RFC 3731 [2], is specified using the Extensible Markup Language (XML) 1.0 [3] and XML Schema notation ([4], [5]).

The EPP core protocol specification [1] provides a complete description of EPP command and response structures. A thorough understanding of the base protocol specification is necessary to understand the mapping described in this document. Familiarity with the Domain Name System (DNS) described in RFC 1034 [11] and RFC 1035 [12] and with DNS security extensions described in RFC 4033 [13], RFC 4034 [6], and RFC 4035 [7] is required to understand the DNS security concepts described in this document.

The EPP mapping described in this document specifies a mechanism for the provisioning and management of DNS security extensions in a shared central repository. Information exchanged via this mapping can be extracted from the repository and used to publish DNSSEC delegation signer (DS) resource records as described in RFC 4034 [6].

1.1. Conventions Used in This Document

The key words "MUST", "MUST NOT", "REQUIRED", "SHALL", "SHALL NOT", "SHOULD", "SHOULD NOT", "RECOMMENDED", "MAY", and "OPTIONAL" in this document are to be interpreted as described in BCP 14, RFC 2119 [8].

In examples, "C:" represents lines sent by a protocol client, and "S:" represents lines returned by a protocol server. "////" is used to note element values that have been shortened to better fit page boundaries. Indentation and white space in examples is provided only to illustrate element relationships and is not a mandatory feature of this protocol.

XML is case sensitive. Unless stated otherwise, XML specifications and examples provided in this document MUST be interpreted in the character case presented in order to develop a conforming implementation.

2. Object Attributes

This extension adds additional elements to the EPP domain name mapping [2]. Only new element descriptions are described here.

This document describes operational scenarios in which a client can create, add, remove, and replace delegation signer (DS) information. Key data associated with the DS information MAY be provided by the client, but the server is not obligated to use the key data. The server operator MAY also issue out-of-band DNS queries to retrieve the key data from the registered domain's apex in order to evaluate the received DS information. It is RECOMMENDED that the child zone operator have this key data online in the DNS tree to allow the parent zone administrator to validate the data as necessary. The key data SHOULD have the Secure Entry Point (SEP) bit set as described in RFC 3757 [9].

2.1. Delegation Signer Information

Delegation signer (DS) information is published by a DNS server to indicate that a child zone is digitally signed and that the parent zone recognizes the indicated key as a valid zone key for the child zone. A DS RR contains four fields: a key tag field, a key algorithm number octet, an octet identifying the digest algorithm used, and a digest field. See RFC 4034 [6] for specific field formats.

2.1.1. Public Key Information

Public key information provided by a client maps to the DNSKEY RR presentation field formats described in section 2.2 of RFC 4034 [6]. A DNSKEY RR contains four fields: flags, a protocol octet, an algorithm number octet, and a public key.

2.2. Booleans

Boolean values MUST be represented in the XML Schema format described in Part 2 of the W3C XML Schema recommendation [5].

2.3. Maximum Signature Lifetime Values

Maximum signature lifetime values MUST be represented in seconds using an extended XML Schema "int" format. The base "int" format, which allows negative numbers, is described in Part 2 of the W3C XML Schema recommendation [5]. This format is further restricted to enforce a minimum value of one.

3. EPP Command Mapping

A detailed description of the EPP syntax and semantics can be found in the EPP core protocol specification [1]. The command mappings described here are specifically for use in provisioning and managing DNS security extensions via EPP.

3.1. EPP Query Commands

EPP provides three commands to retrieve object information: <check> to determine if an object is known to the server, <info> to retrieve detailed information associated with an object, and <transfer> to retrieve object transfer status information.

3.1.1. EPP <check> Command

This extension does not add any elements to the EPP <check> command or <check> response described in the EPP domain mapping [2].

3.1.2. EPP <info> Command

This extension does not add any elements to the EPP <info> command described in the EPP domain mapping [2]. Additional elements are defined for the <info> response.

When an <info> command has been processed successfully, the EPP <resData> element MUST contain child elements as described in the EPP domain mapping [2]. In addition, the EPP <extension> element MUST contain a child <secDNS:infData> element that identifies the extension namespace and the location of the extension schema. The <secDNS:infData> element contains the following child elements:

> One or more <secDNS:dsData> elements that describe the delegation signer data provided by the client for the domain. The <secDNS:dsData> element contains the following child elements:
>
>> A <secDNS:keyTag> element that contains a key tag value as described in section 5.1.1 of RFC 4034 [6].
>>
>> A <secDNS:alg> element that contains an algorithm value as described in section 5.1.2 of RFC 4034 [6].
>>
>> A <secDNS:digestType> element that contains a digest type value as described in section 5.1.3 of RFC 4034 [6].
>>
>> A <secDNS:digest> element that contains a digest value as described in section 5.1.4 of RFC 4034 [6].
>>
>> An OPTIONAL <secDNS:maxSigLife> element that indicates a child's preference for the number of seconds after signature generation when the parent's signature on the DS information provided by the child will

expire. A client SHOULD specify the same <secDNS:maxSigLife> value for all <secDNS:dsData> elements associated with a domain. If the <secDNS:maxSigLife> is not present, or if multiple <secDNS:maxSigLife> values are requested, the default signature expiration policy of the server operator (as determined using an out-of-band mechanism) applies.

An OPTIONAL <secDNS:keyData> element that describes the key data used as input in the DS hash calculation. The <secDNS:keyData> element contains the following child elements:

A <secDNS:flags> element that contains a flags field value as described in section 2.1.1 of RFC 4034 [6].

A <secDNS:protocol> element that contains a protocol field value as described in section 2.1.2 of RFC 4034 [6].

A <secDNS:alg> element that contains an algorithm number field value as described in sections 2.1.3 of RFC 4034 [6].

A <secDNS:pubKey> element that contains an encoded public key field value as described in sections 2.1.4 of RFC 4034 [6].

Example <info> Response for a Secure Delegation:

```
S:<?xml version="1.0" encoding="UTF-8" standalone="no"?>
S:<epp xmlns="urn:ietf:params:xml:ns:epp-1.0"
S:     xmlns:xsi="http://www.w3.org/2001/XMLSchema-instance"
S:     xsi:schemaLocation="urn:ietf:params:xml:ns:epp-1.0
S:     epp-1.0.xsd">
S:  <response>
S:    <result code="1000">
S:      <msg>Command completed successfully</msg>
S:    </result>
S:    <resData>
S:      <domain:infData
S:        xmlns:domain="urn:ietf:params:xml:ns:domain-1.0"
S:        xsi:schemaLocation="urn:ietf:params:xml:ns:domain-1.0
S:        domain-1.0.xsd">
S:        <domain:name>example.com</domain:name>
S:        <domain:roid>EXAMPLE1-REP</domain:roid>
S:        <domain:status s="ok"/>
S:        <domain:registrant>jd1234</domain:registrant>
S:        <domain:contact type="admin">sh8013</domain:contact>
S:        <domain:contact type="tech">sh8013</domain:contact>
S:        <domain:ns>
S:          <domain:hostObj>ns1.example.com</domain:hostObj>
S:          <domain:hostObj>ns2.example.com</domain:hostObj>
S:        </domain:ns>
S:        <domain:host>ns1.example.com</domain:host>
S:        <domain:host>ns2.example.com</domain:host>
S:        <domain:clID>ClientX</domain:clID>
S:        <domain:crID>ClientY</domain:crID>
S:        <domain:crDate>1999-04-03T22:00:00.0Z</domain:crDate>
```

```
S:          <domain:upID>ClientX</domain:upID>
S:          <domain:upDate>1999-12-03T09:00:00.0Z</domain:upDate>
S:          <domain:exDate>2005-04-03T22:00:00.0Z</domain:exDate>
S:          <domain:trDate>2000-04-08T09:00:00.0Z</domain:trDate>
S:          <domain:authInfo>
S:            <domain:pw>2fooBAR</domain:pw>
S:          </domain:authInfo>
S:        </domain:infData>
S:      </resData>
S:      <extension>
S:        <secDNS:infData
S:         xmlns:secDNS="urn:ietf:params:xml:ns:secDNS-1.0"
S:         xsi:schemaLocation="urn:ietf:params:xml:ns:secDNS-1.0
S:         secDNS-1.0.xsd">
S:          <secDNS:dsData>
S:            <secDNS:keyTag>12345</secDNS:keyTag>
S:            <secDNS:alg>3</secDNS:alg>
S:            <secDNS:digestType>1</secDNS:digestType>
S:            <secDNS:digest>49FD46E6C4B45C55D4AC</secDNS:digest>
S:          </secDNS:dsData>
S:        </secDNS:infData>
S:      </extension>
S:      <trID>
S:        <clTRID>ABC-12345</clTRID>
S:        <svTRID>54322-XYZ</svTRID>
S:      </trID>
S:    </response>
S:</epp>
```

Example <info> Response for a Secure Delegation with OPTIONAL Data:

```
S:<?xml version="1.0" encoding="UTF-8" standalone="no"?>
S:<epp xmlns="urn:ietf:params:xml:ns:epp-1.0"
S:     xmlns:xsi="http://www.w3.org/2001/XMLSchema-instance"
S:     xsi:schemaLocation="urn:ietf:params:xml:ns:epp-1.0
S:     epp-1.0.xsd">
S:  <response>
S:    <result code="1000">
S:      <msg>Command completed successfully</msg>
S:    </result>
S:    <resData>
S:      <domain:infData
S:       xmlns:domain="urn:ietf:params:xml:ns:domain-1.0"
S:       xsi:schemaLocation="urn:ietf:params:xml:ns:domain-1.0
S:       domain-1.0.xsd">
S:        <domain:name>example.com</domain:name>
S:        <domain:roid>EXAMPLE1-REP</domain:roid>
S:        <domain:status s="ok"/>
S:        <domain:registrant>jd1234</domain:registrant>
S:        <domain:contact type="admin">sh8013</domain:contact>
S:        <domain:contact type="tech">sh8013</domain:contact>
S:        <domain:ns>
```

```
S:            <domain:hostObj>ns1.example.com</domain:hostObj>
S:            <domain:hostObj>ns2.example.com</domain:hostObj>
S:          </domain:ns>
S:          <domain:host>ns1.example.com</domain:host>
S:          <domain:host>ns2.example.com</domain:host>
S:          <domain:clID>ClientX</domain:clID>
S:          <domain:crID>ClientY</domain:crID>
S:          <domain:crDate>1999-04-03T22:00:00.0Z</domain:crDate>
S:          <domain:upID>ClientX</domain:upID>
S:          <domain:upDate>1999-12-03T09:00:00.0Z</domain:upDate>
S:          <domain:exDate>2005-04-03T22:00:00.0Z</domain:exDate>
S:          <domain:trDate>2000-04-08T09:00:00.0Z</domain:trDate>
S:          <domain:authInfo>
S:            <domain:pw>2fooBAR</domain:pw>
S:          </domain:authInfo>
S:        </domain:infData>
S:      </resData>
S:      <extension>
S:        <secDNS:infData
S:          xmlns:secDNS="urn:ietf:params:xml:ns:secDNS-1.0"
S:          xsi:schemaLocation="urn:ietf:params:xml:ns:secDNS-1.0
S:          secDNS-1.0.xsd">
S:          <secDNS:dsData>
S:            <secDNS:keyTag>12345</secDNS:keyTag>
S:            <secDNS:alg>3</secDNS:alg>
S:            <secDNS:digestType>1</secDNS:digestType>
S:            <secDNS:digest>49FD46E6C4B45C55D4AC</secDNS:digest>
S:            <secDNS:maxSigLife>604800</secDNS:maxSigLife>
S:            <secDNS:keyData>
S:              <secDNS:flags>256</secDNS:flags>
S:              <secDNS:protocol>3</secDNS:protocol>
S:              <secDNS:alg>1</secDNS:alg>
S:              <secDNS:pubKey>AQPJ////4Q==</secDNS:pubKey>
S:            </secDNS:keyData>
S:          </secDNS:dsData>
S:        </secDNS:infData>
S:      </extension>
S:      <trID>
S:        <clTRID>ABC-12345</clTRID>
S:        <svTRID>54322-XYZ</svTRID>
S:      </trID>
S:    </response>
S:</epp>
```

An EPP error response MUST be returned if an <info> command can not be processed for any reason.

3.1.3. EPP <transfer> Command

This extension does not add any elements to the EPP <transfer> command or <transfer> response described in the EPP domain mapping [2].

3.2. EPP Transform Commands

EPP provides five commands to transform objects: <create> to create an instance of an object, <delete> to delete an instance of an object, <renew> to extend the validity period of an object, <transfer> to manage object sponsorship changes, and <update> to change information associated with an object.

3.2.1. EPP <create> Command

This extension defines additional elements for the EPP <create> command described in the EPP domain mapping [2]. No additional elements are defined for the EPP <create> response.

The EPP <create> command provides a transform operation that allows a client to create a domain object. In addition to the EPP command elements described in the EPP domain mapping [2], the command MUST contain an <extension> element. The <extension> element MUST contain a child <secDNS:create> element that identifies the extension namespace and the location of the extension schema. The <secDNS:create> element MUST contain one or more <secDNS:dsData> elements. Child elements of the <secDNS:dsData> element are described in Section 3.1.2.

The <secDNS:dsData> element contains OPTIONAL <secDNS:maxSigLife> and <secDNS:keyData> elements. The server MUST abort command processing and respond with an appropriate EPP error if the values provided by the client can not be accepted for syntax or policy reasons.

Example <create> Command for a Secure Delegation:

```
C:<?xml version="1.0" encoding="UTF−8" standalone="no"?>
C:<epp xmlns="urn:ietf:params:xml:ns:epp−1.0"
C:      xmlns:xsi="http://www.w3.org/2001/XMLSchema−instance"
C:      xsi:schemaLocation="urn:ietf:params:xml:ns:epp−1.0
C:      epp−1.0.xsd">
C:   <command>
C:     <create>
C:       <domain:create
C:        xmlns:domain="urn:ietf:params:xml:ns:domain−1.0"
C:        xsi:schemaLocation="urn:ietf:params:xml:ns:domain−1.0
C:        domain−1.0.xsd">
C:        <domain:name>example.com</domain:name>
C:        <domain:period unit="y">2</domain:period>
C:        <domain:ns>
C:          <domain:hostObj>ns1.example.com</domain:hostObj>
C:          <domain:hostObj>ns2.example.com</domain:hostObj>
C:        </domain:ns>
C:        <domain:registrant>jd1234</domain:registrant>
C:        <domain:contact type="admin">sh8013</domain:contact>
C:        <domain:contact type="tech">sh8013</domain:contact>
C:        <domain:authInfo>
C:          <domain:pw>2fooBAR</domain:pw>
C:        </domain:authInfo>
C:       </domain:create>
```

```
C:     </create>
C:     <extension>
C:       <secDNS:create
C:        xmlns:secDNS="urn:ietf:params:xml:ns:secDNS-1.0"
C:        xsi:schemaLocation="urn:ietf:params:xml:ns:secDNS-1.0
C:        secDNS-1.0.xsd">
C:         <secDNS:dsData>
C:           <secDNS:keyTag>12345</secDNS:keyTag>
C:           <secDNS:alg>3</secDNS:alg>
C:           <secDNS:digestType>1</secDNS:digestType>
C:           <secDNS:digest>49FD46E6C4B45C55D4AC</secDNS:digest>
C:         </secDNS:dsData>
C:       </secDNS:create>
C:     </extension>
C:     <clTRID>ABC-12345</clTRID>
C:   </command>
C:</epp>
```

Example <create> Command for a Secure Delegation with OPTIONAL data:

```
C:<?xml version="1.0" encoding="UTF-8" standalone="no"?>
C:<epp xmlns="urn:ietf:params:xml:ns:epp-1.0"
C:       xmlns:xsi="http://www.w3.org/2001/XMLSchema-instance"
C:       xsi:schemaLocation="urn:ietf:params:xml:ns:epp-1.0
C:       epp-1.0.xsd">
C:   <command>
C:     <create>
C:       <domain:create
C:        xmlns:domain="urn:ietf:params:xml:ns:domain-1.0"
C:        xsi:schemaLocation="urn:ietf:params:xml:ns:domain-1.0
C:        domain-1.0.xsd">
C:         <domain:name>example.com</domain:name>
C:         <domain:period unit="y">2</domain:period>
C:         <domain:ns>
C:           <domain:hostObj>ns1.example.com</domain:hostObj>
C:           <domain:hostObj>ns2.example.com</domain:hostObj>
C:         </domain:ns>
C:         <domain:registrant>jd1234</domain:registrant>
C:         <domain:contact type="admin">sh8013</domain:contact>
C:         <domain:contact type="tech">sh8013</domain:contact>
C:         <domain:authInfo>
C:           <domain:pw>2fooBAR</domain:pw>
C:         </domain:authInfo>
C:       </domain:create>
C:     </create>
C:     <extension>
C:       <secDNS:create
C:        xmlns:secDNS="urn:ietf:params:xml:ns:secDNS-1.0"
C:        xsi:schemaLocation="urn:ietf:params:xml:ns:secDNS-1.0
C:        secDNS-1.0.xsd">
C:         <secDNS:dsData>
C:           <secDNS:keyTag>12345</secDNS:keyTag>
```

```
C:          <secDNS:alg>3</secDNS:alg>
C:          <secDNS:digestType>1</secDNS:digestType>
C:          <secDNS:digest>49FD46E6C4B45C55D4AC</secDNS:digest>
C:          <secDNS:maxSigLife>604800</secDNS:maxSigLife>
C:          <secDNS:keyData>
C:            <secDNS:flags>256</secDNS:flags>
C:            <secDNS:protocol>3</secDNS:protocol>
C:            <secDNS:alg>1</secDNS:alg>
C:            <secDNS:pubKey>AQPJ////4Q==</secDNS:pubKey>
C:          </secDNS:keyData>
C:        </secDNS:dsData>
C:      </secDNS:create>
C:    </extension>
C:    <clTRID>ABC-12345</clTRID>
C:  </command>
C:</epp>
```

When a <create> command has been processed successfully, the EPP response is as described in the EPP domain mapping [2].

3.2.2. EPP <delete> Command

This extension does not add any elements to the EPP <delete> command or <delete> response described in the EPP domain mapping [2].

3.2.3. EPP <renew> Command

This extension does not add any elements to the EPP <renew> command or <renew> response described in the EPP domain mapping [2].

3.2.4. EPP <transfer> Command

This extension does not add any elements to the EPP <transfer> command or <transfer> response described in the EPP domain mapping [2].

3.2.5. EPP <update> Command

This extension defines additional elements for the EPP <update> command described in the EPP domain mapping [2]. No additional elements are defined for the EPP <update> response.

The EPP <update> command provides a transform operation that allows a client to modify the attributes of a domain object. In addition to the EPP command elements described in the EPP domain mapping, the command MUST contain an <extension> element. The <extension> element MUST contain a child <secDNS:update> element that identifies the extension namespace and the location of the extension schema. The <secDNS:update> element contains a <secDNS:add> element to add security information to a delegation, a

<secDNS:rem> element to remove security information from a delegation, or a <secDNS:chg>
element to replace security information with new security information.

The <secDNS:update> element also contains an OPTIONAL "urgent" attribute that a client
can use to ask the server operator to complete and implement the update request with high
priority. This attribute accepts boolean values as described in Section 2.2; the default value
is boolean false. "High priority" is relative to standard server operator policies that are
determined using an out-of-band mechanism.

The <secDNS:add> element is used to add DS information to an existing set. The <secDNS:add>
element MUST contain one or more <secDNS:dsData> elements as described in Section 3.1.2.

The <secDNS:rem> element contains one or more <secDNS:keyTag> elements that are used
to remove DS data from a delegation. The <secDNS:keyTag> element MUST contain a key tag
value as described in section 5.1.1 of RFC 4034 [6]. Removing all DS information can remove
the ability of the parent to secure the delegation to the child zone.

The <secDNS:chg> element is used to replace existing DS information with new DS information. The <secDNS:chg> element MUST contain one or more <secDNS:dsData> elements as
described in Section 3.1.2. The data in these elements is used to replace whatever other data is
currently archived for the delegation.

The <secDNS:update> element contains an OPTIONAL "urgent" attribute. In addition, the
<secDNS:dsData> element contains OPTIONAL <secDNS:maxSigLife> and <secDNS:keyData>
elements. The server MUST abort command processing and respond with an appropriate EPP
error if the values provided by the client can not be accepted for syntax or policy reasons.

Example <update> Command, Adding DS Data:

```
C:<?xml version="1.0" encoding="UTF-8" standalone="no"?>
C:<epp xmlns="urn:ietf:params:xml:ns:epp-1.0"
C:     xmlns:xsi="http://www.w3.org/2001/XMLSchema-instance"
C:     xsi:schemaLocation="urn:ietf:params:xml:ns:epp-1.0
C:     epp-1.0.xsd">
C:  <command>
C:    <update>
C:      <domain:update
C:        xmlns:domain="urn:ietf:params:xml:ns:domain-1.0"
C:        xsi:schemaLocation="urn:ietf:params:xml:ns:domain-1.0
C:        domain-1.0.xsd">
C:        <domain:name>example.com</domain:name>
C:      </domain:update>
C:    </update>
C:    <extension>
C:      <secDNS:update
C:        xmlns:secDNS="urn:ietf:params:xml:ns:secDNS-1.0"
C:        xsi:schemaLocation="urn:ietf:params:xml:ns:secDNS-1.0
C:        secDNS-1.0.xsd">
C:        <secDNS:add>
C:          <secDNS:dsData>
C:            <secDNS:keyTag>12346</secDNS:keyTag>
C:            <secDNS:alg>3</secDNS:alg>
C:            <secDNS:digestType>1</secDNS:digestType>
```

```
C:                    <secDNS:digest>38EC35D5B3A34B44C39B</secDNS:digest>
C:                  </secDNS:dsData>
C:                </secDNS:add>
C:              </secDNS:update>
C:           </extension>
C:           <clTRID>ABC-12345</clTRID>
C:         </command>
C:</epp>
```

Example <update> Command, Removing DS Data:

```
C:<?xml version="1.0" encoding="UTF-8" standalone="no"?>
C:<epp xmlns="urn:ietf:params:xml:ns:epp-1.0"
C:      xmlns:xsi="http://www.w3.org/2001/XMLSchema-instance"
C:      xsi:schemaLocation="urn:ietf:params:xml:ns:epp-1.0
C:      epp-1.0.xsd">
C:   <command>
C:     <update>
C:       <domain:update
C:        xmlns:domain="urn:ietf:params:xml:ns:domain-1.0"
C:        xsi:schemaLocation="urn:ietf:params:xml:ns:domain-1.0
C:        domain-1.0.xsd">
C:         <domain:name>example.com</domain:name>
C:       </domain:update>
C:     </update>
C:     <extension>
C:       <secDNS:update
C:        xmlns:secDNS="urn:ietf:params:xml:ns:secDNS-1.0"
C:        xsi:schemaLocation="urn:ietf:params:xml:ns:secDNS-1.0
C:        secDNS-1.0.xsd">
C:         <secDNS:rem>
C:            <secDNS:keyTag>12345</secDNS:keyTag>
C:         </secDNS:rem>
C:       </secDNS:update>
C:     </extension>
C:     <clTRID>ABC-12345</clTRID>
C:   </command>
C:</epp>
```

Example Urgent <update> Command, Changing DS Data:

```
C:<?xml version="1.0" encoding="UTF-8" standalone="no"?>
C:<epp xmlns="urn:ietf:params:xml:ns:epp-1.0"
C:      xmlns:xsi="http://www.w3.org/2001/XMLSchema-instance"
C:      xsi:schemaLocation="urn:ietf:params:xml:ns:epp-1.0
C:      epp-1.0.xsd">
C:   <command>
C:     <update>
C:       <domain:update
C:        xmlns:domain="urn:ietf:params:xml:ns:domain-1.0"
C:        xsi:schemaLocation="urn:ietf:params:xml:ns:domain-1.0
C:        domain-1.0.xsd">
```

```
C:            <domain:name>example.com</domain:name>
C:          </domain:update>
C:        </update>
C:        <extension>
C:          <secDNS:update urgent="1"
C:            xmlns:secDNS="urn:ietf:params:xml:ns:secDNS−1.0"
C:            xsi:schemaLocation="urn:ietf:params:xml:ns:secDNS−1.0
C:            secDNS−1.0.xsd">
C:            <secDNS:chg>
C:              <secDNS:dsData>
C:                <secDNS:keyTag>12345</secDNS:keyTag>
C:                <secDNS:alg>3</secDNS:alg>
C:                <secDNS:digestType>1</secDNS:digestType>
C:                <secDNS:digest>49FD46E6C4B45C55D4AC</secDNS:digest>
C:              </secDNS:dsData>
C:            </secDNS:chg>
C:          </secDNS:update>
C:        </extension>
C:        <clTRID>ABC−12345</clTRID>
C:      </command>
C:</epp>
```

Example <update> Command, Changing Data to Include OPTIONAL Data:

```
C:<?xml version="1.0" encoding="UTF−8" standalone="no"?>
C:<epp xmlns="urn:ietf:params:xml:ns:epp−1.0"
C:      xmlns:xsi="http://www.w3.org/2001/XMLSchema−instance"
C:      xsi:schemaLocation="urn:ietf:params:xml:ns:epp−1.0
C:      epp−1.0.xsd">
C:    <command>
C:      <update>
C:        <domain:update
C:          xmlns:domain="urn:ietf:params:xml:ns:domain−1.0"
C:          xsi:schemaLocation="urn:ietf:params:xml:ns:domain−1.0
C:          domain−1.0.xsd">
C:          <domain:name>example.com</domain:name>
C:        </domain:update>
C:      </update>
C:      <extension>
C:        <secDNS:update
C:          xmlns:secDNS="urn:ietf:params:xml:ns:secDNS−1.0"
C:          xsi:schemaLocation="urn:ietf:params:xml:ns:secDNS−1.0
C:          secDNS−1.0.xsd">
C:          <secDNS:chg>
C:            <secDNS:dsData>
C:              <secDNS:keyTag>12345</secDNS:keyTag>
C:              <secDNS:alg>3</secDNS:alg>
C:              <secDNS:digestType>1</secDNS:digestType>
C:              <secDNS:digest>49FD46E6C4B45C55D4AC</secDNS:digest>
C:              <secDNS:maxSigLife>604800</secDNS:maxSigLife>
C:              <secDNS:keyData>
C:                <secDNS:flags>256</secDNS:flags>
```

```
C:                    <secDNS:protocol>3</secDNS:protocol>
C:                    <secDNS:alg>1</secDNS:alg>
C:                    <secDNS:pubKey>AQPJ////4Q==</secDNS:pubKey>
C:                 </secDNS:keyData>
C:               </secDNS:dsData>
C:             </secDNS:chg>
C:           </secDNS:update>
C:         </extension>
C:         <clTRID>ABC-12345</clTRID>
C:    </command>
C:</epp>
```

When an extended <update> command has been processed successfully, the EPP response is as described in the EPP domain mapping [2]. A server operator MUST return an EPP error result code of 2306 if an urgent update (noted with an "urgent" attribute value of boolean true) can not be completed with high priority.

4. Formal Syntax

An EPP object mapping is specified in XML Schema notation. The formal syntax presented here is a complete schema representation of the object mapping suitable for automated validation of EPP XML instances. The BEGIN and END tags are not part of the schema; they are used to note the beginning and ending of the schema for URI registration purposes.

```
BEGIN
<?xml version="1.0" encoding="UTF-8"?>

<schema targetNamespace="urn:ietf:params:xml:ns:secDNS-1.0"
        xmlns:secDNS="urn:ietf:params:xml:ns:secDNS-1.0"
        xmlns="http://www.w3.org/2001/XMLSchema"
        elementFormDefault="qualified">

   <annotation>
     <documentation>
       Extensible Provisioning Protocol v1.0
       domain name extension schema for provisioning
       DNS security (DNSSEC) extensions.
     </documentation>
   </annotation>

<!--
Child elements found in EPP commands.
-->
   <element name="create" type="secDNS:dsType"/>
   <element name="update" type="secDNS:updateType"/>

<!--
Child elements of the <create> command.
-->
```

```
<complexType name="dsType">
  <sequence>
    <element name="dsData" type="secDNS:dsDataType"
      maxOccurs="unbounded"/>
  </sequence>
</complexType>

<complexType name="dsDataType">
  <sequence>
    <element name="keyTag" type="unsignedShort"/>
    <element name="alg" type="unsignedByte"/>
    <element name="digestType" type="unsignedByte"/>
    <element name="digest" type="hexBinary"/>
    <element name="maxSigLife" type="secDNS:maxSigLifeType"
      minOccurs="0"/>
    <element name="keyData" type="secDNS:keyDataType"
      minOccurs="0"/>
  </sequence>
</complexType>

<simpleType name="maxSigLifeType">
  <restriction base="int">
    <minInclusive value="1"/>
  </restriction>
</simpleType>

<complexType name="keyDataType">
  <sequence>
    <element name="flags" type="unsignedShort"/>
    <element name="protocol" type="unsignedByte"/>
    <element name="alg" type="unsignedByte"/>
    <element name="pubKey" type="secDNS:keyType"/>
  </sequence>
</complexType>

<simpleType name="keyType">
  <restriction base="base64Binary">
    <minLength value="1"/>
  </restriction>
</simpleType>

<!--
Child elements of the <update> command.
-->
<complexType name="updateType">
  <choice>
    <element name="add" type="secDNS:dsType"/>
    <element name="chg" type="secDNS:dsType"/>
    <element name="rem" type="secDNS:remType"/>
  </choice>
  <attribute name="urgent" type="boolean" default="false"/>
```

```
    </complexType>

    <complexType name="remType">
      <sequence>
        <element name="keyTag" type="unsignedShort"
          maxOccurs="unbounded"/>
      </sequence>
    </complexType>

  <!--
  Child response elements.
  -->
    <element name="infData" type="secDNS:dsType"/>

  <!--
  End of schema.
  -->
  </schema>
  END
```

5. Internationalization Considerations

EPP is represented in XML, which provides native support for encoding information using the Unicode character set and its more compact representations including UTF-8 [14]. Conformant XML processors recognize both UTF-8 and UTF-16 [15]. Though XML includes provisions to identify and use other character encodings through use of an "encoding" attribute in an <?xml?> declaration, use of UTF-8 is RECOMMENDED in environments where parser encoding support incompatibility exists.

As an extension of the EPP domain mapping [2], the elements, element content, attributes, and attribute values described in this document MUST inherit the internationalization conventions used to represent higher-layer domain and core protocol structures present in an XML instance that includes this extension.

6. IANA Considerations

This document uses URNs to describe XML namespaces and XML schemas conforming to a registry mechanism described in RFC 3688 [10]. Two URI assignments have been completed by the IANA.

Registration request for the extension namespace:

URI: urn:ietf:params:xml:ns:secDNS-1.0

Registrant Contact: IESG

XML: None. Namespace URIs do not represent an XML specification.

Registration request for the extension XML schema:

URI: urn:ietf:params:xml:schema:secDNS-1.0

Registrant Contact: IESG

XML: See the "Formal Syntax" section of this document.

7. Security Considerations

The mapping extensions described in this document do not provide any security services beyond those described by EPP [1], the EPP domain name mapping [2], and protocol layers used by EPP. The security considerations described in these other specifications apply to this specification as well.

As with other domain object transforms, the EPP transform operations described in this document MUST be restricted to the sponsoring client as authenticated using the mechanisms described in sections 2.9.1.1 and 7 of RFC 3730 [1]. Any attempt to perform a transform operation on a domain object by any client other than the sponsoring client MUST be rejected with an appropriate EPP authorization error.

The provisioning service described in this document involves the exchange of information that can have an operational impact on the DNS. A trust relationship MUST exist between the EPP client and server, and provisioning of public key information MUST only be done after the identities of both parties have been confirmed using a strong authentication mechanism.

An EPP client might be acting as an agent for a zone administrator who wants to send delegation information to be signed and published by the server operator. Man-in-the-middle attacks are thus possible as a result of direct client activity or inadvertent client data manipulation.

Acceptance of a false key by a server operator can produce significant operational consequences. The child and parent zones MUST be consistent to secure the delegation properly. In the absence of consistent signatures, the delegation will not appear in the secure name space, yielding untrustworthy query responses. If a key is compromised, a client can either remove the compromised information or update the delegation information via EPP commands using the "urgent" attribute.

Operational scenarios requiring quick removal of a secure domain delegation can be implemented using a two-step process. First, security credentials can be removed using an "urgent" update as just described. The domain can then be removed from the parent zone by changing the status of the domain to either of the EPP "clientHold" or "serverHold" domain status values. The domain can also be removed from the zone using the EPP <delete> command, but this is a more drastic step that needs to be considered carefully before use.

Data validity checking at the server requires computational resources. A purposeful or inadvertent denial-of-service attack is possible if a client requests some number of update operations that exceed a server's processing capabilities. Server operators SHOULD take steps to manage command load and command processing requirements to minimize the risk of a denial-of-service attack.

The signature lifetime values provided by clients are requests that can be rejected. Blind acceptance by a server operator can have an adverse impact on a server's processing capabilities.

Server operators SHOULD seriously consider adopting implementation rules to limit the range of acceptable signature lifetime values to counter potential adverse situations.

8. Acknowledgements

The author would like to thank the following people who have provided significant contributions to the development of this document:

David Blacka, Olafur Gudmundsson, Mark Kosters, Ed Lewis, Dan Massey, Marcos Sanz, Sam Weiler, and Ning Zhang.

9. References

9.1. Normative References

[1]   Hollenbeck, S., "Extensible Provisioning Protocol (EPP)", RFC 3730, March 2004.

[2]   Hollenbeck, S., "Extensible Provisioning Protocol (EPP) Domain Name Mapping", RFC 3731, March 2004.

[3]   Paoli, J., Sperberg-McQueen, C., Bray, T., and E. Maler, "Extensible Markup Language (XML) 1.0 (Second Edition)", W3C FirstEdition REC-xml-20001006, October 2000.

[4]   Maloney, M., Beech, D., Mendelsohn, N., and H. Thompson, "XML Schema Part 1: Structures", W3C REC REC-xmlschema-1-20010502, May 2001.

[5]   Malhotra, A. and P. Biron, "XML Schema Part 2: Datatypes", W3C REC REC-xmlschema-2-20010502, May 2001.

[6]   Arends, R., Austein, R., Larson, M., Massey, D., and S. Rose, "Resource Records for the DNS Security Extensions", RFC 4034, March 2005.

[7]   Arends, R., Austein, R., Larson, M., Massey, D., and S. Rose, "Protocol Modifications for the DNS Security Extensions", RFC 4035, March 2005.

[8]   Bradner, S., "Key words for use in RFCs to Indicate Requirement Levels", BCP 14, RFC 2119, March 1997.

[9]   Kolkman, O., Schlyter, J., and E. Lewis, "Domain Name System KEY (DNSKEY) Resource Record (RR) Secure Entry Point (SEP) Flag", RFC 3757, April 2004.

[10]   Mealling, M., "The IETF XML Registry", BCP 81, RFC 3688, January 2004.

9.2. Informative References

[11]   Mockapetris, P., "Domain names - concepts and facilities", STD 13, RFC 1034, November 1987.

[12]   Mockapetris, P., "Domain names - implementation and specification", STD 13, RFC 1035, November 1987.

[13]   Arends, R., Austein, R., Larson, M., Massey, D., and S. Rose, "DNS Security Introduction and Requirements", RFC 4033, March 2005.

[14]   Yergeau, F., "UTF-8, a transformation format of ISO 10646", STD 63, RFC 3629, November 2003.

[15]   Hoffman, P. and F. Yergeau, "UTF-16, an encoding of ISO 10646", RFC 2781, February 2000.

Author's Address

Scott Hollenbeck
VeriSign, Inc.
21345 Ridgetop Circle
Dulles, VA 20166-6503
US

EMail: shollenbeck@verisign.com

Full Copyright Statement

Intellectual Property

The IETF takes no position regarding the validity or scope of any Intellectual Property Rights or other rights that might be claimed to pertain to the implementation or use of the technology described in this document or the extent to which any license under such rights might or might not be available; nor does it represent that it has made any independent effort to identify any such rights. Information on the procedures with respect to rights in RFC documents can be found in BCP 78 and BCP 79.

Copies of IPR disclosures made to the IETF Secretariat and any assurances of licenses to be made available, or the result of an attempt made to obtain a general license or permission for the use of such proprietary rights by implementers or users of this specification can be obtained from the IETF on-line IPR repository at http://www.ietf.org/ipr.

The IETF invites any interested party to bring to its attention any copyrights, patents or patent applications, or other proprietary rights that may cover technology that may be required to implement this standard. Please address the information to the IETF at ietf-ipr@ietf.org.

Acknowledgement

Funding for the RFC Editor function is currently provided by the Internet Society.

RFC 4431
The DNSSEC Lookaside Validation (DLV) DNS Resource Record

Network Working Group
Request for Comments: 4431
Category: Informational

M. Andrews
Internet Systems Consortium
S. Weiler
SPARTA, Inc.
February 2006

Status of This Memo

This memo provides information for the Internet community. It does not specify an Internet standard of any kind. Distribution of this memo is unlimited.

Copyright Notice

Abstract

This document defines a new DNS resource record, called the DNSSEC Lookaside Validation (DLV) RR, for publishing DNSSEC trust anchors outside of the DNS delegation chain.

RFC 4431 Contents

1. Introduction

DNSSEC [1] [2] [3] authenticates DNS data by building public-key signature chains along the DNS delegation chain from a trust anchor, ideally a trust anchor for the DNS root.

This document defines a new resource record for publishing such trust anchors outside of the DNS's normal delegation chain. Use of these records by DNSSEC validators is outside the scope of this document, but it is expected that these records will help resolvers validate DNSSEC-signed data from zones whose ancestors either aren't signed or refuse to publish delegation signer (DS) records for their children.

2. DLV Resource Record

The DLV resource record has exactly the same wire and presentation formats as the DS resource record, defined in RFC 4034, Section 5. It uses the same IANA-assigned values in the algorithm and digest type fields as the DS record. (Those IANA registries are known as the "DNS Security Algorithm Numbers" and "DS RR Type Algorithm Numbers" registries.) The DLV record is a normal DNS record type without any special processing requirements. In particular, the DLV record does not inherit any of the special processing or handling requirements of the DS record type (described in Section 3.1.4.1 of RFC 4035). Unlike the DS record, the DLV record may not appear on the parent's side of a zone cut. A DLV record may, however, appear at the apex of a zone.

3. Security Considerations

For authoritative servers and resolvers that do not attempt to use DLV RRs as part of DNSSEC validation, there are no particular security concerns – DLV RRs are just like any other DNS data.

Software using DLV RRs as part of DNSSEC validation will almost certainly want to impose constraints on their use, but those constraints are best left to be described by the documents that more fully describe the particulars of how the records are used. At a minimum, it would be unwise to use the records without some sort of cryptographic authentication. More likely than not, DNSSEC itself will be used to authenticate the DLV RRs. Depending on how a DLV RR is used, failure to properly authenticate it could lead to significant additional security problems including failure to detect spoofed DNS data.

RFC 4034, Section 8, describes security considerations specific to the DS RR. Those considerations are equally applicable to DLV RRs. Of particular note, the key tag field is used to help select DNSKEY RRs efficiently, but it does not uniquely identify a single DNSKEY RR. It is possible for two distinct DNSKEY RRs to have the same owner name, the same algorithm type, and the same key tag. An implementation that uses only the key tag to select a DNSKEY RR might select the wrong public key in some circumstances.

For further discussion of the security implications of DNSSEC, see RFC 4033, RFC 4034, and RFC 4035.

4. IANA Considerations

IANA has assigned DNS type code 32769 to the DLV resource record from the Specification Required portion of the DNS Resource Record Type registry, as defined in [4].

The DLV resource record reuses the same algorithm and digest type registries already used for the DS resource record, currently known as the "DNS Security Algorithm Numbers" and "DS RR Type Algorithm Numbers" registries.

5. Normative References

[1]   Arends, R., Austein, R., Larson, M., Massey, D., and S. Rose, "DNS Security Introduction and Requirements", RFC 4033, March 2005.

[2]   Arends, R., Austein, R., Larson, M., Massey, D., and S. Rose, "Resource Records for the DNS Security Extensions", RFC 4034, March 2005.

[3]   Arends, R., Austein, R., Larson, M., Massey, D., and S. Rose, "Protocol Modifications for the DNS Security Extensions", RFC 4035, March 2005.

[4]   Eastlake, D., Brunner-Williams, E., and B. Manning, "Domain Name System (DNS) IANA Considerations", BCP 42, RFC 2929, September 2000.

Authors' Addresses

Mark Andrews
Internet Systems Consortium
950 Charter St.
Redwood City, CA 94063
US

EMail: Mark_Andrews@isc.org

Samuel Weiler
SPARTA, Inc.
7075 Samuel Morse Drive
Columbia, Maryland 21046
US

EMail: weiler@tislabs.com

Full Copyright Statement

Intellectual Property

Acknowledgement

Funding for the RFC Editor function is provided by the IETF Administrative Support Activity (IASA).

RFC 4470
Minimally Covering NSEC Records and DNSSEC On-line Signing

Network Working Group
Request for Comments: 4470
Updates: 4035, 4034
Category: Standards Track

S. Weiler
SPARTA, Inc.
J. Ihren
Autonomica AB
April 2006

Status of This Memo

This document specifies an Internet standards track protocol for the Internet community, and requests discussion and suggestions for improvements. Please refer to the current edition of the "Internet Official Protocol Standards" (STD 1) for the standardization state and status of this protocol. Distribution of this memo is unlimited.

Copyright Notice

Abstract

This document describes how to construct DNSSEC NSEC resource records that cover a smaller range of names than called for by RFC 4034. By generating and signing these records on demand, authoritative name servers can effectively stop the disclosure of zone contents otherwise made possible by walking the chain of NSEC records in a signed zone.

RFC 4470 Contents

1. Introduction

With DNSSEC [1], an NSEC record lists the next instantiated name in its zone, proving that no names exist in the "span" between the NSEC's owner name and the name in the "next name" field. In this document, an NSEC record is said to "cover" the names between its owner name and next name.

Through repeated queries that return NSEC records, it is possible to retrieve all of the names in the zone, a process commonly called "walking" the zone. Some zone owners have policies forbidding zone transfers by arbitrary clients; this side effect of the NSEC architecture subverts those policies.

This document presents a way to prevent zone walking by constructing NSEC records that cover fewer names. These records can make zone walking take approximately as many queries as simply asking for all possible names in a zone, making zone walking impractical. Some of these records must be created and signed on demand, which requires on-line private keys. Anyone contemplating use of this technique is strongly encouraged to review the discussion of the risks of on-line signing in Section 5.

1.2. Keywords

The keywords "MUST", "MUST NOT", "REQUIRED", "SHALL", "SHALL NOT", "SHOULD", "SHOULD NOT", "RECOMMENDED", "MAY", and "OPTIONAL" in this document are to be interpreted as described in RFC 2119 [4].

2. Applicability of This Technique

The technique presented here may be useful to a zone owner that wants to use DNSSEC, is concerned about exposure of its zone contents via zone walking, and is willing to bear the costs of on-line signing.

As discussed in Section 5, on-line signing has several security risks, including an increased likelihood of private keys being disclosed and an increased risk of denial of service attack. Anyone contemplating use of this technique is strongly encouraged to review the discussion of the risks of on-line signing in Section 5.

Furthermore, at the time this document was published, the DNSEXT working group was actively working on a mechanism to prevent zone walking that does not require on-line signing (tentatively called NSEC3). The new mechanism is likely to expose slightly more information about the zone than this technique (e.g., the number of instantiated names), but it may be preferable to this technique.

3. Minimally Covering NSEC Records

This mechanism involves changes to NSEC records for instantiated names, which can still be generated and signed in advance, as well as the on-demand generation and signing of new NSEC records whenever a name must be proven not to exist.

In the "next name" field of instantiated names' NSEC records, rather than list the next instantiated name in the zone, list any name that falls lexically after the NSEC's owner name and before the next instantiated name in the zone, according to the ordering function in RFC 4034 [2] Section 6.1. This relaxes the requirement in Section 4.1.1 of RFC 4034 that the "next name" field contains the next owner name in the zone. This change is expected to be fully compatible with all existing DNSSEC validators. These NSEC records are returned whenever proving something specifically about the owner name (e.g., that no resource records of a given type appear at that name).

Whenever an NSEC record is needed to prove the non-existence of a name, a new NSEC record is dynamically produced and signed. The new NSEC record has an owner name lexically before the QNAME but lexically following any existing name and a "next name" lexically following the QNAME but before any existing name.

The generated NSEC record's type bitmap MUST have the RRSIG and NSEC bits set and SHOULD NOT have any other bits set. This relaxes the requirement in Section 2.3 of RFC4035 that NSEC RRs not appear at names that did not exist before the zone was signed.

The functions to generate the lexically following and proceeding names need not be perfect or consistent, but the generated NSEC records must not cover any existing names. Furthermore, this technique works best when the generated NSEC records cover as few names as possible. In this document, the functions that generate the nearby names are called "epsilon" functions, a reference to the mathematical convention of using the greek letter epsilon to represent small deviations.

An NSEC record denying the existence of a wildcard may be generated in the same way. Since the NSEC record covering a non-existent wildcard is likely to be used in response to many queries, authoritative name servers using the techniques described here may want to pregenerate or cache that record and its corresponding RRSIG.

For example, a query for an A record at the non-instantiated name example.com might produce the following two NSEC records, the first denying the existence of the name example.com and the second denying the existence of a wildcard:

> exampld.com 3600 IN NSEC example−.com (RRSIG NSEC)

> \).com 3600 IN NSEC +.com (RRSIG NSEC)

Before answering a query with these records, an authoritative server must test for the existence of names between these endpoints. If the generated NSEC would cover existing names (e.g., exampldd.com or *bizarre.example.com), a better epsilon function may be used or the covered name closest to the QNAME could be used as the NSEC owner name or next name, as appropriate. If an existing name is used as the NSEC owner name, that name's real NSEC record MUST be returned. Using the same example, assuming an exampldd.com delegation exists, this record might be returned from the parent:

exampldd.com 3600 IN NSEC example-.com (NS DS RRSIG NSEC)

Like every authoritative record in the zone, each generated NSEC record MUST have corresponding RRSIGs generated using each algorithm (but not necessarily each DNSKEY) in the zone's DNSKEY RRset, as described in RFC 4035 [3] Section 2.2. To minimize the number of signatures that must be generated, a zone may wish to limit the number of algorithms in its DNSKEY RRset.

4. Better Epsilon Functions

Section 6.1 of RFC 4034 defines a strict ordering of DNS names. Working backward from that definition, it should be possible to define epsilon functions that generate the immediately following and preceding names, respectively. This document does not define such functions. Instead, this section presents functions that come reasonably close to the perfect ones. As described above, an authoritative server should still ensure than no generated NSEC covers any existing name.

To increment a name, add a leading label with a single null (zero-value) octet.

To decrement a name, decrement the last character of the leftmost label, then fill that label to a length of 63 octets with octets of value 255. To decrement a null (zero-value) octet, remove the octet – if an empty label is left, remove the label. Defining this function numerically: fill the leftmost label to its maximum length with zeros (numeric, not ASCII zeros) and subtract one.

In response to a query for the non-existent name foo.example.com, these functions produce NSEC records of the following:

```
fon\255\255\255\255\255\255\255\255\255\255\255\255\255\255
\255\255\255\255\255\255\255\255\255\255\255\255\255\255\255
\255\255\255\255\255\255\255\255\255\255\255\255\255\255\255
\255\255\255\255\255\255\255\255\255\255\255\255\255\255\255
\255.example.com  3600  IN  NSEC  \000.foo.example.com  ( NSEC RRSIG )

\)\255\255\255\255\255\255\255\255\255\255\255\255\255\255
\255\255\255\255\255\255\255\255\255\255\255\255\255\255\255
\255\255\255\255\255\255\255\255\255\255\255\255\255\255\255
\255\255\255\255\255\255\255\255\255\255\255\255\255\255\255
\255\255.example.com 3600  IN  NSEC  \000.*.example.com  ( NSEC RRSIG )
```

The first of these NSEC RRs proves that no exact match for foo.example.com exists, and the second proves that there is no wildcard in example.com.

Both of these functions are imperfect: they do not take into account constraints on number of labels in a name nor total length of a name. As noted in the previous section, though, this technique does not depend on the use of perfect epsilon functions: it is sufficient to test whether any instantiated names fall into the span covered by the generated NSEC and, if so, substitute those instantiated owner names for the NSEC owner name or next name, as appropriate.

5. Security Considerations

This approach requires on-demand generation of RRSIG records. This creates several new vulnerabilities.

First, on-demand signing requires that a zone's authoritative servers have access to its private keys. Storing private keys on well-known Internet-accessible servers may make them more vulnerable to unintended disclosure.

Second, since generation of digital signatures tends to be computationally demanding, the requirement for on-demand signing makes authoritative servers vulnerable to a denial of service attack.

Last, if the epsilon functions are predictable, on-demand signing may enable a chosen-plaintext attack on a zone's private keys. Zones using this approach should attempt to use cryptographic algorithms that are resistant to chosen-plaintext attacks. It is worth noting that although DNSSEC has a "mandatory to implement" algorithm, that is a requirement on resolvers and validators – there is no requirement that a zone be signed with any given algorithm.

The success of using minimally covering NSEC records to prevent zone walking depends greatly on the quality of the epsilon functions chosen. An increment function that chooses a name obviously derived from the next instantiated name may be easily reverse engineered, destroying the value of this technique. An increment function that always returns a name close to the next instantiated name is likewise a poor choice. Good choices of epsilon functions are the ones that produce the immediately following and preceding names, respectively, though zone administrators may wish to use less perfect functions that return more human-friendly names than the functions described in Section 4 above.

Another obvious but misguided concern is the danger from synthesized NSEC records being replayed. It is possible for an attacker to replay an old but still validly signed NSEC record after a new name has been added in the span covered by that NSEC, incorrectly proving that there is no record at that name. This danger exists with DNSSEC as defined in [3]. The techniques described here actually decrease the danger, since the span covered by any NSEC record is smaller than before. Choosing better epsilon functions will further reduce this danger.

6. Acknowledgements

Many individuals contributed to this design. They include, in addition to the authors of this document, Olaf Kolkman, Ed Lewis, Peter Koch, Matt Larson, David Blacka, Suzanne Woolf, Jaap Akkerhuis, Jakob Schlyter, Bill Manning, and Joao Damas.

In addition, the editors would like to thank Ed Lewis, Scott Rose, and David Blacka for their careful review of the document.

7. Normative References

[1]   Arends, R., Austein, R., Larson, M., Massey, D., and S. Rose, "DNS Security Introduction and Requirements", RFC 4033, March 2005.

[2]   Arends, R., Austein, R., Larson, M., Massey, D., and S. Rose, "Resource Records for the DNS Security Extensions", RFC 4034, March 2005.

[3]   Arends, R., Austein, R., Larson, M., Massey, D., and S. Rose, "Protocol Modifications for the DNS Security Extensions", RFC 4035, March 2005.

[4]   Bradner, S., "Key words for use in RFCs to Indicate Requirement Levels", BCP 14, RFC 2119, March 1997.

Authors' Addresses

Samuel Weiler
SPARTA, Inc.
7075 Samuel Morse Drive
Columbia, Maryland 21046
US

EMail: weiler@tislabs.com

Johan Ihren
Autonomica AB
Bellmansgatan 30
Stockholm SE-118 47
Sweden

EMail: johani@autonomica.se

Full Copyright Statement

Intellectual Property

The IETF takes no position regarding the validity or scope of any Intellectual Property Rights or other rights that might be claimed to pertain to the implementation or use of the technology described in this document or the extent to which any license under such rights might or might not be available; nor does it represent that it has made any independent effort to identify any such rights. Information on the procedures with respect to rights in RFC documents can be found in BCP 78 and BCP 79.

Copies of IPR disclosures made to the IETF Secretariat and any assurances of licenses to be made available, or the result of an attempt made to obtain a general license or permission for the use of such proprietary rights by implementers or users of this specification can be obtained from the IETF on-line IPR repository at http://www.ietf.org/ipr.

The IETF invites any interested party to bring to its attention any copyrights, patents or patent applications, or other proprietary rights that may cover technology that may be required to implement this standard. Please address the information to the IETF at ietf-ipr@ietf.org.

Acknowledgement

Funding for the RFC Editor function is provided by the IETF Administrative Support Activity (IASA).

RFC 4059
Use of SHA-256 in DNSSEC Delegation Signer (DS) Resource Records (RRs)

Network Working Group
Request for Comments: 4509
Category: Standards Track

W. Hardaker
Sparta
May 2006

Status of This Memo

This document specifies an Internet standards track protocol for the Internet community, and requests discussion and suggestions for improvements. Please refer to the current edition of the "Internet Official Protocol Standards" (STD 1) for the standardization state and status of this protocol. Distribution of this memo is unlimited.

Copyright Notice

Abstract

This document specifies how to use the SHA-256 digest type in DNS Delegation Signer (DS) Resource Records (RRs). DS records, when stored in a parent zone, point to DNSKEYs in a child zone.

RFC 4059 Contents

1. Introduction

The DNSSEC [RFC4033] [RFC4034] [RFC4035] DS RR is published in parent zones to distribute a cryptographic digest of one key in a child's DNSKEY RRset. The DS RRset is signed by at least one of the parent zone's private zone data signing keys for each algorithm in use by the parent. Each signature is published in an RRSIG resource record, owned by the same domain as the DS RRset, with a type covered of DS.

In this document, the key words "MUST", "MUST NOT", "REQUIRED", "SHALL", "SHALL NOT", "SHOULD", "SHOULD NOT", "RECOMMENDED", "MAY", and "OPTIONAL" are to be interpreted as described in [RFC2119].

2. Implementing the SHA-256 Algorithm for DS Record Support

This document specifies that the digest type code 2 has been assigned to SHA-256 [SHA256] [SHA256CODE] for use within DS records. The results of the digest algorithm MUST NOT be truncated, and the entire 32 byte digest result is to be published in the DS record.

2.1. DS Record Field Values

Using the SHA-256 digest algorithm within a DS record will make use of the following DS-record fields:

Digest type: 2

Digest: A SHA-256 bit digest value calculated by using the following formula ("—" denotes concatenation). The resulting value is not truncated, and the entire 32 byte result is to be used in the resulting DS record and related calculations.

    digest = SHA_256 (DNSKEY owner name | DNSKEY RDATA)

where DNSKEY RDATA is defined by [RFC4034] as:

    DNSKEY RDATA = Flags | Protocol | Algorithm | Public Key

The Key Tag field and Algorithm fields remain unchanged by this document and are specified in the [RFC4034] specification.

2.2. DS Record with SHA-256 Wire Format

The resulting on-the-wire format for the resulting DS record will be as follows:

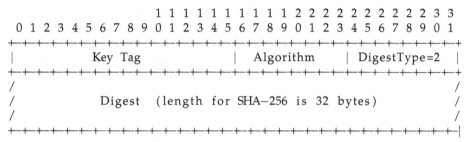

2.3. Example DS Record Using SHA-256

The following is an example DNSKEY and matching DS record. This DNSKEY record comes from the example DNSKEY/DS records found in section 5.4 of [RFC4034].

The DNSKEY record:

```
dskey.example.com. 86400 IN DNSKEY 256 3 5  ( AQOeiiR0GOMYkDshWoSKz9Xz
                                              fwJr1AYtsmx3TGkJaNXVbfi/
                                              2pHm822aJ5iI9BMzNXxeYCmZ
                                              DRD99WYwYqUSdjMmmAphXdvx
                                              egXd/M5+X7OrzKBaMbCVdFLU
                                              Uh6DhweJBjEVv5f2wwjM9Xzc
                                              nOf+EPbtG9DMBmADjFDc2w/r
                                              ljwvFw==
                                              ) ;  key id = 60485
```

The resulting DS record covering the above DNSKEY record using a SHA-256 digest:

```
dskey.example.com. 86400 IN DS 60485 5 2   ( D4B7D520E7BB5F0F67674A0C
                                             CEB1E3E0614B93C4F9E99B83
                                             83F6A1E4469DA50A )
```

3. Implementation Requirements

Implementations MUST support the use of the SHA-256 algorithm in DS RRs. Validator implementations SHOULD ignore DS RRs containing SHA-1 digests if DS RRs with SHA-256 digests are present in the DS RRset.

4. Deployment Considerations

If a validator does not support the SHA-256 digest type and no other DS RR exists in a zone's DS RRset with a supported digest type, then the validator has no supported authentication path leading from the parent to the child. The resolver should treat this case as it would the case of an authenticated NSEC RRset proving that no DS RRset exists, as described in [RFC4035], Section 5.2.

Because zone administrators cannot control the deployment speed of support for SHA-256 in validators that may be referencing any of their zones, zone operators should consider deploying both SHA-1 and SHA-256 based DS records. This should be done for every DNSKEY for which DS records are being generated. Whether to make use of both digest types and for how long is a policy decision that extends beyond the scope of this document.

5. IANA Considerations

Only one IANA action is required by this document:

The Digest Type to be used for supporting SHA-256 within DS records has been assigned by IANA.

At the time of this writing, the current digest types assigned for use in DS records are as follows:

VALUE	Digest Type	Status
0	Reserved	—
1	SHA–1	MANDATORY
2	SHA–256	MANDATORY
3–255	Unassigned	—

6. Security Considerations

6.1. Potential Digest Type Downgrade Attacks

A downgrade attack from a stronger digest type to a weaker one is possible if all of the following are true:

- A zone includes multiple DS records for a given child's DNSKEY, each of which uses a different digest type.

- A validator accepts a weaker digest even if a stronger one is present but invalid.

For example, if the following conditions are all true:

- Both SHA-1 and SHA-256 based digests are published in DS records within a parent zone for a given child zone's DNSKEY.

- The DS record with the SHA-1 digest matches the digest computed using the child zone's DNSKEY.

- The DS record with the SHA-256 digest fails to match the digest computed using the child zone's DNSKEY.

Then, if the validator accepts the above situation as secure, then this can be used as a downgrade attack since the stronger SHA-256 digest is ignored.

6.2. SHA-1 vs. SHA-256 Considerations for DS Records

Users of DNSSEC are encouraged to deploy SHA-256 as soon as software implementations allow for it. SHA-256 is widely believed to be more resilient to attack than SHA-1, and confidence in SHA-1's strength is being eroded by recently announced attacks. Regardless of whether the attacks on SHA-1 will affect DNSSEC, it is believed (at the time of this writing) that SHA-256 is the better choice for use in DS records.

At the time of this publication, the SHA-256 digest algorithm is considered sufficiently strong for the immediate future. It is also considered sufficient for use in DNSSEC DS RRs for the immediate future. However, future published attacks may weaken the usability of this algorithm within the DS RRs. It is beyond the scope of this document to speculate extensively on the cryptographic strength of the SHA-256 digest algorithm.

Likewise, it is also beyond the scope of this document to specify whether or for how long SHA-1 based DS records should be simultaneously published alongside SHA-256 based DS records.

7. Acknowledgements

This document is a minor extension to the existing DNSSEC documents and those authors are gratefully appreciated for the hard work that went into the base documents.

The following people contributed to portions of this document in some fashion: Mark Andrews, Roy Arends, Olafur Gudmundsson, Paul Hoffman, Olaf M. Kolkman, Edward Lewis, Scott Rose, Stuart E. Schechter, Sam Weiler.

8. References

8.1. Normative References

[RFC2119] Bradner, S., "Key words for use in RFCs to Indicate Requirement Levels", BCP 14, RFC 2119, March 1997.

[RFC4033] Arends, R., Austein, R., Larson, M., Massey, D., and S. Rose, "DNS Security Introduction and Requirements", RFC 4033, March 2005.

[RFC4034] Arends, R., Austein, R., Larson, M., Massey, D., and S. Rose, "Resource Records for the DNS Security Extensions", RFC 4034, March 2005.

[RFC4035] Arends, R., Austein, R., Larson, M., Massey, D., and S. Rose, "Protocol Modifications for the DNS Security Extensions", RFC 4035, March 2005.

[SHA256] National Institute of Standards and Technology, "Secure Hash Algorithm. NIST FIPS 180-2", August 2002.

8.2. Informative References

[SHA256CODE] Eastlake, D., "US Secure Hash Algorithms (SHA)", Work in Progress.

Author's Address

Wes Hardaker
Sparta
P.O. Box 382
Davis, CA 95617
USA

EMail: hardaker@tislabs.com

Full Copyright Statement

Intellectual Property

Copies of IPR disclosures made to the IETF Secretariat and any assurances of licenses to be made available, or the result of an attempt made to obtain a general license or permission for the use of such proprietary rights by implementers or users of this specification can be obtained from the IETF on-line IPR repository at http://www.ietf.org/ipr.

The IETF invites any interested party to bring to its attention any copyrights, patents or patent applications, or other proprietary rights that may cover technology that may be required to implement this standard. Please address the information to the IETF at ietf-ipr@ietf.org.

Acknowledgement

Funding for the RFC Editor function is provided by the IETF Administrative Support Activity (IASA).

RFC 4641
DNSSEC Operational Practices

Network Working Group
Request for Comments: 4641
Obsoletes: 2541
Category: Informational

O. Kolkman
R. Gieben
NLnet Labs
September 2006

Status of This Memo

Copyright Notice

Abstract

This document describes a set of practices for operating the DNS with security extensions (DNSSEC). The target audience is zone administrators deploying DNSSEC.

The document discusses operational aspects of using keys and signatures in the DNS. It discusses issues of key generation, key storage, signature generation, key rollover, and related policies.

This document obsoletes RFC 2541, as it covers more operational ground and gives more up-to-date requirements with respect to key sizes and the new DNSSEC specification.

RFC 4641 Contents

1. Introduction

This document describes how to run a DNS Security (DNSSEC)-enabled environment. It is intended for operators who have knowledge of the DNS (see RFC 1034 [1] and RFC 1035 [2]) and want to deploy DNSSEC. See RFC 4033 [4] for an introduction to DNSSEC, RFC 4034 [5] for the newly introduced Resource Records (RRs), and RFC 4035 [6] for the protocol changes.

During workshops and early operational deployment tests, operators and system administrators have gained experience about operating the DNS with security extensions (DNSSEC). This document translates these experiences into a set of practices for zone administrators. At the time of writing, there exists very little experience with DNSSEC in production environments; this document should therefore explicitly not be seen as representing 'Best Current Practices'.

The procedures herein are focused on the maintenance of signed zones (i.e., signing and publishing zones on authoritative servers). It is intended that maintenance of zones such as re-signing or key rollovers be transparent to any verifying clients on the Internet.

The structure of this document is as follows. In Section 2, we discuss the importance of keeping the "chain of trust" intact. Aspects of key generation and storage of private keys are discussed in Section 3; the focus in this section is mainly on the private part of the key(s). Section 4 describes considerations concerning the public part of the keys. Since these public keys appear in the DNS one has to take into account all kinds of timing issues, which are discussed in Section 4.1. Section 4.2 and Section 4.3 deal with the rollover, or supercession, of keys. Finally, Section 4.4 discusses considerations on how parents deal with their children's public keys in order to maintain chains of trust.

The typographic conventions used in this document are explained in Appendix C.

Since this is a document with operational suggestions and there are no protocol specifications, the RFC 2119 [7] language does not apply.

This document obsoletes RFC 2541 [12] to reflect the evolution of the underlying DNSSEC protocol since then. Changes in the choice of cryptographic algorithms, DNS record types and type names, and the parent-child key and signature exchange demanded a major rewrite and additional information and explanation.

1.1. The Use of the Term 'key'

It is assumed that the reader is familiar with the concept of asymmetric keys on which DNSSEC is based (public key cryptography [17]). Therefore, this document will use the term 'key' rather loosely. Where it is written that 'a key is used to sign data' it is assumed that the reader understands that it is the private part of the key pair that is used for signing. It is also assumed that the reader understands that the public part of the key pair is published in the DNSKEY Resource Record and that it is the public part that is used in key exchanges.

1.2. Time Definitions

In this document, we will be using a number of time-related terms. The following definitions apply:

- "Signature validity period" The period that a signature is valid. It starts at the time specified in the signature inception field of the RRSIG RR and ends at the time specified in the expiration field of the RRSIG RR.

- "Signature publication period" Time after which a signature (made with a specific key) is replaced with a new signature (made with the same key). This replacement takes place by publishing the relevant RRSIG in the master zone file. After one stops publishing an RRSIG in a zone, it may take a while before the RRSIG has expired from caches and has actually been removed from the DNS.

- "Key effectivity period" The period during which a key pair is expected to be effective. This period is defined as the time between the first inception time stamp and the last expiration date of any signature made with this key, regardless of any discontinuity in the use of the key. The key effectivity period can span multiple signature validity periods.

- "Maximum/Minimum Zone Time to Live (TTL)" The maximum or minimum value of the TTLs from the complete set of RRs in a zone. Note that the minimum TTL is not the same as the MINIMUM field in the SOA RR. See [11] for more information.

2. Keeping the Chain of Trust Intact

Maintaining a valid chain of trust is important because broken chains of trust will result in data being marked as Bogus (as defined in [4] Section 5), which may cause entire (sub)domains to become invisible to verifying clients. The administrators of secured zones have to realize that their zone is, to verifying clients, part of a chain of trust.

As mentioned in the introduction, the procedures herein are intended to ensure that maintenance of zones, such as re-signing or key rollovers, will be transparent to the verifying clients on the Internet.

Administrators of secured zones will have to keep in mind that data published on an authoritative primary server will not be immediately seen by verifying clients; it may take some time for the data to be transferred to other secondary authoritative nameservers and clients may be fetching data from caching non-authoritative servers. In this light, note that the time for a zone transfer from master to slave is negligible when using NOTIFY [9] and incremental transfer (IXFR) [8]. It increases when full zone transfers (AXFR) are used in combination with NOTIFY. It increases even more if you rely on full zone transfers based on only the SOA timing parameters for refresh.

For the verifying clients, it is important that data from secured zones can be used to build chains of trust regardless of whether the data came directly from an authoritative server, a caching nameserver, or some middle box. Only by carefully using the available timing parameters can a zone administrator ensure that the data necessary for verification can be obtained.

The responsibility for maintaining the chain of trust is shared by administrators of secured zones in the chain of trust. This is most obvious in the case of a 'key compromise' when a trade-off between maintaining a valid chain of trust and replacing the compromised keys as soon as possible must be made. Then zone administrators will have to make a trade-off, between keeping the chain of trust intact – thereby allowing for attacks with the compromised key – or deliberately breaking the chain of trust and making secured subdomains invisible to security-aware resolvers. Also see Section 4.3.

3. Keys Generation and Storage

This section describes a number of considerations with respect to the security of keys. It deals with the generation, effectivity period, size, and storage of private keys.

3.1. Zone and Key Signing Keys

The DNSSEC validation protocol does not distinguish between different types of DNSKEYs. All DNSKEYs can be used during the validation. In practice, operators use Key Signing and Zone Signing Keys and use the so-called Secure Entry Point (SEP) [3] flag to distinguish between them during operations. The dynamics and considerations are discussed below.

To make zone re-signing and key rollover procedures easier to implement, it is possible to use one or more keys as Key Signing Keys (KSKs). These keys will only sign the apex DNSKEY RRSet in a zone. Other keys can be used to sign all the RRSets in a zone and are referred to as Zone Signing Keys (ZSKs). In this document, we assume that KSKs are the subset of keys that are used for key exchanges with the parent and potentially for configuration as trusted anchors – the SEP keys. In this document, we assume a one-to-one mapping between KSK and SEP keys and we assume the SEP flag to be set on all KSKs.

3.1.1. Motivations for the KSK and ZSK Separation

Differentiating between the KSK and ZSK functions has several advantages:

- No parent/child interaction is required when ZSKs are updated.
- The KSK can be made stronger (i.e., using more bits in the key material). This has little operational impact since it is only used to sign a small fraction of the zone data. Also, the KSK is only used to verify the zone's key set, not for other RRSets in the zone.

- As the KSK is only used to sign a key set, which is most probably updated less frequently than other data in the zone, it can be stored separately from and in a safer location than the ZSK.

- A KSK can have a longer key effectivity period.

For almost any method of key management and zone signing, the KSK is used less frequently than the ZSK. Once a key set is signed with the KSK, all the keys in the key set can be used as ZSKs. If a ZSK is compromised, it can be simply dropped from the key set. The new key set is then re-signed with the KSK.

Given the assumption that for KSKs the SEP flag is set, the KSK can be distinguished from a ZSK by examining the flag field in the DNSKEY RR. If the flag field is an odd number it is a KSK. If it is an even number it is a ZSK.

The Zone Signing Key can be used to sign all the data in a zone on a regular basis. When a Zone Signing Key is to be rolled, no interaction with the parent is needed. This allows for signature validity periods on the order of days.

The Key Signing Key is only to be used to sign the DNSKEY RRs in a zone. If a Key Signing Key is to be rolled over, there will be interactions with parties other than the zone administrator. These can include the registry of the parent zone or administrators of verifying resolvers that have the particular key configured as secure entry points. Hence, the key effectivity period of these keys can and should be made much longer. Although, given a long enough key, the key effectivity period can be on the order of years, we suggest planning for a key effectivity on the order of a few months so that a key rollover remains an operational routine.

3.1.2. KSKs for High-Level Zones

Higher-level zones are generally more sensitive than lower-level zones. Anyone controlling or breaking the security of a zone thereby obtains authority over all of its subdomains (except in the case of resolvers that have locally configured the public key of a subdomain, in which case this, and only this, subdomain wouldn't be affected by the compromise of the parent zone). Therefore, extra care should be taken with high-level zones, and strong keys should be used.

The root zone is the most critical of all zones. Someone controlling or compromising the security of the root zone would control the entire DNS namespace of all resolvers using that root zone (except in the case of resolvers that have locally configured the public key of a subdomain). Therefore, the utmost care must be taken in the securing of the root zone. The strongest and most carefully handled keys should be used. The root zone private key should always be kept off-line.

Many resolvers will start at a root server for their access to and authentication of DNS data. Securely updating the trust anchors in an enormous population of resolvers around the world will be extremely difficult.

3.2. Key Generation

Careful generation of all keys is a sometimes overlooked but absolutely essential element in any cryptographically secure system. The strongest algorithms used with the longest keys are still of no use if an adversary can guess enough to lower the size of the likely key space so that it can be exhaustively searched. Technical suggestions for the generation of random keys will be found in RFC 4086 [14]. One should carefully assess if the random number generator used during key generation adheres to these suggestions.

Keys with a long effectivity period are particularly sensitive as they will represent a more valuable target and be subject to attack for a longer time than short-period keys. It is strongly recommended that long-term key generation occur off-line in a manner isolated from the network via an air gap or, at a minimum, high-level secure hardware.

3.3. Key Effectivity Period

For various reasons, keys in DNSSEC need to be changed once in a while. The longer a key is in use, the greater the probability that it will have been compromised through carelessness, accident, espionage, or cryptanalysis. Furthermore, when key rollovers are too rare an event, they will not become part of the operational habit and there is risk that nobody on-site will remember the procedure for rollover when the need is there.

From a purely operational perspective, a reasonable key effectivity period for Key Signing Keys is 13 months, with the intent to replace them after 12 months. An intended key effectivity period of a month is reasonable for Zone Signing Keys.

For key sizes that match these effectivity periods, see Section 3.5.

As argued in Section 3.1.2, securely updating trust anchors will be extremely difficult. On the other hand, the "operational habit" argument does also apply to trust anchor reconfiguration. If a short key effectivity period is used and the trust anchor configuration has to be revisited on a regular basis, the odds that the configuration tends to be forgotten is smaller. The trade-off is against a system that is so dynamic that administrators of the validating clients will not be able to follow the modifications.

Key effectivity periods can be made very short, as in a few minutes. But when replacing keys one has to take the considerations from Section 4.1 and Section 4.2 into account.

3.4. Key Algorithm

There are currently three different types of algorithms that can be used in DNSSEC: RSA, DSA, and elliptic curve cryptography. The latter is fairly new and has yet to be standardized for usage in DNSSEC.

RSA has been developed in an open and transparent manner. As the patent on RSA expired in 2000, its use is now also free.

DSA has been developed by the National Institute of Standards and Technology (NIST). The creation of signatures takes roughly the same time as with RSA, but is 10 to 40 times as slow for verification [17].

We suggest the use of RSA/SHA-1 as the preferred algorithm for the key. The current known attacks on RSA can be defeated by making your key longer. As the MD5 hashing algorithm is showing cracks, we recommend the usage of SHA-1.

At the time of publication, it is known that the SHA-1 hash has cryptanalysis issues. There is work in progress on addressing these issues. We recommend the use of public key algorithms based on hashes stronger than SHA-1 (e.g., SHA-256), as soon as these algorithms are available in protocol specifications (see [19] and [20]) and implementations.

3.5. Key Sizes

When choosing key sizes, zone administrators will need to take into account how long a key will be used, how much data will be signed during the key publication period (see Section 8.10 of [17]), and, optionally, how large the key size of the parent is. As the chain of trust really is "a chain", there is not much sense in making one of the keys in the chain several times larger then the others. As always, it's the weakest link that defines the strength of the entire chain. Also see Section 3.1.1 for a discussion of how keys serving different roles (ZSK vs. KSK) may need different key sizes.

Generating a key of the correct size is a difficult problem; RFC 3766 [13] tries to deal with that problem. The first part of the selection procedure in Section 1 of the RFC states:

1. Determine the attack resistance necessary to satisfy the security requirements of the application. Do this by estimating the minimum number of computer operations that the attacker will be forced to do in order to compromise the security of the system and then take the logarithm base two of that number. Call that logarithm value "n".

    A 1996 report recommended 90 bits as a good all-around choice for system security. The 90 bit number should be increased by about 2/3 bit/year, or about 96 bits in 2005.

[13] goes on to explain how this number "n" can be used to calculate the key sizes in public key cryptography. This culminated in the table given below (slightly modified for our purpose):

System requirement for attack resistance (bits)	Symmetric key size (bits)	RSA or DSA modulus size (bits)
70	70	947
80	80	1228
90	90	1553
100	100	1926
150	150	4575
200	200	8719
250	250	14596

The key sizes given are rather large. This is because these keys are resilient against a trillionaire attacker. Assuming this rich attacker will not attack your key and that the key is rolled over once a year, we come to the following recommendations about KSK sizes: 1024 bits for low-value domains, 1300 bits for medium-value domains, and 2048 bits for high-value domains.

Whether a domain is of low, medium, or high value depends solely on the views of the zone owner. One could, for instance, view leaf nodes in the DNS as of low value, and top-level domains (TLDs) or the root zone of high value. The suggested key sizes should be safe for the next 5 years.

As ZSKs can be rolled over more easily (and thus more often), the key sizes can be made smaller. But as said in the introduction of this paragraph, making the ZSKs' key sizes too small (in relation to the KSKs' sizes) doesn't make much sense. Try to limit the difference in size to about 100 bits.

Note that nobody can see into the future and that these key sizes are only provided here as a guide. Further information can be found in [16] and Section 7.5 of [17]. It should be noted though that [16] is already considered overly optimistic about what key sizes are considered safe.

One final note concerning key sizes. Larger keys will increase the sizes of the RRSIG and DNSKEY records and will therefore increase the chance of DNS UDP packet overflow. Also, the time it takes to validate and create RRSIGs increases with larger keys, so don't needlessly double your key sizes.

3.6. Private Key Storage

It is recommended that, where possible, zone private keys and the zone file master copy that is to be signed be kept and used in off-line, non-network-connected, physically secure machines only. Periodically, an application can be run to add authentication to a zone by adding RRSIG and NSEC RRs. Then the augmented file can be transferred.

When relying on dynamic update to manage a signed zone [10], be aware that at least one private key of the zone will have to reside on the master server. This key is only as secure as the amount of exposure the server receives to unknown clients and the security of the host. Although not mandatory, one could administer the DNS in the following way. The master that processes the dynamic updates is unavailable from generic hosts on the Internet, it is not listed in the NS RR set, although its name appears in the SOA RRs MNAME field. The nameservers in the NS RRSet are able to receive zone updates through NOTIFY, IXFR, AXFR, or an out-of-band distribution mechanism. This approach is known as the "hidden master" setup.

The ideal situation is to have a one-way information flow to the network to avoid the possibility of tampering from the network. Keeping the zone master file on-line on the network and simply cycling it through an off-line signer does not do this. The on-line version could still be tampered with if the host it resides on is compromised. For maximum security, the master copy of the zone file should be off-net and should not be updated based on an unsecured network mediated communication.

In general, keeping a zone file off-line will not be practical and the machines on which zone files are maintained will be connected to a network. Operators are advised to take security measures to shield unauthorized access to the master copy.

For dynamically updated secured zones [10], both the master copy and the private key that is used to update signatures on updated RRs will need to be on-line.

4. Signature Generation, Key Rollover, and Related Policies

4.1. Time in DNSSEC

Without DNSSEC, all times in the DNS are relative. The SOA fields REFRESH, RETRY, and EXPIRATION are timers used to determine the time elapsed after a slave server synchronized with a master server. The Time to Live (TTL) value and the SOA RR minimum TTL parameter [11] are used to determine how long a forwarder should cache data after it has been fetched from an authoritative server. By using a signature validity period, DNSSEC introduces the notion of an absolute time in the DNS. Signatures in DNSSEC have an expiration date after which the signature is marked as invalid and the signed data is to be considered Bogus.

4.1.1. Time Considerations

Because of the expiration of signatures, one should consider the following:

- We suggest the Maximum Zone TTL of your zone data to be a fraction of your signature validity period.

    If the TTL would be of similar order as the signature validity period, then all RRSets fetched during the validity period would be cached until the signature expiration time. Section 7.1 of [4] suggests that "the resolver may use the time remaining before expiration of the signature validity period of a signed RRSet as an upper bound for the TTL". As a result, query load on authoritative servers would peak at signature expiration time, as this is also the time at which records simultaneously expire from caches.

    To avoid query load peaks, we suggest the TTL on all the RRs in your zone to be at least a few times smaller than your signature validity period.

- We suggest the signature publication period to end at least one Maximum Zone TTL duration before the end of the signature validity period.

    Re-signing a zone shortly before the end of the signature validity period may cause simultaneous expiration of data from caches. This in turn may lead to peaks in the load on authoritative servers.

- We suggest the Minimum Zone TTL to be long enough to both fetch and verify all the RRs in the trust chain. In workshop environments, it has been demonstrated [18] that a low TTL (under 5 to 10 minutes) caused disruptions because of the following two problems:

1.   During validation, some data may expire before the validation is complete. The validator should be able to keep all data until it is completed. This applies to all RRs needed to complete the chain of trust: DSes, DNSKEYs, RRSIGs, and the final answers, i.e., the RRSet that is returned for the initial query.

2.   Frequent verification causes load on recursive nameservers. Data at delegation points, DSes, DNSKEYs, and RRSIGs benefit from caching. The TTL on those should be relatively long.

- Slave servers will need to be able to fetch newly signed zones well before the RRSIGs in the zone served by the slave server pass their signature expiration time.

When a slave server is out of sync with its master and data in a zone is signed by expired signatures, it may be better for the slave server not to give out any answer.

Normally, a slave server that is not able to contact a master server for an extended period will expire a zone. When that happens, the server will respond differently to queries for that zone. Some servers issue SERVFAIL, whereas others turn off the 'AA' bit in the answers. The time of expiration is set in the SOA record and is relative to the last successful refresh between the master and the slave servers. There exists no coupling between the signature expiration of RRSIGs in the zone and the expire parameter in the SOA.

If the server serves a DNSSEC zone, then it may well happen that the signatures expire well before the SOA expiration timer counts down to zero. It is not possible to completely prevent this from happening by tweaking the SOA parameters. However, the effects can be minimized where the SOA expiration time is equal to or shorter than the signature validity period. The consequence of an authoritative server not being able to update a zone, whilst that zone includes expired signatures, is that non-secure resolvers will continue to be able to resolve data served by the particular slave servers while security-aware resolvers will experience problems because of answers being marked as Bogus.

We suggest the SOA expiration timer being approximately one third or one fourth of the signature validity period. It will allow problems with transfers from the master server to be noticed before the actual signature times out. We also suggest that operators of nameservers that supply secondary services develop 'watch dogs' to spot upcoming signature expirations in zones they slave, and take appropriate action.

When determining the value for the expiration parameter one has to take the following into account: What are the chances that all my secondaries expire the zone? How quickly can I reach an administrator of secondary servers to load a valid zone? These questions are not DNSSEC specific but may influence the choice of your signature validity intervals.

4.2. Key Rollovers

A DNSSEC key cannot be used forever (see Section 3.3). So key rollovers – or supercessions, as they are sometimes called – are a fact of life when using DNSSEC. Zone administrators who are in the process of rolling their keys have to take into account that data published in previous versions of their zone still lives in caches. When deploying DNSSEC, this becomes an important consideration; ignoring data that may be in caches may lead to loss of service for clients.

The most pressing example of this occurs when zone material signed with an old key is being validated by a resolver that does not have the old zone key cached. If the old key is no longer present in the current zone, this validation fails, marking the data "Bogus". Alternatively, an attempt could be made to validate data that is signed with a new key against an old key that lives in a local cache, also resulting in data being marked "Bogus".

4.2.1. Zone Signing Key Rollovers

For "Zone Signing Key rollovers", there are two ways to make sure that during the rollover data still cached can be verified with the new key sets or newly generated signatures can be verified with the keys still in caches. One schema, described in Section 4.2.1.2, uses double signatures; the other uses key pre-publication (Section 4.2.1.1). The pros, cons, and recommendations are described in Section 4.2.1.3.

4.2.1.1. Pre-Publish Key Rollover

This section shows how to perform a ZSK rollover without the need to sign all the data in a zone twice – the "pre-publish key rollover". This method has advantages in the case of a key compromise. If the old key is compromised, the new key has already been distributed in the DNS. The zone administrator is then able to quickly switch to the new key and remove the compromised key from the zone. Another major advantage is that the zone size does not double, as is the case with the double signature ZSK rollover. A small "how-to" for this kind of rollover can be found in Appendix B.

Pre-publish key rollover involves four stages as follows:

initial	new DNSKEY	new RRSIGs	DNSKEY removal
SOA0	SOA1	SOA2	SOA3
RRSIG10 (SOA0)	RRSIG10 (SOA1)	RRSIG11 (SOA2)	RRSIG11 (SOA3)
DNSKEY1	DNSKEY1	DNSKEY1	DNSKEY1
DNSKEY10	DNSKEY10	DNSKEY10	DNSKEY11
DNSKEY11	DNSKEY11		
RRSIG1 (DNSKEY)	RRSIG1 (DNSKEY)	RRSIG1 (DNSKEY)	RRSIG1 (DNSKEY)
RRSIG10 (DNSKEY)	RRSIG10 (DNSKEY)	RRSIG11 (DNSKEY)	RRSIG11 (DNSKEY)

Pre−Publish Key Rollover

initial: Initial version of the zone: DNSKEY 1 is the Key Signing Key. DNSKEY 10 is used to sign all the data of the zone, the Zone Signing Key.

new DNSKEY: DNSKEY 11 is introduced into the key set. Note that no signatures are generated with this key yet, but this does not secure against brute force attacks on the public key. The minimum duration of this pre-roll phase is the time it takes for the data to propagate to the authoritative servers plus TTL value of the key set.

new RRSIGs: At the "new RRSIGs" stage (SOA serial 2), DNSKEY 11 is used to sign the data in the zone exclusively (i.e., all the signatures from DNSKEY 10 are removed from the zone). DNSKEY 10 remains published in the key set. This way data that was loaded into caches from version 1 of the zone can still be verified with key sets fetched from version 2 of the zone. The minimum time that the key set including DNSKEY 10 is to be published is the time that it takes for zone data from the previous version of the zone to expire from old caches, i.e., the time it takes for this zone to propagate to all authoritative servers plus the Maximum Zone TTL value of any of the data in the previous version of the zone.

DNSKEY removal: DNSKEY 10 is removed from the zone. The key set, now only containing DNSKEY 1 and DNSKEY 11, is re-signed with the DNSKEY 1.

The above scheme can be simplified by always publishing the "future" key immediately after the rollover. The scheme would look as follows (we show two rollovers); the future key is introduced in "new DNSKEY" as DNSKEY 12 and again a newer one, numbered 13, in "new DNSKEY (II)":

initial	new RRSIGs	new DNSKEY
SOA0	SOA1	SOA2
RRSIG10 (SOA0)	RRSIG11 (SOA1)	RRSIG11 (SOA2)
DNSKEY1	DNSKEY1	DNSKEY1
DNSKEY10	DNSKEY10	DNSKEY11
DNSKEY11	DNSKEY11	DNSKEY12
RRSIG1 (DNSKEY)	RRSIG1 (DNSKEY)	RRSIG1 (DNSKEY)
RRSIG10 (DNSKEY)	RRSIG11 (DNSKEY)	RRSIG11 (DNSKEY)

new RRSIGs (II)	new DNSKEY (II)
SOA3	SOA4
RRSIG12 (SOA3)	RRSIG12 (SOA4)
DNSKEY1	DNSKEY1
DNSKEY11	DNSKEY12
DNSKEY12	DNSKEY13
RRSIG1 (DNSKEY)	RRSIG1 (DNSKEY)
RRSIG12 (DNSKEY)	RRSIG12 (DNSKEY)

Pre—Publish Key Rollover, Showing Two Rollovers

Note that the key introduced in the "new DNSKEY" phase is not used for production yet; the private key can thus be stored in a physically secure manner and does not need to be 'fetched' every time a zone needs to be signed.

4.2.1.2. Double Signature Zone Signing Key Rollover

This section shows how to perform a ZSK key rollover using the double zone data signature scheme, aptly named "double signature rollover".

During the "new DNSKEY" stage the new version of the zone file will need to propagate to all authoritative servers and the data that exists in (distant) caches will need to expire, requiring at least the Maximum Zone TTL.

Double signature ZSK rollover involves three stages as follows:

initial	new DNSKEY	DNSKEY removal
SOA0	SOA1	SOA2
RRSIG10 (SOA0)	RRSIG10 (SOA1)	RRSIG11 (SOA2)
RRSIG11 (SOA1)		
DNSKEY1	DNSKEY1	DNSKEY1
DNSKEY10	DNSKEY10	DNSKEY11
DNSKEY11		
RRSIG1 (DNSKEY)	RRSIG1 (DNSKEY)	RRSIG1 (DNSKEY)
RRSIG10 (DNSKEY)	RRSIG10 (DNSKEY)	RRSIG11 (DNSKEY)
RRSIG11 (DNSKEY)		

Double Signature Zone Signing Key Rollover

initial: Initial Version of the zone: DNSKEY 1 is the Key Signing Key. DNSKEY 10 is used to sign all the data of the zone, the Zone Signing Key.

new DNSKEY: At the "New DNSKEY" stage (SOA serial 1) DNSKEY 11 is introduced into the key set and all the data in the zone is signed with DNSKEY 10 and DNSKEY 11. The rollover period will need to continue until all data from version 0 of the zone has expired from remote caches. This will take at least the Maximum Zone TTL of version 0 of the zone.

DNSKEY removal: DNSKEY 10 is removed from the zone. All the signatures from DNSKEY 10 are removed from the zone. The key set, now only containing DNSKEY 11, is re-signed with DNSKEY 1.

At every instance, RRSIGs from the previous version of the zone can be verified with the DNSKEY RRSet from the current version and the other way around. The data from the current version can be verified with the data from the previous version of the zone. The duration of the "new DNSKEY" phase and the period between rollovers should be at least the Maximum Zone TTL.

Making sure that the "new DNSKEY" phase lasts until the signature expiration time of the data in initial version of the zone is recommended. This way all caches are cleared of the old signatures. However, this duration could be considerably longer than the Maximum Zone TTL, making the rollover a lengthy procedure.

Note that in this example we assumed that the zone was not modified during the rollover. New data can be introduced in the zone as long as it is signed with both keys.

4.2.1.3. Pros and Cons of the Schemes

Pre-publish key rollover: This rollover does not involve signing the zone data twice. Instead, before the actual rollover, the new key is published in the key set and thus is available for cryptanalysis attacks. A small disadvantage is that this process requires four steps. Also the pre-publish scheme involves more parental work when used for KSK rollovers as explained in Section 4.2.3.

Double signature ZSK rollover: The drawback of this signing scheme is that during the rollover the number of signatures in your zone doubles; this may be prohibitive if you have very big zones. An advantage is that it only requires three steps.

4.2.2. Key Signing Key Rollovers

For the rollover of a Key Signing Key, the same considerations as for the rollover of a Zone Signing Key apply. However, we can use a double signature scheme to guarantee that old data (only the apex key set) in caches can be verified with a new key set and vice versa. Since only the key set is signed with a KSK, zone size considerations do not apply.

initial	new DNSKEY	DS change	DNSKEY removal
Parent:			
SOA0	——————>	SOA1	——————>
RRSIGpar(SOA0)	——————>	RRSIGpar(SOA1)	——————>
DS1	——————>	DS2	——————>
RRSIGpar(DS)	——————>	RRSIGpar(DS)	——————>
Child:			
SOA0	SOA1	——————>	SOA2
RRSIG10(SOA0)	RRSIG10(SOA1)	——————>	RRSIG10(SOA2)
		——————>	
DNSKEY1	DNSKEY1	——————>	DNSKEY2
	DNSKEY2	——————>	

DNSKEY10	DNSKEY10	————>	DNSKEY10
RRSIG1 (DNSKEY)	RRSIG1 (DNSKEY)	————>	RRSIG2 (DNSKEY)
	RRSIG2 (DNSKEY)	————>	
RRSIG10 (DNSKEY)	RRSIG10 (DNSKEY)	————>	RRSIG10 (DNSKEY)

Stages of Deployment for a Double Signature Key Signing Key Rollover

initial: Initial version of the zone. The parental DS points to DNSKEY1. Before the rollover starts, the child will have to verify what the TTL is of the DS RR that points to DNSKEY1 – it is needed during the rollover and we refer to the value as TTL_DS.

new DNSKEY: During the "new DNSKEY" phase, the zone administrator generates a second KSK, DNSKEY2. The key is provided to the parent, and the child will have to wait until a new DS RR has been generated that points to DNSKEY2. After that DS RR has been published on all servers authoritative for the parent's zone, the zone administrator has to wait at least TTL_DS to make sure that the old DS RR has expired from caches.

DS change: The parent replaces DS1 with DS2.

DNSKEY removal: DNSKEY1 has been removed.

The scenario above puts the responsibility for maintaining a valid chain of trust with the child. It also is based on the premise that the parent only has one DS RR (per algorithm) per zone. An alternative mechanism has been considered. Using an established trust relation, the interaction can be performed in-band, and the removal of the keys by the child can possibly be signaled by the parent. In this mechanism, there are periods where there are two DS RRs at the parent. Since at the moment of writing the protocol for this interaction has not been developed, further discussion is out of scope for this document.

4.2.3. Difference Between ZSK and KSK Rollovers

Note that KSK rollovers and ZSK rollovers are different in the sense that a KSK rollover requires interaction with the parent (and possibly replacing of trust anchors) and the ensuing delay while waiting for it.

A zone key rollover can be handled in two different ways: pre-publish (Section 4.2.1.1) and double signature (Section 4.2.1.2).

As the KSK is used to validate the key set and because the KSK is not changed during a ZSK rollover, a cache is able to validate the new key set of the zone. The pre-publish method would also work for a KSK rollover. The records that are to be pre-published are the parental DS RRs. The pre-publish method has some drawbacks for KSKs. We first describe the rollover scheme and then indicate these drawbacks.

initial	new DS	new DNSKEY	DS/DNSKEY removal

Parent:

```
SOA0           SOA1           ———————>    SOA2
RRSIGpar(SOA0) RRSIGpar(SOA1) ———————>    RRSIGpar(SOA2)
DS1            DS1            ———————>    DS2
               DS2            ———————>
RRSIGpar(DS)   RRSIGpar(DS)   ———————>    RRSIGpar(DS)

Child:
SOA0           ———————>    SOA1           SOA1
RRSIG10(SOA0)  ———————>    RRSIG10(SOA1)  RRSIG10(SOA1)
               ———————>
DNSKEY1        ———————>    DNSKEY2        DNSKEY2
               ———————>
DNSKEY10       ———————>    DNSKEY10       DNSKEY10
RRSIG1 (DNSKEY) ———————>   RRSIG2(DNSKEY) RRSIG2 (DNSKEY)
RRSIG10(DNSKEY) ———————>   RRSIG10(DNSKEY) RRSIG10(DNSKEY)
```

Stages of Deployment for a Pre–Publish Key Signing Key Rollover

When the child zone wants to roll, it notifies the parent during the "new DS" phase and submits the new key (or the corresponding DS) to the parent. The parent publishes DS1 and DS2, pointing to DNSKEY1 and DNSKEY2, respectively. During the rollover ("new DNSKEY" phase), which can take place as soon as the new DS set propagated through the DNS, the child replaces DNSKEY1 with DNSKEY2. Immediately after that ("DS/DNSKEY removal" phase), it can notify the parent that the old DS record can be deleted.

The drawbacks of this scheme are that during the "new DS" phase the parent cannot verify the match between the DS2 RR and DNSKEY2 using the DNS – as DNSKEY2 is not yet published. Besides, we introduce a "security lame" key (see Section 4.4.3). Finally, the child-parent interaction consists of two steps. The "double signature" method only needs one interaction.

4.2.4. Automated Key Rollovers

As keys must be renewed periodically, there is some motivation to automate the rollover process. Consider the following:

- ZSK rollovers are easy to automate as only the child zone is involved.

- A KSK rollover needs interaction between parent and child. Data exchange is needed to provide the new keys to the parent; consequently, this data must be authenticated and integrity must be guaranteed in order to avoid attacks on the rollover.

4.3. Planning for Emergency Key Rollover

This section deals with preparation for a possible key compromise. Our advice is to have a documented procedure ready for when a key compromise is suspected or confirmed.

When the private material of one of your keys is compromised it can be used for as long as a valid trust chain exists. A trust chain remains intact for

- as long as a signature over the compromised key in the trust chain is valid,

- as long as a parental DS RR (and signature) points to the compromised key,

- as long as the key is anchored in a resolver and is used as a starting point for validation (this is generally the hardest to update).

While a trust chain to your compromised key exists, your namespace is vulnerable to abuse by anyone who has obtained illegitimate possession of the key. Zone operators have to make a trade-off if the abuse of the compromised key is worse than having data in caches that cannot be validated. If the zone operator chooses to break the trust chain to the compromised key, data in caches signed with this key cannot be validated. However, if the zone administrator chooses to take the path of a regular rollover, the malicious key holder can spoof data so that it appears to be valid.

4.3.1. KSK Compromise

A zone containing a DNSKEY RRSet with a compromised KSK is vulnerable as long as the compromised KSK is configured as trust anchor or a parental DS points to it.

A compromised KSK can be used to sign the key set of an attacker's zone. That zone could be used to poison the DNS.

Therefore, when the KSK has been compromised, the trust anchor or the parental DS should be replaced as soon as possible. It is local policy whether to break the trust chain during the emergency rollover. The trust chain would be broken when the compromised KSK is removed from the child's zone while the parent still has a DS pointing to the compromised KSK (the assumption is that there is only one DS at the parent. If there are multiple DSes this does not apply – however the chain of trust of this particular key is broken).

Note that an attacker's zone still uses the compromised KSK and the presence of a parental DS would cause the data in this zone to appear as valid. Removing the compromised key would cause the attacker's zone to appear as valid and the child's zone as Bogus. Therefore, we advise not to remove the KSK before the parent has a DS to a new KSK in place.

4.3.1.1. Keeping the Chain of Trust Intact

If we follow this advice, the timing of the replacement of the KSK is somewhat critical. The goal is to remove the compromised KSK as soon as the new DS RR is available at the parent. And also make sure that the signature made with a new KSK over the key set with the compromised KSK in it expires just after the new DS appears at the parent, thus removing the old cruft in one swoop.

The procedure is as follows:

1.   Introduce a new KSK into the key set, keep the compromised KSK in the key set.

2.   Sign the key set, with a short validity period. The validity period should expire shortly after the DS is expected to appear in the parent and the old DSes have expired from caches.

3.   Upload the DS for this new key to the parent.

4.   Follow the procedure of the regular KSK rollover: Wait for the DS to appear in the authoritative servers and then wait as long as the TTL of the old DS RRs. If necessary re-sign the DNSKEY RRSet and modify/extend the expiration time.

5.   Remove the compromised DNSKEY RR from the zone and re-sign the key set using your "normal" validity interval.

An additional danger of a key compromise is that the compromised key could be used to facilitate a legitimate DNSKEY/DS rollover and/or nameserver changes at the parent. When that happens, the domain may be in dispute. An authenticated out-of-band and secure notify mechanism to contact a parent is needed in this case.

Note that this is only a problem when the DNSKEY and or DS records are used for authentication at the parent.

4.3.1.2. Breaking the Chain of Trust

There are two methods to break the chain of trust. The first method causes the child zone to appear 'Bogus' to validating resolvers. The other causes the child zone to appear 'insecure'. These are described below.

In the method that causes the child zone to appear 'Bogus' to validating resolvers, the child zone replaces the current KSK with a new one and re-signs the key set. Next it sends the DS of the new key to the parent. Only after the parent has placed the new DS in the zone is the child's chain of trust repaired.

An alternative method of breaking the chain of trust is by removing the DS RRs from the parent zone altogether. As a result, the child zone would become insecure.

4.3.2. ZSK Compromise

Primarily because there is no parental interaction required when a ZSK is compromised, the situation is less severe than with a KSK compromise. The zone must still be re-signed with a new ZSK as soon as possible. As this is a local operation and requires no communication between the parent and child, this can be achieved fairly quickly. However, one has to take into account that just as with a normal rollover the immediate disappearance of the old compromised key may lead to verification problems. Also note that as long as the RRSIG over the compromised ZSK is not expired the zone may be still at risk.

4.3.3. Compromises of Keys Anchored in Resolvers

A key can also be pre-configured in resolvers. For instance, if DNSSEC is successfully deployed the root key may be pre-configured in most security aware resolvers.

If trust-anchor keys are compromised, the resolvers using these keys should be notified of this fact. Zone administrators may consider setting up a mailing list to communicate the fact that a SEP key is about to be rolled over. This communication will of course need to be authenticated, e.g., by using digital signatures.

End-users faced with the task of updating an anchored key should always validate the new key. New keys should be authenticated out-of-band, for example, through the use of an announcement website that is secured using secure sockets (TLS) [21].

4.4. Parental Policies

4.4.1. Initial Key Exchanges and Parental Policies Considerations

The initial key exchange is always subject to the policies set by the parent. When designing a key exchange policy one should take into account that the authentication and authorization mechanisms used during a key exchange should be as strong as the authentication and authorization mechanisms used for the exchange of delegation information between parent and child. That is, there is no implicit need in DNSSEC to make the authentication process stronger than it was in DNS.

Using the DNS itself as the source for the actual DNSKEY material, with an out-of-band check on the validity of the DNSKEY, has the benefit that it reduces the chances of user error. A DNSKEY query tool can make use of the SEP bit [3] to select the proper key from a DNSSEC key set, thereby reducing the chance that the wrong DNSKEY is sent. It can validate the self-signature over a key; thereby verifying the ownership of the private key material. Fetching the DNSKEY from the DNS ensures that the chain of trust remains intact once the parent publishes the DS RR indicating the child is secure.

Note: the out-of-band verification is still needed when the key material is fetched via the DNS. The parent can never be sure whether or not the DNSKEY RRs have been spoofed.

4.4.2. Storing Keys or Hashes?

When designing a registry system one should consider which of the DNSKEYs and/or the corresponding DSes to store. Since a child zone might wish to have a DS published using a message digest algorithm not yet understood by the registry, the registry can't count on being able to generate the DS record from a raw DNSKEY. Thus, we recommend that registry systems at least support storing DS records.

It may also be useful to store DNSKEYs, since having them may help during troubleshooting and, as long as the child's chosen message digest is supported, the overhead of generating DS records from them is minimal. Having an out-of-band mechanism, such as a registry directory (e.g., Whois), to find out which keys are used to generate DS Resource Records for specific owners and/or zones may also help with troubleshooting.

The storage considerations also relate to the design of the customer interface and the method by which data is transferred between registrant and registry; Will the child zone administrator be able to upload DS RRs with unknown hash algorithms or does the interface only allow DNSKEYs? In the registry-registrar model, one can use the DNSSEC extensions to the Extensible Provisioning Protocol (EPP) [15], which allows transfer of DS RRs and optionally DNSKEY RRs.

4.4.3. Security Lameness

Security lameness is defined as what happens when a parent has a DS RR pointing to a non-existing DNSKEY RR. When this happens, the child's zone may be marked "Bogus" by verifying DNS clients.

As part of a comprehensive delegation check, the parent could, at key exchange time, verify that the child's key is actually configured in the DNS. However, if a parent does not understand the hashing algorithm used by child, the parental checks are limited to only comparing the key id.

Child zones should be very careful in removing DNSKEY material, specifically SEP keys, for which a DS RR exists.

Once a zone is "security lame", a fix (e.g., removing a DS RR) will take time to propagate through the DNS.

4.4.4. DS Signature Validity Period

Since the DS can be replayed as long as it has a valid signature, a short signature validity period over the DS minimizes the time a child is vulnerable in the case of a compromise of the child's KSK(s). A signature validity period that is too short introduces the possibility that a zone is marked "Bogus" in case of a configuration error in the signer. There may not be enough time to fix the problems before signatures expire. Something as mundane as operator unavailability during weekends shows the need for DS signature validity periods longer than 2 days. We recommend an absolute minimum for a DS signature validity period of a few days.

The maximum signature validity period of the DS record depends on how long child zones are willing to be vulnerable after a key compromise. On the other hand, shortening the DS signature validity interval increases the operational risk for the parent. Therefore, the parent may have policy to use a signature validity interval that is considerably longer than the child would hope for.

A compromise between the operational constraints of the parent and minimizing damage for the child may result in a DS signature validity period somewhere between a week and months.

In addition to the signature validity period, which sets a lower bound on the number of times the zone owner will need to sign the zone data and which sets an upper bound to the time a child is vulnerable after key compromise, there is the TTL value on the DS RRs. Shortening the TTL means that the authoritative servers will see more queries. But on the other hand, a short TTL lowers the persistence of DS RRSets in caches thereby increasing the speed with which updated DS RRSets propagate through the DNS.

5. Security Considerations

DNSSEC adds data integrity to the DNS. This document tries to assess the operational considerations to maintain a stable and secure DNSSEC service. Not taking into account the 'data propagation' properties in the DNS will cause validation failures and may make secured zones unavailable to security-aware resolvers.

6. Acknowledgments

Most of the ideas in this document were the result of collective efforts during workshops, discussions, and tryouts.

At the risk of forgetting individuals who were the original contributors of the ideas, we would like to acknowledge people who were actively involved in the compilation of this document. In random order: Rip Loomis, Olafur Gudmundsson, Wesley Griffin, Michael Richardson, Scott Rose, Rick van Rein, Tim McGinnis, Gilles Guette Olivier Courtay, Sam Weiler, Jelte Jansen, Niall O'Reilly, Holger Zuleger, Ed Lewis, Hilarie Orman, Marcos Sanz, and Peter Koch.

Some material in this document has been copied from RFC 2541 [12].

Mike StJohns designed the key exchange between parent and child mentioned in the last paragraph of Section 4.2.2

Section 4.2.4 was supplied by G. Guette and O. Courtay.

Emma Bretherick, Adrian Bedford, and Lindy Foster corrected many of the spelling and style issues.

Kolkman and Gieben take the blame for introducing all miscakes (sic).

While working on this document, Kolkman was employed by the RIPE NCC and Gieben was employed by NLnet Labs.

7. References

7.1. Normative References

[1]   Mockapetris, P., "Domain names - concepts and facilities", STD 13, RFC 1034, November 1987.

[2]   Mockapetris, P., "Domain names - implementation and specification", STD 13, RFC 1035, November 1987.

[3]   Kolkman, O., Schlyter, J., and E. Lewis, "Domain Name System KEY (DNSKEY) Resource Record (RR) Secure Entry Point (SEP) Flag", RFC 3757, May 2004.

[4]   Arends, R., Austein, R., Larson, M., Massey, D., and S. Rose, "DNS Security Introduction and Requirements", RFC 4033, March 2005.

[5]   Arends, R., Austein, R., Larson, M., Massey, D., and S. Rose, "Resource Records for the DNS Security Extensions", RFC 4034, March 2005.

[6]   Arends, R., Austein, R., Larson, M., Massey, D., and S. Rose, "Protocol Modifications for the DNS Security Extensions", RFC 4035, March 2005.

7.2. Informative References

[7]   Bradner, S., "Key words for use in RFCs to Indicate Requirement Levels", BCP 14, RFC 2119, March 1997.

[8]   Ohta, M., "Incremental Zone Transfer in DNS", RFC 1995, August 1996.

[9]   Vixie, P., "A Mechanism for Prompt Notification of Zone Changes (DNS NOTIFY)", RFC 1996, August 1996.

[10]   Wellington, B., "Secure Domain Name System (DNS) Dynamic Update", RFC 3007, November 2000.

[11]   Andrews, M., "Negative Caching of DNS Queries (DNS NCACHE)", RFC 2308, March 1998.

[12]   Eastlake, D., "DNS Security Operational Considerations", RFC 2541, March 1999.

[13]   Orman, H. and P. Hoffman, "Determining Strengths For Public Keys Used For Exchanging Symmetric Keys", BCP 86, RFC 3766, April 2004.

[14]   Eastlake, D., Schiller, J., and S. Crocker, "Randomness Requirements for Security", BCP 106, RFC 4086, June 2005.

[15]   Hollenbeck, S., "Domain Name System (DNS) Security Extensions Mapping for the Extensible Provisioning Protocol (EPP)", RFC 4310, December 2005.

[16]   Lenstra, A. and E. Verheul, "Selecting Cryptographic Key Sizes", The Journal of Cryptology 14 (255-293), 2001.

[17]   Schneier, B., "Applied Cryptography: Protocols, Algorithms, and Source Code in C", ISBN (hardcover) 0-471-12845-7, ISBN (paperback) 0-471-59756-2, Published by John Wiley & Sons Inc., 1996.

[18]   Rose, S., "NIST DNSSEC workshop notes", June 2001.

[19]   Jansen, J., "Use of RSA/SHA-256 DNSKEY and RRSIG Resource Records in DNSSEC", Work in Progress, January 2006.

[20]   Hardaker, W., "Use of SHA-256 in DNSSEC Delegation Signer (DS) Resource Records (RRs)", RFC 4509, May 2006.

[21]   Blake-Wilson, S., Nystrom, M., Hopwood, D., Mikkelsen, J., and T. Wright, "Transport Layer Security (TLS) Extensions", RFC 4366, April 2006.

Appendix A. Terminology

In this document, there is some jargon used that is defined in other documents. In most cases, we have not copied the text from the documents defining the terms but have given a more elaborate explanation of the meaning. Note that these explanations should not be seen as authoritative.

Anchored key: A DNSKEY configured in resolvers around the globe. This key is hard to update, hence the term anchored.

Bogus: Also see Section 5 of [4]. An RRSet in DNSSEC is marked "Bogus" when a signature of an RRSet does not validate against a DNSKEY.

Key Signing Key or KSK: A Key Signing Key (KSK) is a key that is used exclusively for signing the apex key set. The fact that a key is a KSK is only relevant to the signing tool.

Key size: The term 'key size' can be substituted by 'modulus size' throughout the document. It is mathematically more correct to use modulus size, but as this is a document directed at operators we feel more at ease with the term key size.

Private and public keys: DNSSEC secures the DNS through the use of public key cryptography. Public key cryptography is based on the existence of two (mathematically related) keys, a public key and a private key. The public keys are published in the DNS by use of the DNSKEY Resource Record (DNSKEY RR). Private keys should remain private.

Key rollover: A key rollover (also called key supercession in some environments) is the act of replacing one key pair with another at the end of a key effectivity period.

Secure Entry Point (SEP) key: A KSK that has a parental DS record pointing to it or is configured as a trust anchor. Although not required by the protocol, we recommend that the SEP flag [3] is set on these keys.

Self-signature: This only applies to signatures over DNSKEYs; a signature made with DNSKEY x, over DNSKEY x is called a self-signature. Note: without further information, self-signatures convey no trust. They are useful to check the authenticity of the DNSKEY, i.e., they can be used as a hash.

Singing the zone file: The term used for the event where an administrator joyfully signs its zone file while producing melodic sound patterns.

Signer: The system that has access to the private key material and signs the Resource Record sets in a zone. A signer may be configured to sign only parts of the zone, e.g., only those RRSets for which existing signatures are about to expire.

Zone Signing Key (ZSK): A key that is used for signing all data in a zone. The fact that a key is a ZSK is only relevant to the signing tool.

Zone administrator: The 'role' that is responsible for signing a zone and publishing it on the primary authoritative server.

Appendix B. Zone Signing Key Rollover How-To

Using the pre-published signature scheme and the most conservative method to assure oneself that data does not live in caches, here follows the "how-to".

Step 0: The preparation: Create two keys and publish both in your key set. Mark one of the keys "active" and the other "published". Use the "active" key for signing your zone data. Store the private part of the "published" key, preferably off-line. The protocol does not provide for attributes to mark a key as active or published. This is something you have to do on your own, through the use of a notebook or key management tool.

Step 1: Determine expiration: At the beginning of the rollover make a note of the highest expiration time of signatures in your zone file created with the current key marked as active. Wait until the expiration time marked in Step 1 has passed.

Step 2: Then start using the key that was marked "published" to sign your data (i.e., mark it "active"). Stop using the key that was marked "active"; mark it "rolled".

Step 3: It is safe to engage in a new rollover (Step 1) after at least one signature validity period.

Appendix C. Typographic Conventions

The following typographic conventions are used in this document:

Key notation: A key is denoted by DNSKEYx, where x is a number or an identifier, x could be thought of as the key id.

RRSet notations: RRs are only denoted by the type. All other information – owner, class, rdata, and TTL–is left out. Thus: "example.com 3600 IN A 192.0.2.1" is reduced to "A". RRSets are a list of RRs. A example of this would be "A1, A2", specifying the RRSet containing two "A" records. This could again be abbreviated to just "A".

Signature notation: Signatures are denoted as RRSIGx(RRSet), which means that RRSet is signed with DNSKEYx.

Zone representation: Using the above notation we have simplified the representation of a signed zone by leaving out all unnecessary details such as the names and by representing all data by "SOAx"

SOA representation: SOAs are represented as SOAx, where x is the serial number.

Using this notation the following signed zone:

```
example.net.          86400   IN SOA  ns.example.net.  bert.example.net.  (
                                2006022100    ; serial
                                86400         ; refresh (  24 hours)
                                7200          ; retry   (   2 hours)
                                3600000       ; expire  (1000 hours)
                                28800 )       ; minimum (   8 hours)
                      86400   RRSIG   SOA 5 2 86400 20130522213204 (
                                      20130422213204 14 example.net.
                                      cmL62SI6iAX46xGNQAdQ... )
                      86400   NS      a.iana-servers.net.
                      86400   NS      b.iana-servers.net.
                      86400   RRSIG   NS 5 2 86400 20130507213204 (
                                      20130407213204 14 example.net.
                                      SO5epiJei19AjXoUpFnQ ... )
                      86400   DNSKEY  256 3 5 (
                                      EtRB9MP5/AvOuVO0I8XDxy0... ) ; id = 14
                      86400   DNSKEY  257 3 5 (
                                      gsPW/Yy19GzYIY+Gnr8HABU... ) ; id = 15
                      86400   RRSIG   DNSKEY 5 2 86400 20130522213204 (
                                      20130422213204 14 example.net.
                                      J4zCe8QX4tXVGjV4e1r9 ... )
                      86400   RRSIG   DNSKEY 5 2 86400 20130522213204 (
                                      20130422213204 15 example.net.
                                      keVDCOpsSeDReyV6O ... )
                      86400   RRSIG   NSEC 5 2 86400 20130507213204 (
                                      20130407213204 14 example.net.
                                      obj3HEp1GjnmhRjX ... )
a.example.net.        86400   IN TXT  "A label"
                      86400   RRSIG   TXT 5 3 86400 20130507213204 (
                                      20130407213204 14 example.net.
                                      IkDMlRdYLmXH7QJnuF3v ... )
                      86400   NSEC    b.example.com. TXT RRSIG NSEC
                      86400   RRSIG   NSEC 5 3 86400 20130507213204 (
                                      20130407213204 14 example.net.
                                      bZMjoZ3bHjnEz0nIsPMM ... )
                        ...
```

is reduced to the following representation:

```
SOA2006022100
RRSIG14(SOA2006022100)
DNSKEY14
DNSKEY15

RRSIG14(KEY)
RRSIG15(KEY)
```

The rest of the zone data has the same signature as the SOA record, i.e., an RRSIG created with DNSKEY 14.

Authors' Addresses

Olaf M. Kolkman
NLnet Labs
Kruislaan 419
Amsterdam 1098 VA
The Netherlands

EMail: olaf@nlnetlabs.nl
URI: http://www.nlnetlabs.nl

R. (Miek) Gieben

EMail: miek@miek.nl

Full Copyright Statement

Intellectual Property

Acknowledgement

Funding for the RFC Editor function is provided by the IETF Administrative Support Activity (IASA).

RFC 4955
DNS Security (DNSSEC) Experiments

Network Working Group
Request for Comments: 4955
Category: Standards Track

D. Blacka
VeriSign, Inc.
July 2007

Status of This Memo

This document specifies an Internet standards track protocol for the Internet community, and requests discussion and suggestions for improvements. Please refer to the current edition of the "Internet Official Protocol Standards" (STD 1) for the standardization state and status of this protocol. Distribution of this memo is unlimited.

Copyright Notice

Abstract

This document describes a methodology for deploying alternate, non- backwards-compatible, DNS Security (DNSSEC) methodologies in an experimental fashion without disrupting the deployment of standard DNSSEC.

RFC 4955 Contents

1. Overview

Historically, experimentation with DNSSEC alternatives has been a problematic endeavor. There has typically been a desire to both introduce non-backwards-compatible changes to DNSSEC and to try these changes on real zones in the public DNS. This creates a problem when the change to DNSSEC would make all or part of the zone using those changes appear bogus (bad) or otherwise broken to existing security- aware resolvers.

This document describes a standard methodology for setting up DNSSEC experiments. This methodology addresses the issue of coexistence with standard DNSSEC and DNS by using unknown algorithm identifiers to hide the experimental DNSSEC protocol modifications from standard security-aware resolvers.

2. Definitions and Terminology

Throughout this document, familiarity with the DNS system (RFC 1035 [5]) and the DNS security extensions (RFC 4033 [2], RFC 4034 [3], and RFC 4035 [4]) is assumed.

The key words "MUST", "MUST NOT", "REQUIRED", "SHALL", "SHALL NOT", "SHOULD", "SHOULD NOT", "RECOMMENDED", "MAY", and "OPTIONAL" in this document are to be interpreted as described in RFC 2119 [1].

3. Experiments

When discussing DNSSEC experiments, it is necessary to classify these experiments into two broad categories:

Backwards-Compatible: describes experimental changes that, while not strictly adhering to the DNSSEC standard, are nonetheless interoperable with clients and servers that do implement the DNSSEC standard.

Non-Backwards-Compatible: describes experiments that would cause a standard security-aware resolver to (incorrectly) determine that all or part of a zone is bogus, or to otherwise not interoperate with standard DNSSEC clients and servers.

Not included in these terms are experiments with the core DNS protocol itself.

The methodology described in this document is not necessary for backwards-compatible experiments, although it certainly may be used if desired.

4. Method

The core of the methodology is the use of strictly unknown algorithm identifiers when signing the experimental zone, and more importantly, having only unknown algorithm identifiers in the DS records for the delegation to the zone at the parent.

This technique works because of the way DNSSEC-compliant validators are expected to work in the presence of a DS set with only unknown algorithm identifiers. From RFC 4035 [4], Section 5.2:

> If the validator does not support any of the algorithms listed in an authenticated DS RRset, then the resolver has no supported authentication path leading from the parent to the child. The resolver should treat this case as it would the case of an authenticated NSEC RRset proving that no DS RRset exists, as described above.

And further:

> If the resolver does not support any of the algorithms listed in an authenticated DS RRset, then the resolver will not be able to verify the authentication path to the child zone. In this case, the resolver SHOULD treat the child zone as if it were unsigned.

Although this behavior isn't strictly mandatory (as marked by MUST), it is unlikely for a validator to implement a substantially different behavior. Essentially, if the validator does not have a usable chain of trust to a child zone, then it can only do one of two things: treat responses from the zone as insecure (the recommended behavior), or treat the responses as bogus. If the validator chooses the latter, this will both violate the expectation of the zone owner and defeat the purpose of the above rule. However, with local policy, it is within the right of a validator to refuse to trust certain zones based on any criteria, including the use of unknown signing algorithms.

Because we are talking about experiments, it is RECOMMENDED that private algorithm numbers be used (see RFC 4034 [3], Appendix A.1.1. Note that secure handling of private algorithms requires special handing by the validator logic. See "Clarifications and Implementation Notes for DNSSECbis" [6] for further details.) Normally, instead of actually inventing new signing algorithms, the recommended path is to create alternate algorithm identifiers that are aliases for the existing, known algorithms. While, strictly speaking, it is only necessary to create an alternate identifier for the mandatory algorithms, it is suggested that all optional defined algorithms be aliased as well.

It is RECOMMENDED that for a particular DNSSEC experiment, a particular domain name base is chosen for all new algorithms, then the algorithm number (or name) is prepended to it. For example, for experiment A, the base name of "dnssec-experiment-a.example.com" is chosen. Then, aliases for algorithms 3 (DSA) and 5 (RSASHA1) are defined to be "3.dnssec-experiment-a.example.com" and "5.dnssec-experiment-a.example.com". However, any unique identifier will suffice.

Using this method, resolvers (or, more specifically, DNSSEC validators) essentially indicate their ability to understand the DNSSEC experiment's semantics by understanding what the new algorithm identifiers signify.

This method creates two classes of security-aware servers and resolvers: servers and resolvers that are aware of the experiment (and thus recognize the experiment's algorithm identifiers and experimental semantics), and servers and resolvers that are unaware of the experiment.

This method also precludes any zone from being both in an experiment and in a classic DNSSEC island of security. That is, a zone is either in an experiment and only possible to validate experimentally, or it is not.

5. Defining an Experiment

The DNSSEC experiment MUST define the particular set of (previously unknown) algorithm identifiers that identify the experiment and define what each unknown algorithm identifier means. Typically, unless the experiment is actually experimenting with a new DNSSEC algorithm, this will be a mapping of private algorithm identifiers to existing, known algorithms.

Normally the experiment will choose a DNS name as the algorithm identifier base. This DNS name SHOULD be under the control of the authors of the experiment. Then the experiment will define a mapping between known mandatory and optional algorithms into this private algorithm identifier space. Alternately, the experiment MAY use the Object Identifier (OID) private algorithm space instead (using algorithm number 254), or MAY choose non-private algorithm numbers, although this would require an IANA allocation.

For example, an experiment might specify in its description the DNS name "dnssec-experiment-a.example.com" as the base name, and declare that "3.dnssec-experiment-a.example.com" is an alias of DNSSEC algorithm 3 (DSA), and that "5.dnssec-experiment-a.example.com" is an alias of DNSSEC algorithm 5 (RSASHA1).

Resolvers MUST only recognize the experiment's semantics when present in a zone signed by one or more of these algorithm identifiers. This is necessary to isolate the semantics of one experiment from any others that the resolver might understand.

In general, resolvers involved in the experiment are expected to understand both standard DNSSEC and the defined experimental DNSSEC protocol, although this isn't required.

6. Considerations

There are a number of considerations with using this methodology.

1. If an unaware validator does not correctly follow the rules laid out in RFC 4035 (e.g., the validator interprets a DNSSEC record prior to validating it), or if the experiment is broader in scope that just modifying the DNSSEC semantics, the experiment may not be sufficiently masked by this technique. This may cause unintended resolution failures.

2. It will not be possible for security-aware resolvers unaware of the experiment to build a chain of trust through an experimental zone.

7. Use in Non-Experiments

This general methodology MAY be used for non-backwards compatible DNSSEC protocol changes that start out as or become standards. In this case:

- The protocol change SHOULD use public IANA allocated algorithm identifiers instead of private algorithm identifiers. This will help identify the protocol change as a standard, rather than an experiment.

- Resolvers MAY recognize the protocol change in zones not signed (or not solely signed) using the new algorithm identifiers.

8. Security Considerations

Zones using this methodology will be considered insecure by all resolvers except those aware of the experiment. It is not generally possible to create a secure delegation from an experimental zone that will be followed by resolvers unaware of the experiment.

Implementers should take into account any security issues that may result from environments being configured to trust both experimental and non-experimental zones. If the experimental zone is more vulnerable to attacks, it could, for example, be used to promote trust in zones not part of the experiment, possibly under the control of an attacker.

9. References

9.1. Normative References

[1]   Bradner, S., "Key words for use in RFCs to Indicate Requirement Levels", BCP 14, RFC 2119, March 1997.

[2]   Arends, R., Austein, R., Larson, M., Massey, D., and S. Rose, "DNS Security Introduction and Requirements", RFC 4033, March 2005.

[3]   Arends, R., Austein, R., Larson, M., Massey, D., and S. Rose, "Resource Records for the DNS Security Extensions", RFC 4034, March 2005.

[4]   Arends, R., Austein, R., Larson, M., Massey, D., and S. Rose, "Protocol Modifications for the DNS Security Extensions", RFC 4035, March 2005.

9.2. Informative References

[5]   Mockapetris, P., "Domain names - implementation and specification", STD 13, RFC 1035, November 1987.

[6]   Weiler, S. and R. Austein, "Clarifications and Implementation Notes for DNSSECbis", Work in Progress, March 2007.

Author's Address

David Blacka
VeriSign, Inc.
21355 Ridgetop Circle
Dulles, VA 20166
US

Phone: +1 703 948 3200
EMail: davidb@verisign.com
URI: http://www.verisignlabs.com

Full Copyright Statement

Intellectual Property

Acknowledgement

Funding for the RFC Editor function is currently provided by the Internet Society.

RFC 4956
DNS Security (DNSSEC) Opt-In

Network Working Group
Request for Comments: 4956
Category: Experimental

R. Arends
Nominet
M. Kosters
D. Blacka
VeriSign, Inc.
July 2007

Status of This Memo

This memo defines an Experimental Protocol for the Internet community. It does not specify an Internet standard of any kind. Discussion and suggestions for improvement are requested. Distribution of this memo is unlimited.

Copyright Notice

Abstract

In the DNS security (DNSSEC) extensions, delegations to unsigned subzones are cryptographically secured. Maintaining this cryptography is not always practical or necessary. This document describes an experimental "Opt-In" model that allows administrators to omit this cryptography and manage the cost of adopting DNSSEC with large zones.

RFC 4956 Contents

1. Overview

The cost to cryptographically secure delegations to unsigned zones is high for large delegation-centric zones and zones where insecure delegations will be updated rapidly. For these zones, the costs of maintaining the NextSECure (NSEC) record chain may be extremely high relative to the gain of cryptographically authenticating existence of unsecured zones.

This document describes an experimental method of eliminating the superfluous cryptography present in secure delegations to unsigned zones. Using "Opt-In", a zone administrator can choose to remove insecure delegations from the NSEC chain. This is accomplished by extending the semantics of the NSEC record by using a redundant bit in the type map.

2. Definitions and Terminology

Throughout this document, familiarity with the DNS system (RFC 1035 [1]), DNS security extensions ([4], [5], and [6], referred to in this document as "standard DNSSEC"), and DNSSEC terminology (RFC 3090 [10]) is assumed.

The following abbreviations and terms are used in this document:

RR: is used to refer to a DNS resource record.

RRset: refers to a Resource Record Set, as defined by [8]. In this document, the RRset is also defined to include the covering RRSIG records, if any exist.

signed name: refers to a DNS name that has, at minimum, a (signed) NSEC record.

unsigned name: refers to a DNS name that does not (at least) have an NSEC record.

covering NSEC record/RRset: is the NSEC record used to prove (non)existence of a particular name or RRset. This means that for a RRset or name 'N', the covering NSEC record has the name 'N', or has an owner name less than 'N' and "next" name greater than 'N'.

delegation: refers to an NS RRset with a name different from the current zone apex (non-zone-apex), signifying a delegation to a subzone.

secure delegation: refers to a signed name containing a delegation (NS RRset), and a signed DS RRset, signifying a delegation to a signed subzone.

insecure delegation: refers to a signed name containing a delegation (NS RRset), but lacking a DS RRset, signifying a delegation to an unsigned subzone.

Opt-In insecure delegation: refers to an unsigned name containing only a delegation NS RRset. The covering NSEC record uses the Opt-In methodology described in this document.

The key words "MUST, "MUST NOT", "REQUIRED", "SHALL", "SHALL NOT", "SHOULD", "SHOULD NOT", "RECOMMENDED", "MAY, and "OPTIONAL" in this document are to be interpreted as described in RFC 2119 [2].

3. Experimental Status

This document describes an EXPERIMENTAL extension to DNSSEC. It interoperates with non-experimental DNSSEC using the technique described in [7]. This experiment is identified with the following private algorithms (using algorithm 253):

"3.optin.verisignlabs.com": is an alias for DNSSEC algorithm 3, DSA, and

"5.optin.verisignlabs.com": is an alias for DNSSEC algorithm 5, RSASHA1.

Servers wishing to sign and serve zones that utilize Opt-In MUST sign the zone with only one or more of these private algorithms and MUST NOT use any other algorithms.

Resolvers MUST NOT apply the Opt-In validation rules described in this document unless a zone is signed using one or more of these private algorithms.

This experimental protocol relaxes the restriction that validators MUST ignore the setting of the NSEC bit in the type map as specified in RFC 4035 [6] Section 5.4.

The remainder of this document assumes that the servers and resolvers involved are aware of and are involved in this experiment.

4. Protocol Additions

In DNSSEC, delegation NS RRsets are not signed, but are instead accompanied by an NSEC RRset of the same name and (possibly) a DS record. The security status of the subzone is determined by the presence or absence of the DS RRset, cryptographically proven by the NSEC record. Opt-In expands this definition by allowing insecure delegations to exist within an otherwise signed zone without the corresponding NSEC record at the delegation's owner name. These insecure delegations are proven insecure by using a covering NSEC record.

Since this represents a change of the interpretation of NSEC records, resolvers must be able to distinguish between RFC standard DNSSEC NSEC records and Opt-In NSEC records. This is accomplished by "tagging" the NSEC records that cover (or potentially cover) insecure delegation nodes. This tag is indicated by the absence of the NSEC bit in the type map. Since the NSEC bit in the type map merely indicates the existence of the record itself, this bit is redundant and safe for use as a tag.

An Opt-In tagged NSEC record does not assert the (non)existence of the delegations that it covers (except for a delegation with the same name). This allows for the addition or removal of these delegations without recalculating or resigning records in the NSEC chain. However, Opt-In tagged NSEC records do assert the (non)existence of other RRsets.

An Opt-In NSEC record MAY have the same name as an insecure delegation. In this case, the delegation is proven insecure by the lack of a DS bit in the type map, and the signed NSEC record does assert the existence of the delegation.

Zones using Opt-In MAY contain a mixture of Opt-In tagged NSEC records and standard DNSSEC NSEC records. If an NSEC record is not Opt-In, there MUST NOT be any insecure delegations (or any other records) between it and the RRsets indicated by the 'next domain name' in the NSEC RDATA. If it is Opt-In, there MUST only be insecure delegations between it and the next node indicated by the 'next domain name' in the NSEC RDATA.

In summary,

- An Opt-In NSEC type is identified by a zero-valued (or not- specified) NSEC bit in the type bit map of the NSEC record.

- A standard DNSSEC NSEC type is identified by a one-valued NSEC bit in the type bit map of the NSEC record.

and

- An Opt-In NSEC record does not assert the non-existence of a name between its owner name and "next" name, although it does assert that any name in this span MUST be an insecure delegation.

- An Opt-In NSEC record does assert the (non)existence of RRsets with the same owner name.

4.1. Server Considerations

Opt-In imposes some new requirements on authoritative DNS servers.

4.1.1. Delegations Only

This specification dictates that only insecure delegations may exist between the owner and "next" names of an Opt-In tagged NSEC record. Signing tools MUST NOT generate signed zones that violate this restriction. Servers MUST refuse to load and/or serve zones that violate this restriction. Servers also MUST reject AXFR or IXFR responses that violate this restriction.

4.1.2. Insecure Delegation Responses

When returning an Opt-In insecure delegation, the server MUST return the covering NSEC RRset in the Authority section.

In standard DNSSEC, NSEC records already must be returned along with the insecure delegation. The primary difference that this proposal introduces is that the Opt-In tagged NSEC record will have a different owner name from the delegation RRset. This may require implementations to search for the covering NSEC RRset.

4.1.3. Dynamic Update

Opt-In changes the semantics of Secure DNS Dynamic Update [9]. In particular, it introduces the need for rules that describe when to add or remove a delegation name from the NSEC chain. This document does not attempt to define these rules. Until these rules are defined, servers MUST NOT process DNS Dynamic Update requests against zones that use Opt-In NSEC records. Servers SHOULD return responses to update requests with RCODE=REFUSED.

4.2. Client Considerations

Opt-In imposes some new requirements on security-aware resolvers (caching or otherwise).

4.2.1. Delegations Only

As stated in Section 4.1 above, this specification restricts the namespace covered by Opt-In tagged NSEC records to insecure delegations only. Clients are not expected to take any special measures to enforce this restriction; instead, it forms an underlying assumption that clients may rely on.

4.2.2. Validation Process Changes

This specification does not change the resolver's resolution algorithm. However, it does change the DNSSEC validation process.

4.2.2.1. Referrals

Resolvers MUST be able to use Opt-In tagged NSEC records to cryptographically prove the validity and security status (as insecure) of a referral. Resolvers determine the security status of the referred-to zone as follows:

- In standard DNSSEC, the security status is proven by the existence or absence of a DS RRset at the same name as the delegation. The existence of the DS RRset indicates that the referred-to zone is signed. The absence of the DS RRset is proven using a verified NSEC record of the same name that does not have the DS bit set in the type map. This NSEC record MAY also be tagged as Opt-In.

- Using Opt-In, the security status is proven by the existence of a DS record (for signed) or the presence of a verified Opt-In tagged NSEC record that covers the delegation name. That is, the NSEC record does not have the NSEC bit set in the type map, and the delegation name falls between the NSEC's owner and "next" name.

Using Opt-In does not substantially change the nature of following referrals within DNSSEC. At every delegation point, the resolver will have cryptographic proof that the referred-to subzone is signed or unsigned.

4.2.2.2. Queries for DS Resource Records

Since queries for DS records are directed to the parent side of a zone cut (see [5], Section 5), negative responses to these queries may be covered by an Opt-In flagged NSEC record.

Resolvers MUST be able to use Opt-In tagged NSEC records to cryptographically prove the validity and security status of negative responses to queries for DS records. In particular, a NOERROR/NODATA (i.e., RCODE=3, but the answer section is empty) response to a DS query may be proven by an Opt-In flagged covering NSEC record, rather than an NSEC record matching the query name.

4.2.3. NSEC Record Caching

Caching resolvers MUST be able to retrieve the appropriate covering Opt-In NSEC record when returning referrals that need them. This requirement differs from standard DNSSEC in that the covering NSEC will not have the same owner name as the delegation. Some implementations may have to use new methods for finding these NSEC records.

4.2.4. Use of the AD bit

The AD bit, as defined by [3] and [6], MUST NOT be set when:

- sending a Name Error (RCODE=3) response where the covering NSEC is tagged as Opt-In.

- sending an Opt-In insecure delegation response, unless the covering (Opt-In) NSEC record's owner name equals the delegation name.

- sending a NOERROR/NODATA response when query type is DS and the covering NSEC is tagged as Opt-In, unless NSEC record's owner name matches the query name.

This rule is based on what the Opt-In NSEC record actually proves: for names that exist between the Opt-In NSEC record's owner and "next" names, the Opt-In NSEC record cannot prove the non-existence or existence of the name. As such, not all data in the response has been cryptographically verified, so the AD bit cannot be set.

5. Benefits

Using Opt-In allows administrators of large and/or changing delegation-centric zones to minimize the overhead involved in maintaining the security of the zone.

Opt-In accomplishes this by eliminating the need for NSEC records for insecure delegations. This, in a zone with a large number of delegations to unsigned subzones, can lead to substantial space savings (both in memory and on disk). Additionally, Opt-In allows for the addition or removal of insecure delegations without modifying the NSEC record chain. Zones that are frequently updating insecure delegations (e.g., Top-Level Domains (TLDs)) can avoid the substantial overhead of modifying and resigning the affected NSEC records.

6. Example

Consider the zone EXAMPLE shown below. This is a zone where all of the NSEC records are tagged as Opt-In.

Example A: Fully Opt-In Zone.

```
EXAMPLE.                    SOA     . . .
EXAMPLE.                    RRSIG   SOA . . .
EXAMPLE.                    NS      FIRST-SECURE.EXAMPLE.
EXAMPLE.                    RRSIG   NS . . .
EXAMPLE.                    DNSKEY  . . .
EXAMPLE.                    RRSIG   DNSKEY . . .
EXAMPLE.                    NSEC    FIRST-SECURE.EXAMPLE. (
                                    SOA NS RRSIG DNSKEY )
EXAMPLE.                    RRSIG   NSEC . . .

FIRST-SECURE.EXAMPLE.       A       . . .
FIRST-SECURE.EXAMPLE.       RRSIG   A . . .
FIRST-SECURE.EXAMPLE.       NSEC    NOT-SECURE-2.EXAMPLE. A RRSIG
FIRST-SECURE.EXAMPLE.       RRSIG   NSEC . . .

NOT-SECURE.EXAMPLE.         NS      NS.NOT-SECURE.EXAMPLE.
NS.NOT-SECURE.EXAMPLE.      A       . . .

NOT-SECURE-2.EXAMPLE.       NS      NS.NOT-SECURE.EXAMPLE.
NOT-SECURE-2.EXAMPLE        NSEC    SECOND-SECURE.EXAMPLE NS RRSIG
NOT-SECURE-2.EXAMPLE        RRSIG   NSEC . . .

SECOND-SECURE.EXAMPLE.  NS          NS.ELSEWHERE.
SECOND-SECURE.EXAMPLE.  DS          . . .
SECOND-SECURE.EXAMPLE.  RRSIG       DS . . .
SECOND-SECURE.EXAMPLE.  NSEC        EXAMPLE. NS RRSIG DNSKEY
SECOND-SECURE.EXAMPLE.  RRSIG       NSEC . . .

UNSIGNED.EXAMPLE.           NS      NS.UNSIGNED.EXAMPLE.
NS.UNSIGNED.EXAMPLE.        A       . . .
```

Example A.

In this example, a query for a signed RRset (e.g., "FIRST- SECURE.EXAMPLE A") or a secure delegation ("WWW.SECOND-SECURE.EXAMPLE A") will result in a standard DNSSEC response.

A query for a nonexistent RRset will result in a response that differs from standard DNSSEC by the following: the NSEC record will be tagged as Opt-In, there may be no NSEC record proving the non- existence of a matching wildcard record, and the AD bit will not be set.

A query for an insecure delegation RRset (or a referral) will return both the answer (in the Authority section) and the corresponding Opt-In NSEC record to prove that it is not secure.

Example A.1: Response to query for WWW.UNSIGNED.EXAMPLE. A

```
    RCODE=NOERROR,  AD=0

    Answer Section:

    Authority Section:
    UNSIGNED.EXAMPLE.          NS      NS.UNSIGNED.EXAMPLE
    SECOND-SECURE.EXAMPLE.  NSEC    EXAMPLE. NS RRSIG DS
    SECOND-SECURE.EXAMPLE.  RRSIG   NSEC ...

    Additional Section:
    NS.UNSIGNED.EXAMPLE.       A       ...
```

Example A.1

In the Example A.1 zone, the EXAMPLE. node MAY use either style of NSEC record, because there are no insecure delegations that occur between it and the next node, FIRST-SECURE.EXAMPLE. In other words, Example A would still be a valid zone if the NSEC record for EXAMPLE. was changed to the following RR:

```
    EXAMPLE.                   NSEC    FIRST-SECURE.EXAMPLE.  (SOA NS
                                       RRSIG DNSKEY NSEC )
```

However, the other NSEC records (FIRST-SECURE.EXAMPLE. and SECOND-SECURE.EXAMPLE.) MUST be tagged as Opt-In because there are insecure delegations in the range they define. (NOT-SECURE.EXAMPLE. and UNSIGNED.EXAMPLE., respectively).

NOT-SECURE-2.EXAMPLE. is an example of an insecure delegation that is part of the NSEC chain and also covered by an Opt-In tagged NSEC record. Because NOT-SECURE-2.EXAMPLE. is a signed name, it cannot be removed from the zone without modifying and resigning the prior NSEC record. Delegations with names that fall between NOT-SECURE- 2.EXAMPLE. and SECOND-SECURE.EXAMPLE. may be added or removed without resigning any NSEC records.

7. Transition Issues

Opt-In is not backwards compatible with standard DNSSEC and is considered experimental. Standard DNSSEC-compliant implementations would not recognize Opt-In tagged NSEC records as different from standard NSEC records. Because of this, standard DNSSEC implementations, if they were to validate Opt-In style responses, would reject all Opt-In insecure delegations within a zone as invalid. However, by only signing with private algorithms, standard DNSSEC implementations will treat Opt-In responses as unsigned.

It should be noted that all elements in the resolution path between (and including) the validator and the authoritative name server must be aware of the Opt-In experiment and implement the Opt-In semantics for successful validation to be possible. In particular, this includes any caching middleboxes between the validator and authoritative name server.

8. Security Considerations

Opt-In allows for unsigned names, in the form of delegations to unsigned subzones, to exist within an otherwise signed zone. All unsigned names are, by definition, insecure, and their validity or existence cannot be cryptographically proven.

In general:

- Records with unsigned names (whether or not existing) suffer from the same vulnerabilities as records in an unsigned zone. These vulnerabilities are described in more detail in [12] (note in particular Sections 2.3, "Name Games" and 2.6, "Authenticated Denial").

- Records with signed names have the same security whether or not Opt-In is used.

Note that with or without Opt-In, an insecure delegation may have its contents undetectably altered by an attacker. Because of this, the primary difference in security that Opt-In introduces is the loss of the ability to prove the existence or nonexistence of an insecure delegation within the span of an Opt-In NSEC record.

In particular, this means that a malicious entity may be able to insert or delete records with unsigned names. These records are normally NS records, but this also includes signed wildcard expansions (while the wildcard record itself is signed, its expanded name is an unsigned name), which can be undetectably removed or used to replace an existing unsigned delegation.

For example, if a resolver received the following response from the example zone above:

Example S.1: Response to query for WWW.DOES-NOT-EXIST.EXAMPLE. A

```
RCODE=NOERROR

Answer Section:

Authority Section:
DOES–NOT–EXIST.EXAMPLE. NS     NS.FORGED.
EXAMPLE.                 NSEC   FIRST–SECURE.EXAMPLE. SOA NS \
                                RRSIG DNSKEY
EXAMPLE.                 RRSIG  NSEC ...

Additional Section:

        Attacker has forged a name
```

The resolver would have no choice but to believe that the referral to NS.FORGED. is valid. If a wildcard existed that would have been expanded to cover "WWW.DOES-NOT-EXIST.EXAMPLE.", an attacker could have undetectably removed it and replaced it with the forged delegation.

Note that being able to add a delegation is functionally equivalent to being able to add any record type: an attacker merely has to forge a delegation to the nameserver under his/her control and place whatever records are needed at the subzone apex.

While in particular cases, this issue may not present a significant security problem, in general it should not be lightly dismissed. Therefore, it is strongly RECOMMENDED that Opt-In be used sparingly. In particular, zone signing tools SHOULD NOT default to Opt-In, and MAY choose not to support Opt-In at all.

9. Acknowledgments

The contributions, suggestions, and remarks of the following persons (in alphabetic order) to this document are acknowledged:

Mats Kolkman, Edward Lewis, Ted Lindgreen, Rip Loomis, Bill Manning, Dan Massey, Scott Rose, Mike Schiraldi, Jakob Schlyter, Brian Wellington.

10. References

10.1. Normative References

[1]   Mockapetris, P., "Domain names - implementation and specification", STD 13, RFC 1035, November 1987.

[2]   Bradner, S., "Key words for use in RFCs to Indicate Requirement Levels", BCP 14, RFC 2119, March 1997.

[3]   Wellington, B. and O. Gudmundsson, "Redefinition of DNS Authenticated Data (AD) bit", RFC 3655, November 2003.

[4]   Arends, R., Austein, R., Larson, M., Massey, D., and S. Rose, "DNS Security Introduction and Requirements", RFC 4033, March 2005.

[5]   Arends, R., Austein, R., Larson, M., Massey, D., and S. Rose, "Resource Records for the DNS Security Extensions", RFC 4034, March 2005.

[6]   Arends, R., Austein, R., Larson, M., Massey, D., and S. Rose, "Protocol Modifications for the DNS Security Extensions", RFC 4035, March 2005.

[7]   Blacka, D., "DNSSEC Experiments", RFC 4955, July 2007.

10.2. Informative References

[8]   Elz, R. and R. Bush, "Clarifications to the DNS Specification", RFC 2181, July 1997.

[9]   Wellington, B., "Secure Domain Name System (DNS) Dynamic Update", RFC 3007, November 2000.

[10]   Lewis, E., "DNS Security Extension Clarification on Zone Status", RFC 3090, March 2001.

[11]   Conrad, D., "Indicating Resolver Support of DNSSEC", RFC 3225, December 2001.

[12]   Atkins, D. and R. Austein, "Threat Analysis of the Domain Name System (DNS)", RFC 3833, August 2004.

Appendix A. Implementing Opt-In Using "Views"

In many cases, it may be convenient to implement an Opt-In zone by combining two separately maintained "views" of a zone at request time. In this context, "view" refers to a particular version of a zone, not to any specific DNS implementation feature.

In this scenario, one view is the secure view, the other is the insecure (or legacy) view. The secure view consists of an entirely signed zone using Opt-In tagged NSEC records. The insecure view contains no DNSSEC information. It is helpful, although not necessary, for the secure view to be a subset (minus DNSSEC records) of the insecure view.

In addition, the only RRsets that may solely exist in the insecure view are non-zone-apex NS RRsets. That is, all non-NS RRsets (and the zone apex NS RRset) MUST be signed and in the secure view.

These two views may be combined at request time to provide a virtual, single Opt-In zone. The following algorithm is used when responding to each query:

V_A is the secure view as described above.

V_B is the insecure view as described above.

R_A is a response generated from V_A, following standard DNSSEC.

R_B is a response generated from V_B, following DNS resolution as per RFC 1035 [1].

R_C is the response generated by combining R_A with R_B, as described below.

A query is DNSSEC-aware if it either has the DO bit [11] turned on or is for a DNSSEC-specific record type.

1. If V_A is a subset of V_B and the query is not DNSSEC-aware, generate and return R_B, otherwise

2. Generate R_A.

3. If R_A's RCODE != NXDOMAIN, return R_A, otherwise

4. Generate R_B and combine it with R_A to form R_C:

For each section (ANSWER, AUTHORITY, ADDITIONAL), copy the records from R_A into R_B, EXCEPT the AUTHORITY section SOA record, if R_B's RCODE = NOERROR.

5. Return R_C.

Authors' Addresses

Roy Arends
Nominet
Sandford Gate
Sandy Lane West
Oxford OX4 6LB
UNITED KINGDOM

Phone: +44 1865 332211
EMail: roy@nominet.org.uk

Mark Kosters
VeriSign, Inc.
21355 Ridgetop Circle
Dulles, VA 20166
US

Phone: +1 703 948 3200
EMail: mkosters@verisign.com
URI: http://www.verisignlabs.com

David Blacka
VeriSign, Inc.
21355 Ridgetop Circle
Dulles, VA 20166
US

Phone: +1 703 948 3200
EMail: davidb@verisign.com
URI: http://www.verisignlabs.com

Full Copyright Statement

BY (IF ANY), THE INTERNET SOCIETY, THE IETF TRUST AND THE INTERNET ENGI-
NEERING TASK FORCE DISCLAIM ALL WARRANTIES, EXPRESS OR IMPLIED, INCLUD-
ING BUT NOT LIMITED TO ANY WARRANTY THAT THE USE OF THE INFORMATION
HEREIN WILL NOT INFRINGE ANY RIGHTS OR ANY IMPLIED WARRANTIES OF MER-
CHANTABILITY OR FITNESS FOR A PARTICULAR PURPOSE.

Intellectual Property

The IETF takes no position regarding the validity or scope of any Intellectual Property Rights
or other rights that might be claimed to pertain to the implementation or use of the technology
described in this document or the extent to which any license under such rights might or might
not be available; nor does it represent that it has made any independent effort to identify any
such rights. Information on the procedures with respect to rights in RFC documents can be
found in BCP 78 and BCP 79.

Copies of IPR disclosures made to the IETF Secretariat and any assurances of licenses to be
made available, or the result of an attempt made to obtain a general license or permission
for the use of such proprietary rights by implementers or users of this specification can be
obtained from the IETF on-line IPR repository at http://www.ietf.org/ipr.

The IETF invites any interested party to bring to its attention any copyrights, patents or patent
applications, or other proprietary rights that may cover technology that may be required to
implement this standard. Please address the information to the IETF at ietf-ipr@ietf.org.

Acknowledgement

Funding for the RFC Editor function is currently provided by the Internet Society.

RFC 4986
Requirements Related to DNS Security (DNSSEC) Trust Anchor Rollover

Network Working Group
Request for Comments: 4986
Category: Informational

H. Eland
Afilias Limited
R. Mundy
SPARTA, Inc.
S. Crocker
Shinkuro Inc.
S. Krishnaswamy
SPARTA, Inc.
August 2007

Status of This Memo

This memo provides information for the Internet community. It does not specify an Internet standard of any kind. Distribution of this memo is unlimited.

Abstract

Every DNS security-aware resolver must have at least one Trust Anchor to use as the basis for validating responses from DNS signed zones. For various reasons, most DNS security-aware resolvers are expected to have several Trust Anchors. For some operations, manual monitoring and updating of Trust Anchors may be feasible, but many operations will require automated methods for updating Trust Anchors in their security-aware resolvers. This document identifies the requirements that must be met by an automated DNS Trust Anchor rollover solution for security-aware DNS resolvers.

RFC 4986 Contents

1. Introduction

The Domain Name System Security Extensions (DNSSEC), as described in [2], [3], and [4], define new records and protocol modifications to DNS that permit security-aware resolvers to validate DNS Resource Records (RRs) from one or more Trust Anchors held by such security-aware resolvers.

Security-aware resolvers will have to initially obtain their Trust Anchors in a trustworthy manner to ensure the Trust Anchors are correct and valid. There are a number of ways that this initial step can be accomplished; however, details of this step are beyond the scope of this document. Once an operator has obtained Trust Anchors, initially entering the Trust Anchors into their security-aware resolvers will in many instances be a manual operation.

For some operational environments, manual management of Trust Anchors might be a viable approach. However, many operational environments will require a more automated, specification-based method for updating and managing Trust Anchors. This document provides a list of requirements that can be used to measure the effectiveness of any proposed automated Trust Anchor rollover mechanism in a consistent manner.

2. Terminology

The key words "MUST", "MUST NOT", "REQUIRED", "SHALL", "SHALL NOT", "SHOULD", "SHOULD NOT", "RECOMMENDED", "MAY", and "OPTIONAL" in this document are to be interpreted as described in RFC 2119 [1].

The use of RFC 2119 words in the requirements is intended to unambiguously describe a requirement. If a tradeoff is to be made between conflicting requirements when choosing a solution, the requirement with MUST language will have higher preference than requirements with SHOULD, MAY, or RECOMMENDED language. It is understood that a tradeoff may need to be made between requirements that both contain RFC 2119 language.

3. Background

DNS resolvers need to have one or more starting points to use in obtaining DNS answers. The starting points for stub resolvers are normally the IP addresses for one or more recursive name servers. The starting points for recursive name servers are normally IP addresses for DNS

Root name servers. Similarly, security-aware resolvers must have one or more starting points to use for building the authenticated chain to validate a signed DNS response. Instead of IP addresses, DNSSEC requires that each resolver trust one or more DNSKEY RRs or DS RRs as their starting point. Each of these starting points is called a Trust Anchor.

It should be noted that DNSKEY RRs and DS RRs are not Trust Anchors when they are created by the signed zone operator nor are they Trust Anchors because the records are published in the signed zone. A DNSKEY RR or DS RR becomes a Trust Anchor when an operator of a security-aware resolver determines that the public key or hash will be used as a Trust Anchor. Thus, the signed zone operator that created and/or published these RRs may not know if any of the DNSKEY RRs or DS RRs associated with their zone are being used as Trust Anchors by security-aware resolvers. The obvious exceptions are the DNSKEY RRs for the Root Zone, which will be used as Trust Anchors by many security-aware resolvers. For various reasons, DNSKEY RRs or DS RRs from zones other than Root can be used by operators of security-aware resolvers as Trust Anchors. It follows that responsibility lies with the operator of the security-aware resolver to ensure that the DNSKEY and/or DS RRs they have chosen to use as Trust Anchors are valid at the time they are used by the security-aware resolver as the starting point for building the authentication chain to validate a signed DNS response.

When operators of security-aware resolvers choose one or more Trust Anchors, they must also determine the method(s) they will use to ensure that they are using valid RRs and that they are able to determine when RRs being used as Trust Anchors should be replaced or removed. Early adopters of DNS signed zones have published information about the processes and methods they will use when their DNSKEY and/or DS RRs change so that operators of security-aware resolvers can manually change the Trust Anchors at the appropriate time. This manual approach will not scale and, therefore, drives the need for an automated specification-based approach for rollover of Trust Anchors for security-aware resolvers.

4. Definitions

This document uses the definitions contained in RFC 4033, section 2, plus the following additional definitions:

Trust Anchor: From RFC 4033, "A configured DNSKEY RR or DS RR hash of a DNSKEY RR. A validating security-aware resolver uses this public key or hash as a starting point for building the authentication chain to a signed DNS response." Additionally, a DNSKEY RR or DS RR is associated with precisely one point in the DNS hierarchy, i.e., one DNS zone. Multiple Trust Anchors MAY be associated with each DNS zone and MAY be held by any number of security-aware resolvers. Security-aware resolvers MAY have Trust Anchors from multiple DNS zones. Those responsible for the operation of security-aware resolvers are responsible for determining the set of RRs that will be used as Trust Anchors by that resolver.

Initial Trust Relationship: Operators of security-aware resolvers must ensure that they initially obtain any Trust Anchors in a trustworthy manner. For example, the correctness of the Root Zone DNSKEY RR(s) could be verified by comparing what the operator believes to be the Root Trust Anchor(s) with several 'well-known' sources such as the IANA web site, the DNS published Root Zone and the publication of the public key in well-known hard-copy forms. For other Trust Anchors, the operator must ensure the accuracy and validity of the DNSKEY and/or DS RRs before designating them Trust Anchors. This might be accomplished through a combination of technical, procedural, and contractual relationships, or use other existing trust relationships outside the current DNS protocol.

Trust Anchor Distribution: The method or methods used to convey the DNSKEY and/or DS RR(s) between the signed zone operator and the security-aware resolver operator. The method or methods MUST be deemed sufficiently trustworthy by the operator of the security-aware resolver to ensure source authenticity and integrity of the new RRs to maintain the Initial Trust Relationship required to designate those RRs as Trust Anchors.

Trust Anchor Maintenance: Any change in a validating security-aware resolver to add a new Trust Anchor, delete an existing Trust Anchor, or replace an existing Trust Anchor with another. This change might be accomplished manually or in some automated manner. Those responsible for the operation of the security-aware resolver are responsible for establishing policies and procedures to ensure that a sufficient Initial Trust Relationship is in place before adding Trust Anchors for a particular DNS zone to their security-aware resolver configuration.

Trust Anchor Revocation and Removal: The invalidation of a particular Trust Anchor that results when the operator of the signed zone revokes or removes a DNSKEY RR or DS RR that is being used as a Trust Anchor by any security-aware resolver. It is possible that a zone administrator may invalidate more than one RR at one point in time; therefore, it MUST be clear to both the zone administrator and the security-aware resolver the exact RR(s) that have been revoked or removed so the proper Trust Anchor or Trust Anchors are removed.

Trust Anchor Rollover: The method or methods necessary for the secure replacement of one or multiple Trust Anchors held by security-aware resolvers. Trust Anchor Rollover should be considered a subset of Trust Anchor Maintenance.

Normal or Pre-Scheduled Trust Anchor Rollover: The operator of a DNSSEC signed zone has issued a new DNSKEY and/or DS RR(s) as a part of an operational routine.

Emergency or Non-Scheduled Trust Anchor Rollover: The operator of a signed zone has issued a new DNSKEY and/or DS RR(s) as part of an exceptional event.

Emergency Trust Anchor Revocation: The operator of a signed zone wishes to indicate that the current DNSKEY and/or DS RR(s) are no longer valid as part of an exceptional event.

5. Requirements

Following are the requirements for DNSSEC automated specification-based Trust Anchor Rollover:

5.1. Scalability

The automated Trust Anchor Rollover solution MUST be capable of scaling to Internet-wide usage. The probable largest number of instances of security-aware resolvers needing to rollover a Trust Anchor will be those that use the public key(s) for the Root Zone as Trust Anchor(s). This number could be extremely large if a number of applications have embedded security-aware resolvers.

The automated Trust Anchor Rollover solution MUST be able to support Trust Anchors for multiple zones and multiple Trust Anchors for each DNS zone. The number of Trust Anchors that might be configured into any one validating security-aware resolver is not known with certainty at this time; in most cases it will be less than 20 but it may even be as high as one thousand.

5.2. No Known Intellectual Property Encumbrance

Because trust anchor rollover is likely to be "mandatory-to-implement", section 8 of [5] requires that the technical solution chosen must not be known to be encumbered or must be available under royalty-free terms.

For this purpose, "royalty-free" is defined as follows: worldwide, irrevocable, perpetual right to use, without fee, in commerce or otherwise, where "use" includes descriptions of algorithms, distribution and/or use of hardware implementations, distribution and/or use of software systems in source and/or binary form, in all DNS or DNSSEC applications including registry, registrar, domain name service including authority, recursion, caching, forwarding, stub resolver, or similar.

In summary, no implementor, distributor, or operator of the technology chosen for trust anchor management shall be expected or required to pay any fee to any IPR holder for the right to implement, distribute, or operate a system which includes the chosen mandatory-to-implement solution.

5.3. General Applicability

The solution MUST provide the capability to maintain Trust Anchors in security-aware resolvers for any and all DNS zones.

5.4. Support Private Networks

The solution MUST support private networks with their own DNS hierarchy.

5.5. Detection of Stale Trust Anchors

The Trust Anchor Rollover solution MUST allow a validating security-aware resolver to be able to detect if the DNSKEY and/or DS RR(s) can no longer be updated given the current set of actual trust-anchors. In these cases, the resolver should inform the operator of the need to reestablish initial trust.

5.6. Manual Operations Permitted

The operator of a security-aware resolver may choose manual or automated rollover, but the rollover protocol must allow the implementation to support both automated and manual Trust Anchor Maintenance operations. Implementation of the rollover protocol is likely to be mandatory, but that's out of scope for this requirements document.

5.7. Planned and Unplanned Rollovers

The solution MUST permit both planned (pre-scheduled) and unplanned (non-scheduled) rollover of Trust Anchors. Support for providing an Initial Trust Relationship is OPTIONAL.

5.8. Timeliness

Resource Records used as Trust Anchors SHOULD be able to be distributed to security-aware resolvers in a timely manner.

Security-aware resolvers need to acquire new and remove revoked DNSKEY and/or DS RRs that are being used as Trust Anchors for a zone such that no old RR is used as a Trust Anchor for long after the zone issues new or revokes existing RRs.

5.9. High Availability

Information about the zone administrator's view of the state of Resource Records used as Trust Anchors SHOULD be available in a trustworthy manner at all times to security-aware resolvers. Information about Resource Records that a zone administrator has invalidated and that are known to be used as Trust Anchors should be available in a trustworthy manner for a reasonable length of time.

5.10. New RR Types

If a Trust Anchor Rollover solution requires new RR types or protocol modifications, this should be considered in the evaluation of solutions. The working group needs to determine whether such changes are a good thing or a bad thing or something else.

5.11. Support for Trust Anchor Maintenance Operations

The Trust Anchor Rollover solution MUST support operations that allow a validating security-aware resolver to add a new Trust Anchor, delete an existing Trust Anchor, or replace an existing Trust Anchor with another.

5.12. Recovery from Compromise

The Trust Anchor Rollover solution MUST allow a security-aware resolver to be able to recover from the compromise of any of its configured Trust Anchors for a zone so long as at least one other key, which is known to have not been compromised, is configured as a Trust Anchor for that same zone at that resolver.

5.13. Non-Degrading Trust

The Trust Anchor Rollover solution MUST provide sufficient means to ensure authenticity and integrity so that the existing trust relation does not degrade by performing the rollover.

6. Security Considerations

This document defines overall requirements for an automated specification-based Trust Anchor Rollover solution for security-aware resolvers but specifically does not define the security mechanisms needed to meet these requirements.

7. Acknowledgements

This document reflects the majority opinion of the DNSEXT Working Group members on the topic of requirements related to DNSSEC trust anchor rollover. The contributions made by various members of the working group to improve the readability and style of this document are graciously acknowledged.

8. Normative References

[1]   Bradner, S., "Key Words for Use in RFCs to Indicate Requirement Levels", RFC 2119, March 1997.

[2]   Arends, R., Austein, R., Larson, M., Massey, D., and S. Rose, "DNS Security Introduction and Requirements", RFC 4033, March 2005.

[3]   Arends, R., Austein, R., Larson, M., Massey, D., and S. Rose, "Resource Records for the DNS Security Extensions", RFC 4034, March 2005.

[4]   Arends, R., Austein, R., Larson, M., Massey, D., and S. Rose, "Protocol Modifications for the DNS Security Extensions", RFC 4035, March 2005.

[5]   Bradner, S., "Intellectual Property Rights in IETF Technology", RFC 3979, March 2005.

Authors' Addresses

Howard Eland
Afilias Limited
300 Welsh Road
Building 3, Suite 105
Horsham, PA 19044
USA

EMail: heland@afilias.info

Russ Mundy
SPARTA, Inc.
7110 Samuel Morse Dr.
Columbia, MD 21046
USA

EMail: mundy@sparta.com

Steve Crocker
Shinkuro Inc.
1025 Vermont Ave, Suite 820
Washington, DC 20005
USA

EMail: steve@shinkuro.com

Suresh Krishnaswamy
SPARTA, Inc.
7110 Samuel Morse Dr.
Columbia, MD 21046
USA

EMail: suresh@sparta.com

Full Copyright Statement

Intellectual Property

The IETF takes no position regarding the validity or scope of any Intellectual Property Rights or other rights that might be claimed to pertain to the implementation or use of the technology described in this document or the extent to which any license under such rights might or might not be available; nor does it represent that it has made any independent effort to identify any such rights. Information on the procedures with respect to rights in RFC documents can be found in BCP 78 and BCP 79.

Copies of IPR disclosures made to the IETF Secretariat and any assurances of licenses to be made available, or the result of an attempt made to obtain a general license or permission for the use of such proprietary rights by implementers or users of this specification can be obtained from the IETF on-line IPR repository at http://www.ietf.org/ipr.

The IETF invites any interested party to bring to its attention any copyrights, patents or patent applications, or other proprietary rights that may cover technology that may be required to implement this standard. Please address the information to the IETF at ietf-ipr@ietf.org.

RFC 5011
Automated Updates of DNS Security (DNSSEC) Trust Anchors

Network Working Group
Request for Comments: 5011
Category: Standards Track

M. StJohns
Independent
September 2007

Status of This Memo

This document specifies an Internet standards track protocol for the Internet community, and requests discussion and suggestions for improvements. Please refer to the current edition of the "Internet Official Protocol Standards" (STD 1) for the standardization state and status of this protocol. Distribution of this memo is unlimited.

Abstract

This document describes a means for automated, authenticated, and authorized updating of DNSSEC "trust anchors". The method provides protection against N-1 key compromises of N keys in the trust point key set. Based on the trust established by the presence of a current anchor, other anchors may be added at the same place in the hierarchy, and, ultimately, supplant the existing anchor(s).

This mechanism will require changes to resolver management behavior (but not resolver resolution behavior), and the addition of a single flag bit to the DNSKEY record.

RFC 5011 Contents

1. Introduction

As part of the reality of fielding DNSSEC (Domain Name System Security Extensions) [RFC4033] [RFC4034] [RFC4035], the community has come to the realization that there will not be one signed name space, but rather islands of signed name spaces each originating from specific points (i.e., 'trust points') in the DNS tree. Each of those islands will be identified by the trust point name, and validated by at least one associated public key. For the purpose of this document, we'll call the association of that name and a particular key a 'trust anchor'. A particular trust point can have more than one key designated as a trust anchor.

For a DNSSEC-aware resolver to validate information in a DNSSEC protected branch of the hierarchy, it must have knowledge of a trust anchor applicable to that branch. It may also have more than one trust anchor for any given trust point. Under current rules, a chain of trust for DNSSEC-protected data that chains its way back to ANY known trust anchor is considered 'secure'.

Because of the probable balkanization of the DNSSEC tree due to signing voids at key locations, a resolver may need to know literally thousands of trust anchors to perform its duties (e.g., consider an unsigned ".COM"). Requiring the owner of the resolver to manually manage these many relationships is problematic. It's even more problematic when considering the eventual requirement for key replacement/update for a given trust anchor. The mechanism described herein won't help with the initial configuration of the trust anchors in the resolvers, but should make trust point key replacement/rollover more viable.

As mentioned above, this document describes a mechanism whereby a resolver can update the trust anchors for a given trust point, mainly without human intervention at the resolver. There are some corner cases discussed (e.g., multiple key compromise) that may require manual intervention, but they should be few and far between. This document DOES NOT discuss the general problem of the initial configuration of trust anchors for the resolver.

1.1. Compliance Nomenclature

The key words "MUST", "MUST NOT", "REQUIRED", "SHALL", "SHALL NOT", "SHOULD", "SHOULD NOT", "RECOMMENDED", "MAY", and "OPTIONAL" in this document are to be interpreted as described in BCP 14, [RFC2119].

2. Theory of Operation

The general concept of this mechanism is that existing trust anchors can be used to authenticate new trust anchors at the same point in the DNS hierarchy. When a zone operator adds a new

SEP key (i.e., a DNSKEY with the Secure Entry Point bit set) (see [RFC4034], Section 2.1.1) to a trust point DNSKEY RRSet, and when that RRSet is validated by an existing trust anchor, then the resolver can add the new key to its set of valid trust anchors for that trust point.

There are some issues with this approach that need to be mitigated. For example, a compromise of one of the existing keys could allow an attacker to add their own 'valid' data. This implies a need for a method to revoke an existing key regardless of whether or not that key is compromised. As another example, assuming a single key compromise, we need to prevent an attacker from adding a new key and revoking all the other old keys.

2.1. Revocation

Assume two trust anchor keys A and B. Assume that B has been compromised. Without a specific revocation bit, B could invalidate A simply by sending out a signed trust point key set that didn't contain A. To fix this, we add a mechanism that requires knowledge of the private key of a DNSKEY to revoke that DNSKEY.

A key is considered revoked when the resolver sees the key in a self-signed RRSet and the key has the REVOKE bit (see Section 7 below) set to '1'. Once the resolver sees the REVOKE bit, it MUST NOT use this key as a trust anchor or for any other purpose except to validate the RRSIG it signed over the DNSKEY RRSet specifically for the purpose of validating the revocation. Unlike the 'Add' operation below, revocation is immediate and permanent upon receipt of a valid revocation at the resolver.

A self-signed RRSet is a DNSKEY RRSet that contains the specific DNSKEY and for which there is a corresponding validated RRSIG record. It's not a special DNSKEY RRSet, just a way of describing the validation requirements for that RRSet.

N.B.: A DNSKEY with the REVOKE bit set has a different fingerprint than one without the bit set. This affects the matching of a DNSKEY to DS records in the parent [RFC3755], or the fingerprint stored at a resolver used to configure a trust point.

In the given example, the attacker could revoke B because it has knowledge of B's private key, but could not revoke A.

2.2. Add Hold-Down

Assume two trust point keys A and B. Assume that B has been compromised. An attacker could generate and add a new trust anchor key C (by adding C to the DNSKEY RRSet and signing it with B), and then invalidate the compromised key. This would result in both the attacker and owner being able to sign data in the zone and have it accepted as valid by resolvers.

To mitigate but not completely solve this problem, we add a hold-down time to the addition of the trust anchor. When the resolver sees a new SEP key in a validated trust point DNSKEY RRSet, the resolver starts an acceptance timer, and remembers all the keys that validated the RRSet. If the resolver ever sees the DNSKEY RRSet without the new key but validly signed, it stops the acceptance process for that key and resets the acceptance timer. If all of the keys that were originally used to validate this key are revoked prior to the timer expiring, the resolver stops the acceptance process and resets the timer.

Once the timer expires, the new key will be added as a trust anchor the next time the validated RRSet with the new key is seen at the resolver. The resolver MUST NOT treat the new key as a trust anchor until the hold-down time expires AND it has retrieved and validated a DNSKEY RRSet after the hold-down time that contains the new key.

N.B.: Once the resolver has accepted a key as a trust anchor, the key MUST be considered a valid trust anchor by that resolver until explicitly revoked as described above.

In the given example, the zone owner can recover from a compromise by revoking B and adding a new key D and signing the DNSKEY RRSet with both A and B.

The reason this does not completely solve the problem has to do with the distributed nature of DNS. The resolver only knows what it sees. A determined attacker who holds one compromised key could keep a single resolver from realizing that the key had been compromised by intercepting 'real' data from the originating zone and substituting their own (e.g., using the example, signed only by B). This is no worse than the current situation assuming a compromised key.

2.3. Active Refresh

A resolver that has been configured for an automatic update of keys from a particular trust point MUST query that trust point (e.g., do a lookup for the DNSKEY RRSet and related RRSIG records) no less often than the lesser of 15 days, half the original TTL for the DNSKEY RRSet, or half the RRSIG expiration interval and no more often than once per hour. The expiration interval is the amount of time from when the RRSIG was last retrieved until the expiration time in the RRSIG. That is, queryInterval = MAX(1 hr, MIN (15 days, 1/2*OrigTTL, 1/2*RRSigExpirationInterval))

If the query fails, the resolver MUST repeat the query until satisfied no more often than once an hour and no less often than the lesser of 1 day, 10% of the original TTL, or 10% of the original expiration interval. That is, retryTime = MAX (1 hour, MIN (1 day, .1 * origTTL, .1 * expireInterval)).

2.4. Resolver Parameters

2.4.1. Add Hold-Down Time

The add hold-down time is 30 days or the expiration time of the original TTL of the first trust point DNSKEY RRSet that contained the new key, whichever is greater. This ensures that at least two validated DNSKEY RRSets that contain the new key MUST be seen by the resolver prior to the key's acceptance.

2.4.2. Remove Hold-Down Time

The remove hold-down time is 30 days. This parameter is solely a key management database bookeeping parameter. Failure to remove information about the state of defunct keys from the database will not adversely impact the security of this protocol, but may end up with a database cluttered with obsolete key information.

2.4.3. Minimum Trust Anchors per Trust Point

A compliant resolver MUST be able to manage at least five SEP keys per trust point.

3. Changes to DNSKEY RDATA Wire Format

Bit 8 of the DNSKEY Flags field is designated as the 'REVOKE' flag. If this bit is set to '1', AND the resolver sees an RRSIG(DNSKEY) signed by the associated key, then the resolver MUST consider this key permanently invalid for all purposes except for validating the revocation.

4. State Table

The most important thing to understand is the resolver's view of any key at a trust point. The following state table describes this view at various points in the key's lifetime. The table is a normative part of this specification. The initial state of the key is 'Start'. The resolver's view of the state of the key changes as various events occur.

This is the state of a trust-point key as seen from the resolver. The column on the left indicates the current state. The header at the top shows the next state. The intersection of the two shows the event that will cause the state to transition from the current state to the next.

NEXT STATE

FROM	Start	AddPend	Valid	Missing	Revoked	Removed
Start		NewKey				
AddPend	KeyRem		AddTime			
Valid				KeyRem	Revbit	
Missing			KeyPres		Revbit	
Revoked						RemTime
Removed						

State Table

4.1. Events

NewKey The resolver sees a valid DNSKEY RRSet with a new SEP key. That key will become a new trust anchor for the named trust point after it's been present in the RRSet for at least 'add time'.

KeyPres The key has returned to the valid DNSKEY RRSet.

KeyRem The resolver sees a valid DNSKEY RRSet that does not contain this key.

AddTime The key has been in every valid DNSKEY RRSet seen for at least the 'add time'.

RemTime A revoked key has been missing from the trust-point DNSKEY RRSet for sufficient time to be removed from the trust set.

RevBit The key has appeared in the trust anchor DNSKEY RRSet with its "REVOKED" bit set, and there is an RRSig over the DNSKEY RRSet signed by this key.

4.2. States

Start The key doesn't yet exist as a trust anchor at the resolver. It may or may not exist at the zone server, but either hasn't yet been seen at the resolver or was seen but was absent from the last DNSKEY RRSet (e.g., KeyRem event).

AddPend The key has been seen at the resolver, has its 'SEP' bit set, and has been included in a validated DNSKEY RRSet. There is a hold-down time for the key before it can be used as a trust anchor.

Valid The key has been seen at the resolver and has been included in all validated DNSKEY RRSets from the time it was first seen through the hold-down time. It is now valid for verifying RRSets that arrive after the hold-down time. Clarification: The DNSKEY RRSet does not need to be continuously present at the resolver (e.g., its TTL might expire). If the RRSet is seen and is validated (i.e., verifies against an existing trust anchor), this key MUST be in the RRSet, otherwise a 'KeyRem' event is triggered.

Missing This is an abnormal state. The key remains a valid trust-point key, but was not seen at the resolver in the last validated DNSKEY RRSet. This is an abnormal state because the zone operator should be using the REVOKE bit prior to removal.

Revoked This is the state a key moves to once the resolver sees an RRSIG(DNSKEY) signed by this key where that DNSKEY RRSet contains this key with its REVOKE bit set to '1'. Once in this state, this key MUST permanently be considered invalid as a trust anchor.

Removed After a fairly long hold-down time, information about this key may be purged from the resolver. A key in the removed state MUST NOT be considered a valid trust anchor. (Note: this state is more or less equivalent to the "Start" state, except that it's bad practice to re-introduce previously used keys – think of this as the holding state for all the old keys for which the resolver no longer needs to track state.)

5. Trust Point Deletion

A trust point that has all of its trust anchors revoked is considered deleted and is treated as if the trust point was never configured. If there are no superior configured trust points, data at and below the deleted trust point are considered insecure by the resolver. If there ARE superior configured trust points, data at and below the deleted trust point are evaluated with respect to the superior trust point(s).

Alternately, a trust point that is subordinate to another configured trust point MAY be deleted by a resolver after 180 days, where such a subordinate trust point validly chains to a superior trust point. The decision to delete the subordinate trust anchor is a local configuration decision. Once the subordinate trust point is deleted, validation of the subordinate zone is dependent on validating the chain of trust to the superior trust point.

6. Scenarios - Informative

The suggested model for operation is to have one active key and one stand-by key at each trust point. The active key will be used to sign the DNSKEY RRSet. The stand-by key will not normally sign this RRSet, but the resolver will accept it as a trust anchor if/when it sees the signature on the trust point DNSKEY RRSet.

Since the stand-by key is not in active signing use, the associated private key may (and should) be provided with additional protections not normally available to a key that must be used frequently (e.g., locked in a safe, split among many parties, etc). Notionally, the stand-by key should be less subject to compromise than an active key, but that will be dependent on operational concerns not addressed here.

6.1. Adding a Trust Anchor

Assume an existing trust anchor key 'A'.

1.   Generate a new key pair.

2.   Create a DNSKEY record from the key pair and set the SEP and Zone Key bits.

3.   Add the DNSKEY to the RRSet.

4.   Sign the DNSKEY RRSet ONLY with the existing trust anchor key - 'A'.

5.   Wait for various resolvers' timers to go off and for them to retrieve the new DNSKEY RRSet and signatures.

6.   The new trust anchor will be populated at the resolvers on the schedule described by the state table and update algorithm – see Sections 2 and 4 above.

6.2. Deleting a Trust Anchor

Assume existing trust anchors 'A' and 'B' and that you want to revoke and delete 'A'.

1.   Set the revocation bit on key 'A'.

2.   Sign the DNSKEY RRSet with both 'A' and 'B'. 'A' is now revoked. The operator should include the revoked 'A' in the RRSet for at least the remove hold-down time, but then may remove it from the DNSKEY RRSet.

6.3. Key Roll-Over

Assume existing keys A and B. 'A' is actively in use (i.e. has been signing the DNSKEY RRSet). 'B' was the stand-by key. (i.e. has been in the DNSKEY RRSet and is a valid trust anchor, but wasn't being used to sign the RRSet).

1.   Generate a new key pair 'C'.

2.   Add 'C' to the DNSKEY RRSet.

3.   Set the revocation bit on key 'A'.

4.   Sign the RRSet with 'A' and 'B'.

'A' is now revoked, 'B' is now the active key, and 'C' will be the stand-by key once the hold-down expires. The operator should include the revoked 'A' in the RRSet for at least the remove hold-down time, but may then remove it from the DNSKEY RRSet.

6.4. Active Key Compromised

This is the same as the mechanism for Key Roll-Over (Section 6.3) above, assuming 'A' is the active key.

6.5. Stand-by Key Compromised

Using the same assumptions and naming conventions as Key Roll-Over (Section 6.3) above:

1.   Generate a new key pair 'C'.

2.   Add 'C' to the DNSKEY RRSet.

3.   Set the revocation bit on key 'B'.

4.   Sign the RRSet with 'A' and 'B'.

'B' is now revoked, 'A' remains the active key, and 'C' will be the stand-by key once the hold-down expires. 'B' should continue to be included in the RRSet for the remove hold-down time.

6.6. Trust Point Deletion

To delete a trust point that is subordinate to another configured trust point (e.g., example.com to .com) requires some juggling of the data. The specific process is:

1. Generate a new DNSKEY and DS record and provide the DS record to the parent along with DS records for the old keys.

2. Once the parent has published the DSs, add the new DNSKEY to the RRSet and revoke ALL of the old keys at the same time, while signing the DNSKEY RRSet with all of the old and new keys.

3. After 30 days, stop publishing the old, revoked keys and remove any corresponding DS records in the parent.

Revoking the old trust-point keys at the same time as adding new keys that chain to a superior trust prevents the resolver from adding the new keys as trust anchors. Adding DS records for the old keys avoids a race condition where either the subordinate zone becomes unsecure (because the trust point was deleted) or becomes bogus (because it didn't chain to the superior zone).

7. IANA Considerations

The IANA has assigned a bit in the DNSKEY flags field (see Section 7 of [RFC4034]) for the REVOKE bit (8).

8. Security Considerations

In addition to the following sections, see also Theory of Operation above (Section 2) and especially Section 2.2 for related discussions.

Security considerations for trust anchor rollover not specific to this protocol are discussed in [RFC4986].

8.1. Key Ownership vs. Acceptance Policy

The reader should note that, while the zone owner is responsible for creating and distributing keys, it's wholly the decision of the resolver owner as to whether to accept such keys for the authentication of the zone information. This implies the decision to update trust-anchor keys based on trusting a current trust-anchor key is also the resolver owner's decision.

The resolver owner (and resolver implementers) MAY choose to permit or prevent key status updates based on this mechanism for specific trust points. If they choose to prevent the automated updates, they will need to establish a mechanism for manual or other out-of-band updates, which are outside the scope of this document.

8.2. Multiple Key Compromise

This scheme permits recovery as long as at least one valid trust-anchor key remains uncompromised, e.g., if there are three keys, you can recover if two of them are compromised. The zone owner should determine their own level of comfort with respect to the number of active, valid trust anchors in a zone and should be prepared to implement recovery procedures once they detect a compromise. A manual or other out-of-band update of all resolvers will be required if all trust-anchor keys at a trust point are compromised.

8.3. Dynamic Updates

Allowing a resolver to update its trust anchor set based on in-band key information is potentially less secure than a manual process. However, given the nature of the DNS, the number of resolvers that would require update if a trust anchor key were compromised, and the lack of a standard management framework for DNS, this approach is no worse than the existing situation.

9. Normative References

[RFC2119] Bradner, S., "Key words for use in RFCs to Indicate Requirement Levels", BCP 14, RFC 2119, March 1997.

[RFC3755] Weiler, S., "Legacy Resolver Compatibility for Delegation Signer (DS)", RFC 3755, May 2004.

[RFC4033] Arends, R., Austein, R., Larson, M., Massey, D., and S. Rose, "DNS Security Introduction and Requirements", RFC 4033, March 2005.

[RFC4034] Arends, R., Austein, R., Larson, M., Massey, D., and S. Rose, "Resource Records for the DNS Security Extensions", RFC 4034, March 2005.

[RFC4035] Arends, R., Austein, R., Larson, M., Massey, D., and S. Rose, "Protocol Modifications for the DNS Security Extensions", RFC 4035, March 2005.

10. Informative References

[RFC4986] Eland, H., Mundy, R., Crocker, S., and S. Krishnaswamy, "Requirements Related to DNS Security (DNSSEC) Trust Anchor Rollover", RFC 4986, August 2007.

Author's Address

Michael StJohns
Independent

EMail: mstjohns@comcast.net

Full Copyright Statement

Intellectual Property

The IETF takes no position regarding the validity or scope of any Intellectual Property Rights or other rights that might be claimed to pertain to the implementation or use of the technology described in this document or the extent to which any license under such rights might or might not be available; nor does it represent that it has made any independent effort to identify any such rights. Information on the procedures with respect to rights in RFC documents can be found in BCP 78 and BCP 79.

Copies of IPR disclosures made to the IETF Secretariat and any assurances of licenses to be made available, or the result of an attempt made to obtain a general license or permission for the use of such proprietary rights by implementers or users of this specification can be obtained from the IETF on-line IPR repository at http://www.ietf.org/ipr.

The IETF invites any interested party to bring to its attention any copyrights, patents or patent applications, or other proprietary rights that may cover technology that may be required to implement this standard. Please address the information to the IETF at ietf-ipr@ietf.org.

RFC 5074
DNSSEC Lookaside Validation (DLV)

Network Working Group
Request for Comments: 5074
Category: Informational

S. Weiler
SPARTA, Inc.
November 2007

Status of This Memo

This memo provides information for the Internet community. It does not specify an Internet standard of any kind. Distribution of this memo is unlimited.

Abstract

DNSSEC Lookaside Validation (DLV) is a mechanism for publishing DNS Security (DNSSEC) trust anchors outside of the DNS delegation chain. It allows validating resolvers to validate DNSSEC-signed data from zones whose ancestors either aren't signed or don't publish Delegation Signer (DS) records for their children.

RFC 5074 Contents

1. Introduction

DNSSEC [RFC4033] [RFC4034] [RFC4035] authenticates DNS data by building public-key signature chains along the DNS delegation chain from a trust anchor.

In the present world, with the DNS root and many key top level domains unsigned, the only way for a validating resolver ("validator") to validate the many DNSSEC-signed zones is to maintain a sizable collection of preconfigured trust anchors. Maintaining multiple preconfigured trust anchors in each DNSSEC-aware validator presents a significant management challenge.

This document describes a way to publish trust anchors in the DNS outside of the normal delegation chain, as a way to easily configure many validators within an organization or to "outsource" trust anchor management.

Some design trade-offs leading to the mechanism presented here are described in [INI1999-19].

The key words "MUST", "MUST NOT", "REQUIRED", "SHALL", "SHALL NOT", "SHOULD", "SHOULD NOT", "RECOMMENDED", "MAY", and "OPTIONAL" in this document are to be interpreted as described in RFC 2119 [RFC2119].

2. Architecture

DNSSEC Lookaside Validation allows a set of domains, called "DLV domains", to publish secure entry points for zones that are not their own children.

With DNSSEC, validators may expect a zone to be secure when validators have one of two things: a preconfigured trust anchor for the zone or a validated Delegation Signer (DS) record for the zone in the zone's parent (which presumes a preconfigured trust anchor for the parent or another ancestor). DLV adds a third mechanism: a validated entry in a DLV domain (which presumes a preconfigured trust anchor for the DLV domain). Whenever a DLV domain contains a DLV RRset for a zone, a validator may expect the named zone to be signed. Absence of a DLV RRset for a zone does not necessarily mean that the zone should be expected to be insecure; if the validator has another reason to believe the zone should be secured, validation of that zone's data should still be attempted.

3. DLV Domains

A DLV domain includes trust statements about descendants of a single zone, called the 'target' zone. For example, the DLV domain trustbroker.example.com could target the org zone and the DLV domain bar.example.com could target the root.

A DLV domain contains one or more DLV records [RFC4431] for each of the target's descendant zones that have registered security information with it. For a given zone, the corresponding name in the DLV domain is formed by replacing the target zone name with the DLV domain name.

For example, assuming the DLV domain trustbroker.example.com targets the org zone, any DLV records corresponding to the zone example.org can be found at example.trustbroker.example.com. DLV records corresponding to the org zone can be found at the apex of trustbroker.example.com.

As another example, assuming the DLV domain bar.example.com targets the root zone, DLV records corresponding to the zone example.org can be found at example.org.bar.example.com. DLV records corresponding to the org zone can be found at org.bar.example.com, and DLV records corresponding to the root zone itself can be found at the apex of bar.example.com.

A DLV domain need not contain data other than DLV records, appropriate DNSSEC records validating that data, the apex NS and SOA records, and, optionally, delegations. In most cases, the operator of a DLV domain will probably not want to include any other RR types in the DLV domain.

To gain full benefit from aggressive negative caching, described in Section 6, a DLV domain SHOULD NOT use minimally-covering NSEC records, as described in [RFC4470], and it SHOULD NOT use NSEC3 records, as described in [NSEC3].

4. Overview of Validator Behavior

To minimize the load on the DLV domain's authoritative servers as well as query response time, a validator SHOULD first attempt validation using any applicable (non-DLV) trust anchors. If the validation succeeds (with a result of Secure), DLV processing need not occur.

When configured with a trust anchor for a DLV domain, a validator SHOULD attempt to validate all responses at and below the target of that DLV domain.

To do validation using DLV, a validator looks for a (validated) DLV RRset applicable to the query, as described in the following section, and uses it as though it were a DS RRset to validate the answer using the normal procedures in Section 5 of RFC 4035.

For each response, the validator attempts validation using the "closest enclosing" DLV RRset in the DLV domain, which is the DLV RRset with the longest name that matches the query or could be an ancestor of the QNAME. For example, assuming the DLV domain trustbroker.example.com targets the org zone, and there exist DLV RRsets named trustbroker.example.com (applicable to org), example.trustbroker.example.com (applicable to example.org), and
sub.example.trustbroker.example.com (applicable to sub.example.org), a validator would use the sub.example.trustbroker.example.com DLV RRset for validating responses to a query for sub.example.org.

The choice of which DLV record(s) to use has a significant impact on the query load seen at DLV domains' authoritative servers. The particular DLV selection rule described in this document results in a higher query load than some other selection rules, but it has some advantages in terms of the security policies that it can implement. More detailed discussion of this DLV selection rule as well as several alternatives that were considered along the way can be found in [INI1999-19].

5. Details of Validator Behavior

As above, to minimize the load on the DLV domain's authoritative servers as well as query response time, a validator SHOULD first attempt validation using any applicable (non-DLV) trust anchors. If the validation succeeds (with a result of Secure), DLV processing need not occur.

To find the closest enclosing DLV RRset for a given query, the validator starts by looking for a DLV RRset corresponding to the QNAME. If it doesn't find a DLV RRset for that name (as confirmed by the presence of a validated NSEC record) and that name is not the apex of the DLV domain, the validator removes the leading label from the name and tries again. This process is repeated until a DLV RRset is found or it is proved that there is no enclosing DLV RRset applicable to the QNAME. In all cases, a validator SHOULD check its cache for the desired DLV RRset before issuing a query. Section 8 discusses a slight optimization to this strategy.

Having found the closest enclosing DLV RRset or received proof that no applicable DLV RRset exists, the validator MUST validate the RRset or non-existence proof using the normal procedures in Section 5 of RFC 4035. In particular, any delegations within the DLV domain need to be followed, with normal DNSSEC validation applied. If validation of the DLV RRset leads to a result of Bogus, then it MUST NOT be used and the validation result for the original response SHOULD be Bogus, also. If validation of the DLV RRset leads to a result of Insecure (i.e., the DLV record is in an unsecured portion of the DLV domain), then it MUST NOT be used and the validation result for the original response SHOULD be Insecure, also. (It should be very odd, indeed, to find part of a DLV domain marked as Insecure: this is likely to happen only when there are delegations within the DLV domain and some portions of that domain use different cryptographic signing algorithms.) If the validation of the DLV RRset leads to a result of Secure, the validator then treats that DLV RRset as though it were a DS RRset for the applicable zone and attempts validation using the procedures described in Section 5 of RFC 4035.

In the interest of limiting complexity, validators SHOULD NOT attempt to use DLV to validate data from another DLV domain.

6. Aggressive Negative Caching

To minimize load on authoritative servers for DLV domains, particularly those with few entries, DLV validators SHOULD implement aggressive negative caching, as defined in this section.

Previously, cached negative responses were indexed by QNAME, QCLASS, QTYPE, and the setting of the CD bit (see RFC 4035, Section 4.7), and only queries matching the index key would be answered from the cache. With aggressive negative caching, the validator, in addition to checking to see if the answer is in its cache before sending a query, checks to see whether any cached and validated NSEC record denies the existence of the sought record(s).

Using aggressive negative caching, a validator will not make queries for any name covered by a cached and validated NSEC record. Furthermore, a validator answering queries from clients will synthesize a negative answer whenever it has an applicable validated NSEC in its cache unless the CD bit was set on the incoming query.

6.1. Implementation Notes

Implementing aggressive negative caching suggests that a validator will need to build an ordered data structure of NSEC records in order to efficiently find covering NSEC records. Only NSEC records from DLV domains need to be included in this data structure.

Also note that some DLV validator implementations do not synthesize negative answers to insert into outgoing responses – they only use aggressive negative caching when looking up DLV RRs as part of their internal DLV validation.

7. Overlapping DLV Domains

It is possible to have multiple DLV domains targeting overlapping portions of the DNS hierarchy. For example, two DLV domains, perhaps operated by different parties, might target the org zone, or one DLV domain might target the root while another targets org.

If a validator supports multiple DLV domains, the choice of precedence in case of overlap is left up to the implementation and SHOULD be exposed as a configuration option to the user (as compared to the choice of DLV records within each domain, a precedence for which is clearly specified in this document). As a very simple default, a validator could give precedence to the most specific DLV domain.

Some other reasonable options include:

1.   Searching all applicable DLV domains until an applicable DLV record is found that results in a successful validation of the response. In the case where no applicable DLV record is found in any DLV domain, the answer will be treated as Unsecure.

2.   Applying some sort of precedence to the DLV domains based on their perceived trustworthiness.

3.   Searching all applicable DLV domains for applicable DLV records and using only the most specific of those DLV records.

4.   If multiple DLV domains provide applicable DLV records, use a threshold or scoring system (e.g., "best 2 out of 3") to determine the validation result.

The above list is surely not complete, and it's possible for validators to have different precedence rules and configuration options for these cases. [INI1999-19] discusses different policies for selecting from multiple DLV records within the same DLV domain. That discussion may also be applicable to the question of which DLV domain to use and may be of interest to implementers of validators that support multiple DLV domains.

8. Optimization

This section documents an optimization to further reduce query load on DLV servers and improve validator response time.

Authoritative servers, when processing a query for a DLV RRset, SHOULD include all DLV RRsets potentially applicable to a query (specifically, all DLV RRsets applicable to the QNAME and any of its ancestors) in the Additional section of the response as well as NSEC records proving the non-existence of any other applicable DLV records in the DLV domain. Authoritative servers need only include DLV RRsets they're aware of – RRsets in sub-zones may be omitted.

Validators still seek out of the closest enclosing DLV RRset first. If they receive any data about other DLV RRsets in the zone, they MAY cache and use it (assuming that it validates), thus avoiding further round-trips to the DLV domain's authoritative servers.

9. Security Considerations

Validators MUST NOT use a DLV record unless it has been successfully authenticated. Normally, validators will have a trust anchor for the DLV domain and use DNSSEC to validate the data in it.

Aggressive negative caching increases the need for validators to do some basic validation of incoming NSEC records before caching them. In particular, the 'next name' field in the NSEC record MUST be within the zone that generated (and signed) the NSEC. Otherwise, a malicious zone operator could generate an NSEC that reaches out of its zone – into its ancestor zones, even up into the root zone – and use that NSEC to spoof away any name that sorts after the name of the NSEC. We call these overreaching NSECs. More insidiously, an attacker could use an overreaching NSEC in combination with a signed wildcard record to substitute a signed positive answer in place of the real data. This checking is not a new requirement – these attacks are a risk even without aggressive negative caching. However, aggressive negative caching makes the checking more important. Before aggressive negative caching, NSECs were cached only as metadata associated with a particular query. An overreaching NSEC that resulted from a broken zone signing tool or some misconfiguration would only be used by a cache for those queries that it had specifically made before. Only an overreaching NSEC actively served by an attacker could cause misbehavior. With aggressive negative caching, an overreaching NSEC can cause broader problems even in the absence of an active attacker. This threat can be easily mitigated by checking the bounds on the NSEC.

As a reminder, validators MUST NOT use the mere presence of an RRSIG or apex DNSKEY RRset as a trigger for doing validation, whether through the normal DNSSEC hierarchy or DLV. Otherwise, an attacker might perpetrate a downgrade attack by stripping off those RRSIGs or DNSKEYs.

Section 8 of RFC 4034 describes security considerations specific to the DS RR. Those considerations are equally applicable to DLV RRs. Of particular note, the key tag field is used to help select DNSKEY RRs efficiently, but it does not uniquely identify a single DNSKEY RR. It is possible for two distinct DNSKEY RRs to have the same owner name, the same algorithm type, and the same key tag. An implementation that uses only the key tag to select a DNSKEY RR might select the wrong public key in some circumstances.

For further discussion of the security implications of DNSSEC, see RFCs 4033, 4034, and 4035.

10. IANA Considerations

DLV makes use of the DLV resource record (RR type 32769) previously assigned in [RFC4431].

11. References

11.1. Normative References

[RFC2119] Bradner, S., "Key words for use in RFCs to Indicate Requirement Levels", BCP 14, RFC 2119, March 1997.

[RFC4033] Arends, R., Austein, R., Larson, M., Massey, D., and S. Rose, "DNS Security Introduction and Requirements", RFC 4033, March 2005.

[RFC4034] Arends, R., Austein, R., Larson, M., Massey, D., and S. Rose, "Resource Records for the DNS Security Extensions", RFC 4034, March 2005.

[RFC4035] Arends, R., Austein, R., Larson, M., Massey, D., and S. Rose, "Protocol Modifications for the DNS Security Extensions", RFC 4035, March 2005.

[RFC4431] Andrews, M. and S. Weiler, "The DNSSEC Lookaside Validation (DLV) DNS Resource Record", RFC 4431, February 2006.

11.2. Informative References

[INI1999-19] Weiler, S., "Deploying DNSSEC Without a Signed Root", Technical Report 1999-19, Information Networking Institute, Carnegie Mellon University, April 2004.

[NSEC3] Laurie, B., Sisson, G., Arends, R., and D. Blacka, "DNSSEC Hashed Authenticated Denial of Existence", Work in Progress, July 2007.

[RFC4470] Weiler, S. and J. Ihren, "Minimally Covering NSEC Records and DNSSEC On-line Signing", RFC 4470, April 2006.

Appendix A. Acknowledgments

Johan Ihren, Paul Vixie, and Suzanne Woolf contributed significantly to the exploration of possible validator algorithms that led to this design. More about those explorations is documented in [INI1999-19].

Johan Ihren and the editor share the blame for aggressive negative caching.

Thanks to David B. Johnson and Marvin Sirbu for their patient review of [INI1999-19] which led to this specification being far more complete.

Thanks to Mark Andrews, Rob Austein, David Blacka, Stephane Bortzmeyer, Steve Crocker, Wes Hardaker, Alfred Hoenes, Russ Housley, Peter Koch, Olaf Kolkman, Juergen Quittek, and Suzanne Woolf for their valuable comments on this document.

Author's Address

Samuel Weiler
SPARTA, Inc.
7110 Samuel Morse Drive
Columbia, Maryland 21046
US

EMail: weiler@tislabs.com

Full Copyright Statement

Intellectual Property

RFC 5155
DNS Security (DNSSEC) Hashed Authenticated Denial of Existence

Network Working Group
Request for Comments: 5155
Category: Standards Track

B. Laurie
G. Sisson
R. Arends
Nominet
D. Blacka
VeriSign, Inc.
March 2008

Status of This Memo

Abstract

The Domain Name System Security (DNSSEC) Extensions introduced the NSEC resource record (RR) for authenticated denial of existence. This document introduces an alternative resource record, NSEC3, which similarly provides authenticated denial of existence. However, it also provides measures against zone enumeration and permits gradual expansion of delegation-centric zones.

RFC 5155 Contents

1. Introduction

1.1. Rationale

The DNS Security Extensions included the NSEC RR to provide authenticated denial of existence. Though the NSEC RR meets the requirements for authenticated denial of existence, it introduces a side-effect in that the contents of a zone can be enumerated. This property introduces undesired policy issues.

The enumeration is enabled by the set of NSEC records that exists inside a signed zone. An NSEC record lists two names that are ordered canonically, in order to show that nothing exists between the two names. The complete set of NSEC records lists all the names in a zone. It is trivial to enumerate the content of a zone by querying for names that do not exist.

An enumerated zone can be used, for example, as a source of probable e-mail addresses for spam, or as a key for multiple WHOIS queries to reveal registrant data that many registries may have legal obligations to protect. Many registries therefore prohibit the copying of their zone data; however, the use of NSEC RRs renders these policies unenforceable.

A second problem is that the cost to cryptographically secure delegations to unsigned zones is high, relative to the perceived security benefit, in two cases: large, delegation-centric zones, and zones where insecure delegations will be updated rapidly. In these cases, the costs of maintaining the NSEC RR chain may be extremely high and use of the "Opt-Out" convention may be more appropriate (for these unsecured zones).

This document presents the NSEC3 Resource Record which can be used as an alternative to NSEC to mitigate these issues.

Earlier work to address these issues include [DNSEXT-NO], [RFC4956], and [DNSEXT-NSEC2v2].

1.2. Requirements

The key words "MUST", "MUST NOT", "REQUIRED", "SHALL", "SHALL NOT", "SHOULD", "SHOULD NOT", "RECOMMENDED", "MAY", and "OPTIONAL" in this document are to be interpreted as described in [RFC2119].

1.3. Terminology

The reader is assumed to be familiar with the basic DNS and DNSSEC concepts described in [RFC1034], [RFC1035], [RFC4033], [RFC4034], [RFC4035], and subsequent RFCs that update them: [RFC2136], [RFC2181], and [RFC2308].

The following terminology is used throughout this document:

Zone enumeration: the practice of discovering the full content of a zone via successive queries. Zone enumeration was non-trivial prior to the introduction of DNSSEC.

Original owner name: the owner name corresponding to a hashed owner name.

Hashed owner name: the owner name created after applying the hash function to an owner name.

Hash order: the order in which hashed owner names are arranged according to their numerical value, treating the leftmost (lowest numbered) octet as the most significant octet. Note that this order is the same as the canonical DNS name order specified in [RFC4034], when the hashed owner names are in base32, encoded with an Extended Hex Alphabet [RFC4648].

Empty non-terminal: a domain name that owns no resource records, but has one or more subdomains that do.

Delegation: an NS RRSet with a name different from the current zone apex (non-zone-apex), signifying a delegation to a child zone.

Secure delegation: a name containing a delegation (NS RRSet) and a signed DS RRSet, signifying a delegation to a signed child zone.

Insecure delegation: a name containing a delegation (NS RRSet), but lacking a DS RRSet, signifying a delegation to an unsigned child zone.

Opt-Out NSEC3 resource record: an NSEC3 resource record that has the Opt-Out flag set to 1.

Opt-Out zone: a zone with at least one Opt-Out NSEC3 RR.

Closest encloser: the longest existing ancestor of a name. See also Section 3.3.1 of [RFC4592].

Closest provable encloser: the longest ancestor of a name that can be proven to exist. Note that this is only different from the closest encloser in an Opt-Out zone.

Next closer name: the name one label longer than the closest provable encloser of a name.

Base32: the "Base 32 Encoding with Extended Hex Alphabet" as specified in [RFC4648]. Note that trailing padding characters ("=") are not used in the NSEC3 specification.

To cover: An NSEC3 RR is said to "cover" a name if the hash of the name or "next closer" name falls between the owner name and the next hashed owner name of the NSEC3. In other words, if it proves the nonexistence of the name, either directly or by proving the nonexistence of an ancestor of the name.

To match: An NSEC3 RR is said to "match" a name if the owner name of the NSEC3 RR is the same as the hashed owner name of that name.

2. Backwards Compatibility

This specification describes a protocol change that is not generally backwards compatible with [RFC4033], [RFC4034], and [RFC4035]. In particular, security-aware resolvers that are unaware of this specification (NSEC3-unaware resolvers) may fail to validate the responses introduced by this document.

In order to aid deployment, this specification uses a signaling technique to prevent NSEC3-unaware resolvers from attempting to validate responses from NSEC3-signed zones.

This specification allocates two new DNSKEY algorithm identifiers for this purpose. Algorithm 6, DSA-NSEC3-SHA1 is an alias for algorithm 3, DSA. Algorithm 7, RSASHA1-NSEC3-SHA1 is an alias for algorithm 5, RSASHA1. These are not new algorithms, they are additional identifiers for the existing algorithms.

Zones signed according to this specification MUST only use these algorithm identifiers for their DNSKEY RRs. Because these new identifiers will be unknown algorithms to existing, NSEC3-unaware resolvers, those resolvers will then treat responses from the NSEC3 signed zone as insecure, as detailed in Section 5.2 of [RFC4035].

These algorithm identifiers are used with the NSEC3 hash algorithm SHA1. Using other NSEC3 hash algorithms requires allocation of a new alias (see Section 12.1.3).

Security aware resolvers that are aware of this specification MUST recognize the new algorithm identifiers and treat them as equivalent to the algorithms that they alias.

A methodology for transitioning from a DNSSEC signed zone to a zone signed using NSEC3 is discussed in Section 10.4.

3. The NSEC3 Resource Record

The NSEC3 Resource Record (RR) provides authenticated denial of existence for DNS Resource Record Sets.

The NSEC3 RR lists RR types present at the original owner name of the NSEC3 RR. It includes the next hashed owner name in the hash order of the zone. The complete set of NSEC3 RRs in a zone indicates which RRSets exist for the original owner name of the RR and form a chain of hashed owner names in the zone. This information is used to provide authenticated denial of existence for DNS data. To provide protection against zone enumeration, the owner names used in the NSEC3 RR are cryptographic hashes of the original owner name prepended as a single label to the name of the zone. The NSEC3 RR indicates which hash function is used to construct the hash, which salt is used, and how many iterations of the hash function are performed over the original owner name. The hashing technique is described fully in Section 5.

Hashed owner names of unsigned delegations may be excluded from the chain. An NSEC3 RR whose span covers the hash of an owner name or "next closer" name of an unsigned delegation is referred to as an Opt-Out NSEC3 RR and is indicated by the presence of a flag.

The owner name for the NSEC3 RR is the base32 encoding of the hashed owner name prepended as a single label to the name of the zone.

The type value for the NSEC3 RR is 50.

The NSEC3 RR RDATA format is class independent and is described below.

The class MUST be the same as the class of the original owner name.

The NSEC3 RR SHOULD have the same TTL value as the SOA minimum TTL field. This is in the spirit of negative caching [RFC2308].

3.1. RDATA Fields

3.1.1. Hash Algorithm

The Hash Algorithm field identifies the cryptographic hash algorithm used to construct the hash-value.

The values for this field are defined in the NSEC3 hash algorithm registry defined in Section 11.

3.1.2. Flags

The Flags field contains 8 one-bit flags that can be used to indicate different processing. All undefined flags must be zero. The only flag defined by this specification is the Opt-Out flag.

3.1.2.1. Opt-Out Flag

If the Opt-Out flag is set, the NSEC3 record covers zero or more unsigned delegations.

If the Opt-Out flag is clear, the NSEC3 record covers zero unsigned delegations.

The Opt-Out Flag indicates whether this NSEC3 RR may cover unsigned delegations. It is the least significant bit in the Flags field. See Section 6 for details about the use of this flag.

3.1.3. Iterations

The Iterations field defines the number of additional times the hash function has been performed. More iterations result in greater resiliency of the hash value against dictionary attacks, but at a higher computational cost for both the server and resolver. See Section 5 for details of the use of this field, and Section 10.3 for limitations on the value.

3.1.4. Salt Length

The Salt Length field defines the length of the Salt field in octets, ranging in value from 0 to 255.

3.1.5. Salt

The Salt field is appended to the original owner name before hashing in order to defend against pre-calculated dictionary attacks. See Section 5 for details on how the salt is used.

3.1.6. Hash Length

The Hash Length field defines the length of the Next Hashed Owner Name field, ranging in value from 1 to 255 octets.

3.1.7. Next Hashed Owner Name

The Next Hashed Owner Name field contains the next hashed owner name in hash order. This value is in binary format. Given the ordered set of all hashed owner names, the Next Hashed Owner Name field contains the hash of an owner name that immediately follows the owner name of the given NSEC3 RR. The value of the Next Hashed Owner Name field in the last NSEC3 RR in the zone is the same as the hashed owner name of the first NSEC3 RR in the zone in hash order. Note that, unlike the owner name of the NSEC3 RR, the value of this field does not contain the appended zone name.

3.1.8. Type Bit Maps

The Type Bit Maps field identifies the RRSet types that exist at the original owner name of the NSEC3 RR.

3.2. NSEC3 RDATA Wire Format

The RDATA of the NSEC3 RR is as shown below:

```
                        1 1 1 1 1 1 1 1 1 1 2 2 2 2 2 2 2 2 2 2 3 3
    0 1 2 3 4 5 6 7 8 9 0 1 2 3 4 5 6 7 8 9 0 1 2 3 4 5 6 7 8 9 0 1
   +-+-+-+-+-+-+-+-+-+-+-+-+-+-+-+-+-+-+-+-+-+-+-+-+-+-+-+-+-+-+-+-+
   |   Hash Alg.   |     Flags     |           Iterations          |
   +-+-+-+-+-+-+-+-+-+-+-+-+-+-+-+-+-+-+-+-+-+-+-+-+-+-+-+-+-+-+-+-+
   |  Salt Length  |                     Salt                      /
   +-+-+-+-+-+-+-+-+-+-+-+-+-+-+-+-+-+-+-+-+-+-+-+-+-+-+-+-+-+-+-+-+
   |  Hash Length  |             Next Hashed Owner Name            /
   +-+-+-+-+-+-+-+-+-+-+-+-+-+-+-+-+-+-+-+-+-+-+-+-+-+-+-+-+-+-+-+-+
   /                         Type Bit Maps                         /
   +-+-+-+-+-+-+-+-+-+-+-+-+-+-+-+-+-+-+-+-+-+-+-+-+-+-+-+-+-+-+-+-+
```

Hash Algorithm is a single octet.

Flags field is a single octet, the Opt-Out flag is the least significant bit, as shown below:

```
 0 1 2 3 4 5 6 7
+-+-+-+-+-+-+-+-+
|             |O|
+-+-+-+-+-+-+-+-+
```

Iterations is represented as a 16-bit unsigned integer, with the most significant bit first.

Salt Length is represented as an unsigned octet. Salt Length represents the length of the Salt field in octets. If the value is zero, the following Salt field is omitted.

Salt, if present, is encoded as a sequence of binary octets. The length of this field is determined by the preceding Salt Length field.

Hash Length is represented as an unsigned octet. Hash Length represents the length of the Next Hashed Owner Name field in octets.

The next hashed owner name is not base32 encoded, unlike the owner name of the NSEC3 RR. It is the unmodified binary hash value. It does not include the name of the containing zone. The length of this field is determined by the preceding Hash Length field.

3.2.1. Type Bit Maps Encoding

The encoding of the Type Bit Maps field is the same as that used by the NSEC RR, described in [RFC4034]. It is explained and clarified here for clarity.

The RR type space is split into 256 window blocks, each representing the low-order 8 bits of the 16-bit RR type space. Each block that has at least one active RR type is encoded using a single octet window number (from 0 to 255), a single octet bitmap length (from 1 to 32) indicating the number of octets used for the bitmap of the window block, and up to 32 octets (256 bits) of bitmap.

Blocks are present in the NSEC3 RR RDATA in increasing numerical order.

> Type Bit Maps Field = (Window Block # — Bitmap Length — Bitmap)+
>
> where "—" denotes concatenation.

Each bitmap encodes the low-order 8 bits of RR types within the window block, in network bit order. The first bit is bit 0. For window block 0, bit 1 corresponds to RR type 1 (A), bit 2 corresponds to RR type 2 (NS), and so forth. For window block 1, bit 1 corresponds to RR type 257, bit 2 to RR type 258. If a bit is set to 1, it indicates that an RRSet of that type is present for the original owner name of the NSEC3 RR. If a bit is set to 0, it indicates that no RRSet of that type is present for the original owner name of the NSEC3 RR.

Since bit 0 in window block 0 refers to the non-existing RR type 0, it MUST be set to 0. After verification, the validator MUST ignore the value of bit 0 in window block 0.

Bits representing Meta-TYPEs or QTYPEs as specified in Section 3.1 of [RFC2929] or within the range reserved for assignment only to QTYPEs and Meta-TYPEs MUST be set to 0, since they do not appear in zone data. If encountered, they must be ignored upon reading.

Blocks with no types present MUST NOT be included. Trailing zero octets in the bitmap MUST be omitted. The length of the bitmap of each block is determined by the type code with the largest numerical value, within that block, among the set of RR types present at the original owner name of the NSEC3 RR. Trailing octets not specified MUST be interpreted as zero octets.

3.3. Presentation Format

The presentation format of the RDATA portion is as follows:

- The Hash Algorithm field is represented as an unsigned decimal integer. The value has a maximum of 255.

- The Flags field is represented as an unsigned decimal integer. The value has a maximum of 255.

- The Iterations field is represented as an unsigned decimal integer. The value is between 0 and 65535, inclusive.

- The Salt Length field is not represented.

- The Salt field is represented as a sequence of case-insensitive hexadecimal digits. Whitespace is not allowed within the sequence. The Salt field is represented as "-" (without the quotes) when the Salt Length field has a value of 0.

- The Hash Length field is not represented.

- The Next Hashed Owner Name field is represented as an unpadded sequence of case-insensitive base32 digits, without whitespace.

- The Type Bit Maps field is represented as a sequence of RR type mnemonics. When the mnemonic is not known, the TYPE representation as described in Section 5 of [RFC3597] MUST be used.

4. The NSEC3PARAM Resource Record

The NSEC3PARAM RR contains the NSEC3 parameters (hash algorithm, flags, iterations, and salt) needed by authoritative servers to calculate hashed owner names. The presence of an NSEC3PARAM RR at a zone apex indicates that the specified parameters may be used by authoritative servers to choose an appropriate set of NSEC3 RRs for negative responses. The NSEC3PARAM RR is not used by validators or resolvers.

If an NSEC3PARAM RR is present at the apex of a zone with a Flags field value of zero, then there MUST be an NSEC3 RR using the same hash algorithm, iterations, and salt parameters present at every hashed owner name in the zone. That is, the zone MUST contain a complete set of NSEC3 RRs with the same hash algorithm, iterations, and salt parameters.

The owner name for the NSEC3PARAM RR is the name of the zone apex.

The type value for the NSEC3PARAM RR is 51.

The NSEC3PARAM RR RDATA format is class independent and is described below.

The class MUST be the same as the NSEC3 RRs to which this RR refers.

4.1. RDATA Fields

The RDATA for this RR mirrors the first four fields in the NSEC3 RR.

4.1.1. Hash Algorithm

The Hash Algorithm field identifies the cryptographic hash algorithm used to construct the hash-value.

The acceptable values are the same as the corresponding field in the NSEC3 RR.

4.1.2. Flag Fields

The Opt-Out flag is not used and is set to zero.

All other flags are reserved for future use, and must be zero.

NSEC3PARAM RRs with a Flags field value other than zero MUST be ignored.

4.1.3. Iterations

The Iterations field defines the number of additional times the hash is performed.

Its acceptable values are the same as the corresponding field in the NSEC3 RR.

4.1.4. Salt Length

The Salt Length field defines the length of the salt in octets, ranging in value from 0 to 255.

4.1.5. Salt

The Salt field is appended to the original owner name before hashing.

4.2. NSEC3PARAM RDATA Wire Format

The RDATA of the NSEC3PARAM RR is as shown below:

```
                            1 1 1 1 1 1 1 1 1 1 2 2 2 2 2 2 2 2 2 2 3 3
    0 1 2 3 4 5 6 7 8 9 0 1 2 3 4 5 6 7 8 9 0 1 2 3 4 5 6 7 8 9 0 1
   +-+-+-+-+-+-+-+-+-+-+-+-+-+-+-+-+-+-+-+-+-+-+-+-+-+-+-+-+-+-+-+-+
   |   Hash Alg.   |     Flags     |            Iterations         |
   +-+-+-+-+-+-+-+-+-+-+-+-+-+-+-+-+-+-+-+-+-+-+-+-+-+-+-+-+-+-+-+-+
   |  Salt Length  |                    Salt                       /
   +-+-+-+-+-+-+-+-+-+-+-+-+-+-+-+-+-+-+-+-+-+-+-+-+-+-+-+-+-+-+-+-+
```

Hash Algorithm is a single octet.

Flags field is a single octet.

Iterations is represented as a 16-bit unsigned integer, with the most significant bit first.

Salt Length is represented as an unsigned octet. Salt Length represents the length of the following Salt field in octets. If the value is zero, the Salt field is omitted.

Salt, if present, is encoded as a sequence of binary octets. The length of this field is determined by the preceding Salt Length field.

4.3. Presentation Format

The presentation format of the RDATA portion is as follows:

- The Hash Algorithm field is represented as an unsigned decimal integer. The value has a maximum of 255.

- The Flags field is represented as an unsigned decimal integer. The value has a maximum value of 255.

- The Iterations field is represented as an unsigned decimal integer. The value is between 0 and 65535, inclusive.

- The Salt Length field is not represented.

- The Salt field is represented as a sequence of case-insensitive hexadecimal digits. Whitespace is not allowed within the sequence. This field is represented as "-" (without the quotes) when the Salt Length field is zero.

5. Calculation of the Hash

The hash calculation uses three of the NSEC3 RDATA fields: Hash Algorithm, Salt, and Iterations.

Define H(x) to be the hash of x using the Hash Algorithm selected by the NSEC3 RR, k to be the number of Iterations, and —— to indicate concatenation. Then define:

$$IH(salt, x, 0) = H(x \text{------} salt), \text{ and}$$

$$IH(salt, x, k) = H(IH(salt, x, k-1) \text{------} salt), \text{ if } k > 0$$

Then the calculated hash of an owner name is

$$IH(salt, \text{owner name, iterations}),$$

where the owner name is in the canonical form, defined as:

The wire format of the owner name where:

1.   The owner name is fully expanded (no DNS name compression) and fully qualified;

2.   All uppercase US-ASCII letters are replaced by the corresponding lowercase US-ASCII letters;

3.   If the owner name is a wildcard name, the owner name is in its original unexpanded form, including the "*" label (no wildcard substitution);

This form is as defined in Section 6.2 of [RFC4034].

The method to calculate the Hash is based on [RFC2898].

6. Opt-Out

In this specification, as in [RFC4033], [RFC4034] and [RFC4035], NS RRSets at delegation points are not signed and may be accompanied by a DS RRSet. With the Opt-Out bit clear, the security status of the child zone is determined by the presence or absence of this DS RRSet, cryptographically proven by the signed NSEC3 RR at the hashed owner name of the delegation. Setting the Opt-Out flag modifies this by allowing insecure delegations to exist within the signed zone without a corresponding NSEC3 RR at the hashed owner name of the delegation.

An Opt-Out NSEC3 RR is said to cover a delegation if the hash of the owner name or "next closer" name of the delegation is between the owner name of the NSEC3 RR and the next hashed owner name.

An Opt-Out NSEC3 RR does not assert the existence or non-existence of the insecure delegations that it may cover. This allows for the addition or removal of these delegations without recalculating or re-signing RRs in the NSEC3 RR chain. However, Opt-Out NSEC3 RRs do assert the (non)existence of other, authoritative RRSets.

An Opt-Out NSEC3 RR MAY have the same original owner name as an insecure delegation. In this case, the delegation is proven insecure by the lack of a DS bit in the type map and the signed NSEC3 RR does assert the existence of the delegation.

Zones using Opt-Out MAY contain a mixture of Opt-Out NSEC3 RRs and non-Opt-Out NSEC3 RRs. If an NSEC3 RR is not Opt-Out, there MUST NOT be any hashed owner names of insecure delegations (nor any other RRs) between it and the name indicated by the next hashed owner name in the NSEC3 RDATA. If it is Opt-Out, it MUST only cover hashed owner names or hashed "next closer" names of insecure delegations.

The effects of the Opt-Out flag on signing, serving, and validating responses are covered in following sections.

7. Authoritative Server Considerations

7.1. Zone Signing

Zones using NSEC3 must satisfy the following properties:

- Each owner name within the zone that owns authoritative RRSets MUST have a corresponding NSEC3 RR. Owner names that correspond to unsigned delegations MAY have a corresponding NSEC3 RR. However, if there is not a corresponding NSEC3 RR, there MUST be an Opt-Out NSEC3 RR that covers the "next closer" name to the delegation. Other non-authoritative RRs are not represented by NSEC3 RRs.

- Each empty non-terminal MUST have a corresponding NSEC3 RR, unless the empty non-terminal is only derived from an insecure delegation covered by an Opt-Out NSEC3 RR.

- The TTL value for any NSEC3 RR SHOULD be the same as the minimum TTL value field in the zone SOA RR.

- The Type Bit Maps field of every NSEC3 RR in a signed zone MUST indicate the presence of all types present at the original owner name, except for the types solely contributed by an NSEC3 RR itself. Note that this means that the NSEC3 type itself will never be present in the Type Bit Maps.

The following steps describe a method of proper construction of NSEC3 RRs. This is not the only such possible method.

1.   Select the hash algorithm and the values for salt and iterations.

2.   For each unique original owner name in the zone add an NSEC3 RR.

- If Opt-Out is being used, owner names of unsigned delegations MAY be excluded.
- The owner name of the NSEC3 RR is the hash of the original owner name, prepended as a single label to the zone name.
- The Next Hashed Owner Name field is left blank for the moment.
- If Opt-Out is being used, set the Opt-Out bit to one.
- For collision detection purposes, optionally keep track of the original owner name with the NSEC3 RR.

- Additionally, for collision detection purposes, optionally create an additional NSEC3 RR corresponding to the original owner name with the asterisk label prepended (i.e., as if a wildcard existed as a child of this owner name) and keep track of this original owner name. Mark this NSEC3 RR as temporary.

3. For each RRSet at the original owner name, set the corresponding bit in the Type Bit Maps field.

4. If the difference in number of labels between the apex and the original owner name is greater than 1, additional NSEC3 RRs need to be added for every empty non-terminal between the apex and the original owner name. This process may generate NSEC3 RRs with duplicate hashed owner names. Optionally, for collision detection, track the original owner names of these NSEC3 RRs and create temporary NSEC3 RRs for wildcard collisions in a similar fashion to step 1.

5. Sort the set of NSEC3 RRs into hash order.

6. Combine NSEC3 RRs with identical hashed owner names by replacing them with a single NSEC3 RR with the Type Bit Maps field consisting of the union of the types represented by the set of NSEC3 RRs. If the original owner name was tracked, then collisions may be detected when combining, as all of the matching NSEC3 RRs should have the same original owner name. Discard any possible temporary NSEC3 RRs.

7. In each NSEC3 RR, insert the next hashed owner name by using the value of the next NSEC3 RR in hash order. The next hashed owner name of the last NSEC3 RR in the zone contains the value of the hashed owner name of the first NSEC3 RR in the hash order.

8. Finally, add an NSEC3PARAM RR with the same Hash Algorithm, Iterations, and Salt fields to the zone apex.

If a hash collision is detected, then a new salt has to be chosen, and the signing process restarted.

7.2. Zone Serving

This specification modifies DNSSEC-enabled DNS responses generated by authoritative servers. In particular, it replaces the use of NSEC RRs in such responses with NSEC3 RRs.

In the following response cases, the NSEC RRs dictated by DNSSEC [RFC4035] are replaced with NSEC3 RRs that prove the same facts. Responses that would not contain NSEC RRs are unchanged by this specification.

When returning responses containing multiple NSEC3 RRs, all of the NSEC3 RRs MUST use the same hash algorithm, iteration, and salt values. The Flags field value MUST be either zero or one.

7.2.1. Closest Encloser Proof

For many NSEC3 responses a proof of the closest encloser is required. This is a proof that some ancestor of the QNAME is the closest encloser of QNAME.

This proof consists of (up to) two different NSEC3 RRs:

- An NSEC3 RR that matches the closest (provable) encloser.

- An NSEC3 RR that covers the "next closer" name to the closest encloser.

The first NSEC3 RR essentially proposes a possible closest encloser, and proves that the particular encloser does, in fact, exist. The second NSEC3 RR proves that the possible closest encloser is the closest, and proves that the QNAME (and any ancestors between QNAME and the closest encloser) does not exist.

These NSEC3 RRs are collectively referred to as the "closest encloser proof" in the subsequent descriptions.

For example, the closest encloser proof for the nonexistent "alpha.beta.gamma.example." owner name might prove that "gamma.example." is the closest encloser. This response would contain the NSEC3 RR that matches "gamma.example.", and would also contain the NSEC3 RR that covers "beta.gamma.example." (which is the "next closer" name).

It is possible, when using Opt-Out (Section 6), to not be able to prove the actual closest encloser because it is, or is part of an insecure delegation covered by an Opt-Out span. In this case, instead of proving the actual closest encloser, the closest provable encloser is used. That is, the closest enclosing authoritative name is used instead. In this case, the set of NSEC3 RRs used for this proof is referred to as the "closest provable encloser proof".

7.2.2. Name Error Responses

To prove the nonexistence of QNAME, a closest encloser proof and an NSEC3 RR covering the (nonexistent) wildcard RR at the closest encloser MUST be included in the response. This collection of (up to) three NSEC3 RRs proves both that QNAME does not exist and that a wildcard that could have matched QNAME also does not exist.

For example, if "gamma.example." is the closest provable encloser to QNAME, then an NSEC3 RR covering "*.gamma.example." is included in the authority section of the response.

7.2.3. No Data Responses, QTYPE is not DS

The server MUST include the NSEC3 RR that matches QNAME. This NSEC3 RR MUST NOT have the bits corresponding to either the QTYPE or CNAME set in its Type Bit Maps field.

7.2.4. No Data Responses, QTYPE is DS

If there is an NSEC3 RR that matches QNAME, the server MUST return it in the response. The bits corresponding with DS and CNAME MUST NOT be set in the Type Bit Maps field of this NSEC3 RR.

If no NSEC3 RR matches QNAME, the server MUST return a closest provable encloser proof for QNAME. The NSEC3 RR that covers the "next closer" name MUST have the Opt-Out bit set (note that this is true by definition – if the Opt-Out bit is not set, something has gone wrong).

If a server is authoritative for both sides of a zone cut at QNAME, the server MUST return the proof from the parent side of the zone cut.

7.2.5. Wildcard No Data Responses

If there is a wildcard match for QNAME, but QTYPE is not present at that name, the response MUST include a closest encloser proof for QNAME and MUST include the NSEC3 RR that matches the wildcard. This combination proves both that QNAME itself does not exist and that a wildcard that matches QNAME does exist. Note that the closest encloser to QNAME MUST be the immediate ancestor of the wildcard RR (if this is not the case, then something has gone wrong).

7.2.6. Wildcard Answer Responses

If there is a wildcard match for QNAME and QTYPE, then, in addition to the expanded wildcard RRSet returned in the answer section of the response, proof that the wildcard match was valid must be returned.

This proof is accomplished by proving that both QNAME does not exist and that the closest encloser of the QNAME and the immediate ancestor of the wildcard are the same (i.e., the correct wildcard matched).

To this end, the NSEC3 RR that covers the "next closer" name of the immediate ancestor of the wildcard MUST be returned. It is not necessary to return an NSEC3 RR that matches the closest encloser, as the existence of this closest encloser is proven by the presence of the expanded wildcard in the response.

7.2.7. Referrals to Unsigned Subzones

If there is an NSEC3 RR that matches the delegation name, then that NSEC3 RR MUST be included in the response. The DS bit in the type bit maps of the NSEC3 RR MUST NOT be set.

If the zone is Opt-Out, then there may not be an NSEC3 RR corresponding to the delegation. In this case, the closest provable encloser proof MUST be included in the response. The included NSEC3 RR that covers the "next closer" name for the delegation MUST have the Opt-Out flag set to one. (Note that this will be the case unless something has gone wrong).

7.2.8. Responding to Queries for NSEC3 Owner Names

The owner names of NSEC3 RRs are not represented in the NSEC3 RR chain like other owner names. As a result, each NSEC3 owner name is covered by another NSEC3 RR, effectively negating the existence of the NSEC3 RR. This is a paradox, since the existence of an NSEC3 RR can be proven by its RRSIG RRSet.

If the following conditions are all true:

- the QNAME equals the owner name of an existing NSEC3 RR, and

- no RR types exist at the QNAME, nor at any descendant of QNAME,

then the response MUST be constructed as a Name Error response (Section 7.2.2). Or, in other words, the authoritative name server will act as if the owner name of the NSEC3 RR did not exist.

Note that NSEC3 RRs are returned as a result of an AXFR or IXFR query.

7.2.9. Server Response to a Run-Time Collision

If the hash of a non-existing QNAME collides with the owner name of an existing NSEC3 RR, then the server will be unable to return a response that proves that QNAME does not exist. In this case, the server MUST return a response with an RCODE of 2 (server failure).

Note that with the hash algorithm specified in this document, SHA-1, such collisions are highly unlikely.

7.3. Secondary Servers

Secondary servers (and perhaps other entities) need to reliably determine which NSEC3 parameters (i.e., hash, salt, and iterations) are present at every hashed owner name, in order to be able to choose an appropriate set of NSEC3 RRs for negative responses. This is indicated by an NSEC3PARAM RR present at the zone apex.

If there are multiple NSEC3PARAM RRs present, there are multiple valid NSEC3 chains present. The server must choose one of them, but may use any criteria to do so.

7.4. Zones Using Unknown Hash Algorithms

Zones that are signed according to this specification, but are using an unrecognized NSEC3 hash algorithm value, cannot be effectively served. Such zones SHOULD be rejected when loading. Servers SHOULD respond with RCODE=2 (server failure) responses when handling queries that would fall under such zones.

7.5. Dynamic Update

A zone signed using NSEC3 may accept dynamic updates [RFC2136]. However, NSEC3 introduces some special considerations for dynamic updates.

Adding and removing names in a zone MUST account for the creation or removal of empty non-terminals.

- When removing a name with a corresponding NSEC3 RR, any NSEC3 RRs corresponding to empty non-terminals created by that name MUST be removed. Note that more than one name may be asserting the existence of a particular empty non-terminal.

- When adding a name that requires adding an NSEC3 RR, NSEC3 RRs MUST also be added for any empty non-terminals that are created. That is, if there is not an existing NSEC3 RR matching an empty non-terminal, it must be created and added.

The presence of Opt-Out in a zone means that some additions or delegations of names will not require changes to the NSEC3 RRs in a zone.

- When removing a delegation RRSet, if that delegation does not have a matching NSEC3 RR, then it was opted out. In this case, nothing further needs to be done.

- When adding a delegation RRSet, if the "next closer" name of the delegation is covered by an existing Opt-Out NSEC3 RR, then the delegation MAY be added without modifying the NSEC3 RRs in the zone.

The presence of Opt-Out in a zone means that when adding or removing NSEC3 RRs, the value of the Opt-Out flag that should be set in new or modified NSEC3 RRs is ambiguous. Servers SHOULD follow this set of basic rules to resolve the ambiguity.

The central concept to these rules is that the state of the Opt-Out flag of the covering NSEC3 RR is preserved.

- When removing an NSEC3 RR, the value of the Opt-Out flag for the previous NSEC3 RR (the one whose next hashed owner name is modified) should not be changed.

- When adding an NSEC3 RR, the value of the Opt-Out flag is set to the value of the Opt-Out flag of the NSEC3 RR that previously covered the owner name of the NSEC3 RR. That is, the now previous NSEC3 RR.

If the zone in question is consistent with its use of the Opt-Out flag (that is, all NSEC3 RRs in the zone have the same value for the flag) then these rules will retain that consistency. If the zone is not consistent in the use of the flag (i.e., a partially Opt-Out zone), then these rules will not retain the same pattern of use of the Opt-Out flag.

For zones that partially use the Opt-Out flag, if there is a logical pattern for that use, the pattern could be maintained by using a local policy on the server.

8. Validator Considerations

8.1. Responses with Unknown Hash Types

A validator MUST ignore NSEC3 RRs with unknown hash types. The practical result of this is that responses containing only such NSEC3 RRs will generally be considered bogus.

8.2. Verifying NSEC3 RRs

A validator MUST ignore NSEC3 RRs with a Flag fields value other than zero or one.

A validator MAY treat a response as bogus if the response contains NSEC3 RRs that contain different values for hash algorithm, iterations, or salt from each other for that zone.

8.3. Closest Encloser Proof

In order to verify a closest encloser proof, the validator MUST find the longest name, X, such that

- X is an ancestor of QNAME that is matched by an NSEC3 RR present in the response. This is a candidate for the closest encloser, and

- The name one label longer than X (but still an ancestor of – or equal to – QNAME) is covered by an NSEC3 RR present in the response.

One possible algorithm for verifying this proof is as follows:

1. Set SNAME=QNAME. Clear the flag.

2. Check whether SNAME exists:
   - If there is no NSEC3 RR in the response that matches SNAME (i.e., an NSEC3 RR whose owner name is the same as the hash of SNAME, prepended as a single label to the zone name), clear the flag.
   - If there is an NSEC3 RR in the response that covers SNAME, set the flag.
   - If there is a matching NSEC3 RR in the response and the flag was set, then the proof is complete, and SNAME is the closest encloser.
   - If there is a matching NSEC3 RR in the response, but the flag is not set, then the response is bogus.

3. Truncate SNAME by one label from the left, go to step 2.

Once the closest encloser has been discovered, the validator MUST check that the NSEC3 RR that has the closest encloser as the original owner name is from the proper zone. The DNAME type bit must not be set and the NS type bit may only be set if the SOA type bit is set. If this is not the case, it would be an indication that an attacker is using them to falsely deny the existence of RRs for which the server is not authoritative.

In the following descriptions, the phrase "a closest (provable) encloser proof for X" means that the algorithm above (or an equivalent algorithm) proves that X does not exist by proving that an ancestor of X is its closest encloser.

8.4. Validating Name Error Responses

A validator MUST verify that there is a closest encloser proof for QNAME present in the response and that there is an NSEC3 RR that covers the wildcard at the closest encloser (i.e., the name formed by prepending the asterisk label to the closest encloser).

8.5. Validating No Data Responses, QTYPE is not DS

The validator MUST verify that an NSEC3 RR that matches QNAME is present and that both the QTYPE and the CNAME type are not set in its Type Bit Maps field.

Note that this test also covers the case where the NSEC3 RR exists because it corresponds to an empty non-terminal, in which case the NSEC3 RR will have an empty Type Bit Maps field.

8.6. Validating No Data Responses, QTYPE is DS

If there is an NSEC3 RR that matches QNAME present in the response, then that NSEC3 RR MUST NOT have the bits corresponding to DS and CNAME set in its Type Bit Maps field.

If there is no such NSEC3 RR, then the validator MUST verify that a closest provable encloser proof for QNAME is present in the response, and that the NSEC3 RR that covers the "next closer" name has the Opt-Out bit set.

8.7. Validating Wildcard No Data Responses

The validator MUST verify a closest encloser proof for QNAME and MUST find an NSEC3 RR present in the response that matches the wildcard name generated by prepending the asterisk label to the closest encloser. Furthermore, the bits corresponding to both QTYPE and CNAME MUST NOT be set in the wildcard matching NSEC3 RR.

8.8. Validating Wildcard Answer Responses

The verified wildcard answer RRSet in the response provides the validator with a (candidate) closest encloser for QNAME. This closest encloser is the immediate ancestor to the generating wildcard.

Validators MUST verify that there is an NSEC3 RR that covers the "next closer" name to QNAME present in the response. This proves that QNAME itself did not exist and that the correct wildcard was used to generate the response.

8.9. Validating Referrals to Unsigned Subzones

The delegation name in a referral is the owner name of the NS RRSet present in the authority section of the referral response.

If there is an NSEC3 RR present in the response that matches the delegation name, then the validator MUST ensure that the NS bit is set and that the DS bit is not set in the Type Bit Maps field of the NSEC3 RR. The validator MUST also ensure that the NSEC3 RR is from the correct (i.e., parent) zone. This is done by ensuring that the SOA bit is not set in the Type Bit Maps field of this NSEC3 RR.

Note that the presence of an NS bit implies the absence of a DNAME bit, so there is no need to check for the DNAME bit in the Type Bit Maps field of the NSEC3 RR.

If there is no NSEC3 RR present that matches the delegation name, then the validator MUST verify a closest provable encloser proof for the delegation name. The validator MUST verify that the Opt-Out bit is set in the NSEC3 RR that covers the "next closer" name to the delegation name.

9. Resolver Considerations

9.1. NSEC3 Resource Record Caching

Caching resolvers MUST be able to retrieve the appropriate NSEC3 RRs when returning responses that contain them. In DNSSEC [RFC4035], in many cases it is possible to find the correct NSEC RR to return in a response by name (e.g., when returning a referral, the NSEC RR will always have the same owner name as the delegation). With this specification, that will not be true, nor will a cache be able to calculate the name(s) of the appropriate NSEC3 RR(s). Implementations may need to use new methods for caching and retrieving NSEC3 RRs.

9.2. Use of the AD Bit

The AD bit, as defined by [RFC4035], MUST NOT be set when returning a response containing a closest (provable) encloser proof in which the NSEC3 RR that covers the "next closer" name has the Opt-Out bit set.

This rule is based on what this closest encloser proof actually proves: names that would be covered by the Opt-Out NSEC3 RR may or may not exist as insecure delegations. As such, not all the data in responses containing such closest encloser proofs will have been cryptographically verified, so the AD bit cannot be set.

10. Special Considerations

10.1. Domain Name Length Restrictions

Zones signed using this specification have additional domain name length restrictions imposed upon them. In particular, zones with names that, when converted into hashed owner names exceed the 255 octet length limit imposed by [RFC1035], cannot use this specification.

The actual maximum length of a domain name in a particular zone depends on both the length of the zone name (versus the whole domain name) and the particular hash function used.

As an example, SHA-1 produces a hash of 160 bits. The base-32 encoding of 160 bits results in 32 characters. The 32 characters are prepended to the name of the zone as a single label, which includes a length field of a single octet. The maximum length of the zone name, when using SHA-1, is 222 octets (255 - 33).

10.2. DNAME at the Zone Apex

The DNAME specification in Section 3 of [RFC2672] has a 'no-descendants' limitation. If a DNAME RR is present at node N, there MUST be no data at any descendant of N.

If N is the apex of the zone, there will be NSEC3 and RRSIG types present at descendants of N. This specification updates the DNAME specification to allow NSEC3 and RRSIG types at descendants of the apex regardless of the existence of DNAME at the apex.

10.3. Iterations

Setting the number of iterations used allows the zone owner to choose the cost of computing a hash, and therefore the cost of generating a dictionary. Note that this is distinct from the effect of salt, which prevents the use of a single precomputed dictionary for all time.

Obviously the number of iterations also affects the zone owner's cost of signing and serving the zone as well as the validator's cost of verifying responses from the zone. We therefore impose an upper limit on the number of iterations. We base this on the number of iterations that approximates the cost of verifying an RRSet.

The limits, therefore, are based on the size of the smallest zone signing key, rounded up to the nearest table value (or rounded down if the key is larger than the largest table value).

A zone owner MUST NOT use a value higher than shown in the table below for iterations for the given key size. A resolver MAY treat a response with a higher value as insecure, after the validator has verified that the signature over the NSEC3 RR is correct.

Key Size	Iterations
1024	150
2048	500
4096	2,500

This table is based on an approximation of the ratio between the cost of an SHA-1 calculation and the cost of an RSA verification for keys of size 1024 bits (150 to 1), 2048 bits (500 to 1), and 4096 bits (2500 to 1).

The ratio between SHA-1 calculation and DSA verification is higher (1500 to 1 for keys of size 1024). A higher iteration count degrades performance, while DSA verification is already more expensive than RSA for the same key size. Therefore the values in the table MUST be used independent of the key algorithm.

10.4. Transitioning a Signed Zone from NSEC to NSEC3

When transitioning an already signed and trusted zone to this specification, care must be taken to prevent client validation failures during the process.

The basic procedure is as follows:

1. Transition all DNSKEYs to DNSKEYs using the algorithm aliases described in Section 2. The actual method for safely and securely changing the DNSKEY RRSet of the zone is outside the scope of this specification. However, the end result MUST be that all DS RRs in the parent use the specified algorithm aliases.

    After this transition is complete, all NSEC3-unaware clients will treat the zone as insecure. At this point, the authoritative server still returns negative and wildcard responses that contain NSEC RRs.

2. Add signed NSEC3 RRs to the zone, either incrementally or all at once. If adding incrementally, then the last RRSet added MUST be the NSEC3PARAM RRSet.

3. Upon the addition of the NSEC3PARAM RRSet, the server switches to serving negative and wildcard responses with NSEC3 RRs according to this specification.

4. Remove the NSEC RRs either incrementally or all at once.

10.5. Transitioning a Signed Zone from NSEC3 to NSEC

To safely transition back to a DNSSEC [RFC4035] signed zone, simply reverse the procedure above:

1. Add NSEC RRs incrementally or all at once.

2. Remove the NSEC3PARAM RRSet. This will signal the server to use the NSEC RRs for negative and wildcard responses.

3. Remove the NSEC3 RRs either incrementally or all at once.

4. Transition all of the DNSKEYs to DNSSEC algorithm identifiers. After this transition is complete, all NSEC3-unaware clients will treat the zone as secure.

11. IANA Considerations

Although the NSEC3 and NSEC3PARAM RR formats include a hash algorithm parameter, this document does not define a particular mechanism for safely transitioning from one NSEC3 hash algorithm to another. When specifying a new hash algorithm for use with NSEC3, a transition mechanism MUST also be defined.

This document updates the IANA registry "DOMAIN NAME SYSTEM PARAMETERS" (http://www.iana.org/assignments/dns-parameters) in sub-registry "TYPES", by defining two new types. Section 3 defines the NSEC3 RR type 50. Section 4 defines the NSEC3PARAM RR type 51.

This document updates the IANA registry "DNS SECURITY ALGORITHM NUMBERS – per [RFC4035]" (http://www.iana.org/assignments/dns-sec-alg-numbers). Section 2 defines the aliases DSA-NSEC3-SHA1 (6) and RSASHA1-NSEC3-SHA1 (7) for respectively existing registrations DSA and RSASHA1 in combination with NSEC3 hash algorithm SHA1.

Since these algorithm numbers are aliases for existing DNSKEY algorithm numbers, the flags that exist for the original algorithm are valid for the alias algorithm.

This document creates a new IANA registry for NSEC3 flags. This registry is named "DNSSEC NSEC3 Flags". The initial contents of this registry are:

```
 0   1   2   3   4   5   6   7
+---+---+---+---+---+---+---+---+
|   |   |   |   |   |   |   |Opt|
|   |   |   |   |   |   |   |Out|
+---+---+---+---+---+---+---+---+
```

    bit 7 is the Opt-Out flag.

    bits 0 - 6 are available for assignment.

Assignment of additional NSEC3 Flags in this registry requires IETF Standards Action [RFC2434].

This document creates a new IANA registry for NSEC3PARAM flags. This registry is named "DNSSEC NSEC3PARAM Flags". The initial contents of this registry are:

```
 0   1   2   3   4   5   6   7
+---+---+---+---+---+---+---+---+
|   |   |   |   |   |   |   | 0 |
+---+---+---+---+---+---+---+---+
```

    bit 7 is reserved and must be 0.

    bits 0 - 6 are available for assignment.

Assignment of additional NSEC3PARAM Flags in this registry requires IETF Standards Action [RFC2434].

Finally, this document creates a new IANA registry for NSEC3 hash algorithms. This registry is named "DNSSEC NSEC3 Hash Algorithms". The initial contents of this registry are:

0 is Reserved.

1 is SHA-1.

2-255 Available for assignment.

Assignment of additional NSEC3 hash algorithms in this registry requires IETF Standards Action [RFC2434].

12. Security Considerations

12.1. Hashing Considerations

12.1.1. Dictionary Attacks

The NSEC3 RRs are still susceptible to dictionary attacks (i.e., the attacker retrieves all the NSEC3 RRs, then calculates the hashes of all likely domain names, comparing against the hashes found in the NSEC3 RRs, and thus enumerating the zone). These are substantially more expensive than enumerating the original NSEC RRs would have been, and in any case, such an attack could also be used directly against the name server itself by performing queries for all likely names, though this would obviously be more detectable. The expense of this off-line attack can be chosen by setting the number of iterations in the NSEC3 RR.

Zones are also susceptible to a pre-calculated dictionary attack – that is, a list of hashes for all likely names is computed once, then NSEC3 RR is scanned periodically and compared against the precomputed hashes. This attack is prevented by changing the salt on a regular basis.

The salt SHOULD be at least 64 bits long and unpredictable, so that an attacker cannot anticipate the value of the salt and compute the next set of dictionaries before the zone is published.

12.1.2. Collisions

Hash collisions between QNAME and the owner name of an NSEC3 RR may occur. When they do, it will be impossible to prove the non-existence of the colliding QNAME. However, with SHA-1, this is highly unlikely (on the order of 1 in 2^{160}). Note that DNSSEC already relies on the presumption that a cryptographic hash function is second pre-image resistant, since these hash functions are used for generating and validating signatures and DS RRs.

12.1.3. Transitioning to a New Hash Algorithm

Although the NSEC3 and NSEC3PARAM RR formats include a hash algorithm parameter, this document does not define a particular mechanism for safely transitioning from one NSEC3 hash algorithm to another. When specifying a new hash algorithm for use with NSEC3, a transition mechanism MUST also be defined. It is possible that the only practical and palatable transition mechanisms may require an intermediate transition to an insecure state, or to a state that uses NSEC records instead of NSEC3.

12.1.4. Using High Iteration Values

Since validators should treat responses containing NSEC3 RRs with high iteration values as insecure, presence of just one signed NSEC3 RR with a high iteration value in a zone provides attackers with a possible downgrade attack.

The attack is simply to remove any existing NSEC3 RRs from a response, and replace or add a single (or multiple) NSEC3 RR that uses a high iterations value to the response. Validators will then be forced to treat the response as insecure. This attack would be effective only when all of following conditions are met:

- There is at least one signed NSEC3 RR that uses a high iterations value present in the zone.

- The attacker has access to one or more of these NSEC3 RRs. This is trivially true when the NSEC3 RRs with high iteration values are being returned in typical responses, but may also be true if the attacker can access the zone via AXFR or IXFR queries, or any other methodology.

Using a high number of iterations also introduces an additional denial-of-service opportunity against servers, since servers must calculate several hashes per negative or wildcard response.

12.2. Opt-Out Considerations

The Opt-Out Flag (O) allows for unsigned names, in the form of delegations to unsigned zones, to exist within an otherwise signed zone. All unsigned names are, by definition, insecure, and their validity or existence cannot be cryptographically proven.

In general:

- Resource records with unsigned names (whether existing or not) suffer from the same vulnerabilities as RRs in an unsigned zone. These vulnerabilities are described in more detail in [RFC3833] (note in particular Section 2.3, "Name Chaining" and Section 2.6, "Authenticated Denial of Domain Names").

- Resource records with signed names have the same security whether or not Opt-Out is used.

Note that with or without Opt-Out, an insecure delegation may be undetectably altered by an attacker. Because of this, the primary difference in security when using Opt-Out is the loss of the ability to prove the existence or nonexistence of an insecure delegation within the span of an Opt-Out NSEC3 RR.

In particular, this means that a malicious entity may be able to insert or delete RRs with unsigned names. These RRs are normally NS RRs, but this also includes signed wildcard expansions (while the wildcard RR itself is signed, its expanded name is an unsigned name).

Note that being able to add a delegation is functionally equivalent to being able to add any RR type: an attacker merely has to forge a delegation to name server under his/her control and place whatever RRs needed at the subzone apex.

While in particular cases, this issue may not present a significant security problem, in general it should not be lightly dismissed. Therefore, it is strongly RECOMMENDED that Opt-Out be used sparingly. In particular, zone signing tools SHOULD NOT default to using Opt-Out, and MAY choose to not support Opt-Out at all.

12.3. Other Considerations

Walking the NSEC3 RRs will reveal the total number of RRs in the zone (plus empty non-terminals), and also what types there are. This could be mitigated by adding dummy entries, but certainly an upper limit can always be found.

13. References

13.1. Normative References

[RFC1034] Mockapetris, P., "Domain names - concepts and facilities", STD 13, RFC 1034, November 1987.

[RFC1035] Mockapetris, P., "Domain names - implementation and specification", STD 13, RFC 1035, November 1987.

[RFC2119] Bradner, S., "Key words for use in RFCs to Indicate Requirement Levels", BCP 14, RFC 2119, March 1997.

[RFC2136] Vixie, P., Thomson, S., Rekhter, Y., and J. Bound, "Dynamic Updates in the Domain Name System (DNS UPDATE)", RFC 2136, April 1997.

[RFC2181] Elz, R. and R. Bush, "Clarifications to the DNS Specification", RFC 2181, July 1997.

[RFC2308] Andrews, M., "Negative Caching of DNS Queries (DNS NCACHE)", RFC 2308, March 1998.

[RFC2434] Narten, T. and H. Alvestrand, "Guidelines for Writing an IANA Considerations Section in RFCs", BCP 26, RFC 2434, October 1998.

[RFC2929] Eastlake, D., Brunner-Williams, E., and B. Manning, "Domain Name System (DNS) IANA Considerations", BCP 42, RFC 2929, September 2000.

[RFC3597] Gustafsson, A., "Handling of Unknown DNS Resource Record (RR) Types", RFC 3597, September 2003.

[RFC4033] Arends, R., Austein, R., Larson, M., Massey, D., and S. Rose, "DNS Security Introduction and Requirements", RFC 4033, March 2005.

[RFC4034] Arends, R., Austein, R., Larson, M., Massey, D., and S. Rose, "Resource Records for the DNS Security Extensions", RFC 4034, March 2005.

[RFC4035] Arends, R., Austein, R., Larson, M., Massey, D., and S. Rose, "Protocol Modifications for the DNS Security Extensions", RFC 4035, March 2005.

[RFC4648] Josefsson, S., "The Base16, Base32, and Base64 Data Encodings", RFC 4648, October 2006.

13.2. Informative References

[DNSEXT-NO] Josefsson, S., "Authenticating Denial of Existence in DNS with Minimum Disclosure", Work in Progress, July 2000.

[DNSEXT-NSEC2v2] Laurie, B., "DNSSEC NSEC2 Owner and RDATA Format", Work in Progress, December 2004.

[RFC2672] Crawford, M., "Non-Terminal DNS Name Redirection", RFC 2672, August 1999.

[RFC2898] Kaliski, B., "PKCS #5: Password-Based Cryptography Specification Version 2.0", RFC 2898, September 2000.

[RFC3833] Atkins, D. and R. Austein, "Threat Analysis of the Domain Name System (DNS)", RFC 3833, August 2004.

[RFC4592] Lewis, E., "The Role of Wildcards in the Domain Name System", RFC 4592, July 2006.

[RFC4956] Arends, R., Kosters, M., and D. Blacka, "DNS Security (DNSSEC) Opt-In", RFC 4956, July 2007.

Appendix A. Example Zone

This is a zone showing its NSEC3 RRs. They can also be used as test vectors for the hash algorithm.

The overall TTL and class are specified in the SOA RR, and are subsequently omitted for clarity.

The zone is preceded by a list that contains the hashes of the original ownernames.

```
; H(example)       = 0p9mhaveqvm6t7vbl5lop2u3t2rp3tom
; H(a.example)     = 35mthgpgcu1qg68fab165klnsnk3dpvl
; H(ai.example)    = gjeqe526plbf1g8mklp59enfd789njgi
; H(ns1.example)   = 2t7b4g4vsa5smi47k61mv5bv1a22bojr
; H(ns2.example)   = q04jkcevqvmu85r014c7dkba38o0ji5r
; H(w.example)     = k8udemvp1j2f7eg6jebps17vp3n8i58h
; H(*.w.example)   = r53bq7cc2uvmubfu5ocmm6pers9tk9en
; H(x.w.example)   = b4um86eghhds6nea196smvmlo4ors995
```

```
; H(y.w.example)    = ji6neoaepv8b5o6k4ev33abha8ht9fgc
; H(x.y.w.example)  = 2vptu5timamqttgl4luu9kg21e0aor3s
; H(xx.example)     = t644ebqk9bibcna874givr6joj62mlhv
; H(2t7b4g4vsa5smi47k61mv5bv1a22bojr.example)
;                   = kohar7mbb8dc2ce8a9qvl8hon4k53uhi
example. 3600  IN SOA  ns1.example. bugs.x.w.example. 1 3600 300 (
                         3600000 3600 )
               RRSIG   SOA 7 1 3600 20150420235959 20051021000000 (
                         40430 example.
                         Hu25UIyNPmvPIVBrldN+9Mlp9Zql39qaUd8i
                         q4ZLlYWfUUbbAS41pG+68z81q1xhkYAcEyHd
                         VI2LmKusbZsT0Q== )
               NS      ns1.example.
               NS      ns2.example.
               RRSIG   NS 7 1 3600 20150420235959 20051021000000 (
                         40430 example.
                         PVOgtMK1HHeSTau+HwDWC8Ts+6C8qtqd4pQJ
                         qOtdEVgg+MA+ai4fWDEhu3qHJyLcQ9tbD2vv
                         CnMXjtz6SyObxA== )
               MX      1 xx.example.
               RRSIG   MX 7 1 3600 20150420235959 20051021000000 (
                         40430 example.
                         GgQ1A9xs47k42VPvpL/a1BWUz/6XsnHkjotw
                         9So8MQtZtl2wJBsnOQsaoHrRCrRbyriEl/GZ
                         n9Mto/Kx+wBo+w== )
               DNSKEY  256 3 7 AwEAAaetidLzsKWUt4swWR8yu0wPHPiUi8LU (
                         sAD0QPWU+wzt89epO6tHzkMBVDkC7qphQO2h
                         TY4hHn9npWFRw5BYubE= )
               DNSKEY  257 3 7 AwEAAcUlFV1vhmqx6NSOUOq2R/dsR7Xm3upJ (
                         j7IommWSpJABVfW8Q0rOvXdM6kzt+TAu92L9
                         AbsUdblMFin8CVF3n4s= )
               RRSIG   DNSKEY 7 1 3600 20150420235959 (
                         20051021000000 12708 example.
                         AuU4juU9RaxescSmStrQks3Gh9FblGBlVU31
                         uzMZ/U/FpsUb8aC6QZS+sTsJXnLnz7flGOsm
                         MGQZf3bH+QsCtg== )
               NSEC3PARAM 1 0 12 aabbccdd
               RRSIG   NSEC3PARAM 7 1 3600 20150420235959 (
                         20051021000000 40430 example.
                         C1Gl8tPZNtnjlrYWDeeUV/sGLCyy/IHie2re
                         rN05XSA3Pq0U3+4VvGWYWdUMfflOdxqnXHwJ
                         TLQsjlkynhG6Cg== )
0p9mhaveqvm6t7vbl5lop2u3t2rp3tom.example. NSEC3 1 1 12 aabbccdd (
                         2t7b4g4vsa5smi47k61mv5bv1a22bojr MX DNSKEY NS
                         SOA NSEC3PARAM RRSIG )
               RRSIG   NSEC3 7 2 3600 20150420235959 20051021000000 (
                         40430 example.
                         OSgWSm26B+cS+dDL8b5QrWr/dEWhtCsKlwKL
                         IBHYH6blRxK9rC0bMJPwQ4mLIuw85H2EY762
                         BOCXJZMnpuwhpA== )
2t7b4g4vsa5smi47k61mv5bv1a22bojr.example. A 192.0.2.127
```

```
                RRSIG   A 7 2 3600 20150420235959 20051021000000 (
                        40430 example.
                        h6c++bzhRuWWt2bykN6mjaTNBcXNq5UuL5Ed
                        K+iDP4eY8I0kSiKaCjg3tC1SQkeloMeub2GW
                        k8p6xHMPZumXlw== )
                NSEC3   1 1 12 aabbccdd (
                        2vptu5timamqttgl4luu9kg21e0aor3s A RRSIG )
                RRSIG   NSEC3 7 2 3600 20150420235959 20051021000000 (
                        40430 example.
                        OmBvJ1Vgg1hCKMXHFiNeIYHK9XVW0iLDLwJN
                        4TFoNxZuP03gAXEI634YwOc4YBNITrj413iq
                        NI6mRk/r1dOSUw== )
2vptu5timamqttgl4luu9kg21e0aor3s.example. NSEC3 1 1 12 aabbccdd (
                        35mthgpgcu1qg68fab165klnsnk3dpvl MX RRSIG )
                RRSIG   NSEC3 7 2 3600 20150420235959 20051021000000 (
                        40430 example.
                        KL1V2oFYghNV0Hm7Tf2vpJjM6l+0g1JCcVYG
                        VfI0lKrhPmTsOA96cLEACgo1x8I7kApJX+ob
                        TuktZ+sdsZPY1w== )
35mthgpgcu1qg68fab165klnsnk3dpvl.example. NSEC3 1 1 12 aabbccdd (
                        b4um86eghhds6nea196smvmlo4ors995 NS DS RRSIG )
                RRSIG   NSEC3 7 2 3600 20150420235959 20051021000000 (
                        40430 example.
                        g6jPUUpduAJKRljUsN8gB4UagAX0NxY9shwQ
                        Aynzo8EUWH+z6hEIBlUTPGj15eZll6VhQqgZ
                        XtAIR3chwgW+SA== )
a.example.      NS      ns1.a.example.
                NS      ns2.a.example.
                DS      58470 5 1 (
                        3079F1593EBAD6DC121E202A8B766A6A4837206C )
                RRSIG   DS 7 2 3600 20150420235959 20051021000000 (
                        40430 example.
                        XacFcQVHLVzdoc45EJhN616zQ4mEXtE8FzUh
                        M2KWjfy1VfRKD9r1MeVGwwoukOKgJxBPFsWo
                        o722vZ4UZ2dIdA== )
ns1.a.example. A        192.0.2.5
ns2.a.example. A        192.0.2.6
ai.example.    A        192.0.2.9
                RRSIG   A 7 2 3600 20150420235959 20051021000000 (
                        40430 example.
                        hVe+wKYMlObTRPhX0NL67GxeZfdxqr/QeR6F
                        tfdAj5+FgYxyzPEjIzvKWy00hWIl6wD3Vws+
                        rznEn8sQ64UdqA== )
                HINFO   "KLH-10" "ITS"
                RRSIG   HINFO 7 2 3600 20150420235959 20051021000000 (
                        40430 example.
                        Yi42uOq43eyO6qXHNvwwfFnIustWgV5urFcx
                        enkLvs6pKRh00VBjODmf3Z4nMO7IOl6nHSQ1
                        v0wLHpEZG7Xj2w== )
                AAAA    2001:db8:0:0:0:0:f00:baa9
                RRSIG   AAAA 7 2 3600 20150420235959 20051021000000 (
```

```
                    40430 example.
                    LcdxKaCB5bGZwPDg+3JJ4O02zoMBrjxqlf6W
                    uaHQZZfTUpb9Nf2nxFGe2XRPfR5tpJT6GdRG
                    cHueLuXkMjBArQ== )
b4um86eghhds6nea196smvmlo4ors995.example. NSEC3 1 1 12 aabbccdd (
                    gjeqe526plbf1g8mklp59enfd789njgi MX RRSIG )
              RRSIG NSEC3 7 2 3600 20150420235959 20051021000000 (
                    40430 example.
                    ZkPG3M32lmoHM6pa3D6gZFGB/rhL//Bs3Omh
                    5u4m/CUiwtblEVOaAKKZd7S959OeiX43aLX3
                    pOv0TSTyiTxIZg== )
c.example.    NS    ns1.c.example.
              NS    ns2.c.example.
ns1.c.example. A    192.0.2.7
ns2.c.example. A    192.0.2.8
gjeqe526plbf1g8mklp59enfd789njgi.example. NSEC3 1 1 12 aabbccdd (
                    ji6neoaepv8b5o6k4ev33abha8ht9fgc HINFO A AAAA
                    RRSIG )
              RRSIG NSEC3 7 2 3600 20150420235959 20051021000000 (
                    40430 example.
                    IVnezTJ9iqblFF97vPSmfXZ5Zozngx3KX3by
                    LTZC4QBH2dFWhf6scrGFZB980AfCxoD9qbbK
                    Dy+rdGIeRSVNyw== )
ji6neoaepv8b5o6k4ev33abha8ht9fgc.example. NSEC3 1 1 12 aabbccdd (
                    k8udemvp1j2f7eg6jebps17vp3n8i58h )
              RRSIG NSEC3 7 2 3600 20150420235959 20051021000000 (
                    40430 example.
                    gPkFp1s2QDQ6wQzcg1uSebZ61W33rUBDcTj7
                    2F3kQ490fEdp7k1BUIfbcZtPbX3YCpE+sIt0
                    MpzVSKfTwx4uYA== )
k8udemvp1j2f7eg6jebps17vp3n8i58h.example. NSEC3 1 1 12 aabbccdd (
                    kohar7mbb8dc2ce8a9qvl8hon4k53uhi )
              RRSIG NSEC3 7 2 3600 20150420235959 20051021000000 (
                    40430 example.
                    FtXGbvF0+wf8iWkyo73enAuVx03klN+pILBK
                    S6qCcftVtfH4yVzsEZquJ27NHR7ruxJWDNMt
                    Otx7w9WfcIg62A== )
kohar7mbb8dc2ce8a9qvl8hon4k53uhi.example. NSEC3 1 1 12 aabbccdd (
                    q04jkcevqvmu85r014c7dkba38o0ji5r A RRSIG )
              RRSIG NSEC3 7 2 3600 20150420235959 20051021000000 (
                    40430 example.
                    VrDXs2uVW21N08SyQIz88zml+y4ZCInTwgDr
                    6zz43yAg+LFERjOrj3Ojct51ac7Dp4eZbf9F
                    QJazmASFKGxGXg== )
ns1.example.  A     192.0.2.1
              RRSIG A 7 2 3600 20150420235959 20051021000000 (
                    40430 example.
                    bu6kx73n6XEunoVGuRfAgY7EF/AJqHy7hj0j
                    kiqJjB0dOrx3wuz9SaBeGfqWIdn/uta3SavN
                    4FRvZR9SCFHF5Q== )
ns2.example.  A     192.0.2.2
```

```
                    RRSIG    A 7 2 3600 20150420235959 20051021000000 (
                             40430 example.
                             ktQ3TqE0CfRfki0Rb/Ip5BM0VnxelbuejCC4
                             zpLbFKA/7eD7UNAwxMgxJPtbdST+syjYSJaj
                             4IHfeX6n8vfoGA== )
q04jkcevqvmu85r014c7dkba38o0ji5r.example. NSEC3 1 1 12 aabbccdd (
                             r53bq7cc2uvmubfu5ocmm6pers9tk9en A RRSIG )
                    RRSIG    NSEC3 7 2 3600 20150420235959 20051021000000 (
                             40430 example.
                             hV5I89b+4FHJDATp09g4bbN0R1F845CaXpL3
                             ZxlMKimoPAyqletMlEWwLfFia7sdpSzn+ZlN
                             NlkxWcLsIlMmUg== )
r53bq7cc2uvmubfu5ocmm6pers9tk9en.example. NSEC3 1 1 12 aabbccdd (
                             t644ebqk9bibcna874givr6joj62mlhv MX RRSIG )
                    RRSIG    NSEC3 7 2 3600 20150420235959 20051021000000 (
                             40430 example.
                             aupviViruXs4bDg9rCbezzBMf9h1ZlDvbW/C
                             ZFKulIGXXLj8B/fsDJarXVDA9bnUoRhEbKp+
                             HF1FWKW7RIJdtQ== )
t644ebqk9bibcna874givr6joj62mlhv.example. NSEC3 1 1 12 aabbccdd (
                             0p9mhaveqvm6t7vbl5lop2u3t2rp3tom HINFO A AAAA
                             RRSIG )
                    RRSIG    NSEC3 7 2 3600 20150420235959 20051021000000 (
                             40430 example.
                             RAjGECB8P7O+F4Pa4Dx3tC0M+Z3KmlLKImca
                             fb9XWwx+NWUNz7NBEDBQHivIyKPVDkChcePI
                             X1xPl1ATNa+8Dw== )
*.w.example.        MX       1 ai.example.
                    RRSIG    MX 7 2 3600 20150420235959 20051021000000 (
                             40430 example.
                             CikebjQwGQPwijVcxgcZcSJKtfynugtlBiKb
                             9FcBTrmOoyQ4InoWVudhCWsh/URX3lc4WRUM
                             ivEBP6+4KS3ldA== )
x.w.example.        MX       1 xx.example.
                    RRSIG    MX 7 3 3600 20150420235959 20051021000000 (
                             40430 example.
                             IrK3tq/tHFIBF0scHiE/1IwMAvckS/55hAVv
                             QyxTFbkAdDloP3NbZzu+yoSsr3b3OX6qbBpY
                             7WCtwwekLKRAwQ== )
x.y.w.example. MX            1 xx.example.
                    RRSIG    MX 7 4 3600 20150420235959 20051021000000 (
                             40430 example.
                             MqSt5HqJIN8+SLlzTOImrh5h9Xa6gDvAW/Gn
                             nbdPc6Z7nXvCpLPJj/5lCwx3VuzVOjkbvXze
                             8/8Ccl2Zn2hbug== )
xx.example.         A        192.0.2.10
                    RRSIG    A 7 2 3600 20150420235959 20051021000000 (
                             40430 example.
                             T35hBWEZ017VC5u2c4OriKyVn/pu+fVK4AlX
                             YOxJ6iQylfV2HQIKjv6b7DzINB3aF/wjJqgX
                             pQvhq+Ac6+ZiFg== )
```

```
          HINFO    "KLH-10" "TOPS-20"
          RRSIG    HINFO 7 2 3600 20150420235959 20051021000000 (
                   40430 example.
                   KimG+rDd+7VA1zRsu0ITNAQUTRlpnsmqWrih
                   FRnU+bRa93v2e5oFNFYCs3Rqgv62K93N7AhW
                   6Jfqj/8NzWjvKg== )
          AAAA     2001:db8:0:0:0:0:f00:baaa
          RRSIG    AAAA 7 2 3600 20150420235959 20051021000000 (
                   40430 example.
                   IXBcXORITNwd8h3gNwyxtYFvAupS/CYWufVe
                   uBUX0O25ivBCULjZjpDxFSxfohb/KA7YRdxE
                   NzYfMItpIL1/Xw== )
```

Appendix B. Example Responses

The examples in this section show response messages using the signed zone example in Appendix A.

B.1. Name Error

An authoritative name error. The NSEC3 RRs prove that the name does not exist and that there is no wildcard RR that should have been expanded.

```
;; Header: QR AA DO RCODE=3
;;
;; Question
a.c.x.w.example.        IN A

;; Answer
;; (empty)

;; Authority

example.        SOA     ns1.example. bugs.x.w.example. 1 3600 300 (
                        3600000 3600 )
example.        RRSIG   SOA 7 1 3600 20150420235959 20051021000000 (
                        40430 example.
                        Hu25UIyNPmvPIVBrldN+9Mlp9Zql39qaUd8i
                        q4ZLlYWfUUbbAS41pG+68z81q1xhkYAcEyHd
                        VI2LmKusbZsT0Q== )

;; NSEC3 RR that covers the "next closer" name (c.x.w.example)
;; H(c.x.w.example) = 0va5bpr2ou0vk0lbqeeljri88laipsfh

0p9mhaveqvm6t7vbl5lop2u3t2rp3tom.example. NSEC3 1 1 12 aabbccdd (
                        2t7b4g4vsa5smi47k61mv5bv1a22bojr MX DNSKEY NS
                        SOA NSEC3PARAM RRSIG )
0p9mhaveqvm6t7vbl5lop2u3t2rp3tom.example. RRSIG NSEC3 7 2 3600 (
```

```
                20150420235959 20051021000000 40430 example.
                OSgWSm26B+cS+dDL8b5QrWr/dEWhtCsKlwKL
                IBHYH6blRxK9rC0bMJPwQ4mLIuw85H2EY762
                BOCXJZMnpuwhpA==  )

;; NSEC3 RR that matches the closest encloser (x.w.example)
;; H(x.w.example) = b4um86eghhds6nea196smvmlo4ors995

b4um86eghhds6nea196smvmlo4ors995.example. NSEC3 1 1 12 aabbccdd (
                gjeqe526plbf1g8mklp59enfd789njgi MX RRSIG )
b4um86eghhds6nea196smvmlo4ors995.example. RRSIG NSEC3 7 2 3600 (
                20150420235959 20051021000000 40430 example.
                ZkPG3M32lmoHM6pa3D6gZFGB/rhL//Bs3Omh
                5u4m/CUiwtblEVOaAKKZd7S959OeiX43aLX3
                pOv0TSTyiTxIZg==  )

;; NSEC3 RR that covers wildcard at the closest encloser (*.x.w.example)
;; H(*.x.w.example) = 92pqneegtaue7pjatc3l3qnk738c6v5m

35mthgpgcu1qg68fab165klnsnk3dpvl.example. NSEC3 1 1 12 aabbccdd (
                b4um86eghhds6nea196smvmlo4ors995 NS DS RRSIG )
35mthgpgcu1qg68fab165klnsnk3dpvl.example. RRSIG NSEC3 7 2 3600 (
                20150420235959 20051021000000 40430 example.
                g6jPUUpduAJKRljUsN8gB4UagAX0NxY9shwQ
                Aynzo8EUWH+z6hEIBlUTPGj15eZll6VhQqgZ
                XtAIR3chwgW+SA==  )

;; Additional
;; (empty)
```

The query returned three NSEC3 RRs that prove that the requested data does not exist and that no wildcard expansion applies. The negative response is authenticated by verifying the NSEC3 RRs. The corresponding RRSIGs indicate that the NSEC3 RRs are signed by an "example" DNSKEY of algorithm 7 and with key tag 40430. The resolver needs the corresponding DNSKEY RR in order to authenticate this answer.

One of the owner names of the NSEC3 RRs matches the closest encloser. One of the NSEC3 RRs prove that there exists no longer name. One of the NSEC3 RRs prove that there exists no wildcard RRSets that should have been expanded. The closest encloser can be found by applying the algorithm in Section 8.3.

In the above example, the name 'x.w.example' hashes to 'b4um86eghhds6nea196 smvmlo4ors995'. This indicates that this might be the closest encloser. To prove that 'c.x.w.example' and '*.x.w.example' do not exist, these names are hashed to, respectively, '0va5bpr2ou0vk0lbqeeljri88laipsfh' and '92pqneegtaue7pjatc3l3qnk738c6v5m'. The first and last NSEC3 RRs prove that these hashed owner names do not exist.

B.2. No Data Error

A "no data" response. The NSEC3 RR proves that the name exists and that the requested RR type does not.

```
;; Header: QR AA DO RCODE=0
;;
;; Question
ns1.example.              IN MX

;; Answer
;; (empty)

;; Authority
example.          SOA     ns1.example. bugs.x.w.example. 1 3600 300 (
                          3600000 3600 )
example.          RRSIG   SOA 7 1 3600 20150420235959 20051021000000 (
                          40430 example.
                          Hu25UIyNPmvPIVBrldN+9Mlp9Zql39qaUd8i
                          q4ZLlYWfUUbbAS41pG+68z81q1xhkYAcEyHd
                          VI2LmKusbZsT0Q== )
```

;; NSEC3 RR matches the QNAME and shows that the MX type bit is not set.

```
2t7b4g4vsa5smi47k61mv5bv1a22bojr.example. NSEC3 1 1 12 aabbccdd (
                          2vptu5timamqttgl4luu9kg21e0aor3s A RRSIG )
2t7b4g4vsa5smi47k61mv5bv1a22bojr.example. RRSIG NSEC3 7 2 3600 (
                          20150420235959 20051021000000 40430 example.
                          OmBvJ1Vgg1hCKMXHFiNeIYHK9XVW0iLDLwJN
                          4TFoNxZuP03gAXEI634YwOc4YBNITrj413iq
                          NI6mRk/r1dOSUw== )
;; Additional
;; (empty)
```

The query returned an NSEC3 RR that proves that the requested name exists ("ns1.example." hashes to "2t7b4g4vsa5smi47k61mv5bv1a22bojr"), but the requested RR type does not exist (type MX is absent in the type code list of the NSEC3 RR), and was not a CNAME (type CNAME is also absent in the type code list of the NSEC3 RR).

B.2.1. No Data Error, Empty Non-Terminal

A "no data" response because of an empty non-terminal. The NSEC3 RR proves that the name exists and that the requested RR type does not.

```
;; Header: QR AA DO RCODE=0
;;
;; Question
y.w.example.              IN A

;; Answer
;; (empty)

;; Authority
example.          SOA     ns1.example. bugs.x.w.example. 1 3600 300 (
                          3600000 3600 )
```

```
example.          RRSIG    SOA 7 1 3600 20150420235959 20051021000000 (
                           40430 example.
                           Hu25UIyNPmvPIVBrldN+9Mlp9Zql39qaUd8i
                           q4ZLlYWfUUbbAS41pG+68z81q1xhkYAcEyHd
                           VI2LmKusbZsT0Q==  )
```

;; NSEC3 RR matches the QNAME and shows that the A type bit is not set.

```
ji6neoaepv8b5o6k4ev33abha8ht9fgc.example. NSEC3 1 1 12 aabbccdd (
                           k8udemvp1j2f7eg6jebps17vp3n8i58h  )
ji6neoaepv8b5o6k4ev33abha8ht9fgc.example. RRSIG NSEC3 7 2 3600 (
                           20150420235959 20051021000000 40430 example.
                           gPkFp1s2QDQ6wQzcg1uSebZ61W33rUBDcTj7
                           2F3kQ490fEdp7k1BUIfbcZtPbX3YCpE+sIt0
                           MpzVSKfTwx4uYA==  )
```

;; Additional
;; (empty)

The query returned an NSEC3 RR that proves that the requested name exists ("y.w.example." hashes to "ji6neoaepv8b5o6k4ev33abha8ht9fgc"), but the requested RR type does not exist (Type A is absent in the Type Bit Maps field of the NSEC3 RR). Note that, unlike an empty non-terminal proof using NSECs, this is identical to a No Data Error. This example is solely mentioned to be complete.

B.3. Referral to an Opt-Out Unsigned Zone

The NSEC3 RRs prove that nothing for this delegation was signed. There is no proof that the unsigned delegation exists.

```
;; Header: QR DO RCODE=0
;;
;; Question
mc.c.example.          IN MX

;; Answer
;; (empty)

;; Authority
c.example.          NS        ns1.c.example.
                    NS        ns2.c.example.
```

;; NSEC3 RR that covers the "next closer" name (c.example)
;; H(c.example) = 4g6p9u5gvfshp30pqecj98b3maqbn1ck

```
35mthgpgcu1qg68fab165klnsnk3dpvl.example. NSEC3 1 1 12 aabbccdd (
                           b4um86eghhds6nea196smvmlo4ors995 NS DS RRSIG  )
35mthgpgcu1qg68fab165klnsnk3dpvl.example. RRSIG NSEC3 7 2 3600 (
                           20150420235959 20051021000000 40430 example.
                           g6jPUUpduAJKRljUsN8gB4UagAX0NxY9shwQ
```

```
                        Aynzo8EUWH+z6hEIBlUTPGj15eZll6VhQqgZ
                        XtAIR3chwgW+SA==  )

;; NSEC3 RR that matches the closest encloser (example)
;; H(example) = 0p9mhaveqvm6t7vbl5lop2u3t2rp3tom

0p9mhaveqvm6t7vbl5lop2u3t2rp3tom.example. NSEC3 1 1 12 aabbccdd (
                        2t7b4g4vsa5smi47k61mv5bv1a22bojr MX DNSKEY NS
                        SOA NSEC3PARAM RRSIG  )
0p9mhaveqvm6t7vbl5lop2u3t2rp3tom.example. RRSIG NSEC3 7 2 3600 (
                        20150420235959 20051021000000 40430 example.
                        OSgWSm26B+cS+dDL8b5QrWr/dEWhtCsKlwKL
                        IBHYH6blRxK9rC0bMJPwQ4mLIuw85H2EY762
                        BOCXJZMnpuwhpA==  )

;; Additional
ns1.c.example. A       192.0.2.7
ns2.c.example. A       192.0.2.8
```

The query returned a referral to the unsigned "c.example." zone. The response contains the closest provable encloser of "c.example" to be "example", since the hash of "c.example" ("4g6p9u5gvfshp30pqecj98b3maqbn1ck") is covered by the first NSEC3 RR and its Opt-Out bit is set.

B.4. Wildcard Expansion

A query that was answered with a response containing a wildcard expansion. The label count in the RRSIG RRSet in the answer section indicates that a wildcard RRSet was expanded to produce this response, and the NSEC3 RR proves that no "next closer" name exists in the zone.

```
;; Header: QR AA DO RCODE=0
;;
;; Question
a.z.w.example. IN MX

;; Answer
a.z.w.example. MX     1 ai.example.
a.z.w.example. RRSIG  MX 7 2 3600 20150420235959 20051021000000 (
                      40430 example.
                      CikebjQwGQPwijVcxgcZcSJKtfynugtlBiKb
                      9FcBTrmOoyQ4InoWVudhCWsh/URX3lc4WRUM
                      ivEBP6+4KS3ldA==  )

;; Authority
example.       NS     ns1.example.
example.       NS     ns2.example.
example.       RRSIG  NS 7 1 3600 20150420235959 20051021000000 (
                      40430 example.
                      PVOgtMK1HHeSTau+HwDWO8Ts+6C8qtqd4pQJ
                      qOtdEVgg+MA+ai4fWDEhu3qHJyLcQ9tbD2vv
```

```
                    CnMXjtz6SyObxA==  )

;; NSEC3 RR that covers the "next closer" name (z.w.example)
;; H(z.w.example) = qlu7gtfaeh0ek0c05ksfhdpbcgglbe03

q04jkcevqvmu85r014c7dkba38o0ji5r.example. NSEC3 1 1 12 aabbccdd (
                    r53bq7cc2uvmubfu5ocmm6pers9tk9en A RRSIG )
q04jkcevqvmu85r014c7dkba38o0ji5r.example. RRSIG NSEC3 7 2 3600 (
                    20150420235959 20051021000000 40430 example.
                    hV5I89b+4FHJDATp09g4bbN0R1F845CaXpL3
                    ZxlMKimoPAyqletMlEWwLfFia7sdpSzn+ZlN
                    NlkxWcLsIlMmUg==  )
;; Additional
ai.example.     A       192.0.2.9
ai.example.     RRSIG   A 7 2 3600 20150420235959 20051021000000 (
                    40430 example.
                    hVe+wKYMlObTRPhX0NL67GxeZfdxqr/QeR6F
                    tfdAj5+FgYxyzPEjIzvKWy00hWIl6wD3Vws+
                    rznEn8sQ64UdqA==  )
ai.example.     AAAA    2001:db8:0:0:0:0:f00:baa9
ai.example.     RRSIG   AAAA 7 2 3600 20150420235959 20051021000000 (
                    40430 example.
                    LcdxKaCB5bGZwPDg+3JJ4O02zoMBrjxqlf6W
                    uaHQZZfTUpb9Nf2nxFGe2XRPfR5tpJT6GdRG
                    cHueLuXkMjBArQ==  )
```

The query returned an answer that was produced as a result of a wildcard expansion. The answer section contains a wildcard RRSet expanded as it would be in a traditional DNS response. The RRSIG Labels field value of 2 indicates that the answer is the result of a wildcard expansion, as the "a.z.w.example" name contains 4 labels. This also shows that "w.example" exists, so there is no need for an NSEC3 RR that matches the closest encloser.

The NSEC3 RR proves that no closer match could have been used to answer this query.

B.5. Wildcard No Data Error

A "no data" response for a name covered by a wildcard. The NSEC3 RRs prove that the matching wildcard name does not have any RRs of the requested type and that no closer match exists in the zone.

```
;; Header: QR AA DO RCODE=0
;;
;; Question
a.z.w.example.      IN AAAA

;; Answer
;; (empty)

;; Authority
example.        SOA     ns1.example. bugs.x.w.example. 1 3600 300 (
```

```
                     3600000  3600  )
    example.         RRSIG   SOA 7 1 3600 20150420235959 20051021000000 (
                             40430 example.
                             Hu25UIyNPmvPIVBrldN+9Mlp9Zql39qaUd8i
                             q4ZLlYWfUUbbAS41pG+68z81q1xhkYAcEyHd
                             VI2LmKusbZsT0Q==  )
;; NSEC3 RR that matches the closest encloser (w.example)
;; H(w.example) = k8udemvp1j2f7eg6jebps17vp3n8i58h

k8udemvp1j2f7eg6jebps17vp3n8i58h.example. NSEC3 1 1 12 aabbccdd (
                        kohar7mbb8dc2ce8a9qvl8hon4k53uhi )
k8udemvp1j2f7eg6jebps17vp3n8i58h.example. RRSIG NSEC3 7 2 3600 (
                        20150420235959 20051021000000 40430 example.
                        FtXGbvF0+wf8iWkyo73enAuVx03klN+pILBK
                        S6qCcftVtfH4yVzsEZquJ27NHR7ruxJWDNMt
                        Otx7w9WfcIg62A==  )

;; NSEC3 RR that covers the "next closer" name (z.w.example)
;; H(z.w.example) = qlu7gtfaeh0ek0c05ksfhdpbcgglbe03

q04jkcevqvmu85r014c7dkba38o0ji5r.example. NSEC3 1 1 12 aabbccdd (
                        r53bq7cc2uvmubfu5ocmm6pers9tk9en A RRSIG )
q04jkcevqvmu85r014c7dkba38o0ji5r.example. RRSIG NSEC3 7 2 3600 (
                        20150420235959 20051021000000 40430 example.
                        hV5I89b+4FHJDATp09g4bbN0R1F845CaXpL3
                        ZxlMKimoPAyqletMlEWwLfFia7sdpSzn+ZlN
                        NlkxWcLsIlMmUg==  )

;; NSEC3 RR that matches a wildcard at the closest encloser.
;; H(*.w.example) = r53bq7cc2uvmubfu5ocmm6pers9tk9en

r53bq7cc2uvmubfu5ocmm6pers9tk9en.example. NSEC3 1 1 12 aabbccdd (
                        t644ebqk9bibcna874givr6joj62mlhv MX RRSIG )
r53bq7cc2uvmubfu5ocmm6pers9tk9en.example. RRSIG NSEC3 7 2 3600 (
                        20150420235959 20051021000000 40430 example.
                        aupviViruXs4bDg9rCbezzBMf9h1ZlDvbW/C
                        ZFKulIGXXLj8B/fsDJarXVDA9bnUoRhEbKp+
                        HF1FWKW7RIJdtQ==  )

;; Additional
;; (empty)
```

The query returned the NSEC3 RRs that prove that the requested data does not exist and no wildcard RR applies.

B.6. DS Child Zone No Data Error

A "no data" response for a QTYPE=DS query that was mistakenly sent to a name server for the child zone.

```
;; Header: QR AA DO RCODE=0
```

```
;;
;; Question
example.                IN  DS

;; Answer
;; (empty)

;; Authority
example.        SOA     ns1.example. bugs.x.w.example. 1 3600 300 (
                        3600000 3600 )
example.        RRSIG   SOA 7 1 3600 20150420235959 20051021000000 (
                        40430 example.
                        Hu25UIyNPmvPIVBrldN+9Mlp9Zql39qaUd8i
                        q4ZLlYWfUUbbAS41pG+68z81q1xhkYAcEyHd
                        VI2LmKusbZsT0Q==  )

;; NSEC3 RR matches the QNAME and shows that the DS type bit is not set.

0p9mhaveqvm6t7vbl5lop2u3t2rp3tom.example. NSEC3 1 1 12 aabbccdd (
                        2t7b4g4vsa5smi47k61mv5bv1a22bojr MX DNSKEY NS
                        SOA NSEC3PARAM RRSIG )
0p9mhaveqvm6t7vbl5lop2u3t2rp3tom.example. RRSIG NSEC3 7 2 3600
                        20150420235959 20051021000000 40430 example.
                        OSgWSm26B+cS+dDL8b5QrWr/dEWhtCsKlwKL
                        IBHYH6blRxK9rC0bMJPwQ4mLIuw85H2EY762
                        BOCXJZMnpuwhpA==  )

;; Additional
;; (empty)
```

The query returned an NSEC3 RR showing that the requested was answered by the server authoritative for the zone "example". The NSEC3 RR indicates the presence of an SOA RR, showing that this NSEC3 RR is from the apex of the child, not from the zone cut of the parent. Queries for the "example" DS RRSet should be sent to the parent servers (which are in this case the root servers).

Appendix C. Special Considerations

The following paragraphs clarify specific behavior and explain special considerations for implementations.

C.1. Salting

Augmenting original owner names with salt before hashing increases the cost of a dictionary of pre-generated hash-values. For every bit of salt, the cost of a precomputed dictionary doubles (because there must be an entry for each word combined with each possible salt value). The NSEC3 RR can use a maximum of 2040 bits (255 octets) of salt, multiplying the cost by 2^{2040}.

This means that an attacker must, in practice, recompute the dictionary each time the salt is changed.

Including a salt, regardless of size, does not affect the cost of constructing NSEC3 RRs. It does increase the size of the NSEC3 RR.

There MUST be at least one complete set of NSEC3 RRs for the zone using the same salt value.

The salt SHOULD be changed periodically to prevent pre-computation using a single salt. It is RECOMMENDED that the salt be changed for every re-signing.

Note that this could cause a resolver to see RRs with different salt values for the same zone. This is harmless, since each RR stands alone (that is, it denies the set of owner names whose hashes, using the salt in the NSEC3 RR, fall between the two hashes in the NSEC3 RR) – it is only the server that needs a complete set of NSEC3 RRs with the same salt in order to be able to answer every possible query.

There is no prohibition with having NSEC3 RRs with different salts within the same zone. However, in order for authoritative servers to be able to consistently find covering NSEC3 RRs, the authoritative server MUST choose a single set of parameters (algorithm, salt, and iterations) to use when selecting NSEC3 RRs.

C.2. Hash Collision

Hash collisions occur when different messages have the same hash value. The expected number of domain names needed to give a 1 in 2 chance of a single collision is about $2^{(n/2)}$ for a hash of length n bits (i.e., 2^{80} for SHA-1). Though this probability is extremely low, the following paragraphs deal with avoiding collisions and assessing possible damage in the event of an attack using hash collisions.

C.2.1. Avoiding Hash Collisions During Generation

During generation of NSEC3 RRs, hash values are supposedly unique. In the (academic) case of a collision occurring, an alternative salt MUST be chosen and all hash values MUST be regenerated.

C.2.2. Second Preimage Requirement Analysis

A cryptographic hash function has a second-preimage resistance property. The second-preimage resistance property means that it is computationally infeasible to find another message with the same hash value as a given message, i.e., given preimage X, to find a second preimage $X' \neq X$ such that hash(X) = hash(X'). The work factor for finding a second preimage is of the order of 2^{160} for SHA-1. To mount an attack using an existing NSEC3 RR, an adversary needs to find a second preimage.

Assuming an adversary is capable of mounting such an extreme attack, the actual damage is that a response message can be generated that claims that a certain QNAME (i.e., the second pre-image) does exist, while in reality QNAME does not exist (a false positive), which will either cause a security-aware resolver to re-query for the non-existent name, or to fail the initial query. Note that the adversary can't mount this attack on an existing name, but only on a name that the adversary can't choose and that does not yet exist.

Authors' Addresses

Ben Laurie
Nominet
17 Perryn Road
London W3 7LR
England

Phone: +44 20 8735 0686
EMail: ben@links.org

Geoffrey Sisson
Nominet
Minerva House
Edmund Halley Road
Oxford Science Park
Oxford OX4 4DQ
UNITED KINGDOM

Phone: +44 1865 332211
EMail: geoff-s@panix.com

Roy Arends
Nominet
Minerva House
Edmund Halley Road
Oxford Science Park
Oxford OX4 4DQ
UNITED KINGDOM

Phone: +44 1865 332211
EMail: roy@nominet.org.uk

David Blacka
VeriSign, Inc.
21355 Ridgetop Circle
Dulles, VA 20166
US

Phone: +1 703 948 3200
EMail: davidb@verisign.com

Full Copyright Statement

This document is subject to the rights, licenses and restrictions contained in BCP 78, and except as set forth therein, the authors retain all their rights.

This document and the information contained herein are provided on an "AS IS" basis and THE CONTRIBUTOR, THE ORGANIZATION HE/SHE REPRESENTS OR IS SPONSORED BY (IF ANY), THE INTERNET SOCIETY, THE IETF TRUST AND THE INTERNET ENGINEERING TASK FORCE DISCLAIM ALL WARRANTIES, EXPRESS OR IMPLIED, INCLUDING BUT NOT LIMITED TO ANY WARRANTY THAT THE USE OF THE INFORMATION HEREIN WILL NOT INFRINGE ANY RIGHTS OR ANY IMPLIED WARRANTIES OF MERCHANTABILITY OR FITNESS FOR A PARTICULAR PURPOSE.

Intellectual Property

The IETF takes no position regarding the validity or scope of any Intellectual Property Rights or other rights that might be claimed to pertain to the implementation or use of the technology described in this document or the extent to which any license under such rights might or might not be available; nor does it represent that it has made any independent effort to identify any such rights. Information on the procedures with respect to rights in RFC documents can be found in BCP 78 and BCP 79.

Copies of IPR disclosures made to the IETF Secretariat and any assurances of licenses to be made available, or the result of an attempt made to obtain a general license or permission for the use of such proprietary rights by implementers or users of this specification can be obtained from the IETF on-line IPR repository at http://www.ietf.org/ipr.

The IETF invites any interested party to bring to its attention any copyrights, patents or patent applications, or other proprietary rights that may cover technology that may be required to implement this standard. Please address the information to the IETF at ietf-ipr@ietf.org.

Index

www.ingramcontent.com/pod-product-compliance
Lightning Source LLC
Chambersburg PA
CBHW080151060326
40689CB00018B/3932

* 9 7 8 0 9 7 9 0 3 4 2 7 5 *